Microsoft

WINDOWS 3.1

A QUICK STUDY

MARGARET BROWN

DDC

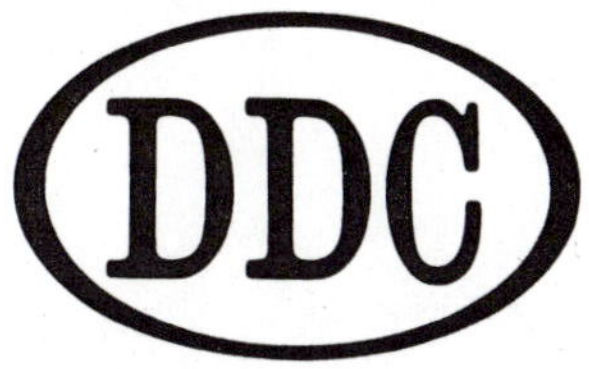

DICTATION DISC COMPANY

To my mother and father, Hazel and Jess.
Everyone should have such nice, loving parents.

Acknowledgments

Special Thanks for Extraordinary Patience and Help
Karl Schwartz
Staten Island, New York

Desktop Publishers
Karl and Joanne Schwartz
Staten Island, New York

Editor
Kristen Cassereau
San Mateo, California

Cover Design and Design Consultation
Irwin Bag
Bethel, Connecticut

Technical Editor
Suzanne Moreland
Humboldt County, California

About this Book

This is a beginning Microsoft Windows® book whose goal is to introduce you to Windows by simplifying terms and concepts; by furnishing frequent reinforcing worksheets; and by providing short, task-oriented, step-by-step exercises.

The book has two sections: a Getting Started section and the Lessons section, made up of hands-on exercises.

Getting Started

The Getting Started section consists of 16 topics, followed by a section of worksheets for the topics. Most topics have simple explanations and definitions on the right page, and illustrations to demonstrate the topic on the facing left page. The Getting Started section introduces you to the computer and to Windows terms and concepts.

Lessons

Eight lessons, with a total of 96 exercises, make up the main part of the book. There are practice exercises at the end of each lesson that review the tasks performed in the lesson. Each lesson is followed by a *review of the lesson's terms and concepts,* and by *one or more worksheets.*

Groups of Exercises

Some groups of exercises should be done during the same session. This is noted immediately under the "task name" in the narrow column when appropriate.

"OR" Boxes

"OR" boxes are faintly dotted boxes around different directions to perform the same action. Do <u>only one</u> option when you come to "OR" boxes.

Hands-On Exercises

- Each exercise performs a task.
  The tasks are listed sequentially (page xiv) and alphabetically (page xv).
- Each task is defined.
- New terms are defined.
- New Windows elements are pointed out.
- Frequent illustrations show what is happening on your screen.
- Exercise instructions are shown in the wide column.
- Exercise steps are clearly numbered.
- Exercise instructions usually use the mouse.
- Keyboard instructions are included in the narrow column.
- Tasks that are reviewed often have referring page numbers.
- Notes explain more about the exercise.
- Assumptions, warnings, important comments, and notes appear in the narrow column when needed.

Appendix

Appendix A provides a list for you to check off worksheets and printouts as you complete them, if you desire. Appendix B has instructions to Rebuild Group Windows. Appendix C has instructions to Reproduce the Original Windows Desktop. Appendix D has answers to the 32 worksheets in the book.

Table of Contents — At a Glance

Table of Contents

Continued ...

LESSON THREE — HELP

LESSON FOUR — WRITE

LESSON FIVE — PAINTBRUSH

LESSON SIX — FILE MANAGER

LESSON SEVEN — INTEGRATION

LESSON EIGHT — OTHER FEATURES

Read Me

Windows provides a wonderfully changeable environment. With a little exposure to Windows, you will become familiar with this easily manipulated graphics environment, and you will discover how to customize Windows to meet your needs. At first, you may be a little confused as you see windows and icons moving around quickly and sometimes disappearing. If you are used to a stable computer atmosphere, the changeable Windows environment may take some getting used to. As you become acquainted with the many varied aspects of Windows, you will find it easy to use, convenient, practical, and fun.

Follow Directions Precisely

The *starting Windows screen* can be easily altered by mistake or by experimenting. If Windows is being used in a training environment, remember that other people have to use the program and that a consistent environment is important for working through lessons in this book. Therefore, <u>it is recommended that you follow the exercise directions as precisely as possible.</u>

Common Problems and Solutions

Several common errors, and solutions to correct them, are covered on pages x and xi.

Reproduce the Original "Starting Windows Screen"

It is easy to create a messed-up desktop. If this happens, you will be thankful to have an opportunity to return the *starting Windows screen* to its original state. Two processes are offered to help return the *starting Windows screen* to its original condition. Appendix C has instructions to "Reproduce the Original Windows Desktop," and Appendix B has instructions to "Rebuild Group Windows." It is best to perform the instructions to "Reproduce the Original Windows Desktop" when the program is newly installed or as soon afterwards as possible.

Windows Program Differences May Occur

Microsoft has licensed some companies to sell their own customized versions of Windows, thereby creating slight differences in the Windows program that the various vendors provide. Although this book anticipates many different possible conditions, program differences may cause some unanticipated results when doing the exercises in this book.

Where Can I Get Additional Reference Material for Windows 3.1?

Dictation Disc Company (DDC) publishes the "Quick Reference Guide for Microsoft Windows 3.1" by Karl and Joanne Schwartz. This reference guide is designed to help you master any Windows operation without searching through lengthy manuals. Step-by-step instructions show how to perform Windows procedures. Look for it in bookstores or call DDC at (800)528-3897 to order it.

Do Windows Tutorial First

The Windows tutorial is short and well done. It will help you become familiar with basic Windows commands in a way that prevents accidental actions that may easily occur in the real program. For a better understanding of concepts, you should complete the Windows Tutorial before you continue with this book.

NOTE: Windows Tutorial will not run unless you have a color monitor.

If you are new at using a mouse,

Do The Mouse Lesson:

1. Start Windows, if it is not already started (page 52).
2. Press and hold **Alt** <u>while</u> you tap **H** (Help), then release **Alt**.
   The Help drop-down menu should appear.
3. Press **W** (Windows Tutorial).
   The Windows Tutorial program starts.
4. Press **M** (Mouse).
   The mouse lesson starts.
5. Read the information and follow directions to complete the tutorial.

To quit at any time and return to the program:
1. Press **Esc**.
2. Press **Y** (Yes).

*NOTE: If the <u>left</u> mouse button does not work correctly, it may have been changed in the Mouse Lesson of the Windows Tutorial. The default setting for the mouse button is **R** (for right-handed users). The **R** default means that the <u>left</u> mouse button is used for **clicking, double-clicking,** and **dragging** (most of the time). You can change it back to the default from the Mouse Lesson. Select Help, Windows Tutorial, then M(ouse Lesson). Select **R** when given the opportunity, and then either exit the tutorial or continue with the lesson.*

Do The Windows Basics Lesson:

1. Start Windows, if it is not already started (page 52).
2. Either click on Help (on the menu bar) OR press and hold **Alt** <u>while</u> you press **H** (Help), then release **Alt**.
   The Help drop-down menu should appear.
3. Either click on Windows Tutorial OR press **W** (Windows Tutorial).
   The Windows Tutorial program starts.
4. Press **W** (Windows Basics lesson).
   The Windows Basics lesson starts.
5. Read the information and follow directions to complete the tutorial.

To quit at any time and return to the program:
1. Press **Esc**.
2. Press **Y** (Yes).

Common Problems and Solutions

NOTE: Page references in the "Possible solutions" sections below all point you to the next topic, Basic Windows Commands at a Glance.

a window disappears
Possible causes
- As you open new windows, they appear in front of existing windows, partially or completely covering them.
- The "Minimize on Use" setting may be selected. It is located in the Options menu on the Program Manager's menu bar. When checked, this option causes the Program Manager to become an icon when you open another application.
- The window may have been closed.
- You may have moved and sized group windows and the Program Manager window until some windows do not show. If this happens, the Program Manager window will have scroll bars.

Possible solutions
- Select an application window (p. xiii).
- Select a group window (p. xiii).
- Arrange group windows (p. xii).
- Arrange icons (p. xii).
- Move a window (p. xiii).
- Deselect the "Minimize on Use" option:
  - First *select* the Program Manager window (p. xiii).
  - Then Press **Alt** + **O** (Options).
  - If Minimize on Use is checked, press **M**; otherwise, press **Alt** to cancel the menu without making a change.

a window suddenly fills the entire screen
Possible causes
- You may have double-clicked on the window's title bar instead of ▭ (the control box).
- You may have clicked on ▲ (the maximize button).

Possible solution
- Restore the window (p. xiii).

a box appears that offers you choices or asks you to do something (a dialog box)
Possible causes
- You may have clicked on a menu on the menu bar and then selected a menu command that opened a *dialog box* (one with an ellipsis (...)).

Possible solutions
- Press **Esc**.
  OR press **Alt** + **F4**.
  OR double-click on ▭ (the control box).
  OR click on | Cancel |.
  OR click on | No |.

a drop-down menu appears that you do not want
Possible causes
- You clicked on one of the menus on the menu bar.
- You may have pressed **Alt** + the underlined letter of a menu.

Possible solutions
- Press **Alt**.

icons become disorganized
Possible causes
- When you tried to click or double-click on icons, they got *dragged* out of their original positions.

Possible solutions
- Arrange icons (p. xii).

a window appears that you do not want open

Possible causes

- You pressed the ⏎ key (causing any highlighted program icon or group window icon to open to a window).
- You double-clicked on a program icon or group window icon.

Possible solutions

- Close a group window (p. xii).
- Exit a program (p. xii).

part of the window does not show

Possible causes

- You may have dragged an application window off the screen or dragged a group window beyond the border of the Program Manager window.

Possible solutions

- Arrange group windows (p. xii).
- Move a window (p. xii).
- Size a window (p. xiii).

the program manager window is empty or completely jumbled

Possible causes

- You may have moved and sized group windows and the Program Manager window until some windows do not show. If this happens, the Program Manager window will have scroll bars.
- You may have closed all the group windows and sized the Program Manager's borders smaller, thus hiding the group window icons.
- You may have opened many group and/or application windows and moved and resized them.

Possible solutions

- Select the Program Manager (application) window (p. xiii).
- Arrange group windows (p. xii).
- Arrange icons (p. xii).
- Close group windows (p. xii).
- Exit a program (p. xii).

a window has changed size

Possible causes

- When the pointer contacts a window border, it becomes a double-headed arrow. If you press the left mouse button and drag the mouse when the pointer is a double-headed arrow, it will move the border in the direction that the mouse is dragged, thus changing the window size.

- You may have clicked on the maximize, minimize, or restore buttons, or double-clicked on a window's title bar.

Possible solutions

- Size a window (p. xiii).
- Restore a window (p. xiii).

options that should not have a check mark by them

Possible causes

- In the normal course of examining the Windows environment, many people open the Options menu and click on one or more of the menu commands. The following options are best left unchecked until you understand what they do:

    Auto Arrange,
    Minimize on Use, and
    Save Settings on Exit.

Possible solutions

- Click on the Options menu to open it and look at it.
    If an option has a check mark by it, click on that option (to deselect it).
    If no option has a check mark by it, click on Options again to close the menu.
    Repeat the procedure until all check marks are gone.

Basic Windows Commands at a Glance

arrange group windows
    Cascade: Press **Shift** + **F5** (shortcut key to cascade).
                      OR Click on Window, then on Cascade.
    Tile: Press **Shift** + **F4** (shortcut key to tile).
                      OR Click on Window, then on Tile.

arrange icons
    group window icons: Click once on any group window icon (to highlight its name);
                          and click on Window, then on Arrange Icons.
    program-item icons: Click once on any program-item icon (to highlight its name);
                          and click on Window, then on Arrange Icons.

cancel
    Click on [Cancel].
    OR Press **ESC**.

close a group window
    Double-click on ⊟ (the group window's control box).
    OR With the desired group window's title bar highlighted, press **Ctrl** + **F4**.

exit a program
    Double-click on ⊟ (the control box).
    OR Click on File, then on Exit.
    OR Click on ⊟, then on Close.
    OR Press **Alt** + **F4**.
        If a dialog box appears asking if you want to "save current changes," click on [No]
        or press **N**.

exit Windows
    Double-click on ⊟ (the control box), then click on [OK].
    OR Press **Alt** + **F**, **X** (exit), then press **↵**.
    OR Press **Alt** + **F4**, then press **↵**.

maximize a window
    Application window:
        Double-click on the window's title bar.
        OR Click on ▲ (the maximize button).
        OR Press **Alt** + **Space** (spacebar), then press **X** (Maximize).
    Group (or Document) window:
        Double-click on the window's title bar.
        OR Click on ▲ (the group window's maximize button).
        OR Press **Alt** + **—** (hyphen), then press **X** (Maximize).

minimize a window
    Application window:
        Click on ▼ (the top minimize button).
        OR Press **Alt** + **Space** (spacebar), then press **N** (Minimize).
    Document (or Group) window:
        Click on ▼ (the group window's minimize button).
        OR Press **Alt** + **—** (hyphen), then press **N** (Minimize).

move a window
    Position the pointer on the title bar, and drag it to the desired location.

Continued ...

move icons

> Position the cursor on the desired icon, and drag it to the desired location.

open a group window

> Double-click on the group window icon.
> OR Click on the group window icon, then click on <u>R</u>estore.
> OR Press **Ctrl** + **Tab** until the group window name is highlighted, and then press **↵**.

restore a window (that has been maximized — it has **⬍** in top right corner)

> Application window:
> Double-click on the window's title bar.
> OR Click on **⬍** (the top restore button).
> OR Press **Alt** + **Space** (spacebar), then press **R** (<u>R</u>estore).
> Document (or Group) window:
> Click on **⬍** (the group window's restore button).
> OR Press **Alt** + **—** (hyphen), then press **R** (<u>R</u>estore).

scroll through a window

> When scroll bars appear:
> Drag the scroll box within the scroll bar.
> OR Click on the scroll arrow in the direction you want to scroll.
> OR Click just before the scroll arrow in the direction you want to scroll.

select a group window (it will display a highlighted title bar)

> Use menu bar: Click on <u>W</u>indow, then on the desired group window name.
> Click-on method: Click on any visible part of the desired window.
> Rotate method: Hold down **Ctrl** <u>while</u> you tap **Tab** until the desired group
>   window appears, then release both keys.

select an application window (it will display a highlighted title bar)

> Click-on method: Click on any part of the window that is visible.
> Rotate method: Hold down **Alt** <u>while</u> you tap **Tab** until the desired window
>   appears, then release both keys.
> Task List method: Double-click on the desktop, then on the desired window's title.
>   OR Press **Ctrl** + **Esc**, use arrows to highlight the desired window,
>   and then press **↵**.

size a window

> Position the pointer on any of the window borders or corners (it turns into a double-
> headed arrow), and drag the border or corner to the desired size.

start a program

> Double-click on the program-item icon.
> OR With the desired group window open and its title bar highlighted, use the arrow
>   keys to highlight the program-item icon, and then press **↵**.

start Windows

> Type **W** **I** **N** at the DOS prompt, C:\, then press **↵**.

use the menu bar

> Click on the desired menu, then on the desired drop-down menu command.
> OR Press **Alt** + [*the underlined letter of the desired menu*], then press the underlined
> letter of the desired command.

Tasks—Sequential List

Getting Started

Table of Contents

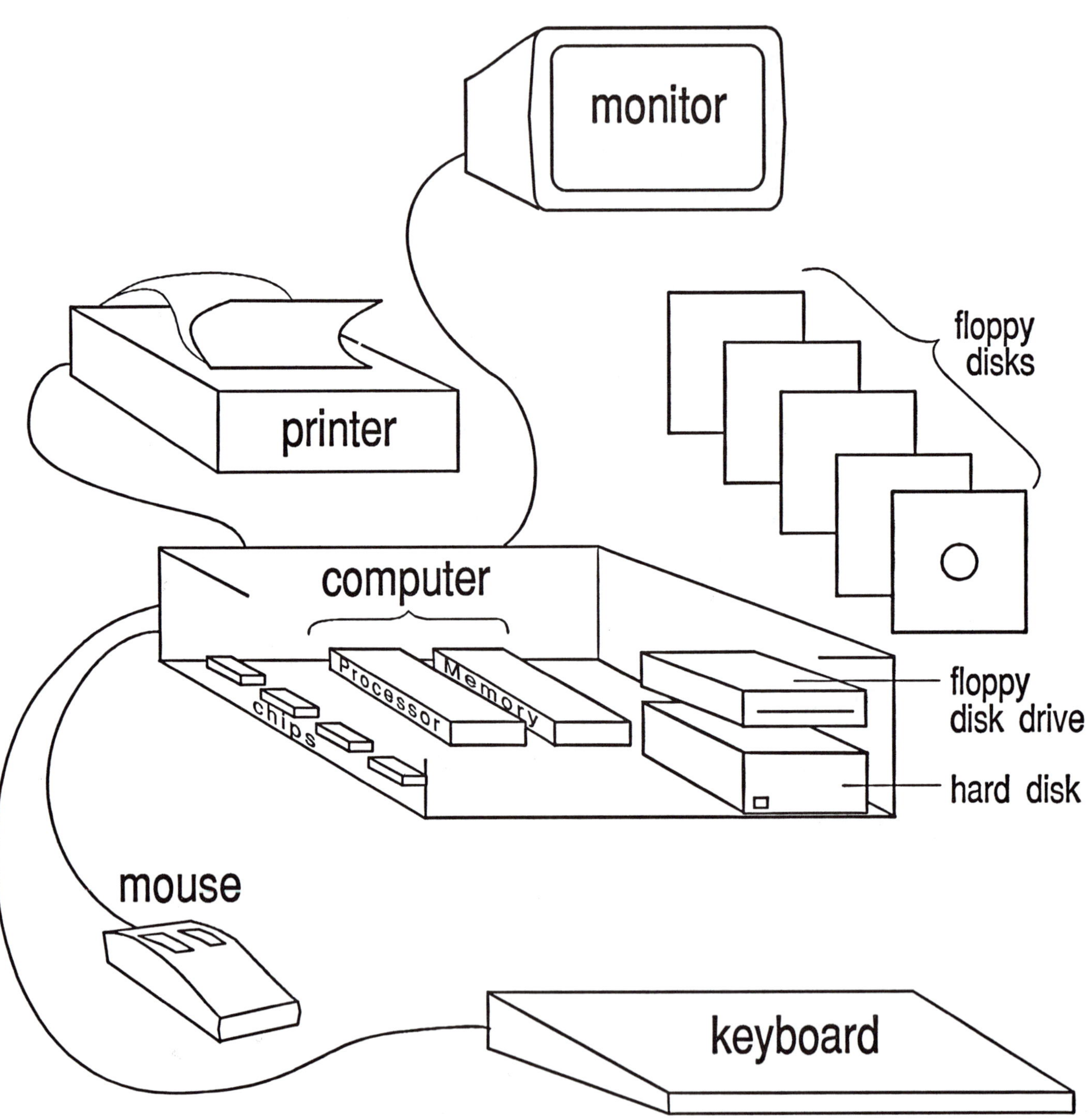
monitor
printer
floppy
disks
computer
Processor
Memory
chips
floppy
disk drive
hard disk
mouse
keyboard

Hardware is the group of parts that make up the computer system and that can be seen and touched.

A **computer** is an electronic device that performs complex tasks at high speed and with great accuracy. There are two main parts of a computer — the **processor** and the **memory.**

1) The **processor** is the "brains" of the computer — it processes instructions in the computer's memory. The 286, 386, and 486 chips are all **processors** (see page 29). The **processor** is also called the central processing unit (CPU) or microprocessor chip.

2) The **memory** is the area of the computer that holds instructions (programs) and information you give it. When the computer is turned off, everything in the memory disappears. The **memory** is also called random access memory (RAM) or main memory.

A **disk drive** is a device that transfers information back and forth between the computer and a disk.

Floppy disks are magnetically coated disks on which information (both programs and data typed from the keyboard) can be stored and **retrieved.** Floppy disks are put into and taken out of a disk drive.

The **hard disk** is a large capacity, permanent storage area that offers fast access to the information stored on it. Unlike floppy disks, the hard disk (along with its drive) is enclosed in a unit (usually within the computer case) that you do not handle.

Chips are small pieces of silicon wafers which often hold instructions to perform behind-the-scenes tasks, making it possible for you to use the computer. The *processor* and *memory* are special kinds of chips.

The **monitor** is a screen that displays the information in the computer.

The **keyboard** is used to enter data into and issue commands to the computer.

The **mouse** is a small, hand-held device used to control a pointer on the screen.

The **printer** transfers information from the computer to paper.

SOFTWARE

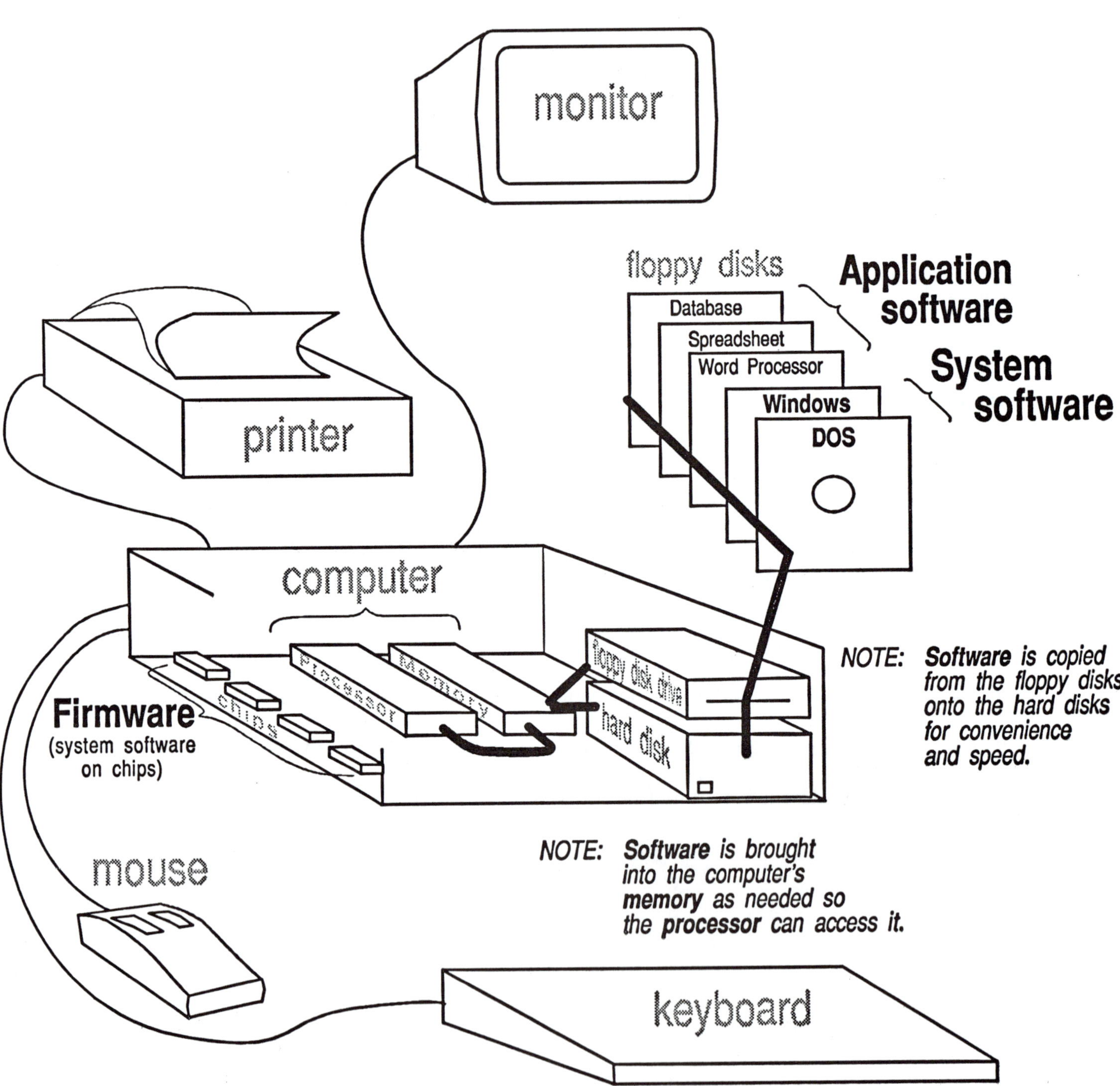

Software is the set of instructions (programs) that tell the computer what to do. While **software** is often stored on a disk, it is not the disk itself, but rather the *instructions* that are stored *on* the disk. **Software** cannot be seen or touched. **Software** typically falls into two main categories — **system software** and **application software.**

1. **System software** runs the computer system — it communicates between the parts that make up the computer system, making it possible for you to operate the computer. Two types of **system software** are *firmware* and *DOS*.

    1) **Firmware** is a kind of *system software* that is built into the computer system on chips.

    2) **DOS** (Disk Operating System) is a kind of *system software* that comes on disks and acts as a link between *application software* and the system's hardware. **DOS** must be in the computer's memory before application software can be used.

2. **Application software** (also called programs) does a specific task, such as word processing.

Microsoft Windows is a special kind of *software* that provides a *graphics environment*, that is, *an icon-based **link*** between you, application software, and DOS.

IMPORTANT: The terms *application* and *program* mean the same thing and are used interchangeably in this book.

<u>QUESTION</u>:   **What is the most common problem new computer users have?**

<u>ANSWER</u>:   **Confusing the computer's memory with the disk's storage area.**

Everything you use in the computer has to be in the **computer's memory**.
(so the *processor* can access it)

The *program* is brought into the **computer's memory**.
(this happens when you choose a program to use)

What you *type* goes *directly* into the **computer's memory**.
(not to the disk)

When you turn the computer off, however, the **computer's memory** is lost.
(this is why it is called *temporary* memory)

So...   in order <u>not</u> to lose your work, you use the **disk's storage area** to hold your information.
(this happens when you use the *SAVE* command)
(and this is why the disk's memory is called *permanent* storage)

When you want to use your information again, you get it from the **disk's storage area** and put it into the **computer's memory**.
(this happens when you use the *OPEN* or *RETRIEVE* command)

The Complete Computer System

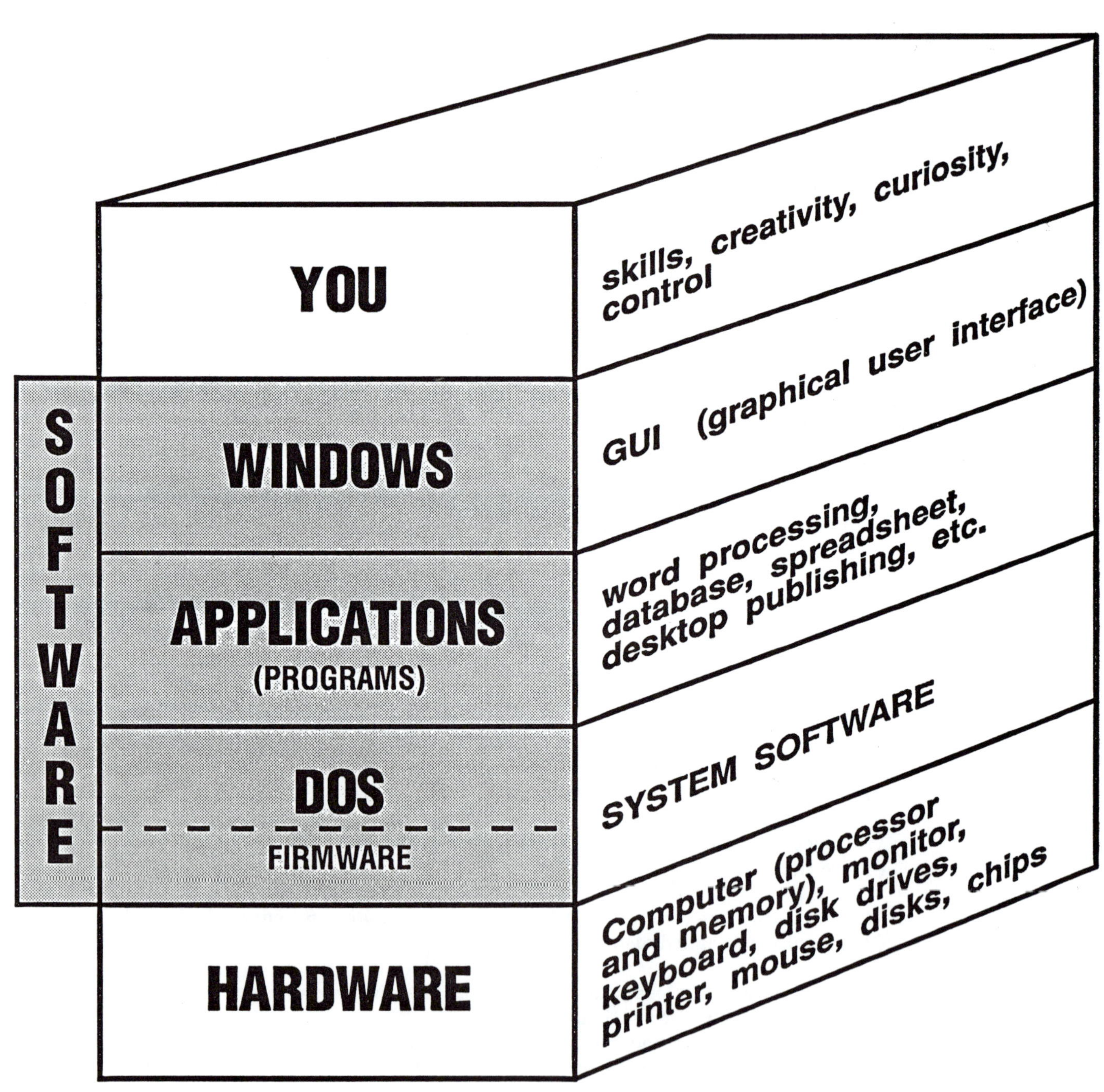

You control the computer system.
Windows acts as a link between you and programs.
DOS acts as a link between the programs and the hardware.

Do Worksheet 5, page 40
(Combined with the next two topics.)

Microsoft Windows is a program that provides a graphics environment that connects you to the computer system in an easy-to-understand, natural way.

Graphical user interface or **GUI** (pronounced "gooey") is a phrase that is commonly used to describe Microsoft Windows and similar programs.

It simply means that Windows has <u>pictures</u> that <u>you use</u> to <u>communicate</u> with the computer.
(graphical)   (user)   (interface)

Microsoft Windows Aspects

GUI (graphical user interface)

Three Basic Windows Parts p. 11
1. windows
    - application
    - document
2. icons
3. desktop

Window Elements p. 13
control box	maximize button
title bar	minimize button
menu bar	restore button
scroll bar	workspace
pointer	window borders & corners

Windows Organization p. 15
Program Manager
- Main
- Accessories
- Games
- Startup
- Applications

Windows Multitasking p. 31
memory-managing programs

Windows Modes p. 29
processor speed
- 286, 386, 486
memory size
- byte, kilobyte, megabyte
Windows modes
- standard
- 386 enhanced

Windows Integration p. 33
clipboard
CUA (common user access)
OLE (object linking and embedding)

Controlling Windows p. 17
menu bar	control box
drop-down menu	button
dialog box	program icon

The Mouse p. 18
- click
- double-click
- drag

The Pointer p. 19
arrow	hand
sizing	I-beam
move	prevent
hourglass	

The Keyboard p. 21
function keys	using keys together
control keys:	using keys in succession
CTRL, ALT,	cursor keys
SHIFT	ESC
shortcut keys	F1

Dialog Boxes p. 23
command button	list box
option buttons	drop-down list box
check boxes	drop-down list box arrow
text box	increment box

File Manager p. 27
Directory Window
directories	files
directory	data file
subdirectory	program file
directory tree	filename
current directory	file extension
directory window	associate

Windows Help p. 25
- contents
- search
- how to use Help
- glossary
- about (application)

Do Worksheet 5, page 40
(Combined with the previous and the next topics.)

What Does Microsoft Windows Do?

Microsoft Windows provides an easy way to organize and start programs.
(the Program Manager does this, page 15)

Microsoft Windows runs more than one program at a time.
(called multitasking, page 31)

Microsoft Windows lets you view more than one program at a time.
(it uses windows to do this, page 11)

Microsoft Windows transfers information between programs in a powerful way.
(called Object Linking and Embedding (OLE), page 33)

Microsoft Windows provides many useful programs of its own.
(called accessories programs, i.e., Write, Paintbrush, Clock, etc., page 15)

Microsoft Windows makes it easy to work with files.
(the File Manager does this, page 27)

How is Microsoft Windows Controlled?

Mouse and Pointer

Icons

Keyboard

Menu bar

Drop-down menus

Shortcut keys

Command buttons

Dialog boxes

Three Basic Parts of Windows

1. Windows
2. Icons
3. Desktop

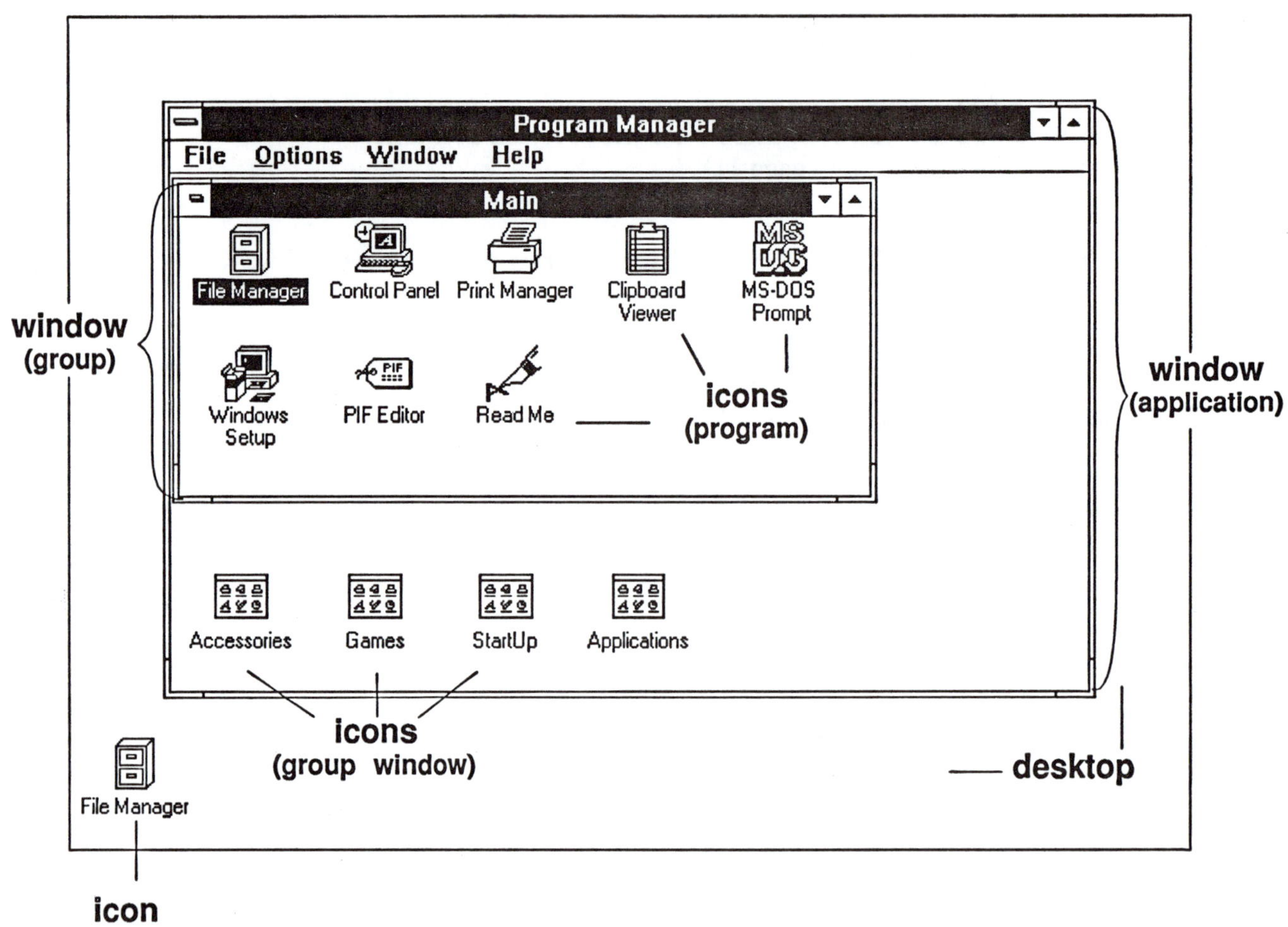

Three Basic Parts of Windows

The three basic parts of Microsoft Windows are
1. **windows,**
2. **icons**, and
3. the **desktop.**

Windows are rectangular areas in which you view a task, application (program), or document. You may open several windows at one time. You may also shrink a window to an **icon**, enlarge it to fill the entire **desktop** (screen), or change it to any desired size in between.

Icons are pictures that represent various elements in Microsoft Windows, such as documents, programs, groups of programs, disk drives, files, and minimized windows.

The **desktop** is the background (screen) upon which **windows** and **icons** appear.

Icon Types

While **icons** are literally any picture, the term most frequently refers to:

application icons -   graphics that represent *minimized, running* programs,
program icons -   graphics that represent *non-running* programs,
group window icons -   graphics that represent *minimized group* windows, and
document icons -   graphics that represent *minimized document* windows.

Window Types

Any screen element that is in a rectangle and has a *title bar* can be called a window, including a dialog box and message window; but the two main types of windows are **application** windows and **document** windows.

Application windows are windows that hold programs. An application window may hold multiple document windows, but it may not hold other application windows. **Application windows** differ in appearance from *document windows* in two ways:
1) they have a *menu bar*, and
2) the *Control box* holds a "spacebar" icon (it is longer than the "hyphen" icon found in the *document window's* Control box).

Document windows are windows that are within an application window. There may be more than one *document* window in an *application* window. *Document* windows do not have their own *menu bar*—they sometimes share the menu bar with the application window they are in. The *document window's Control box* holds a "hyphen" icon.

Group windows are special kinds of document windows that are used to organize programs. They are found only in the Program Manager window (see page 15).

Windows Elements

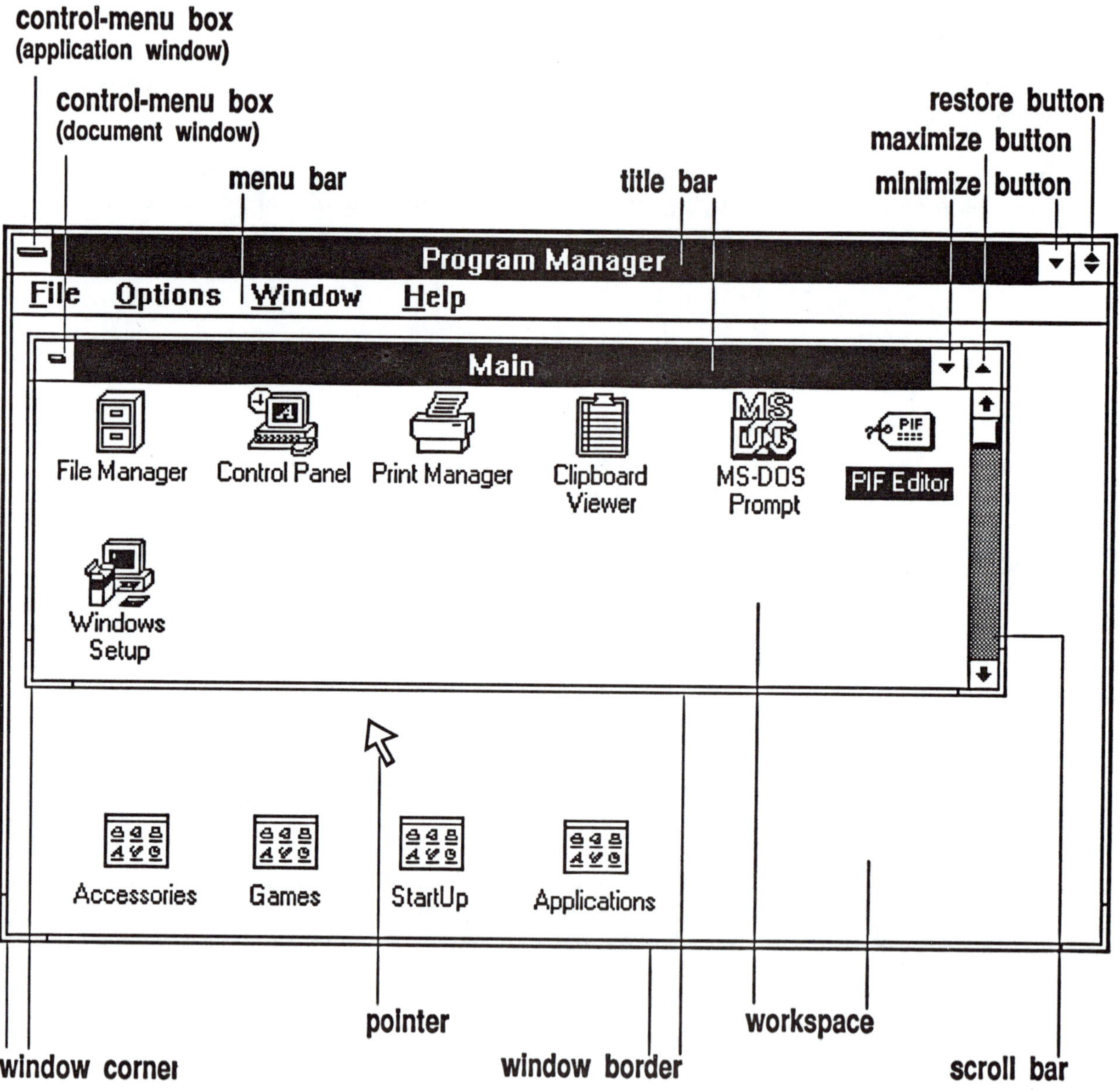

Do Worksheets 6 and 7 on pages 41, 42

Windows Elements

While the three *basic* parts of Microsoft Windows are windows, icons, and the desktop, there are many other elements in Windows. Most of these elements are used to initiate an action.

The **control box** (or Control-menu box) is the box at the left end of the title bar that opens the Control menu. The *control box* for application windows holds a "spacebar" icon (longer), while the *control box* for document windows holds a "hyphen" icon (smaller).

The **title bar** is the horizontal bar at the top of a window that holds the window's name.

The **menu bar** is the horizontal bar (just below the title bar) that holds the names of the *application window's* menus. (*Document windows* do not have a menu bar.)

The **maximize button** is the small box located at the right end of the title bar which holds an up arrow (▲).

The **minimize button** is the small box located at the right of the title bar (just left of the maximize button) which holds a down arrow (▼).

The **restore button** is the small box located at the right end of the title bar (of a maximized window) which holds an up arrow *and* a down arrow (▲▼).

A **scroll bar** is a bar that appears at the right and/or bottom of those windows whose contents are not fully visible.

The **workspace** is the inner part of the window where the work on an application or document is carried out.

The **window borders** and **corners** mark the edges of the window and are used to *size* a window.

The **pointer** (sometimes called *mouse pointer*) is the arrow-shaped cursor that moves with the **mouse** as you slide the mouse over a flat surface. It changes shape depending on the job it can do at any given time.

Windows Organization

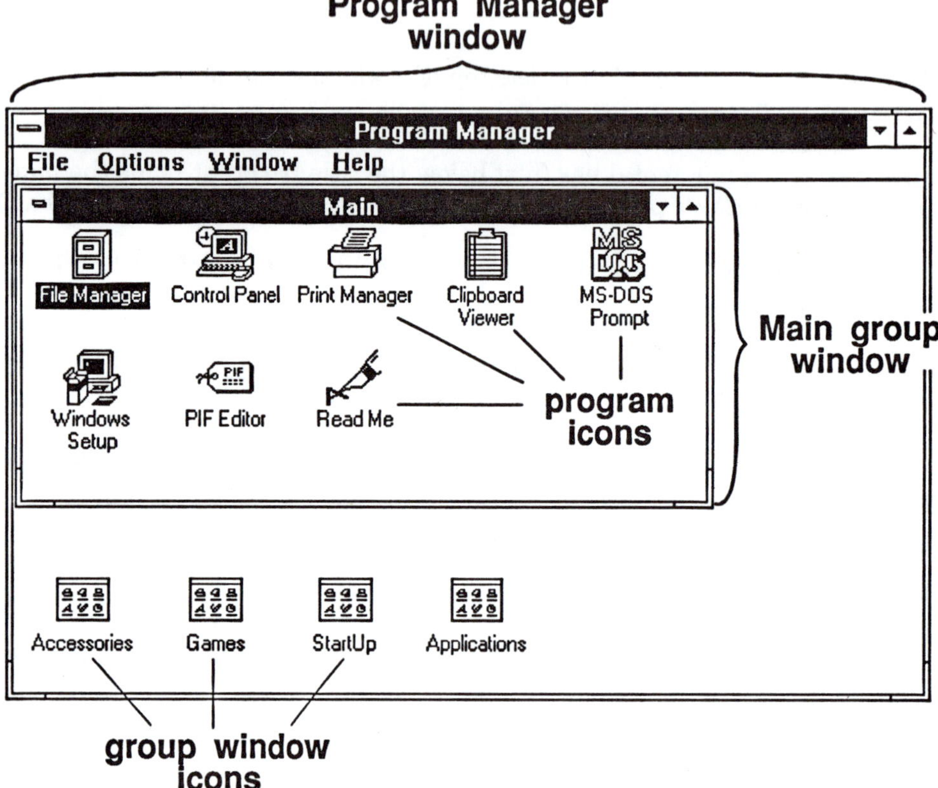

The program icons belonging to the **Main group window** are displayed in the
illustration above. Notice that the name for each icon is shown below the icon.
These icons represent the *commands to start the programs*.

The remaining **group windows** in this illustration are **closed,** but each one is
represented by a **group window icon** at the bottom of the Program Manager's
window.

Do Worksheet 8 on page 43
(combined with next topic)

Windows Organization

The **Program Manager** is a program that lets you organize applications into groups and start them with a *double-click on an icon*. The **Program Manager** is the heart of Microsoft Windows. When you start Windows, you start the Program Manager, and when you exit the Program Manager, you exit Windows. When Microsoft Windows 3.1 is installed, the Program Manager creates the following **groups** of related **programs** (items in the Applications group will probably be different on your system):

PROGRAM MANAGER

Group windows

MAIN	ACCESSORIES	GAMES	STARTUP	APPLICATIONS
File Manager	Write	Solitaire		Microsoft QBASIC
Control Panel	Paintbrush	Minesweeper		MS-DOS Editor
Print Manager	Terminal			Lotus 1-2-3
Clipboard Viewer	Notepad			WordPerfect 5.1 DOS
MS-DOS Prompt	Recorder			WordPerfect 5.1 WIN
Windows Setup	Cardfile			WordPerfect Speller
PIF Editor	Calendar			WordPerfect Thesaurus
Read Me	Calculator			WordPerfect Macro
	Clock			WordPerfect File Manager
	Object Packager			
	Media Player			
	Sound Recorder			

Group windows are a special type of document window that are used to "group" similar kinds of programs together. The icons in the **group windows** represent programs (applications) or, more accurately, *commands to start programs*. New groups can be created and program icons can be easily moved and/or copied between groups. Some programs are very simple, for example, *Clock*, while others are very complex, for example, *File Manager*.

- The programs in **Main** help run Windows.
- The programs in **Accessories** are useful programs that come with Windows.
- The programs in **Games** are games used for fun or for practicing basic mouse skills.
- The **Startup** group has nothing in it when Windows is installed.
- The programs in **Applications** are programs other than Windows, some of which may be designed to work *within* Windows while others may be *non-Windows* programs.

Windows Command Elements

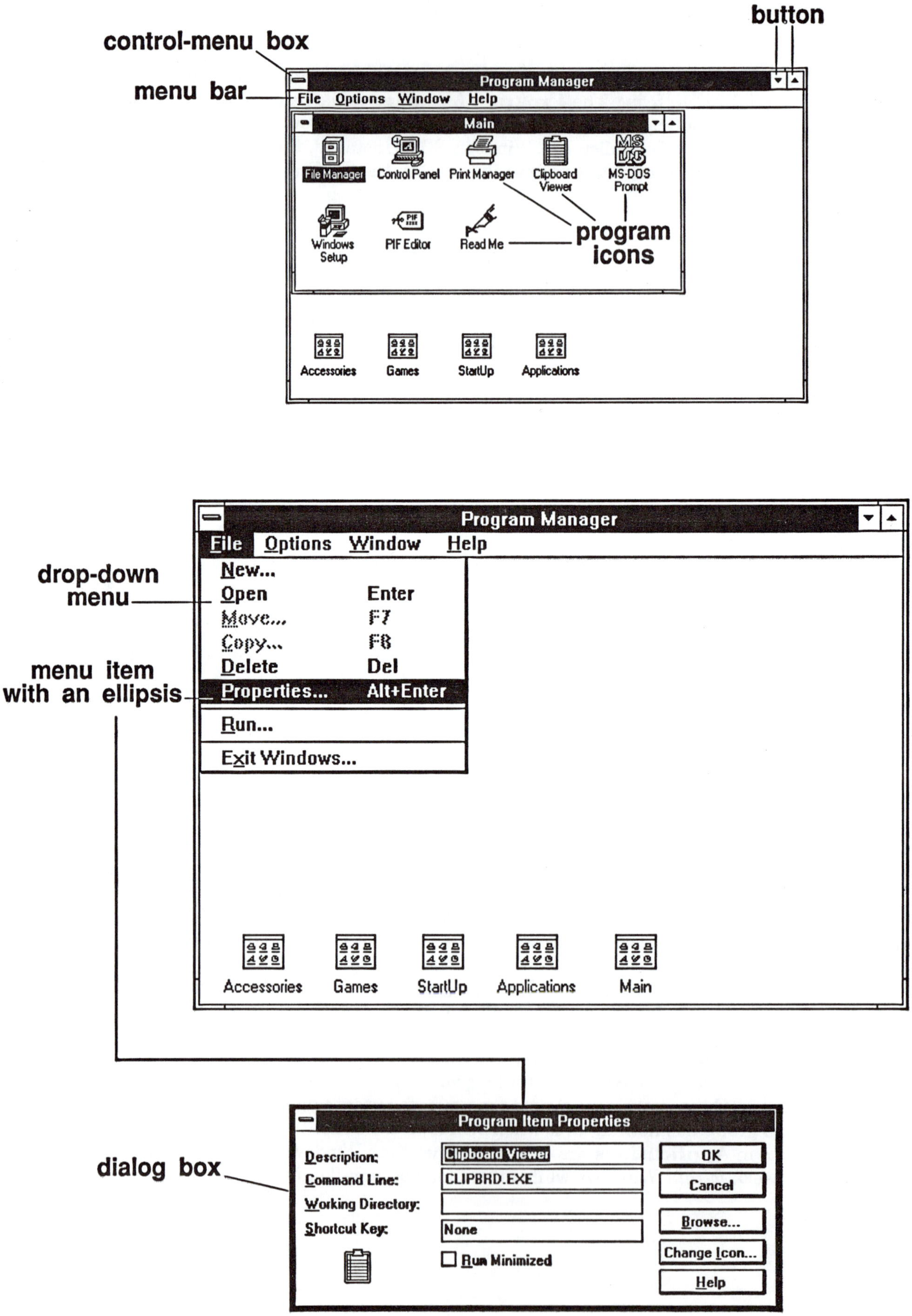

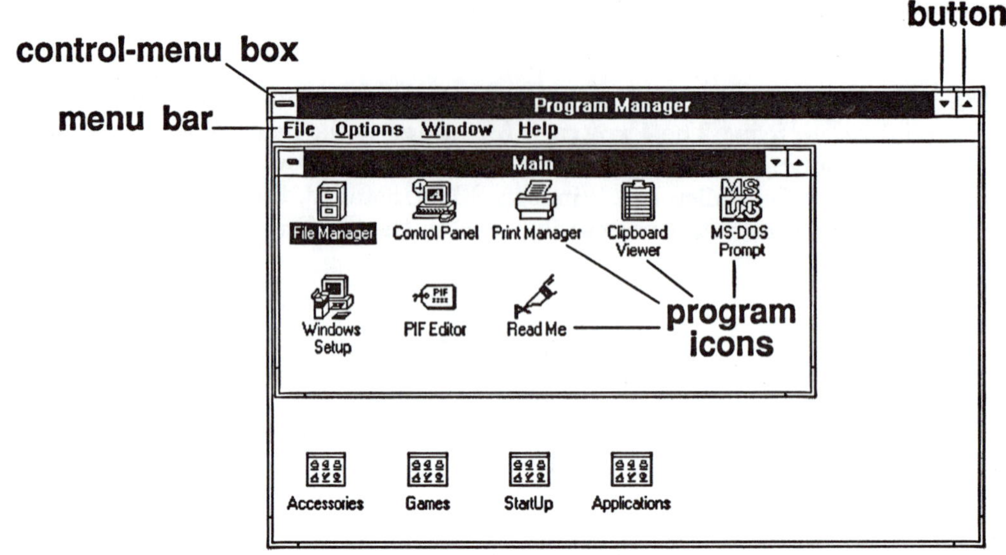

Do Worksheet 8 on page 43
(combined with the previous topic)

Controlling Windows

Windows is controlled by using **commands**. **Commands** are instructions that cause an action to be carried out.

Windows' *graphics environment* is designed to take advantage of the ***mouse*** to issue commands (see next page). Windows commands can also be controlled from the ***keyboard*** (see page 21). And then there are **shortcut keys** for the *keyboard* that can speed access to certain frequently used commands.

This variety means that there may be several ways to activate a single command. While this may be confusing to the beginner who is trying to remember how to issue commands, it offers the flexibility to meet the needs of many different users.

Here are some Windows elements that hold commands:

> The **menu bar** is the second horizontal bar (located under the title bar) in an *application* window. It displays the *menus* for the application.

> A **drop-down menu** is a submenu that *drops down* when a *menu item* is chosen from the *menu bar*.

> A **dialog box** is a window that appears when a menu *item* with an ellipsis (...) is chosen. The dialog box requests additional information before performing the original command. See page 23.

> The **control box** (⊟) opens the *control menu*, which holds commands that manipulate the *window*, such as <u>R</u>estore, <u>M</u>ove, <u>S</u>ize, Ma<u>x</u>imize, Mi<u>n</u>imize, and <u>C</u>lose.

> A **command button** is a small box holding an icon or a word that will carry out a command, for example, ☐ OK ☐ .

> A **program icon** represents a program that can be started from a *group window*.

A **dimmed command**, shown in gray, cannot be used in the current situation.

A **default** is an automatic setting in program. Windows has been designed with many **defaults** that best fit most situations. A command with a ✓ (check), an ☒ (selected check box), or a command button with a *darker outline* represents either a Windows **default** or a selection that a user has made.

NOTE: The following topics (covered on the next few pages) relate to controlling Windows: the mouse and pointer, the keyboard, and dialog boxes.

The Mouse

The **mouse** is a small, hand-held device used to control a pointer on the screen.

There are three mouse actions:

Click
Move the pointer on an item.
Quickly press and release the left button.

Double-click
Move the pointer on an item.
Quickly press and release the left mouse button twice.
NOTE: It may take some practice to perfect this mouse action.

Drag
Move the pointer on an item.
Hold down the left button.
Slide the mouse to a new location.
Release the button.

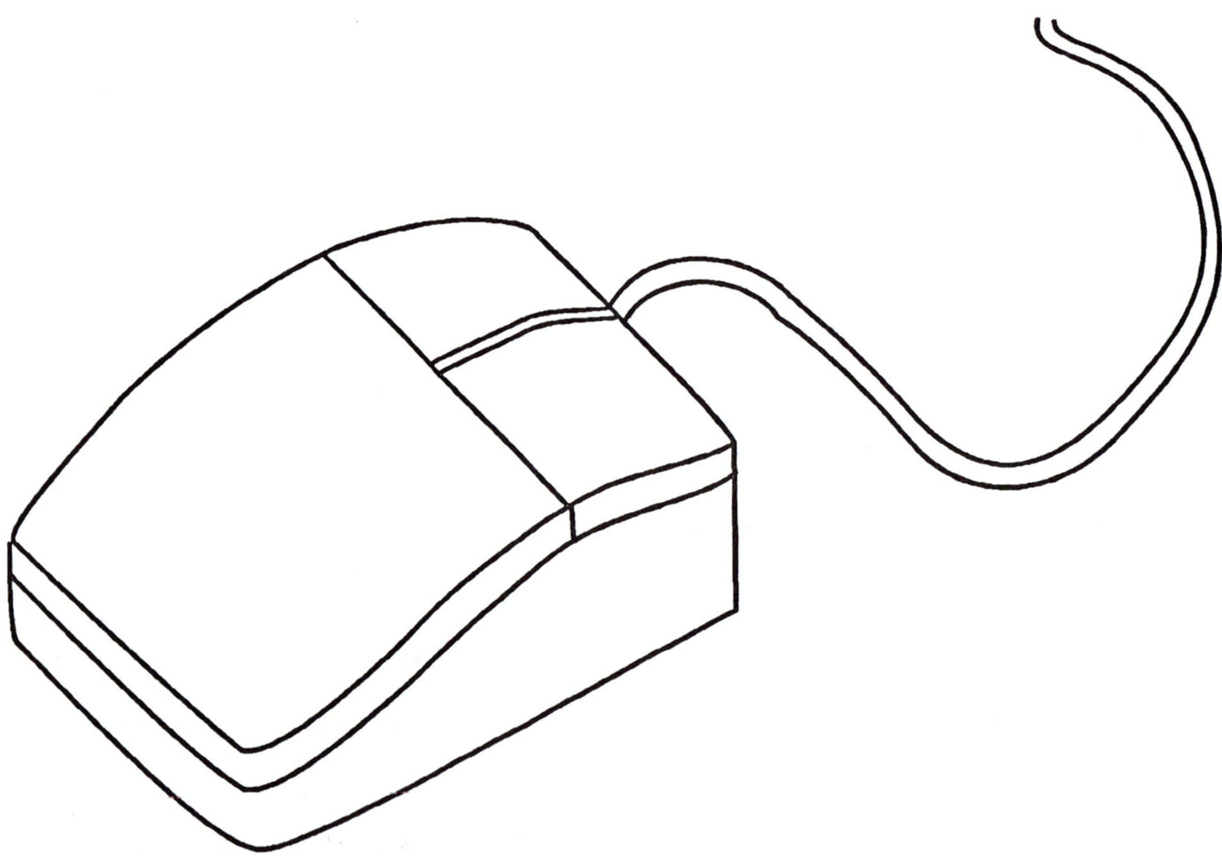

• Always use the left mouse button unless otherwise instructed.

*Do Worksheet 9 on page 44
(combined with the next topic)*

The Mouse and Pointer

The Pointer

The **pointer** (or mouse pointer) is the arrow on the screen that moves with the **mouse** as you slide the mouse over a flat surface. The pointer's shape may change depending on the job it is doing.

Some common pointer shapes, their name, and their function are shown below:

Shape	Name	Function
	Arrow	chooses items, sizes windows, and activates applications
	Sizing	adjusts the size of a window
	Move	moves a window (is displayed when **Move** is chosen from the Control menu)
	Hourglass	signals to wait while Windows processes data
	Hand	jumps between Help topics
	I-beam	text pointer—indicates where text will be entered
	Prevent	indicates that you *cannot* perform an action

The Keyboard

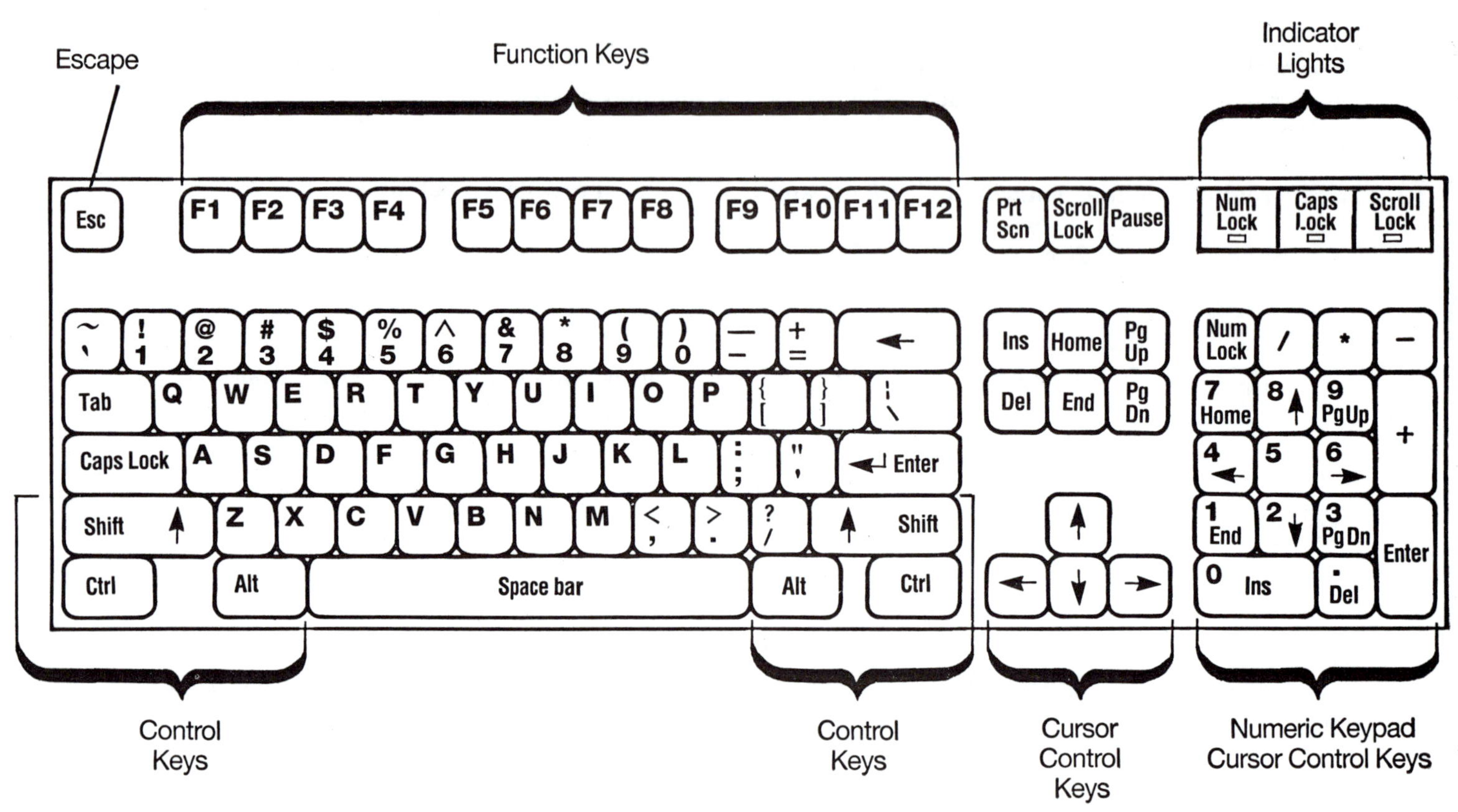

Enhanced keyboard, with 12 function keys across the top.

There are many keyboard variations, but they all have basically the same keys. Notice the special keys shown in this illustration, and locate those keys on your keyboard.

Do Worksheet 9 on page 44
(combined with the previous topic)

The Keyboard

The **keyboard** is used to enter data into and issue commands to the computer.

Function keys are the ten or twelve keys labeled F1, F2, etc., and are located across the top (or at the left side) of the keyboard. They are used to issue commands.

Control keys (Shift, Ctrl, and Alt) are used in combination with other keys to issue commands.

Shortcut keys are key combinations that can be used to activate certain commands instead of using menus. If a command has a **shortcut**, the key combination is shown on the right of the command on the drop-down menu.

Using Keys Together

When two keys are used together to issue a command, a plus sign (+) is shown between the keys.

FOR EXAMPLE:

Alt + Tab   Press and hold down the **Alt** key, tap the **Tab** key, and then release the **Alt** key.

Using Keys in Succession

When two or more keys are pressed one after the other to issue a command, the keys are separated by a comma.

FOR EXAMPLE:

F4, M, E   Press each key in succession.

Two Special Keys

Esc (escape) is used to back out of situations. Occasionally you find yourself in a place you don't want to be, and often, **Esc** will get you out of the situation without doing any damage.

F1 is used to get Help (see page 25).

Dialog Boxes

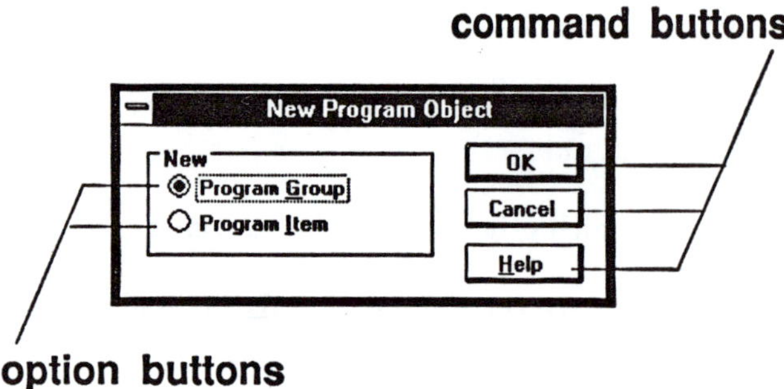

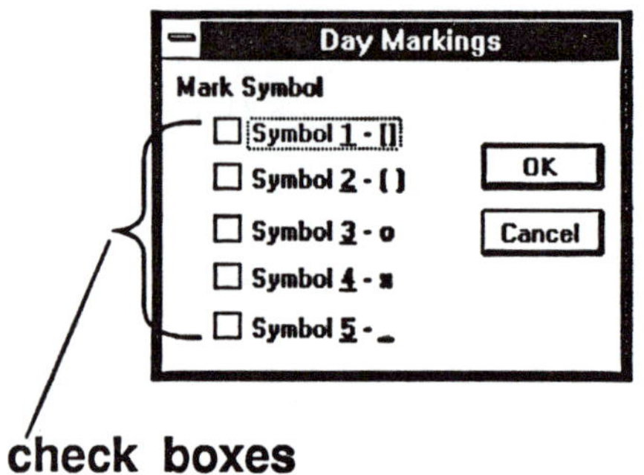

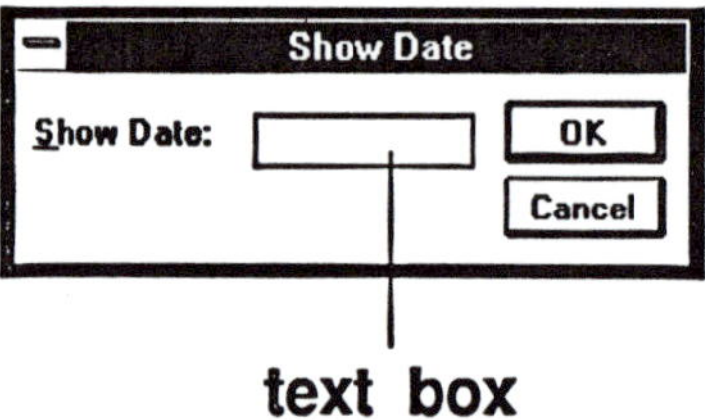

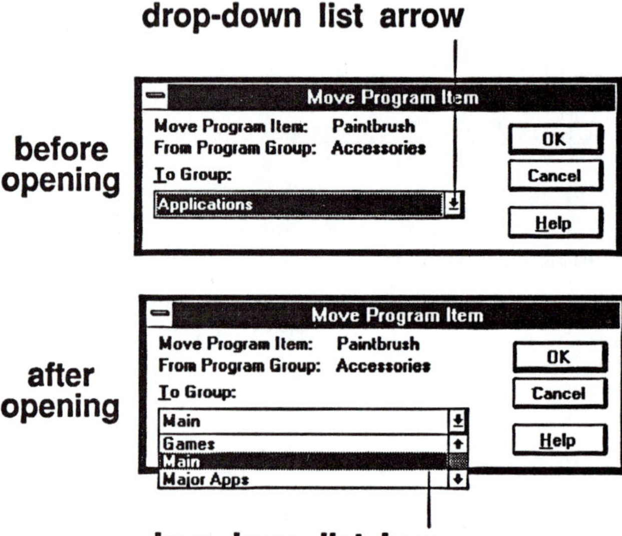

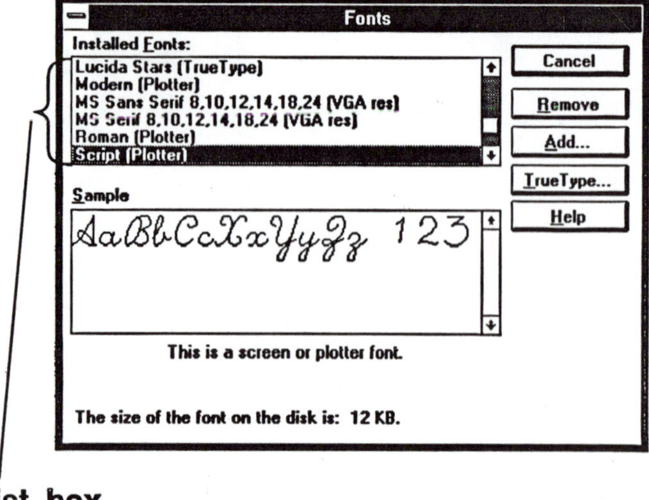

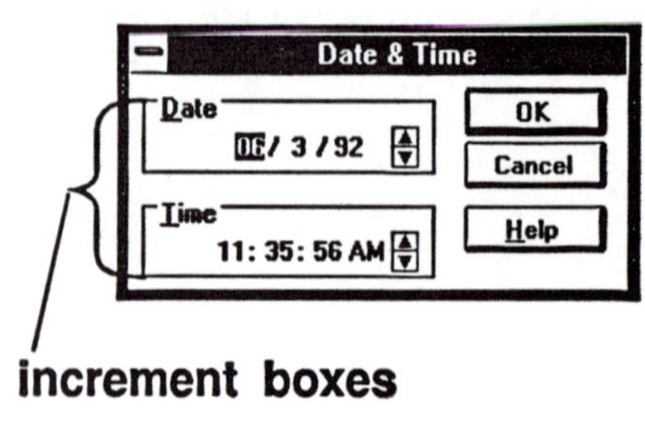

When a command that is followed by an ellipsis (...) is chosen from the menu, a **dialog box** appears. The **dialog box** requests additional information before Windows performs the original command.

Certain control features that are used primarily within **dialog boxes** are listed below:

A **command button** in a dialog box carries out an action such as OK or Cancel.

Option buttons ◯ (or radio buttons) are circles in a dialog box from which you may select *only one of a related group*. A dot in the circle ◉ means an option button is selected.

Check boxes ☐ are squares in a dialog box that you may select as desired. Selected check boxes contain an ☒.

A **text box** is a box in a dialog box that provides space for typing information needed to carry out a command.

A **list box** is a box in a dialog box that displays a list of options from which a choice can be made.

A **drop-down list box** is a box that is similar to a **list box** except that it usually appears in a small or crowded dialog box and must be opened by clicking on the **drop-down list arrow** next to it.

A **drop-down list arrow** ⬇ is an arrow in a dialog box that has a line under it, which indicates that it can open a **drop-down list box**.

An **increment box** is a box in a dialog box used to set a value by providing an up and a down arrow, which, when clicked on, changes the original value. A new value can also be *typed* in.

How many of the control features listed above can you find in this dialog box?

Help Screens

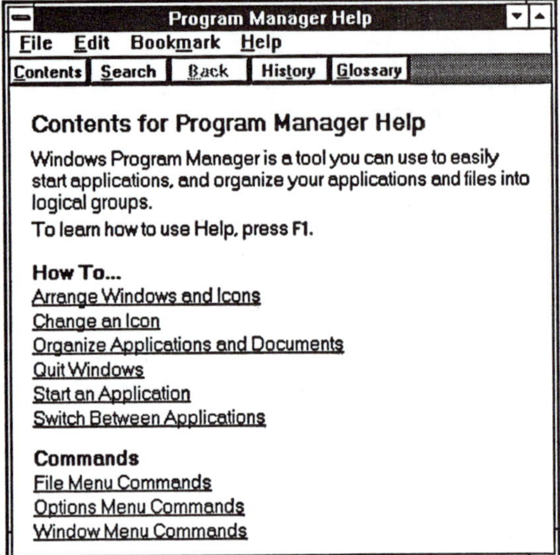

Contents

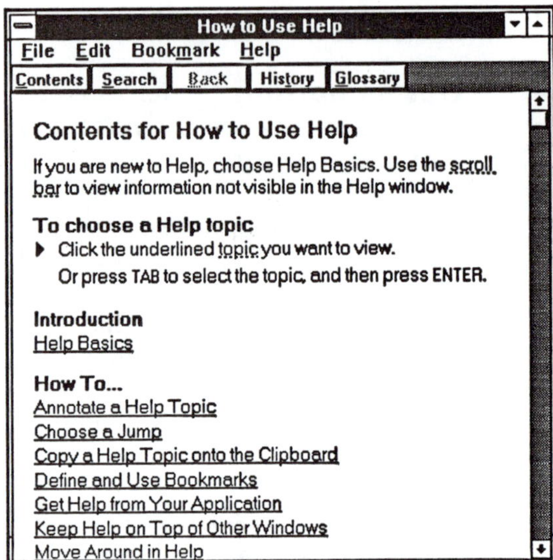

How to Use Help

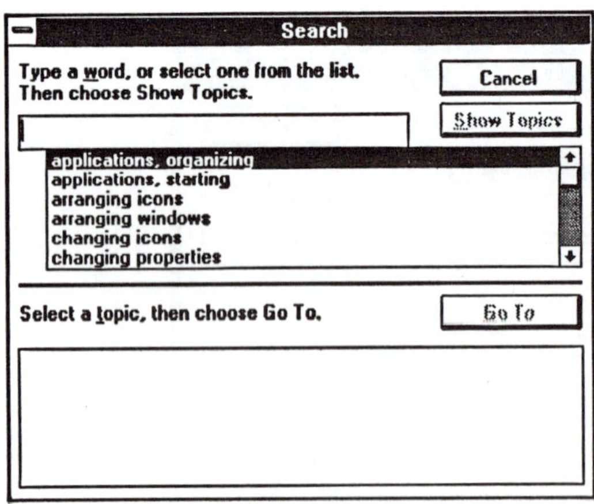

Search for Help On

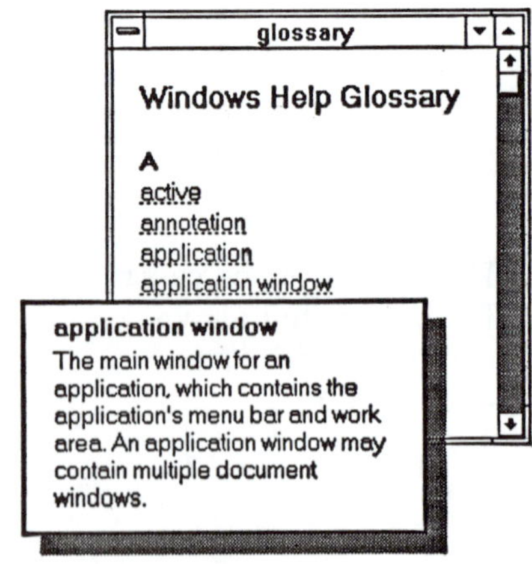

Glossary

Windows Help

Windows **Help** is a quick and easy way to look up information about the feature you are working with. **Help** can be used whenever you see Help on the menu bar or see a Help button (F1 is the *shortcut key* for Help).

The following ways to use Help are found on most Help menus:

Contents is an alphabetic list of the Help *topics* available for the application you are using.

Search for Help On displays a dialog box that is used to locate information about a specific topic.

How to Use Help shows information about how to *use* the Help feature.

Glossary is a list of Windows terms from which you choose a term whose definition will be displayed.

About (application) displays a window with information about the program you are using.

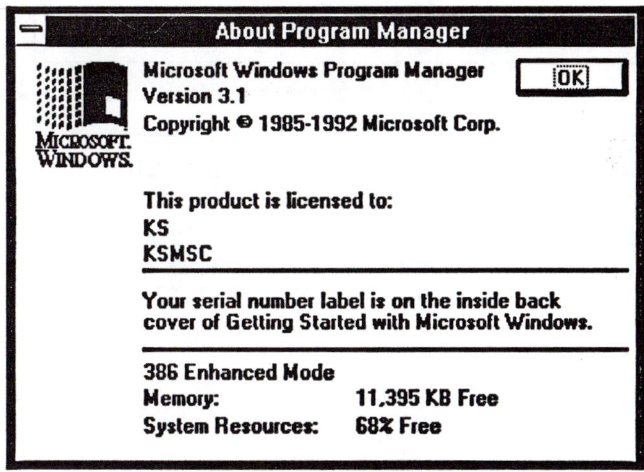

About (Application)

File Manager

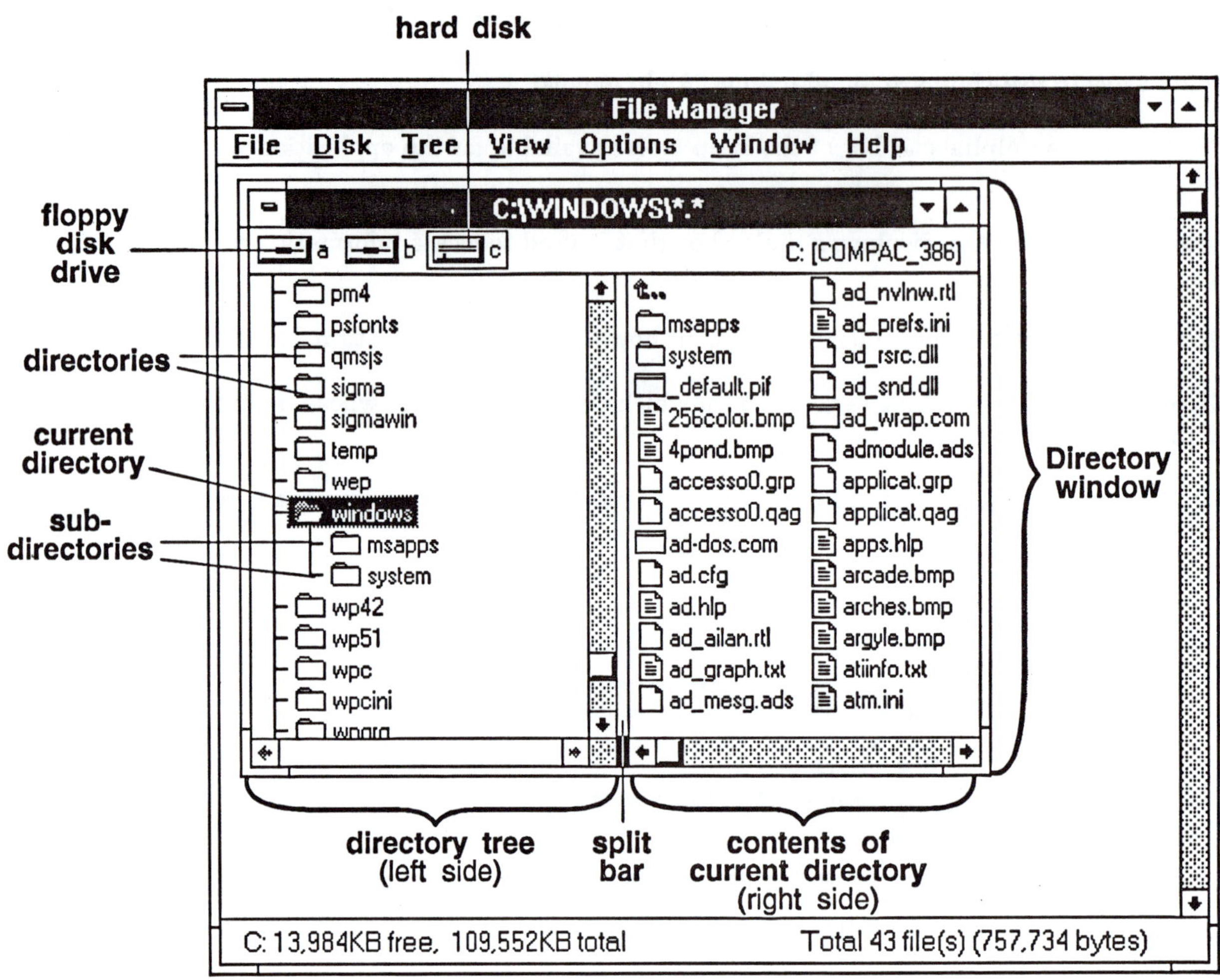

File Manager Icons

floppy disk drive	associated file
hard disk drive	application file
directory	hidden file
current directory	all other files

File Manager

The **File Manager** is a program used to control your files. With **File Manager** you can
- view all your directories, subdirectories, and files
- organize your files and directories
- move and copy files
- sort your files by name, type, size, or date
- start applications
- associate a file with a program

When you first start **File Manager**, a **directory window** that is *split* appears in the File Manager window. The directory window displays
- the *current directory* in its *title bar,*
- the available *disk drives* (as icons)
- the *directory tree* on the *left side,* and
- the *contents of the current directory* (files and subdirectories) on the *right side.*

As you move through the directories in the *directory window,* the files on the *right side* change to reflect the *directory* that is highlighted on the *left side.* The *split screen* is the default for the *directory window* and can be changed.

DIRECTORIES

A **directory** is the part of the disk structure that holds the *files* that are saved on the disk. A directory can also hold other directories (called subdirectories).

A **subdirectory** is a directory that is within another directory.

A **root directory** is the top-level directory; for example, **C:** is the root directory on most hard disks.

A **directory tree** is a display of the directory structure (directories and subdirectories) on a disk.

The **current directory** is the directory you are working in. In the File Manager, the *highlighted* directory is the *current directory.*

The **directory window** is a window within File Manager that displays the *directories, subdirectories,* and *files* on your disk.

FILES

A **file** is a *set of data* that is saved on a disk as a named unit.

A **data file** (or document) is a file that consists of *data that is created in a program,* such as a *letter* typed into a *word processor.*

A **program file** (or application file, or software) is a file that holds a set of instructions that perform a task, such as word processing or database management. Program files contain one of the following extensions: .EXE, .PIF, .COM, or .BAT.

A **filename** is the name you assign to a *set of data* that you save on a disk. The name may have up to eight characters and may include an extension (a period followed by up to three characters), for example: LETTER.WRI

A **filename extension** is the "optional period and up to three characters" at the end of a *filename.* A *file extension* is often used to identify *groups* of related files and is automatically added by some applications.

An **associated file** is a file that has a *filename extension* that identifies it as "belonging" to a certain application, such as Write (.WRI) or Paintbrush (.BMP).

Windows Modes

Standard and **386 Enhanced** Modes
(Processor and Memory Requirements)

Computer's Memory

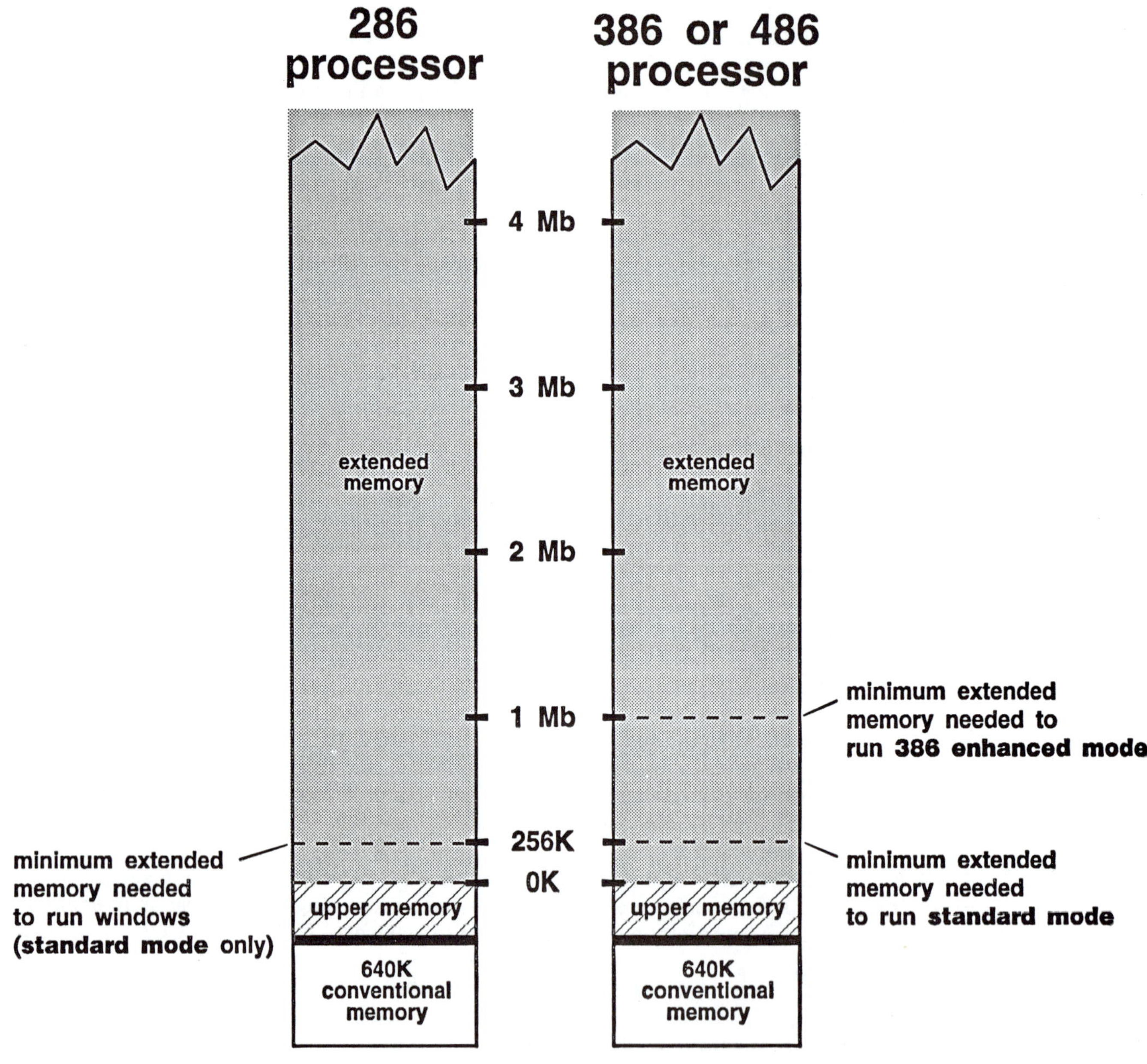

The 286 processor can run Windows in **standard mode** only. The computer must have at least 256K of extended memory to run Windows.

The 386 or 486 processor can run in **386 enhanced mode** if the computer has at least **1** Mb of extended memory. It can run in standard mode if the computer has at least 256K of extended memory.

Do Worksheet 14 on page 49
(combined with the next topic)

Windows Modes

To take advantage of the full power of Microsoft Windows, you need computers with fast **processors** and large **memories**. The faster the *processor* and the larger the *memory*, the better.

Three important factors require this speed and memory:
> Windows' graphics environment,
> larger and more complex programs, and
> multitasking (using more than one program at once; see next two pages).

Speed.   IBM and compatible computers are commonly sold according to their **microprocessor chip**. The higher the number, the faster the **processor**.

> 80286 microprocessor chip is abbreviated **286**
> 80386 microprocessor chip is abbreviated **386**
> 80486 microprocessor chip is abbreviated **486**

Memory. **Memory** size is measured in **bytes**:

> One **byte** of **memory** holds one character, i.e., a or b.
> One **K** (kilobyte) of **memory** holds about 1,000 characters.
> One **Mb** (megabyte) of **memory** holds about 1,000,000 characters.

> **Conventional memory** is the first 640K of computer memory.
> **Upper memory** is additional memory (up to 384K) *above* the 640K of conventional memory, normally reserved for running the computer's hardware.
> **Extended memory** is general purpose memory above conventional and upper memory.

Windows 3.1 can run with a little less than 1 Mb of memory (640K conventional plus 256K extended). However, to realize the full power of Windows 3.1, you need at least 2 Mb and preferably 4 Mb to 8 Mb of memory.

Windows Modes

Window 3.1 can run in two modes, **standard mode** and **386 enhanced mode**, depending on your system's capabilities. When you start Windows (using WIN), the most appropriate mode for your system is automatically used.

> Windows runs in **standard mode** if you have a 286 (or higher) processor with 640K of conventional memory plus at least 256K of extended memory.

> Windows runs in **386 enhanced mode** if you have a 386 (or higher) processor with 640K of conventional memory plus at least 1 Mb of extended memory.

Multitasking

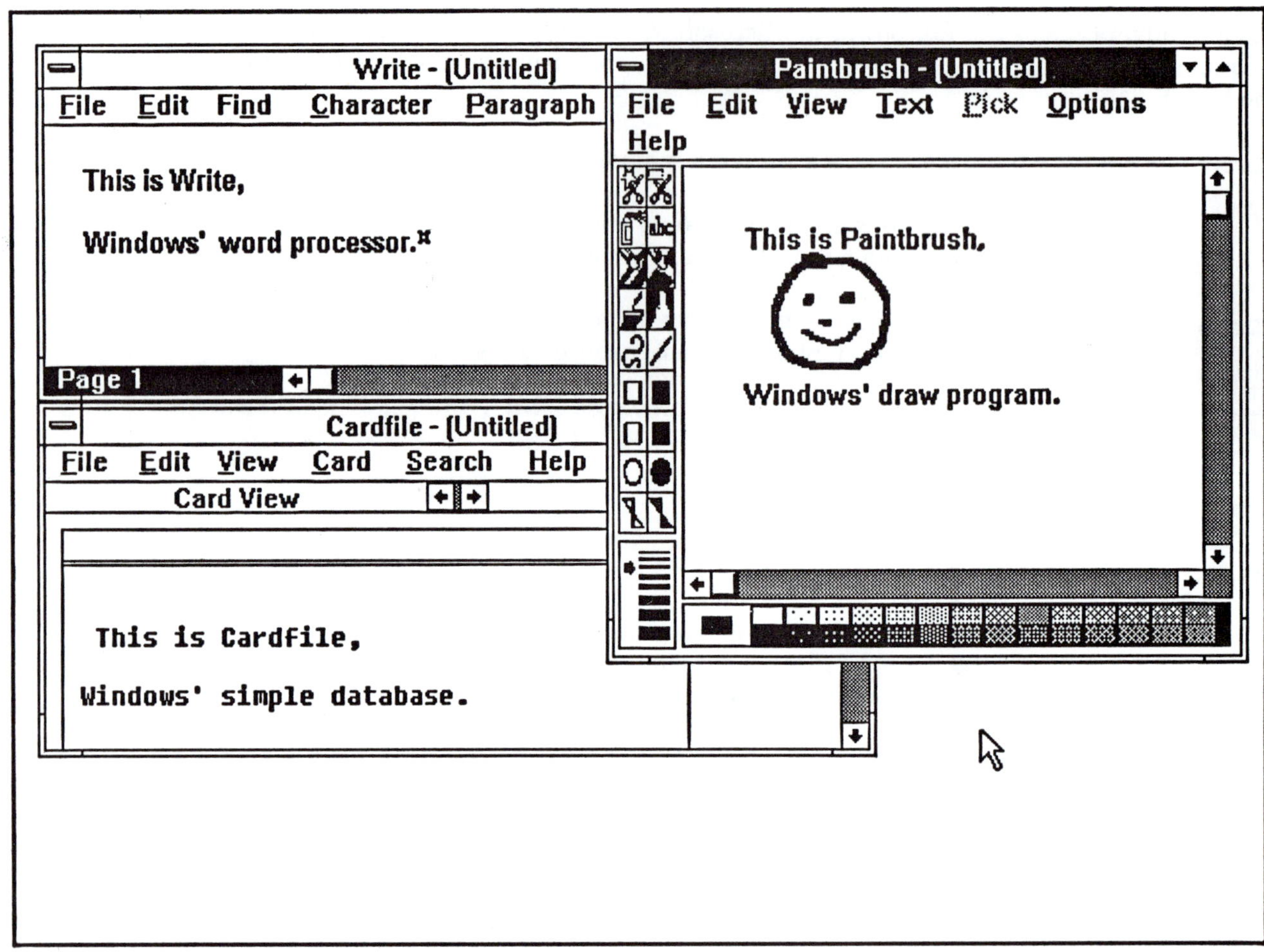

This desktop is arranged to show three *application windows* that are all in the computer's memory at once. Paintbrush is the *active* program as indicated by the highlighted title bar.

Notice the title bar, menu bar, and control box for each window.

Windows Multitasking

Multitasking is the ability to run more than one program at once. Windows has **memory-managing** programs that organize the computer's memory to prevent different programs from using the same memory at the same time.

If you are working in **standard mode** (and sometimes in **386 enhanced mode**), when you switch programs, the program you leave is suspended (exactly as you leave it) while you work with the program you switched into. This is one form of **multitasking**.

A more powerful form of **multitasking** can be accessed when using the **386 enhanced mode**. The computer can *process a time-consuming task* in one program (such as sorting a database) *while you work in another program*. The **standard mode** cannot access this form of multitasking.

<u>View more than one program at once</u>.

When multitasking, it is sometimes useful to size and arrange the application windows so you can view more than one application at a time.

(OLE) Object Linking and Embedding

Embedding	Linking

Embedding

Paintbrush

Make a Paintbrush drawing (*object*), *select* it, and *copy* it.

Write

Embed the *object* (drawing) into Write using *paste*.

Write

Edit the *object* from Write.

Paintbrush

The Paintbrush *object* **does not change.**

Linking

Paintbrush

Make a Paintbrush drawing (*object*), <u>*save*</u> it, *select* it, and *copy* it.

Write

Embed and <u>**link**</u> the *object* (drawing) into Write using <u>*paste link*</u>.

Write

Edit the *object* from Write.

Paintbrush

The Paintbrush *object* **also changes.**

Windows Integration

Integration means
1) that *information* can be easily *transferred* between different programs, and
2) that different programs look and behave alike, reducing the time it takes to learn a new program.

CUA - Common User Access refers to a common set of commands that are used with all Windows applications.

The **clipboard** is used to hold information that is being integrated (transferred) from one program to another.

OLE - Object Linking and Embedding is a powerful way of integrating developed for Microsoft Windows.

An **object** is a selected *set of information* created in a Windows application, such as a *drawing* in Paintbrush. An object can be *embedded in* or *linked to* another application.

To **embed** means to *paste* an *object* that was created in one application *into* another application.

A **link** is an active connection between the same *object* that is *embedded* in more than one application and/or document.

A **client application** is an application whose documents can accept *embedded* or *linked objects*.

A **server application** is an application that creates *objects* that can be *embedded* or *linked* into other documents.

A **source document** is the document in which an *object* is created.

A **destination document** is a document into which an *object* is placed.

Integration is *Powerful!*

Integration means that information can be transferred between different programs. For example, a drawing created in a **drawing** program can be *copied or cut to the clipboard* and then *pasted from the clipboard* into a **word processing** program.

Using simple integration, if you want to change (edit) a drawing in the word processor, you have to:
- delete the drawing from the word processor,
- go back into the drawing program and edit or re-draw the original drawing, and
- copy the picture from the **drawing** document back into the **word processing** document again.

Object Embedding is *More Powerful!*

Object embedding is a way to copy an *object* from a *source program* (for example, Paintbrush) into a *destination program* (for example, Write) so that it can be edited directly from the *destination program* (for example, you can edit a drawing from the word processor).

Object Linking is *Most Powerful!*

Object linking connects an *object* that has been copied from a *source document* and **embedded** in one or more *destination documents* so that when the *object* is *edited* in the source document, all the destination documents are also *edited.*

Getting Started Worksheets

Table of Contents

WORKSHEET 1

THE COMPUTER SYSTEM, HARDWARE

NAME _______________________

DIRECTIONS: Use the following terms to fill in the name of each piece of hardware shown below:

chips	floppy disks	keyboard	mouse
computer	hard disk	memory	floppy disk drive
processor	monitor	printer	

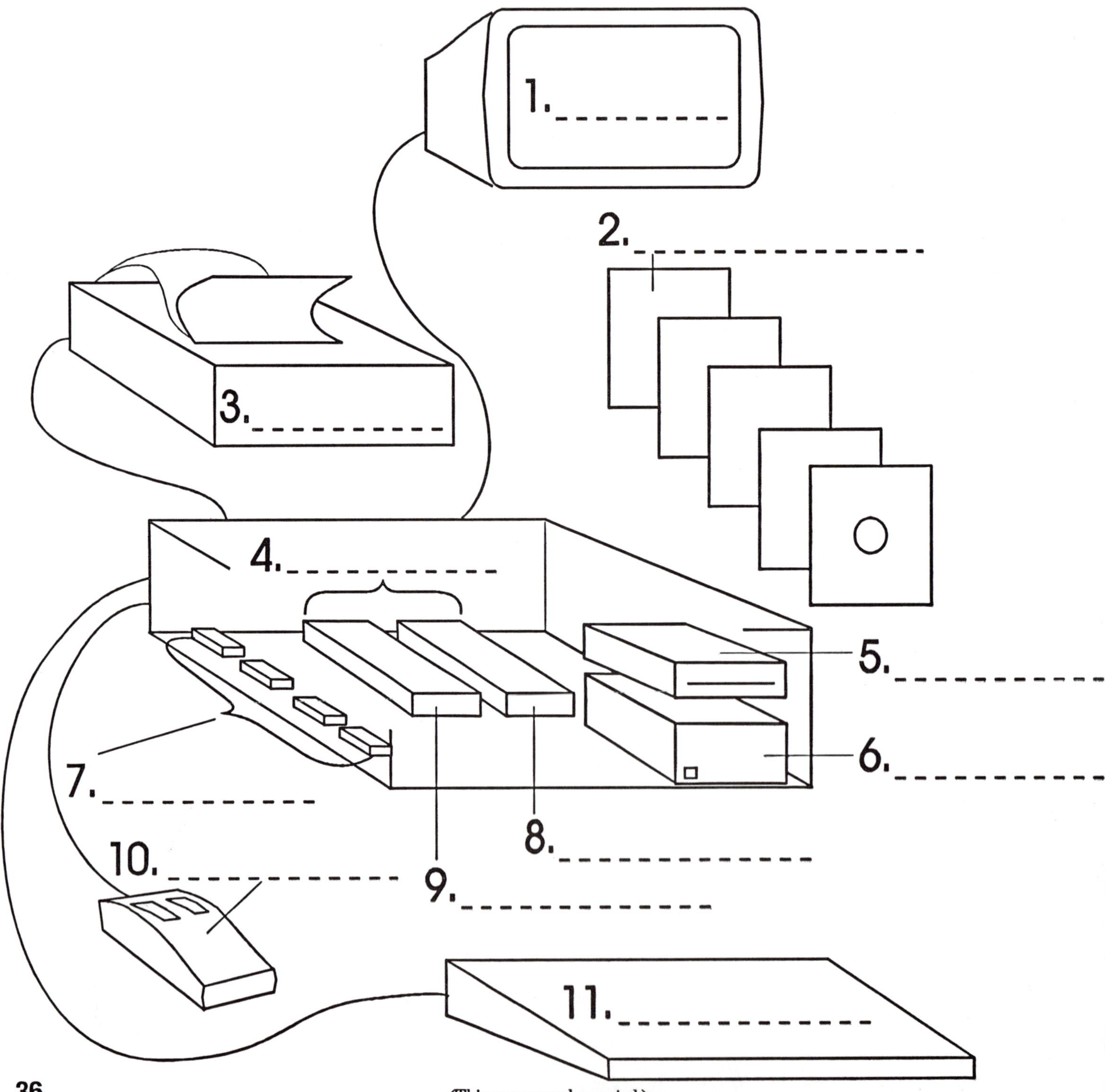

(This page may be copied.)

WORKSHEET 2

THE COMPUTER SYSTEM, HARDWARE

NAME _______________________

DIRECTIONS: Use the following terms to fill in the blanks below:

chips	floppy disks	keyboard	mouse
computer	hard disk	memory	printer
disk drive	hardware	monitor	processor

---

1. What is an electronic device that performs complex tasks at high speed and with great accuracy? It has two main parts, the **processor** and the **memory.**

   1) _______________________

2. What are the small pieces of silicon wafers which often hold instructions to perform behind-the-scenes tasks, making it possible for you to use the computer?

   2) _______________________

3. What is the group of parts that make up the computer system and that <u>can</u> be seen and touched?

   3) _______________________

4. What is the small, hand-held device used to control a pointer on the screen?

   4) _______________________

5. What do you call the large capacity, permanent storage area that offers fast access to the information stored on it?

   5) _______________________

6. What do you call the area of the computer that holds instructions (programs) and information you give it, and forgets everything when the computer is turned off?

   6) _______________________

7. What device transfers information from the computer to paper?

   7) _______________________

8. What is the device that transfers information back and forth between the computer and a disk?

   8) _______________________

9. What do you call the magnetically coated disks on which information (both programs and data typed from the keyboard) can be stored and retrieved?

   9) _______________________

10. What is the "brains" of the computer?

    10) _______________________

11. What is the screen that displays the information in the computer?

    11) _______________________

12. What is used to enter data into and issue commands to the computer?

    12) _______________________

WORKSHEET 3

THE COMPUTER SYSTEM, SOFTWARE

> **DIRECTIONS:** Use the following terms to identify the different types of software and to identify the places software travels:
>
> | | | | |
> |---|---|---|---|
> | firmware | hard disk | floppy disks | application software |
> | memory | processor | system software | |

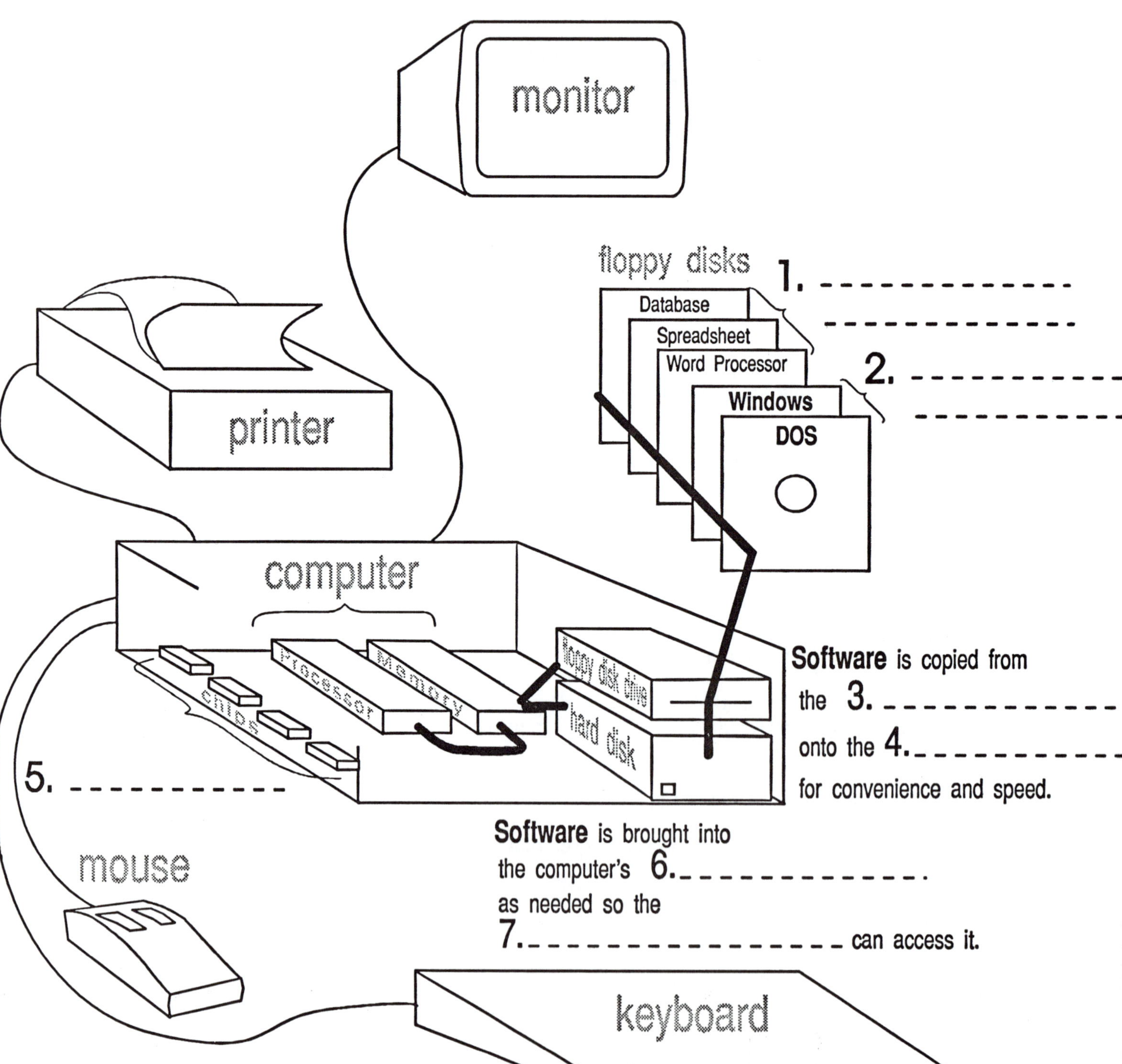

(This page may be copied.)

WORKSHEET 4
THE COMPUTER SYSTEM, SOFTWARE

NAME _______________________

DIRECTIONS: Use the following terms to fill in the blanks below. Some terms are used more than once.

software	system software	application software
program	Microsoft Windows	DOS - disk operating system
firmware		

---

1. What do you call the *set of instructions* that tells the computer what to do, is often stored on disks, and <u>cannot</u> be seen or touched?

   1) _______________________

2. What are the two main kinds of **software**?

   2) a. _______________________

   b. _______________________

3. What are two kinds of **system software**?

   3) a. _______________________

   b. _______________________

4. What kind of **software** runs the computer system (communicates between the parts that make up the computer system)?

   4) _______________________

5. What kind of *system software* is built into the computer system on chips?

   5) _______________________

6. What kind of *system software* comes on disks and acts as a link between *application software* and the system's hardware?

   6) _______________________

7. What kind of **software** does a specific task, such as word processing?

   7) _______________________

8. What is the special kind of *software* that provides a *graphics environment*, that is, an *icon-based* **link** between you, application software, and DOS?

   8) _______________________

9. What word means the same thing as "application"?

   9) _______________________

WORKSHEET 5

NAME ___________________________

ABOUT WINDOWS, WINDOWS ASPECTS, and
THREE BASIC PARTS OF WINDOWS

> DIRECTIONS: Use the following terms to fill in the blanks below.
>
> | | | |
> |---|---|---|
> | windows | multitasking | Program Manager |
> | desktop | application | OLE - object linking and embedding |
> | document | icons | GUI - graphical user interface |

1. What commonly used phrase means that Windows has <u>pictures</u> that <u>you use</u> to <u>communicate</u> with the computer?

    1) ___________________________

2. What Windows program provides an easy way to organize and start programs?

    2) ___________________________

3. What is it called when you run more than one program at a time?

    3) ___________________________

4. What does Windows call its powerful way to transfer information between programs?

    4) ___________________________

5. What are the small pictures that represent various elements in Windows?

    5) ___________________________

6. What are the rectangular work areas for tasks, applications, or documents?

    6) ___________________________

7. What kind of a window holds programs and has a menu bar?

    7) ___________________________

8. What kind of a window is inside an application window and has no menu bar?

    8) ___________________________

9. What is the background (screen) upon which windows and icons appear called?

    9) ___________________________

(This page may be copied.)

WORKSHEET 6

WINDOWS ELEMENTS

NAME _______________________

DIRECTIONS: Use the following terms to fill in the blanks below:

menu bar	maximize button	control box	window borders and corners
title bar	minimize button	workspace	
scroll bar	restore button	pointer	

1. _ _ _ _ _ _ _ _ _ _ _ _ _ _

2. _ _ _ _ _ _ _ _ _ _ _ _ _ _

3. _ _ _ _ _ _ _ _ _ _ _

4. _ _ _ _ _ _ _ _ _ _ _ _ _ _

5. _ _ _ _ _ _ _ _ _ _ _ _ _ _

6. _ _ _ _ _ _ _ _ _ _ _ _ _ _

Program Manager

File   Options   Window   Help

Main

Accessories

Write   Paintbrush   Terminal   Notepad   Recorder   Cardfile

7. _ _ _ _ _ _ _ _ _ _ _

Calendar   Calculator   Clock   Object Packager   Character Map   Media Player

StartUp   Games   Applications

8. _ _ _ _ _ _ _ _ _ _ _ _ _ _

9. _ _ _ _ _ _ _ _ _ _ _ _ _ _

10. _ _ _ _ _ _ _ _ _ _ _ _

WORKSHEET 7

WINDOWS ELEMENTS

NAME _______________________________

> DIRECTIONS: Use the following terms to fill in the blanks below:
>
> | menu bar | maximize button | control box | window borders and corners |
> |----------|-----------------|-------------|----------------------------|
> | title bar | minimize button | workspace | |
> | scroll bars | restore button | pointer | |

1. What do you call the box at the left end of the title bar which holds a hyphen (-) and opens the control menu?

   1) _______________________________

2. What is the arrow-shaped cursor that moves with the **mouse** as you slide the mouse over a flat surface?

   2) _______________________________

3. What is the horizontal bar at the top of a window that holds the window's name?

   3) _______________________________

4. What are bars that appear at the right and/or bottom of *windows whose contents are not fully visible*?

   4) _______________________________

5. What is the horizontal bar (just below the title bar) that holds the names of an *application window's* menus?

   5) _______________________________

6. What is the small box located at the far right end of the title bar which holds an up arrow (▲)?

   6) _______________________________

7. What is the small box located toward the right end of the title bar (just before the maximize button) which holds a down arrow (▼)?

   7) _______________________________

8. What mark the edges of windows and are used to *size* windows?

   8) _______________________________

9. What is the small box located at the far right end of the title bar *of a maximized window* that holds an up arrow *and* a down arrow (⬍)?

   9) _______________________________

10. What do you call the inner part of a *window*, where the work on an application (program) is carried out?

    10) _______________________________

(This page may be copied.)

WORKSHEET 8

NAME ______________________

WINDOWS ORGANIZATION and CONTROLLING WINDOWS

DIRECTIONS: Use the following terms to fill in the blanks below:

mouse	control box	Program Manager	accessories
default	dialog box	drop-down menu	dimmed command
menu bar	program icon	command button	application
main	startup	games	commands

1. What Microsoft Windows program organizes applications into groups and lets you start applications?

1) ______________________

2. List the five **group windows** that are created when Windows is installed.

2) a. ______________________

b. ______________________

c. ______________________

d. ______________________

e. ______________________

3. What are instructions that cause an action to be carried out?

3) ______________________

4. What special control device is Microsoft Windows designed to take advantage of?

4) ______________________

5. In an application window, what is the second horizontal bar (located under the title bar) called?

5) ______________________

6. What do you call the submenu that opens when a menu item is chosen from the menu bar?

6) ______________________

7. What appears when a menu item with an ellipsis (...) is chosen?

7) ______________________

8. What is the box called which holds commands that manipulate the window; for example, move, size, maximize, etc.?

8) ______________________

9. What do you call the small box that holds an icon or a word which carries out a command?

9) ______________________

10. What is used to represent a program that can be started from a group window?

10) ______________________

11. What kind of command is shown in gray and cannot be used in the current situation?

11) ______________________

12. What is an *automatic setting* in a program called?

12) ______________________

WORKSHEET 9

THE MOUSE, THE POINTER and THE KEYBOARD

DIRECTIONS: Use the following terms to fill in the blanks below:

click	ESC	pointer	control keys	shortcut keys
comma	mouse	plus (+)	double-click	Alt, Shift, Ctrl
drag	F1	keyboard	function keys	

---

1. What is the small, hand-held device used to control the pointer on the screen?

1) ________________________

2. What mouse action are you using when you
1) move the pointer on an item, and
2) quickly press and release the left button?

2) ________________________

3. What mouse action are you using when you
1) move the pointer on an item, and 2) quickly press and release the left mouse button *twice*?

3) ________________________

4. What mouse action are you using when you
1) move the pointer on an item,
2) hold down the left button,
3) slide the mouse to a new location, and
4) then release the left button?

4) ________________________

5. What is the arrow on the screen which moves with the *mouse*?

5) ________________________

6. What device is used to enter data into the computer and to issue commands to the computer?

6) ________________________

7. What are two kinds of keys that are used to issue commands from the keyboard?

7) a. ________________________

b. ________________________

8. What are the *control keys*?

8) ________________________

9. What do you call *key combinations* that are used to activate certain commands without using the menu?

9) ________________________

10. When instructions are given to use *two keys together* to issue a command, what sign is shown between the keys?

10) ________________________

11. When instructions are given to use two or more *keys in succession* to issue a command, what separates the keys?

11) ________________________

12. What key is used to back out of situations?

12) ________________________

13. What function key is used to get Help?

13) ________________________

(This page may be copied.)

WORKSHEET 10

DIALOG BOXES

NAME _______________________

1. ___________________________

2. ___________________________

3. ___________________________

4. ___________________________

5. ___________________________

6. ___________________________

7. ___________________________

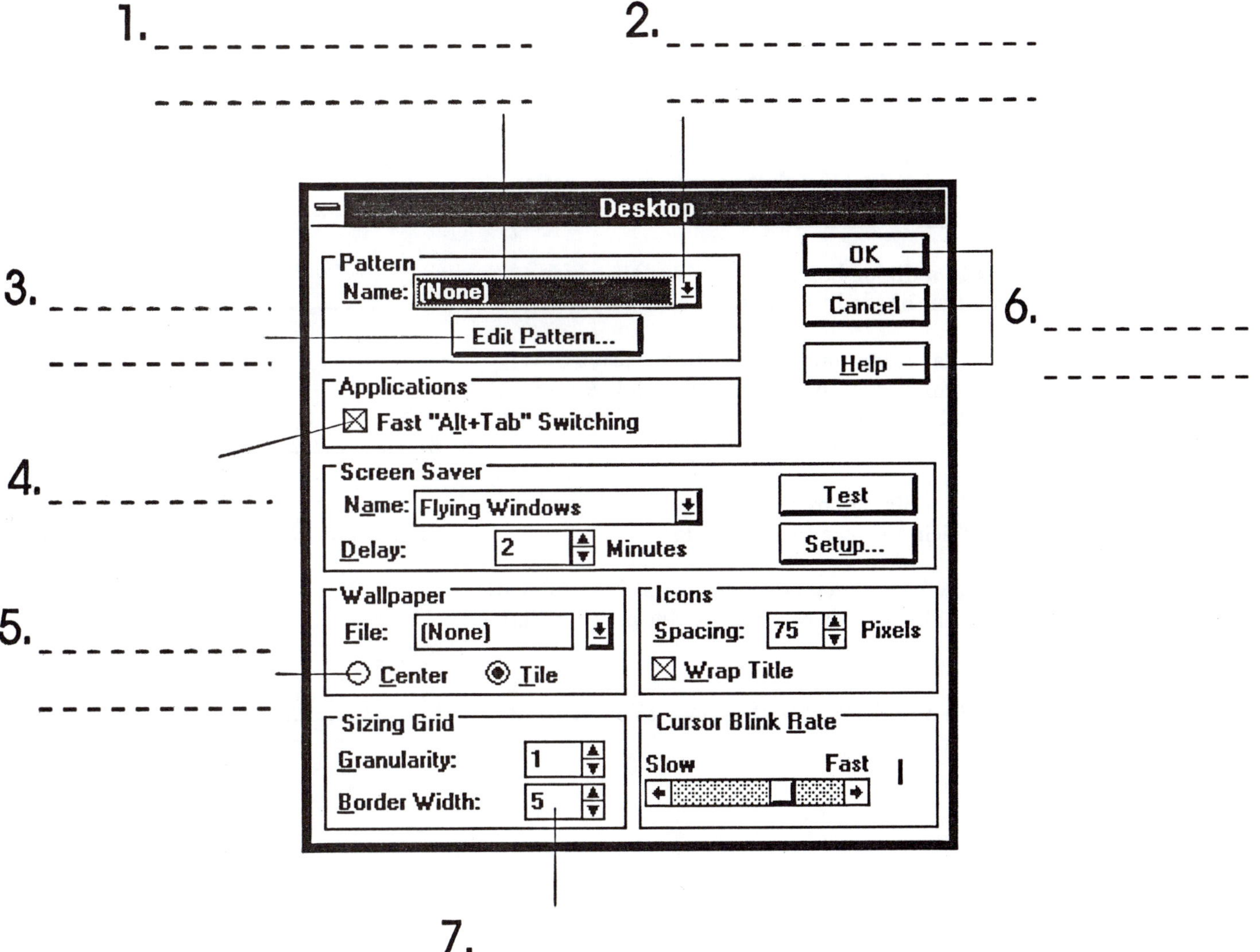

WORKSHEET 11

DIALOG BOXES

DIRECTIONS: Use the following terms to fill in the blanks below:

option buttons	check boxes	drop-down list box
command button	text box	drop-down list arrow
dialog box	list box	increment box

1. What are the circles (◯) in a dialog box from which you may select *only one of a related group?*

   1) ______________________________

2. What appears when a menu item with an ellipsis (...) is chosen?

   2) ______________________________

3. What are the squares (☐) in a dialog box which you may select as desired?

   3) ______________________________

4. In a dialog box, what is a box that carries out an action, such as [OK] or [Cancel], called?

   4) ______________________________

5. What is a box in a dialog box that provides space for typing information needed to carry out a command?

   5) ______________________________

6. What is a box that is similar to a **list box** except that it usually appears in a small or crowded dialog box and must be opened by choosing the **drop-down list arrow** by it?

   6) ______________________________

7. What is a box in a dialog box which displays a list of options from which a choice can be made?

   7) ______________________________

8. What is an arrow in a dialog box that has a line under it (⬇) which indicates that it can open a **drop-down list box?**

   8) ______________________________

9. What is a box in a dialog box that is used to set a value?

   9) ______________________________

(This page may be copied.)

WORKSHEET 12

HELP

NAME ___________________________

1. What is the shortcut key for Help?

    1) ___________________________

2. What Windows feature is a quick and easy way to look up information about the *feature you are working with*?

    2) ___________________________

3. Which Help option displays a list of Windows terms from which you can choose a term so that its definition will be displayed?

    3) ___________________________

4. Which Help option displays an alphabetic list of the Help *topics* available for the application you are using?

    4) ___________________________

5. Which Help option displays a box with information concerning the program you are using?

    5) ___________________________

6. Which Help option displays a dialog box that is used to locate information about a specific topic?

    6) ___________________________

7. Which Help option shows information about how to *use* the Help feature?

    7) ___________________________

WORKSHEET 13

NAME _______________________

FILE MANAGER

DIRECTIONS: Use the following terms to fill in the blanks below. One term is used more than once.

file	data file	program file	directory tree	current directory
filename	directory	File Manager	filename extension	
associated file	subdirectory	root directory	directory window	

---

1. What kind of window displays *directories* on the left side and *files* on the right side?

   1) _______________________

2. What program is used to control your files?

   2) _______________________

3. What is the top-level directory?

   3) _______________________

4. What part of the disk structure holds the *files* that are saved on a disk?

   4) _______________________

5. What is a directory that is within another directory?

   5) _______________________

6. What is the directory you are working in?

   6) _______________________

7. What do you call a display of the directory structure (directories and subdirectories) on your disk?

   7) _______________________

8. What is a window within the File Manager that displays the *directory* and *files* on your disk?

   8) _______________________

9. What is the optional "period and up to three characters" at the end of a *filename* called?

   9) _______________________

10. What is a *set of data* that is saved on a disk as a named unit?

    10) _______________________

11. What kind of file has a filename extension which identifies it as belonging to a certain application, such as Write (.WRI)?

    11) _______________________

12. What kind of file holds a *set of instructions* that does a task, such as word processing, and ends with .EXE, .PIF, .COM, or .BAT?

    12) _______________________

13. What is a file that consists of *data that is created in a program*, such as a letter typed into a word processor?

    13) _______________________

14. What is the name you assign to a *set of data* that you save on a disk?

    14) _______________________

(This page may be copied.)

WORKSHEET 14

WINDOWS MODES and MULTITASKING

NAME ________________________

DIRECTIONS: Use the following terms to fill in the blanks below. Two terms are used more than once.

1,000	1,000,000	extended memory	microprocessor chip
1	multitasking	memory managing	conventional memory
memory	standard mode	complex programs	386 enhanced mode
			graphics environment

---

1. About how many characters will one kilobyte (K) hold?

1) ________________________

2. What is general purpose memory above conventional and upper memory?

2) ________________________

3. What part of the computer determines the computer's *size* as measured in bytes?

3) ________________________

4. What Windows **mode** requires a computer with a 386 or higher processor to run?

4) ________________________

5. How many characters will one byte hold?

5) ________________________

6. What part of the computer determines its *speed*?

6) ________________________

7. What is the first 640K of memory?

7) ________________________

8. List three factors that require computers with fast processors and large memories.

8) a. ________________________

b. ________________________

c. ________________________

9. About how many characters will one megabyte (Mb) hold?

9) ________________________

10. What Windows **mode** will run on a computer with a 286 processor and at least 256K of extended memory?

10) ________________________

11. What is the ability to run more than one program at a time called?

11) ________________________

12. What kind of programs organizes the computer's memory so that different programs do not use the same memory at the same time?

12) ________________________

13. What Windows **mode** will perform the most powerful form of multitasking, whereby the computer can process a time-consuming task while you work on another program?

13) ________________________

WORKSHEET 15

WINDOWS INTEGRATION

NAME _______________________________

DIRECTIONS: Use the following terms to fill in the blanks below. One term is used more than once.

server application	embed	clipboard	destination document
client application	link	integration	CUA - common user access
	object	source document	OLE - object linking and embedding

1. What is the *common set of commands* that is used with all Windows applications?

   1) _______________________________

2. What word refers to the fact that a group of different programs look and behave alike?

   2) _______________________________

3. What is the powerful way of integrating that Microsoft Windows developed?

   3) _______________________________

4. What is the active connector between the same *object* that is *embedded* in more than one document?

   4) _______________________________

5. What word means to *paste* an *object* that was created in a source document into a destination document?

   5) _______________________________

6. What is the process whereby information can be easily transferred between different programs?

   6) _______________________________

7. What is a selected *set of information* created in a Windows application, such as a *drawing* in Paintbrush?

   7) _______________________________

8. What is the document in which an *object* is created?

   8) _______________________________

9. What is used to hold information that is being integrated (transferred) from one program to another?

   9) _______________________________

10. What is the document into which an *object* is placed?

    10) _______________________________

11. What kind of application has documents that can accept embedded or linked objects?

    11) _______________________________

12. What kind of application can create objects that can be embedded or linked into other documents?

    12) _______________________________

(This page may be copied.)

Lesson One — Windows Basics

Table of Contents

EXERCISE 1
Start
Windows

Exercises 1 and 2 should be done during the same session.

ASSUMPTION:

It is assumed that Windows 3.1 has been installed correctly on your computer system.

start Windows
To begin Microsoft Windows from a DOS prompt, and (for some systems) by turning the computer on.

window
The rectangular work area for a task, program, document, or Windows group. There are several kinds of windows: application, document, group, and dialog.

icon
A small picture that represents an element such as a document, program, group of programs, command, or the pointer.

desktop
The background (screen) upon which **windows** and **icons** appear.

title bar
The horizontal bar at the top of a window that holds the window's name.

control box (Control-menu box)
The box at the left end of the title bar which opens the Control menu.

control menu
A menu that you can use to manipulate a window. It contains commands such as restore, move, size, maximize, minimize, close, and open.

IMPORTANT: The "Starting Windows Screen" (below) is the "starting point" for the exercises in this book. See <u>Save Desktop Arrangement</u> (page 86) and <u>Create 'Starting Windows Screen'</u> (page 89) for help in changing your screen to match the one above.

Before you start these exercises, you may want to read
Appendix C: <u>Reproduce Your Original Windows Desktop</u> and
Appendix B: <u>Rebuild Group Windows</u>.

❶ Turn on the monitor and computer.

STOP HERE IF WINDOWS APPEARS ON YOUR SCREEN.

❷ FROM THE DOS PROMPT (C:\>):
- Type W I N.
- Press ↵.

The *Starting Windows screen* appears:

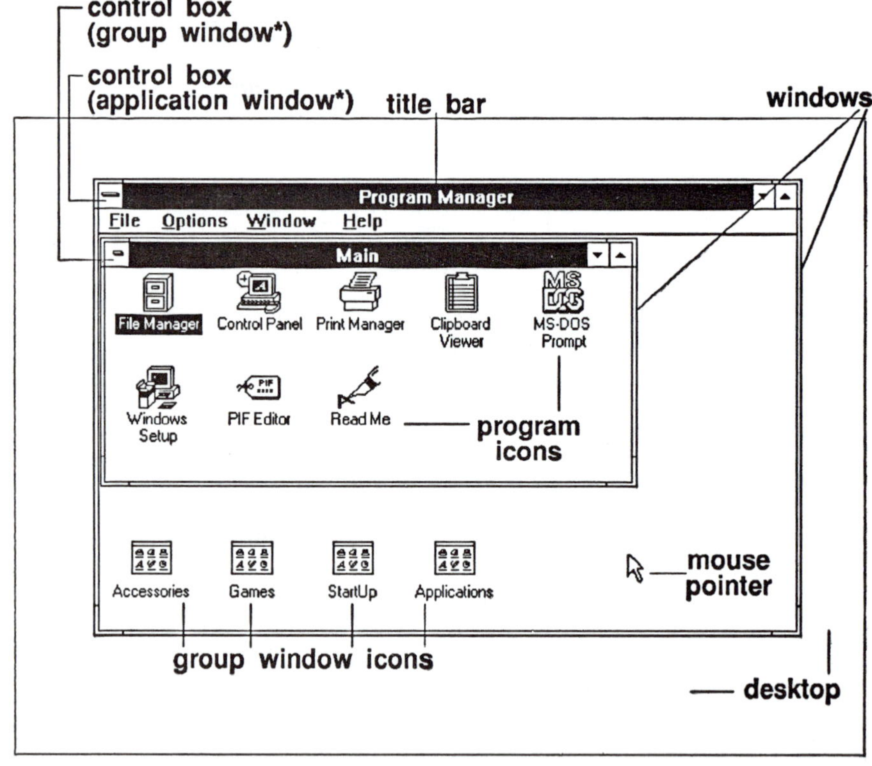

NOTE: The control box for **application and **dialog** windows holds a "spacebar" icon (▭ longer), while the control box for **group** and **document** windows holds a "hyphen" icon (▭ shorter).*

YOUR SCREEN MAY <u>NOT</u> MATCH THE ONE ABOVE.

After Microsoft Windows is installed, the first time it is started the screen is arranged like the one above. But with just a few clicks of the mouse, the opening screen can be changed, and when you **exit** Windows, these changes <u>may</u> be saved, leaving you with the <u>new</u> desktop arrangement when you start Windows again.

If you have upgraded to Windows 3.1 from Windows 3.0, your screen may have slight differences from the screen shown above.

Go on to Exercise 2

IMPORTANT: When clicking the mouse button, <u>always use the left mouse button</u> unless otherwise instructed.

IMPORTANT: Whenever you see dotted boxes with "OR" between them, you should follow the directions in <u>only one</u> of the boxes. The "OR" boxes have instructions for different ways to perform the same action.

FROM THE *STARTING WINDOWS* SCREEN:

- **Double-click** on the **Program Manager's** ⊟ (Control box).
  NOTE: The "double-click" procedure may take some practice. If you accidentally get a menu that you do not want, move the pointer to the desktop and click it once to cancel the menu. Then try again.

OR

- **Click** on **File.**
- **Click** on **Exit Windows... .**

OR

- **Press Alt + F4.**
  (Shortcut keys to exit an application window.)

The *Exit Windows* dialog box appears:

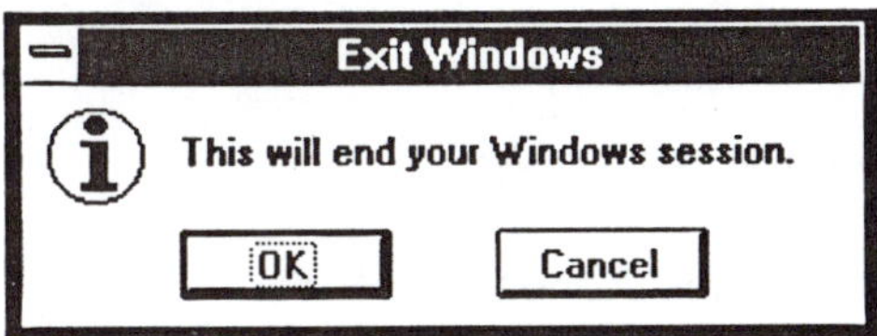

- **Click on** | OK | .

OR

- **Press ↵.**

A screen with just the DOS prompt appears:

IMPORTANT:

Always EXIT Windows before turning off your computer system.

EXERCISE 2
Exit Windows

Continue from Exercise 1, doing both during the same session.

exit Windows
To leave Microsoft Windows and return the computer to a DOS prompt.

click (mouse action)
1. Move the pointer on the desired item.
2. Quickly press and release the left mouse button.

double-click (mouse action)
1. Move the pointer on the desired item.
2. Quickly press and release the left mouse button twice.

dialog box
A box which appears when a menu item with an ellipsis (...) is chosen. A dialog box requests additional information before performing the original command.

Keyboard Users
EXIT WINDOWS

WITH THE PROGRAM MANAGER'S TITLE BAR HIGHLIGHTED:

- **Press Alt + F4**
  (shortcut keys)
- **Press ↵**

OR

- **Press Alt + F**
  (to access File option)
- **Press X** (Exit)
- **Press ↵**

OR

- **Press Alt + Space**
  (to open control box)
- **Press C** (Close)
- **Press ↵**

EXERCISE 3
Open a Group Window

Exercises 3 and 4 should be done during the same session.

open a group window
To enlarge a <u>group window</u> icon to a window. An opened group window displays icons that represent programs.

group windows
Windows within the Program Manager window which hold "groups" of program-item icons. Group windows are a special kind of document window which belong to the Program Manager and cannot be moved outside of the Program Manager window.

group window icons
Icons at the bottom of the Program Manager window which represent <u>group windows</u>.

workspace
The inner part of a window, where the work on an application is done.

Keyboard Users
OPEN A GROUP WINDOW

1. **Press** and **hold** **Ctrl** while **pressing** and **releasing** **Tab** until the desired *group window icon name* is highlighted.
2. **Press** **↵**

---

❶ Start Windows (review, page 52, step 2).

Starting Windows Screen

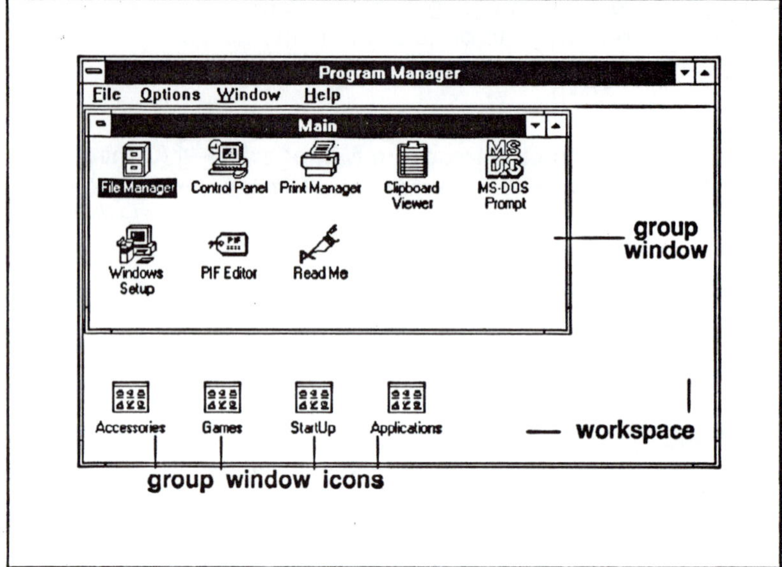

❷ TO OPEN A GROUP WINDOW:

- **Double-click** on the **Accessories** icon.
  NOTE: The "double-click" procedure must be quick and precise, otherwise you may accidently "move" the icon or get the "pop-up" menu. If you do accidently get the "pop-up" menu, move the cursor off the icon and click the mouse to collapse the "pop-up" menu. Try the procedure again.

OR

- **Click** on the **Accessories** icon (a menu pops up).
- **Click** on **Restore**.

Program Manager Window with Accessories Window Opened

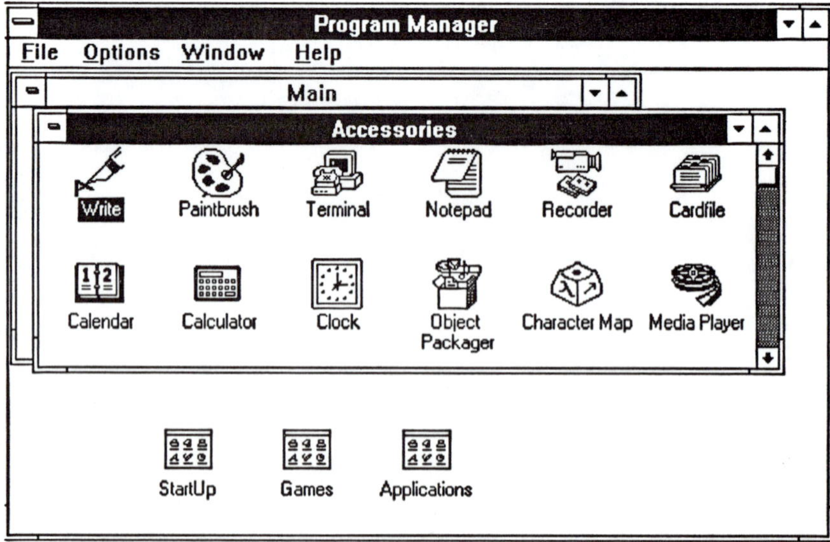

Go on to Exercise 4

EXERCISE 4
Close a Group Window

Continue from Exercise 3, doing both during the same session.

1. - **Double-click** on ▭, the Control box for the **Accessories** window.

   OR

   - **Click** on ▭, the Control box for the **Accessories** window.
   - **Click** on **Close.**

Program Manager Window with Accessories Window Reduced to an Icon

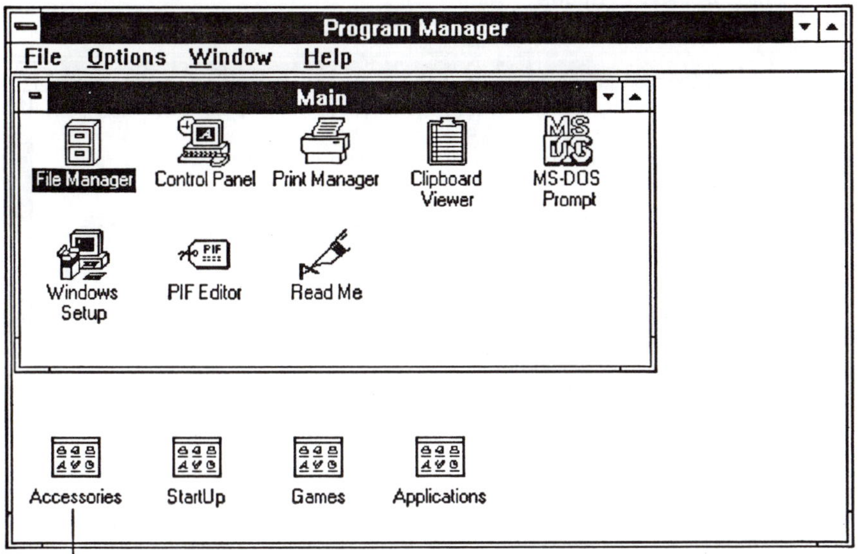

Accessories icon

2. **Click** <u>once</u> on the **Accessories** icon.
   A *pop-up* menu appears:

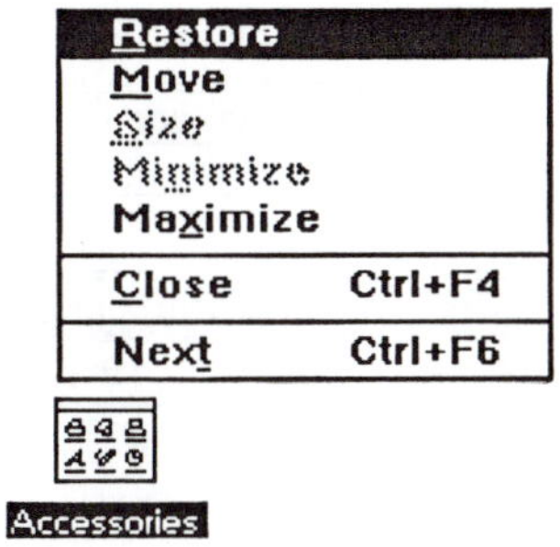

3. OOPS! You do not really want to open the Accessories window.
   - **Click** anywhere <u>outside</u> the **pop-up menu** (to close the menu).

     NOTE: **Alt** *or* **Esc** *also closes a menu.*

4. **Open the Applications** group window.

5. **Close the Applications** group window.

6. **Open the Games** group window.

7. **Close the Games** group window.

8. **Exit Windows** (review, page 53).

close a group window
To reduce a group window to an icon.

click off
To click <u>outside</u> of an area in order to back out of an action.

close a menu
To cancel a menu that has been opened by:
- clicking outside of the menu,
- pressing **Alt**, or
- pressing **Esc**.

<u>WARNING</u>: If you accidentally double-click on the <u>title bar</u> instead of the <u>control box</u>, the window will be maximized. Click on ⇕ (the restore button) to return the window to its original size.

Keyboard Users

CLOSE A GROUP WINDOW

1. **Press and hold** **Ctrl** <u>while</u> **pressing and releasing** **Tab** until the desired group window's *title bar* is highlighted.
2. - **Press** **Ctrl** + **F4** (shortcut keys to close a window)

   OR

   - **Press** **Alt** + **-**
   - **Press** **C** (Close)

EXERCISE 5
Start a Program

Exercises 5 and 6 should be done during the same session.

start a program
To use Windows to run a program.

program icon
A picture in a group window that represents a program (an application).

Keyboard Users

START A PROGRAM

1. To select window:
   Press and **hold** **Ctrl** while **pressing** and **releasing** **Tab** until the desired group window's title bar is highlighted, and then release both **Tab** and **Ctrl**.
2. **Press** **←**, **→**, **↑**, or **↓** until the desired program icon name is highlighted.
3. **Press** **↵**

1 Start Windows (review, page 52).

2 Open the **Accessories** group window (review, page 54).

Program Manager Window with Accessories Group Window Opened

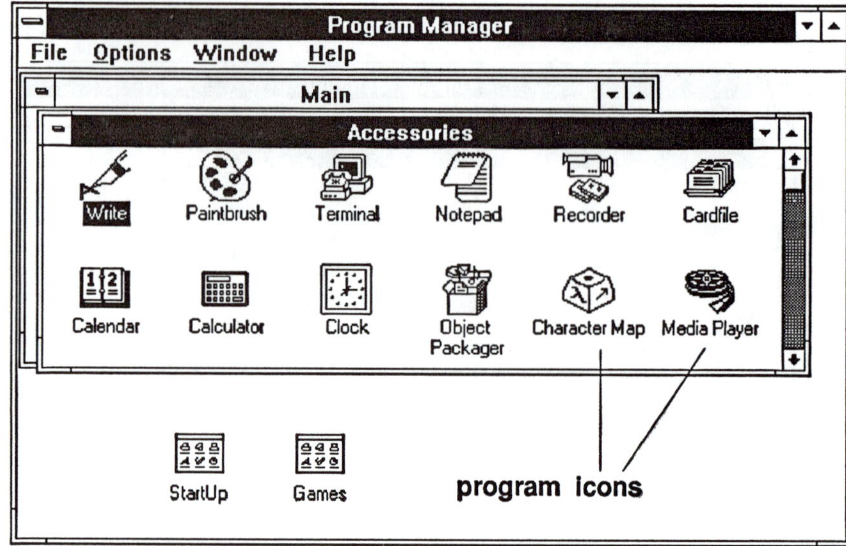

3 Double-click on (the Paintbrush program icon).

The Paintbrush window opens in front of the existing windows, covering all or part of them.

Screen with Paintbrush Running

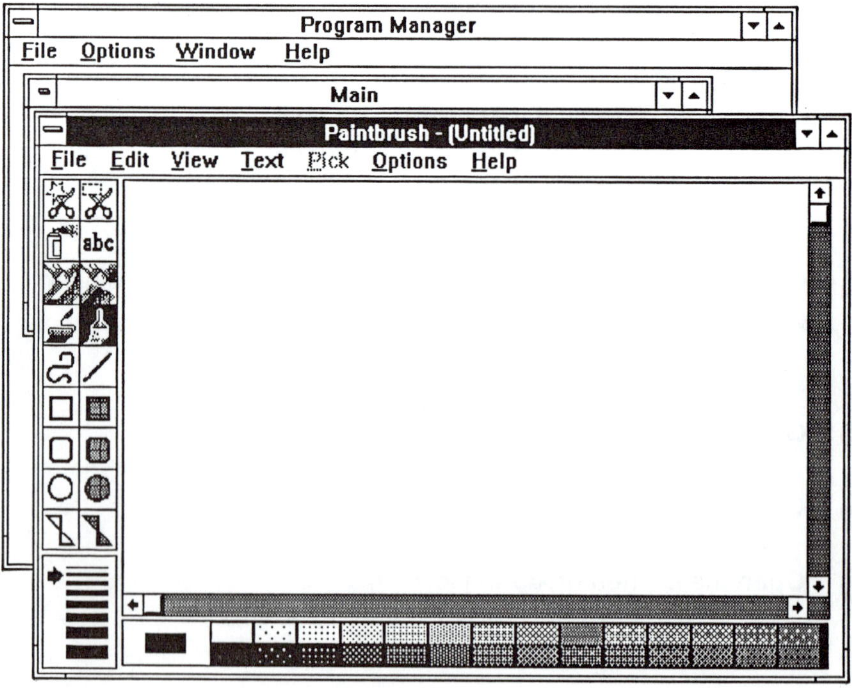

NOTE: You can start any program by double-clicking on its icon.

Go on to Exercise 6

FROM THE SCREEN WITH PAINTBRUSH RUNNING:

1

- **Double-click** on the **Paintbrush** window's ▭ (Control box).

OR

- **Click** on the **Paintbrush** window's ▭ (Control box).
- **Click** on **Close**.

OR

- **Click** on **File**.
- **Click** on **Exit**.

NOTE: IF you make any kind of change in a program (for example, draw a line in Paintbrush or type in Write), when you exit, a dialog box similar to this appears:

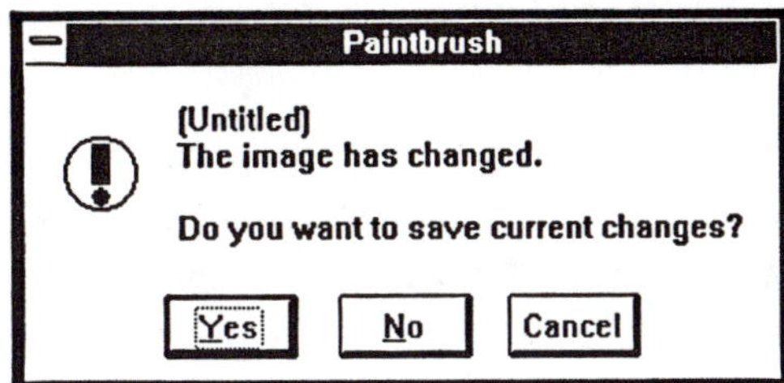

- **Click** on ▢ No ▢ (to **Exit** without saving the changes).

NOTE: Paintbrush becomes a program icon in the Accessories group window.

2 **Start Write.**

3 **Exit Write.**

4 **Start Clock.**

5 **Exit Clock.**

6 **Start Calendar.**

7 **Exit Calendar.**

8 **Close** the **Accessories** window (review, page 55).

9 **Go** on to Exercise 7.

OR

Exit Windows (page 53).

EXERCISE 6
Exit a Program

Continue from Exercise 5, doing both during the same session.

exit a program

To use Windows to leave a program.

NOTE: The term "close" is also used to exit programs. Close is used from the Control box, while Exit is used from the File menu.

Keyboard Users

EXIT A PROGRAM

1. To select window:

   Press and **hold** **Ctrl** while **pressing** and **releasing** **Tab** until the desired window's *title bar* is highlighted.

2.
   - **Press** **Alt** + **F4** (shortcut keys)

   OR

   - **Press** **Alt** + **F** (opens File)
   - **Press** **X** (Exit)

   OR

   - **Press** **Alt** + **Space** (opens Control box)
   - **Press** **C** (Close)

EXERCISE 7
Select an Application Window

Exercises 7 and 8 should be done during the same session.

select an application window
To make an application window active. A <u>highlighted title bar</u> indicates that a window is selected (active).

<u>IMPORTANT</u>: When you select an application window, it moves to the front; the other application windows move to the back. The Program Manager is an application window. <u>Group windows belong to the Program Manager, and they move to the front or back along with the Program Manager window.</u>

application window
A window that holds a program.

active window
The window whose <u>title bar</u> is <u>highlighted</u> (indicating that it is currently selected).

Three ways to select applications
1. **Click** on window (Step 4).
2. **Rotate application windows** (Step 6).
3. **Use Task List** (Step 11).

Keyboard Users

SELECT AN APPLICATION WINDOW

Rotation Method:
- See step 6.

Task list method:
- **Press** `Ctrl` + `Esc`
  (shortcut keys)

OR

- **Press** `Alt` + `Space`
- **Press** `W`
  (S<u>w</u>itch to...)

- Use ↑ and/or ↓ to highlight the desired application.
- **Press** ↵

IMPORTANT: <u>"Selecting application windows" is one of the most important Windows tasks in this book</u>. "Selecting an application window" is how you switch between different windows, thus permitting multitasking (page 31) and aiding you in finding hidden windows. Please take the time to fully understand the three ways to "select" application windows, and use one of these procedures any time you are asked to "select" an application window.

① **Start Windows** (page 52), if necessary.

FROM THE *STARTING WINDOWS* SCREEN:

② **Open** the **Accessories** group window (review, page 54).

③ **Start Calculator** (review, page 56).
The *Calculator* window opens in front of the existing windows. Since it is a small window, it partially covers, but does not hide, the other windows.
NOTE: Calculator is the "selected" (or "active") application as indicated by its highlighted title bar.

④ SELECT AN APPLICATION BY CLICKING ON THE WINDOW:
*NOTE: This method cannot be used to **select** a "hidden" window.*
- **Click** somewhere on the **Program Manager** window (to select it). The Program Manager window now covers most or all of the Calculator window.

⑤ **Start Paintbrush** (review, page 56). Paintbrush opens, covering most or all of the existing windows.
NOTE: Three application windows are now open; Program Manager, Calculator, and Paintbrush.

⑥ SELECT AN APPLICATION WINDOW BY ROTATING OPEN APPLICATIONS:
- **Press** and **hold** `Alt` <u>while</u> **tapping** `Tab` and watch the screen while either:

application names are rotated in a box in the center of the screen.

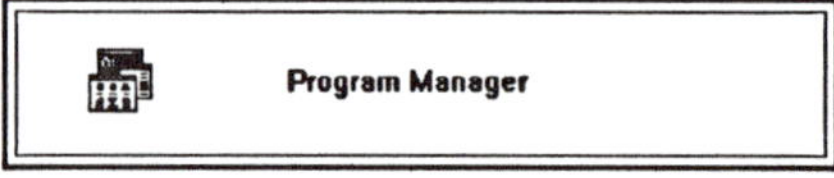

OR

the application *title bars* and/or *icons* are highlighted one after the other.

- Release both keys when **Program Manager** appears (to select it). Program Manager, and the group windows within it, move to the front.
*NOTE: This method can be used to **select** any open application, even if the window is hidden or is an active icon.*

⑦ Use the **rotation** method (step 6) to **select** the **Paintbrush** window. Paintbrush moves to the front.

⑧ Use the **rotation** method (step 6) to **select** the **Calculator** window.

⑨ **Exit** the **Calculator** window (review, page 57).

⑩ Use the **rotation** method (step 6) to **select** the **Program Manager** window.

Continue Exercise 7 on the next page

(11) SELECT AN APPLICATION BY USING THE TASK LIST:

> • **Double-click** anywhere on the **desktop** (outside all windows).

OR

> • **Click** on ☐ (in application window), then on **Switch to...** .

The *Task List* dialog box appears:

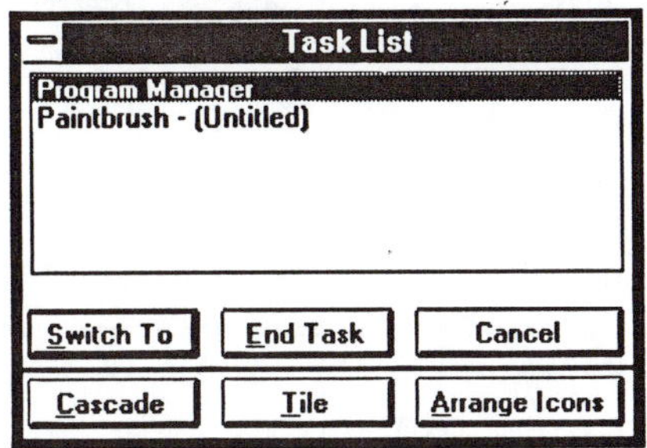

> • **Double-click** on **Paintbrush** (to select it).

(12) • **Exit Paintbrush** (review, page 57).
• **Close** the **Accessories** window (review, page 55).

go on to Exercise 8 below

EXERCISE 8

(1) **Open** the **Accessories group window** (review, page 54).
Two group windows should now be open: Main and Accessories.
NOTE: The Accessories group window's title bar is highlighted, indicating that it is selected.

(2) SELECT A GROUP WINDOW BY CLICKING ON THE WINDOW:
• **Click on** any part of the **"Main"** group window (to select it).
NOTE: You cannot select a "hidden" window using this method. If the Main group window is hidden, go on to step 3.

(3) SELECT A GROUP WINDOW BY USING THE MENU BAR:
• **Click** on **Windows** (on the menu bar), then on **Games**.
NOTE: This method can be used to select "hidden" group windows. If a group window is an icon, this method will also open the group window.

(4) SELECT A GROUP WINDOW BY ROTATING THEM:
• **Press** and **hold** **Ctrl** while tapping **Tab**.
Watch the screen while the **group windows** are <u>selected</u> one after the other by the highlighting of either their *title bar* or their *icon's name*.
• Release both keys when the **Accessories** window is selected.
NOTE: This method can be used to select "hidden" group windows.

(5) **Close** the **Accessories** and **Games** windows (review, page 55).

(6) Go on to Exercise 9.

OR

Exit Windows (review, page 53).

EXERCISE 8
Select a Group Window

Continue from Exercise 7, doing both during the same session.

select a group window
To make a group window active. A <u>highlighted title bar</u> indicates that a window is selected (active).

group window
A special kind of <u>document window</u> that displays program icons that are used to <u>start</u> programs. Group windows belong to the Program Manager application window and cannot be moved outside the Program Manager window.

document window
A window within an application window. A document window <u>belongs</u> to the application window it is in.

<u>IMPORTANT</u>: As you open many windows, some windows may partially or completely overlap other windows. This may cause a window to become hidden, or <u>it may make a window appear to be within another window when it is really just in front of it</u>. Do not confuse these overlapping windows with document windows.

Three ways to select group windows
1. **Click** on group window (step 2).
2. Use the **Menu bar** (step 3).
3. **Rotate** group windows (step 4).

Keyboard Users
SELECT A GROUP WINDOW

See Exercise 8, step 4.

OR

• **Press** **Alt** + **W** (**W**indow)
• **Press** the number of the desired document window.

EXERCISE 9
Use the Menu Bar

use the menu bar
To **select** and **close** a menu from the menu bar, and to **choose** a command from a menu.

menu bar
The bar located under the title bar on application windows that lists the available <u>menus</u>. To use a menu command, you first **select** (highlight) and drop down a menu from the menu bar and then **choose** a command from that menu.

close a menu
To back out of a menu without choosing a command.

choose
To pick an item from a menu that initiates an action. (Contrast with <u>select</u>, page 62.)

shortcut keys
Key combinations that can be used to activate certain commands instead of using menus.

an ellipsis
Three dots (...) that follow the name of menu items which open a <u>dialog box</u> when selected.

menu commands
The options that appear in drop-down menus.

Keyboard Users
SELECT A MENU FROM THE MENU BAR
- Press **Alt** + **F** (<u>F</u>ile) (or some other underlined letter that represents a menu that you want to open).

CLOSE A MENU
- Press **Alt**

1 Start Windows (review, page 52), if necessary.

Starting Windows Screen

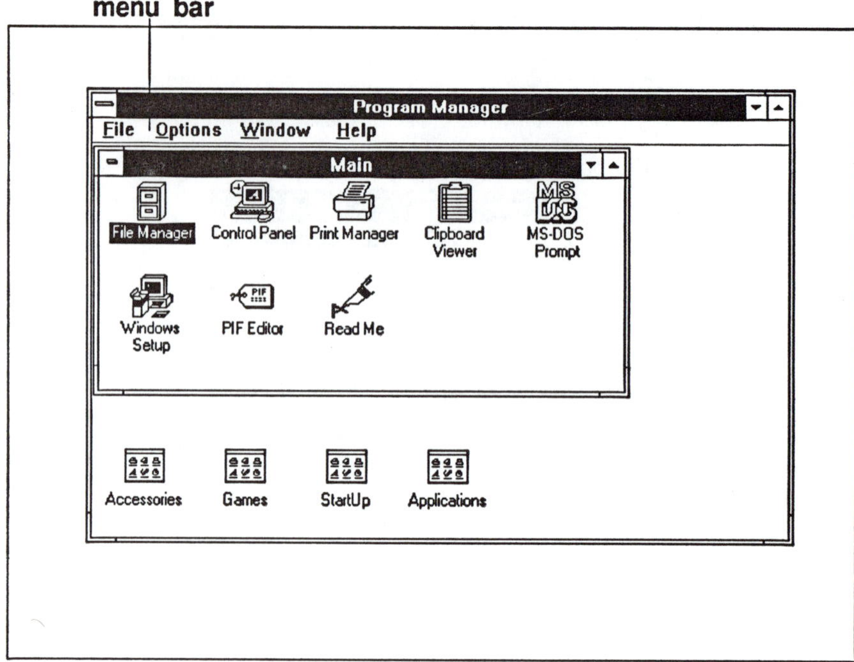

2 **Click** on **F**ile (to *select* the File menu).

The *File* menu drops down:

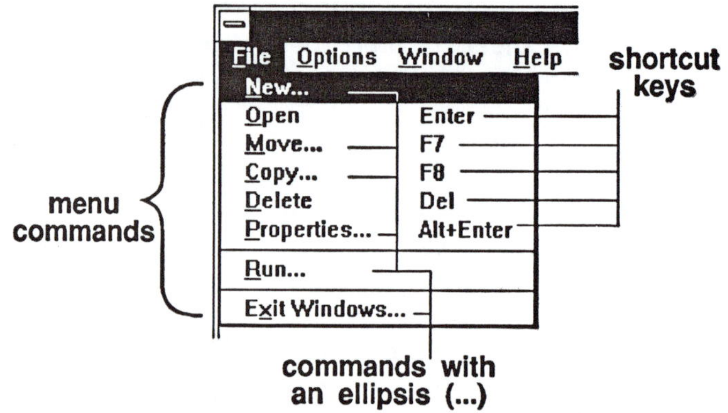

3 CLOSE THE MENU:

- **Click** on **F**ile, again.

OR

- **Click** off (anywhere outside of) the **menu**.
  *NOTE: Be careful <u>not</u> to **click** on some item that you do not want to activate.*

OR

- Press **Alt**. (This takes you off the menu bar.)

OR

- Press **Esc**. (This leaves you on the menu bar.)

4 Repeat steps 2 and 3 several more times, using different ways to *cancel* the menu each time.

Continue Exercise 9 on the next page

5 **Open** the **Accessories** group window (review, page 54).

6 **Start Write** (review, page 56).

7 **Click** on **Edit** (to *select* the Edit menu).
This Edit menu drops down. It has several *dimmed* commands.

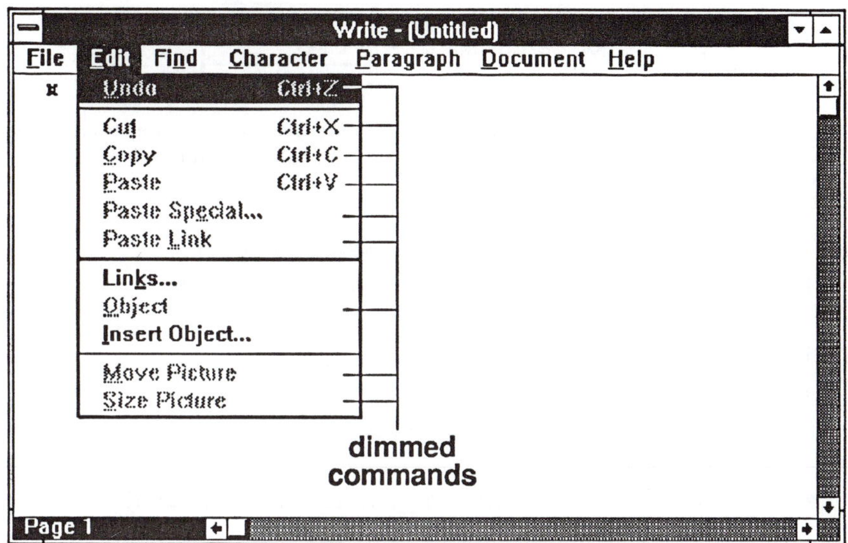

8 **Click** off of the **Edit menu** (to *close* the Edit menu).

9 **Click** on **File** (to *select* the File menu).

10 **Click** on **Exit** (to *choose* the Exit command).
You are returned to the Program Manager window.
*NOTE: If a box appears asking if you want to "save current changes," **click on** [No].*

11 **Click** on **File** (to *select* the Program Manager's File menu).

12 **Click** on **Exit Windows** (to *choose* the Exit command).

13 **Press** [ESC] (to close the dialog box without exiting Windows).

14 **Start Clock** (review, page 56).
NOTE: The clock has only one menu on the menu bar, Settings.

15 **Click** on **Settings** (to *select* the menu).

16 **Click** on **Analog** (to *select* the command), and then **click on Settings** again.

Continue Exercise 9 on the next page

---

dimmed command
A menu command that is shown in gray instead of black. A dimmed command cannot be used in the current situation.

Keyboard Users
CHOOSE A MENU COMMAND

1. To select the menu:
    - **Press** [Alt]

    + the letter that is underlined in the menu you want.

    OR

    - use [→] or [←] to select the menu you want.
    - **Press** [↵]

2. To choose the command:
    - **Press** the letter that is underlined in the command on the menu that you want.

    OR

    - use [↑] or [↓] to select the command you want.
    - **Press** [↵]

USE THE MENU BAR

select

To <u>mark</u> an item so that a subsequent action can activate it. For example, <u>highlighting</u> and <u>using a check mark</u> are two ways to mark a command. (Contrast with <u>choose</u>, page 60.)

analog clock

Displays a round clock with moving hour and minute hands (and, if you choose, a second hand).

digital clock

Displays a clock with a precise numeric readout, for example, 1:15:30 P.M.

The *Settings* menu appears—notice the dimmed *Set Font* command:

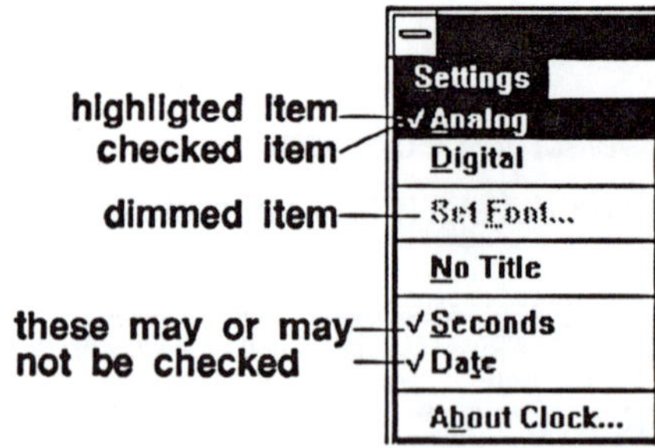

*NOTE: Unlike **selected** commands on some other menus, when you select Analog, Digital, Seconds, and Date, they are both **selected** and **chosen** at the same time.*

(17) **Click** on **Digital**, and then **click** on **Settings** again.
Notice that the *Set Font* command is no longer dimmed.

(18) DESELECT DATE AND SECONDS:
With the Settings menu still displayed from step **17**:
- IF Date has a ✓, **click** on **Date** (to deselect it), and then **click on Settings** again.
- IF Seconds has a ✓, **click** on **Seconds** (to deselect it).

(19) SELECT DATE AND SECONDS:
Use the Settings menu to **select Date** and then **Seconds**.
Are both the date and seconds showing on the clock?

(20) **Click** on **Settings**, and then **click** on **No Title**.
A clock similar to this one appears:

06:51:20 PM
07/21/92

(21) **Double-click** anywhere in the **Clock** window (to make the title bar and menu reappear).

(22) **Click** on **Settings**, and then **click** on **Analog**.

(23) **Exit** the **Clock** by **double-clicking** on ▭ (Control box).

(24) **Close** the **Accessories** window.

(25) **Go** on to Exercise 10.
OR
Exit Windows (review, page 53).

1 Start Windows (review, page 52), if necessary.

2 Click on File.

3 Click on New... .
The *New Program Object* dialog box appears:

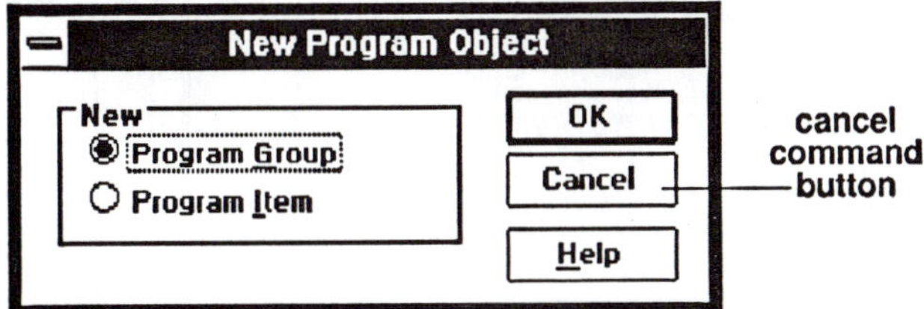

4 Click on Cancel .

5 Click on File again.

6 Click on New... again.

7 Double-click on the *New Program Object* window's ⊟.

8 Click on File once again.

9 Click on New... once again.

10 Press Esc.

11 Open the Accessories window (review, page 54).

12 Start Calendar (review, page 56).

13 Click on File.

14 Click on Page Setup... .

15 Click on Cancel .

16 Exit Calendar (review, page 57).

17 Close the Accessories window (review, page 55).

18 Go on to Exercise 11.
OR
Exit Windows (review, page 53).

EXERCISE 10
Cancel

cancel
To escape (or back out of) a menu or dialog box without completing a command.

ways to cancel (close) a menu
- Click off of the menu.
- Press Alt
- Click on the original menu item again.
- Press Esc
  (The last method leaves the menu bar selected.)

ways to cancel (close) a dialog box:
- Double-click on ⊟
- Click on Cancel
- Press Esc
- Press Alt + F4
- Press Alt + Space , C

ways to cancel (exit or close) an application window:
- Double-click on ⊟
- Click on ⊟ , click on C
- Press Alt + F4
- Press Alt + F , X
- Press Alt + Space , C

ways to cancel (close) a document window:
- Double-click on ⊟
- Click on ⊟ , click on C
- Press Ctrl + F4
- Press Alt + — , C

Keyboard Users
CANCEL
See "ways to cancel" above.

EXERCISE 11
Maximize a Window

Exercises 11 and 12 should be done during the same session.

maximize a window
To enlarge a window to its maximum size.

maximize button ▲
Located at the right end of the title bar, it is used to enlarge a window to its maximum size.

Keyboard Users

MAXIMIZE APPLICATION WINDOW

1. **Select** window to maximize (review, page 58).
2. **Press** Alt + Space (opens Control box)
3. **Press** X (Maximize)

MAXIMIZE DOCUMENT (OR GROUP) WINDOW

1. **Select** window to maximize (review, page 59).
2. **Press** Alt + - (opens Control box)
3. **Press** X (Maximize)

1 **Start Windows** (review, page 52), if necessary.

Starting Windows Screen

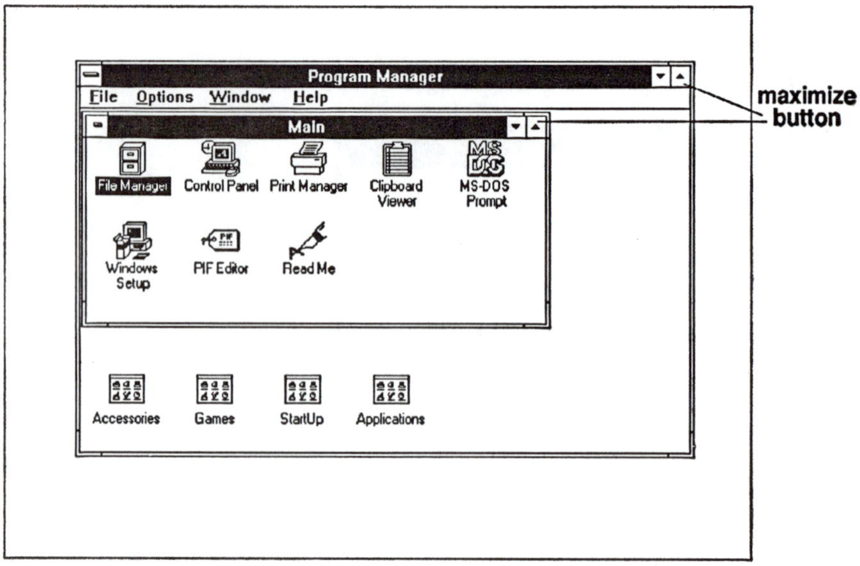

2 MAXIMIZE AN APPLICATION WINDOW:

- **Click** on the **Program Manager's** ▲ (maximize button).

OR

- **Double-click** on the **Program Manager's** title bar.

NOTE: When a window is maximized, ▲ *(maximize button) is replaced with* ⇕ *(restore button).*

Maximized Program Manager Window

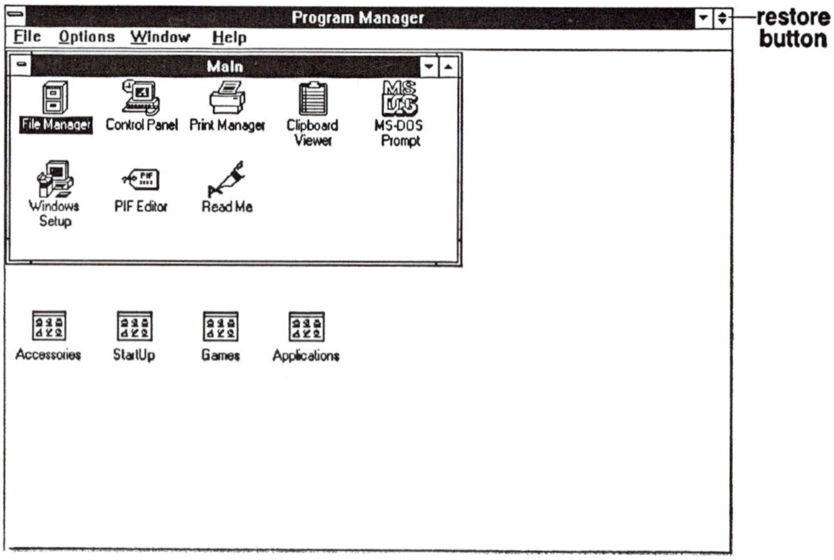

Go on to Exercise 12

1 • **Click** on the **Program Manager's** ⬧ (Restore Button).

OR

• **Double-click** on the **Program Manager's** title bar.

*NOTE: When a window is **restored**, the restore button is replaced with a maximize button.*

2 **MAXIMIZE A <u>DOCUMENT (OR GROUP)</u> WINDOW:**

• **Click** on the **Main** window's ⬧ (maximize button).

Notice the changes:

1. The *Main* window expands to fill the Program Manager's window.
2. The Main window shares the Program Manager's *title bar*, showing "Main" in brackets.
3. The Main window's maximize button is replaced with a restore button (appearing at the right end of the Program Manager's *menu bar*).
4. The Main window's minimize button disappears.
5. The Main window's Control box appears at the left edge of the Program Manager's *menu bar*.

Maximized Main Group Window

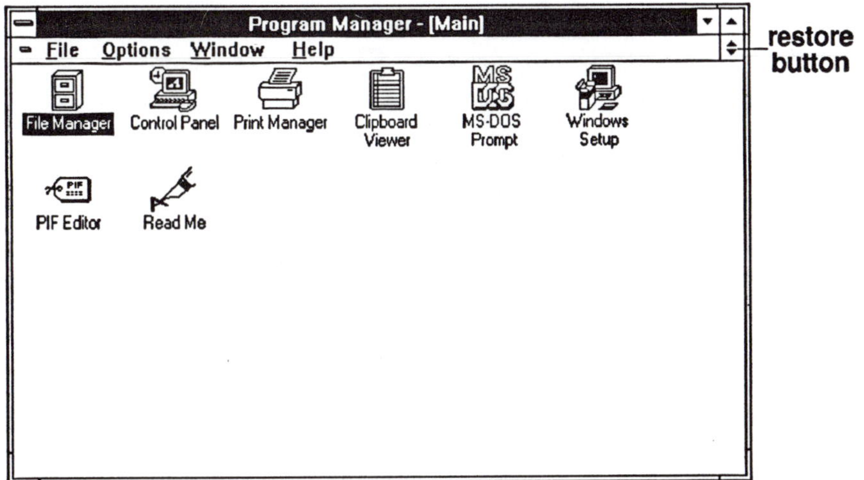

3 **Click** on the **Main** window's ⬧ (restore button), and watch it return to its original state.

4 **Maximize** the **Main** window again.

5 **Maximize** the **Program Manager** window (review, page 64).

*NOTE: Two **restore buttons** now appear in the upper right corner of the screen, one for each of the maximized windows.*

6 **Restore** the **Program Manager** window (top ⬧ button).

7 **Restore** the **Main** window.

8 Go on to Exercise 13.

OR

Exit Windows (review, page 53).

EXERCISE 12
Restore a Window

Continue from Exercise 11, doing both during the same session.

restore a window
To return a maximized window to its previous size.

restore button ⬧
Located at the right end of the title bar of a maximized window, it replaces the maximize button when a window is maximized. The restore button is used to return a maximized window to its previous size.

*NOTE: While **double-clicking** on a maximized application window's title bar will **restore** it, this procedure does <u>not</u> work for a maximized document window.*

Keyboard Users

RESTORE <u>APPLICATION</u> WINDOW

1. **Press** Alt + Space (opens Control box)
2. **Press** R (Restore)

RESTORE <u>DOCUMENT</u> WINDOW

1. **Press** Alt + ▬ (hyphen) (opens Control box)
2. **Press** R (Restore)

EXERCISE 13
Minimize a Window

minimize a window
To shrink a window to an icon.

minimize button ▾
Located at the right of the title bar (just to the left of the maximize button) and used to shrink a window to an icon.

Keyboard Users

MINIMIZE <u>APPLICATION</u> WINDOW

1. **Select** desired window.
2. **Press** Alt + Space
   (opens Control box)
3. **Press** N (Mi<u>n</u>imize)

MINIMIZE <u>DOCUMENT</u> WINDOW

1. **Select** desired window.
2. **Press** Alt + ▬ (hyphen)
   (opens Control box)
3. **Press** N (Mi<u>n</u>imize)

---

❶ **Start Windows** (review, page 52), if necessary.

Starting Windows Screen

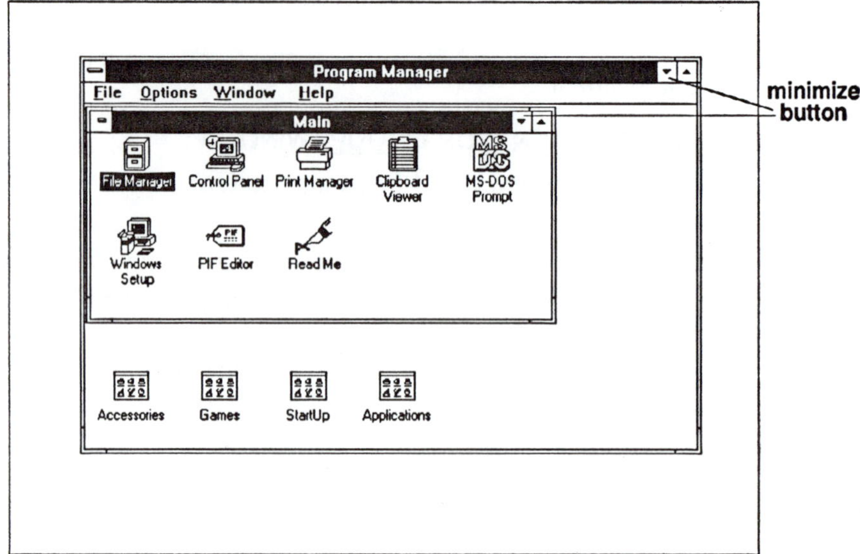

❷ **MINIMIZE A <u>DOCUMENT</u> (OR GROUP) WINDOW:**
Click on the **Main** group window's ▾ (minimize button).

NOTE: The Main group window is closed, and it becomes an icon at the bottom of the Program Manager's window.

Minimized Main Window

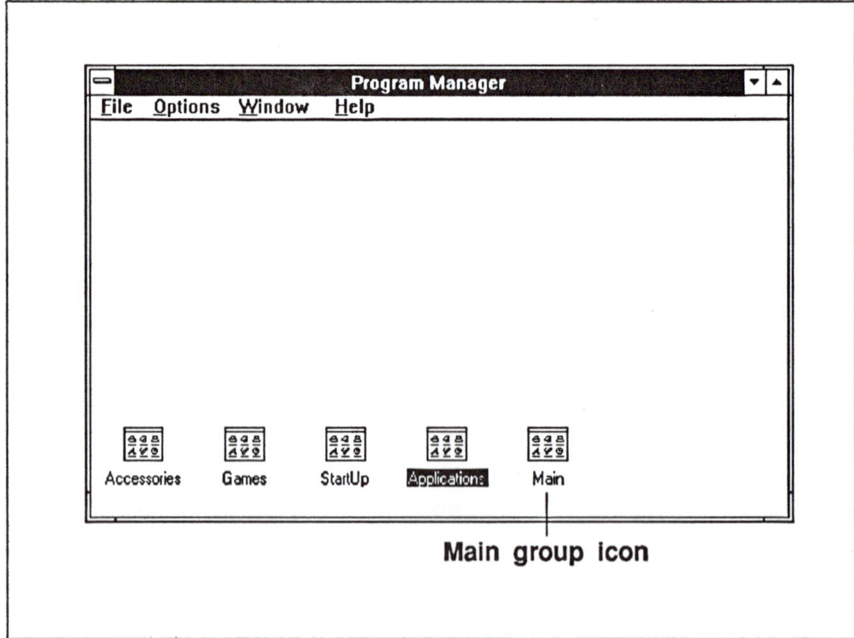

Continue Exercise 13 on the next page

3 **Open** the **Accessories** window (review, page 54).

4 **Start** the **Calendar** program (review, page 56).

5 **MINIMIZE AN <u>APPLICATION</u> WINDOW:**
Click on the **Calendar's** 🔽 minimize button.

NOTE: The Calendar becomes an application icon at the bottom of the desktop...but it is not closed. It is a "running" application icon.

NOTE: *When a **group** window is minimized, it becomes an icon and is closed. However, when a **program** window is minimized, it becomes an icon, but it is not closed.*

Minimized Calendar Window Becomes an Icon

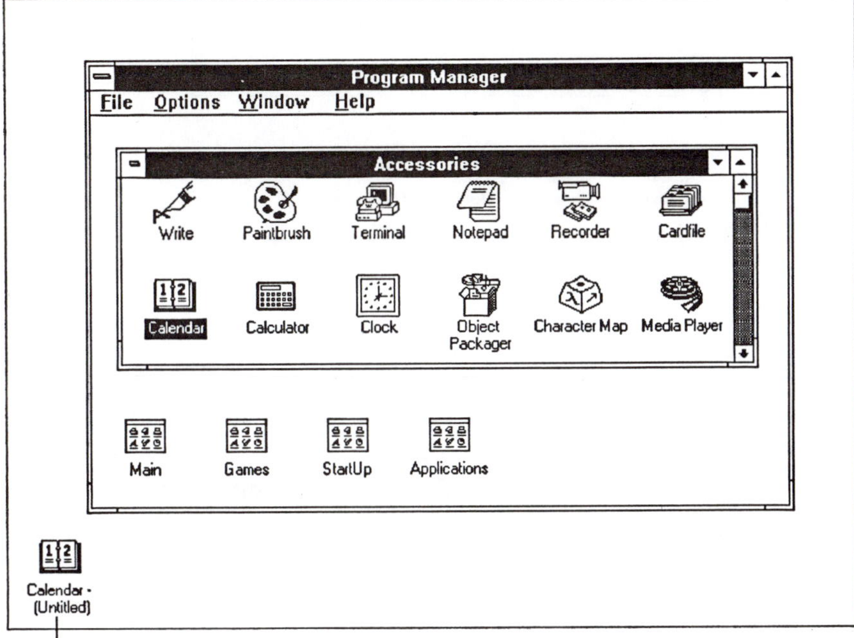

Calendar Icon

6 **Click** on the **Accessories** window's 🔽 (minimize button).

NOTE: The Accessories window shrinks to an icon at the bottom of the Program Manager's window, and it is closed.

7 **Open** the **Main** icon to a window (review, page 54).

NOTE: The screen should look like the "starting Windows screen" with the addition of the calendar icon at the bottom of the desktop.

8 **Double-click** on the **Calendar** icon (to restore it).

9 **Exit** the **Calendar** window (review, page 57).

10 **Exit Windows** (review, page 53).

EXERCISE 14
Move a Window

move a window
To change the location of a window.

title bar
The bar at the top of a window that holds the window's **title**.

drag (mouse action)
- Move the pointer onto an item,
- Press and hold the left button,
- Slide the mouse to a new location, and
- Release the mouse button.

Keyboard Users

MOVE A WINDOW
1. **Select** desired window.
2. Application Window:
   Press Alt + Space
   (opens Control box)
   OR
   Document Window:
   Press Alt + ▬ (hyphen)
   (opens Control box)
3. **Press M** (Move)
4. **Press →, ←, ↑,** or **↓**
   (to move window as desired)
5. **Press ↵**

---

1 Start Windows (review, page 52).

Starting Windows Screen

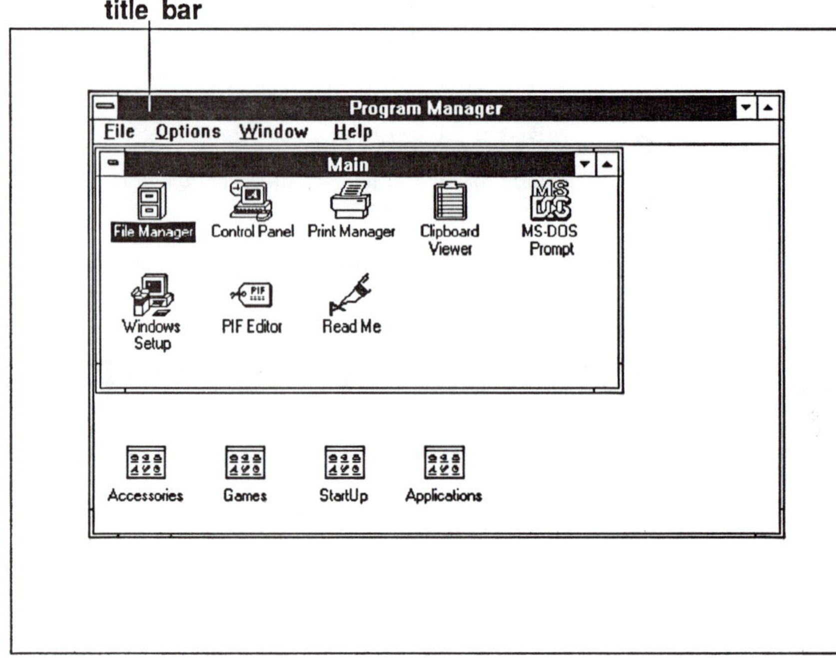

2 Use the **drag** mouse action (described here step-by-step) **to move the** Program Manager's window to the bottom right corner of **the screen:**
- **Move** the pointer onto the **Program Manager's title bar.**
- **Press** and **hold** the left mouse button.
- **Drag** the window to the bottom right corner of the screen.
- **Release** the mouse button.

3 Drag the **Program Manager's Title Bar** back to its original location.

4 Open the **Games** group window (review, page 54).

5 Move the **Game** group window to a new location, but do not leave its *control box* hidden.

6 Close the **Games** group window (review, page 55).

7 Open the **Games** group window again (review, page 54).
NOTE: The Games window opens to its previous size and location.

8 Close the **Games** group window (review, page 55).
NOTE: The screen should look like the "starting Windows screen."

9 Go on to Exercise 15.
OR
Exit Windows (review, page 53).

---

1 Start **Windows** (review, page 52), if necessary.

FROM THE *STARTING WINDOWS* SCREEN:

2 Move the **Program Manager** window to the top left corner of the screen (review, page 68).

3 Move the pointer to the right border of the Program Manager's window so that a *horizontal* **double-headed arrow** (⟺) appears.

4 Use the **drag** mouse action (shown on the previous page) to **drag** the double-headed arrow (and the window's right border) about half an inch to the **right**.

5 Move the pointer to the bottom right **corner** of the Program Manager's border so that a *diagonal* **double-headed arrow** (⤡) appears.

6 **Drag** the double-headed arrow **down** and **right** about half an inch.

7 **Drag** the Program Manager's window right border about one inch to the **left**, BUT DO <u>NOT</u> RELEASE THE MOUSE BUTTON.

8 Press **ESC**.
  *NOTE: **ESC** backs you out of the sizing action – if the mouse button has not been released.*

9 **Size** the Program Manager's window to about its original size.

10 **Move** the **Program Manager** window to the center of the screen (review, page 68).

11 Change the **size** of the Main window.
  NOTE: If you make it smaller, scroll bars appear.

12 **Close** the Main group window (review, page 55).

13 **Open** the Main group window (review, page 54).
  NOTE: The Main window opens to its last size and location.

14 **Size** the Main group window to about its original size, with no scroll bars showing.

15   **Go** on to Exercise 16.

  OR

  Exit Windows (review, page 53).

EXERCISE 15
Size a Window

size a window
To change the size of a window.
NOTE: When you change the size of a window, Windows will remember the new size when you close and then re-open the window (as long as you remain in Windows).

double-headed arrow
The shape the pointer takes when it is used to size a window.

double-headed arrows appear as:

⟺   on right or left edge of window

⇕   on top or bottom edge of window

⤡   on corner of window

Keyboard Users
SIZE A WINDOW
1. **Select** desired window.
2.   <u>Application Window</u>:
   Press **Alt** + **Space**
   (opens Control box)

   OR

   <u>Document Window</u>:
   Press **Alt** + **—** (hyphen)
   (opens Control box)

3. **Press** **S** (Size)
4. **Press** **→**, **←**, **↑**, or **↓** once in the direction of border to be sized.
4. **Press** **→**, **←**, **↑**, or **↓** until desired size is obtained.
5. **Press** **↵**

EXERCISE 16
Scroll through a Window

scroll through a window
To move through information in a window in order to view parts that are beyond the window's borders.

IMPORTANT: If you cannot find what you want in a window, remember to scroll through the window, if there are scroll bars.

scroll bar
A bar that appears at the right and/or bottom of a window whose contents are not completely visible. Each scroll bar contains two scroll arrows and a scroll box.

scroll arrow
The arrow at each end of a scroll bar, used to scroll through the contents of the window.

scroll box
The small box in a scroll bar that shows the position of the information displayed in relation to the entire contents of the window.

NOTE: This exercise has you scroll through group windows. Scroll bars are also used in document windows and dialog boxes.

Keyboard Users
SCROLL THROUGH A WINDOW
1. **Select** the desired window (one that has a scroll bar).
2. Use ⊞ to scroll through the window.

NOTE: You cannot use ⬇ if there is no icon below the highlighted icon.

❶ **Start Windows** (review, page 52), if necessary.

FROM THE *STARTING WINDOWS* SCREEN:

❷ Starting at the right edge, **size** the Main window to about 3 inches wide by 2 inches high (review, page 69).

Main Window Sized to about 3" Wide by 2" High

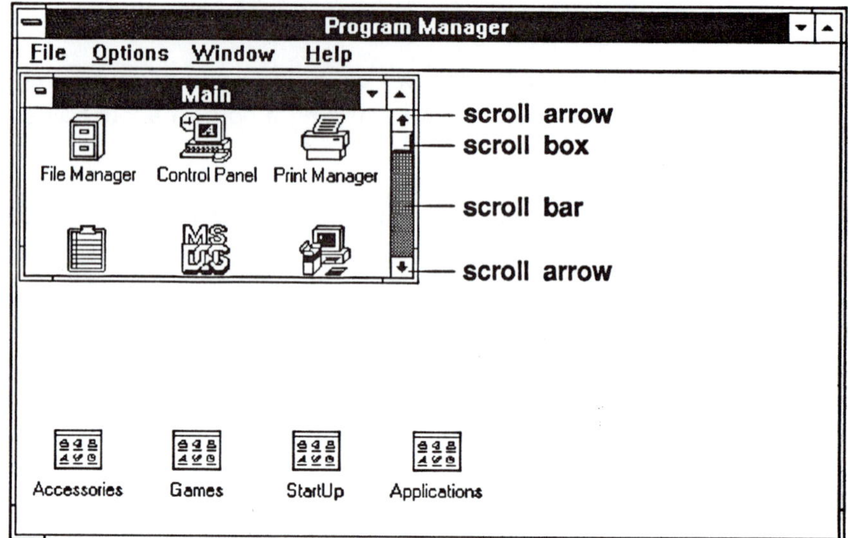

❸ **Click** on the *right (or bottom)* **scroll arrow**, repeatedly, until the **scroll box** moves to the *right edge (or bottom)* of the **scroll bar**.
NOTE: Now you can see the right side (or bottom) of the contents in the window.

❹ **Drag** the **scroll box** to the left edge (or top) of the **scroll bar**.
NOTE: It may take some practice to keep the pointer within the scroll bar.

❺ Practice **dragging** the **scroll box** back and forth (or up and down) in the **scroll bar**. Notice the contents of the window flow back and forth (or up and down) as you drag the scroll box in the scroll bar.

❻ **Click** on the *right (or bottom)* **scroll arrow** several times.

❼ **Click** just before the *left (or top)* **scroll arrow** a few times.
NOTE: It moves in larger jumps than when clicking on the scroll arrow.

❽ **Size** the Main window to about its original size (review, page 69).
NOTE: There is no command to return a newly sized window back to its original size (to do so, you must either size the window again—or, possibly, exit and start Windows).

❾ Scroll the Main window so that all the icons show and, if the window is large enough, the scroll bars will disappear.

❿ Go on to Exercise 17.
OR
Exit Windows (review, page 53).

① Start Windows (review, page 52), if necessary.

FROM THE *STARTING WINDOWS* SCREEN:

② **Close** the **Main** window (review, page 55).

③ **Drag** the **Main** window **icon** to the top right corner of the Program Manager's window.

④ **Drag** the **Accessories** window **icon** to the top left corner of the Program Manager's window.

⑤ ARRANGE ICONS:
- **Click** on <u>W</u>indow (on the menu bar).
- **Click** on **Arrange Icons.**
  NOTE: The group window icons are arranged in a row at the bottom of the Program Manager window.

⑥ **Open** the **Accessories** window (review, page 54).

⑦ **Move** the program icons around <u>just a little (about ¼")</u>.
*NOTE: If you move the icons too far, the **arrange icons** command may change the <u>locations</u> of the icons.*
NOTE: The <u>A</u>uto Arrange command (found in the <u>O</u>ptions menu) must be deselected (no check mark by it) or the program icons will jump back when you try to move them.

⑧ **Arrange** the **icons** using the command (step 5).
NOTE: The program-item icons are arranged within the accessories group window.

⑨ **Start Calendar** (review, page 56).

⑩ **Minimize Calendar** (review, page 66).
*NOTE: Calendar becomes a running **application icon** at the bottom of the desktop.*

⑪ **Drag** the **Calendar icon** to the bottom right corner of the desktop.

⑫ **Drag** the **Calendar icon** back to the bottom left corner of the desktop.

⑬ **Click** on the **Calendar icon** (the Control menu pops up).

⑭ **Click** on <u>C</u>lose.

⑮ **Close** the **Accessories** group window (review, page 55).

⑯ **Move** the **icons** around a little.

⑰ **Arrange** the **icons** using the command.

⑱ **Open** the **Main** group window (review, page 54).

⑲ Go on to Exercise 18.
OR
Exit Windows (review, page 53).

EXERCISE 17
Move and Arrange Icons

move icons
To change the location of:
1) **group window icons** in the Program Manager's workspace, and
2) **application icons** on the desktop.

*NOTE: Moving **program icons** "within a group window" and "from one group to another group" is covered in Ex. 31.*

<u>IMPORTANT</u>: The **arrange icons** command arranges one of two different sets of icons. <u>IF a group window icon</u> is highlighted, the **arrange icons** command will arrange the group window icons in a row at the bottom of the Program Manager window. Or, <u>if a program icon</u> is highlighted, the **arrange icons** command will arrange the program icons within its group window.

Keyboard Users

MOVE <u>APPLICATION</u> ICONS
1. Press **Alt** + **Esc** until the desired *application icon name* is highlighted.
2. Press **Alt** + **Space**
3. Press **M** (<u>M</u>ove)
   (a four-headed arrow appears on the icon)
4. Use the arrow keys to move the icon as desired.
5. Press **↵**

MOVE <u>GROUP WINDOW</u> ICONS
1. Press **Ctrl** + **Tab** until the desired *group window icon* is highlighted.
2. Press **Alt** + **—** (hyphen)
3. Press **M** (<u>M</u>ove)
   (a four-headed arrow appears on the icon)
4. Use the arrow keys to move the icon as desired.
5. Press **↵**

ARRANGE GROUP WINDOW ICONS
With Program Manager selected and a group icon highlighted:
1. Press **Alt** + **F** (<u>F</u>ile)
2. Press **A** (<u>A</u>rrange Icons)

EXERCISE 18
Arrange Group Windows

arrange group windows

Use one of Windows' two methods (cascade or tile) to position the open group windows on the screen so that they can all be seen.

cascade

To resize and layer the open group windows, within the Program Manager workspace, so that the title bar of each group window is visible.

---

1 Start Windows (review, page 52), if necessary.

FROM THE *STARTING WINDOWS* SCREEN:

2 Open the **Accessories** window (review, page 54).

3 Open the **Games** window (review, page 54).

4
- **Click on <u>W</u>indows.**
- **Click on <u>C</u>ascade.**

OR

- **Press Shift + F5.**
  (shortcut keys to cascade windows)

Cascaded Group Windows

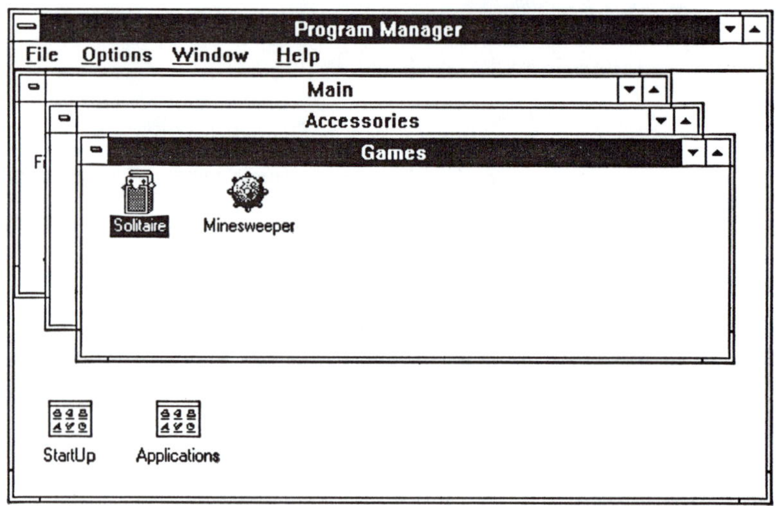

*NOTE: If the Program Manager's window is not large enough to show all the title bars, the group windows may not cascade correctly. In this case, **size** the Program Manager window larger and then give the command to **cascade** again.*

Keyboard Users

ARRANGE GROUP WINDOW

WITH THE PROGRAM MANAGER WINDOW HIGHLIGHTED:

- **Press Shift + F5**
  (shortcut keys to cascade)
  OR
- **Press Shift + F4**
  (shortcut keys to tile)

OR

- **Press Alt + W**
  (to open <u>W</u>indow menu)
- **Press C** (<u>C</u>ascade)
  OR
  Press T (<u>T</u>ile)

Continue Exercise 18 on the next page

5
- Click on <u>W</u>indows.
- Click on <u>T</u>ile.

OR

- Press `Shift` + `F4`.
  (shortcut keys to tile windows)

tile

to resize and arrange the open group windows side by side within the Program Manager workspace.

Tiled Group Windows

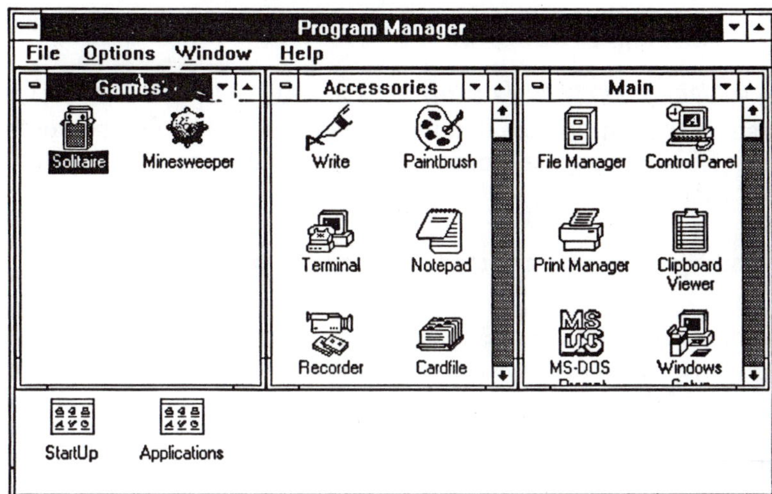

6 **Close** the **Games** window (review, page 55).

7 **Close** the **Accessories** window (review, page 55).

8 **Arrange** the window to **cascade** (review, page 72).

9 **Size** the **Main** window until no scroll bar is showing.

10 **Exit Windows** (review, page 53).

EXERCISE 19
Practice

Lesson One
Windows Basics

Tasks Reviewed:

Start Windows
Move icons
Drag (mouse action)
Use menu bar
Open group windows
Arrange Program Manager
Close group windows
Size a window
Move a window
Exit Windows

1 **Start Windows.**
(The standard "starting Windows screen" should appear.)

2 **Move** the *group window icons*, located at the bottom of the Program Manager window, around a little.

3 **Arrange icons** by using the menu command.

4 Try to **drag** one of the *group window icons* <u>out</u> of the Program Manager window. Notice that the cursor will not drag the icon out of the window.

5 **Drag** a *Main group window* **program icon** <u>out</u> of the window BUT do <u>not</u> release the button. Notice that the pointer turns into a $\bigcirc$ (prevent) shape. Now <u>release</u> the mouse button and watch the icon jump back into its window.

6 **Click** on <u>W</u>indows (to select the Windows menu).

7 **Click** on **Games** (to open Games).
*NOTE: Steps 6 and 7 can be used to **open** or **select** group windows when they are hidden.*

8 **Open** the **Accessories** window.

9 **Open** the **Startup** window.

10 **Arrange** the **group windows** in a **tile** format.

11 **Arrange** the **group windows** in a **cascade** format.
*NOTE: You may have to size the Program Manager window taller so the group windows will **cascade** correctly.*

12 **Close** the **Accessories, Games,** and **Startup** windows.

13 **Size** the **Main** window, making it tall enough to display all the *program icons* without scroll bars showing.

14 **Move** the **Program Manager** window to the bottom center of the screen.

15 **Move** the **Main** window to the right until only half of it shows.

16 **Move** the **Program Manager** window back to its original position (center of the screen) and size it to its original size, if necessary.

17 **Move** the **Main** window back to its original position (on the left edge and just under the menu bar).
*NOTE: If there are **scroll bars** in the Program Manager window, move the **bottom scroll box** to the left side and the **right scroll box** to the top, and the scroll bars should disappear.*

18 **Exit Windows.**

1 Start Windows.
(The standard "starting Windows screen" should appear.)

2 Open the **Accessories** window.

3 Start **Write**.

4 Select **Program Manager** (page 58).

5 Start **Write** again.

6 Select **Program Manager** again.

7 Start **Write** once again.
*NOTE: Starting an application more than once is often done by mistake by new users when they can't find their original application. If you cannot find an application that has been opened, use the **rotation selection** method (Alt + Tab) to cycle through the open applications until you find the one you want.*
NOTE: On the other hand, opening an application more than once is sometimes purposely done in order to transfer data between documents of the same application when that application does not allow multiple document windows.

8 **Exit** the Write that is currently selected.

9 • Press **Ctrl** + **Esc** (to access the Task List).
• **Double-click** on one of the Writes.

10 **Exit** this Write.

11 **Select** the last Write that is open.

12 **Exit** this last Write.

13 **Close** the **Accessories** window.

14 **Click** on **Window**.

15 **Cancel** the **menu**.

16 **Click** on **File**.

17 **Click** on **Properties...** .

18 **Cancel** the **dialog box**.

19 **Go** on to Exercise 21.
OR
Exit Windows.

Tasks Reviewed:
Start Windows
Open group windows
Select application windows
Start programs
Exit programs
Close group windows
Use the menu bar
Cancel
Exit Windows

EXERCISE 21
Practice

Lesson One
Windows Basics

Tasks Reviewed:

Start Windows
Open group windows
Start programs
Maximize a window
Select an application
Minimize application windows
Restore application windows
Exit programs
Exit Windows

1 Start Windows, if necessary.

2 Open the **Accessories** group window.

3 Start Calculator.

4 Select Accessories and **start Paintbrush.**

5 Maximize Paintbrush.

6 Select Calculator using the **rotation** method.
(It appears in Paintbrush's workspace but it is not really <u>within</u> Paintbrush; rather, it has moved <u>in front of</u> the Paintbrush window.)

7 Select Program Manager.

8 Select Paintbrush.

9 Minimize Paintbrush (it becomes a "running" icon).

10 Select Calculator.

11 Minimize Calculator (it becomes a "running" icon).

12 Minimize the Program Manager (it becomes a "running" icon).

13 Restore (double-click on) the **Program Manager.**

14 Restore Paintbrush (to enlarge the icon to a window).

15 Restore Paintbrush again (to resize the window).

16 Exit Paintbrush.

17 Restore Calculator.

18 Exit Calculator.

19 Close Accessories.

20 Go on to Exercise 22.
OR
Exit Windows.

1 Start Windows, if necessary.

2 Open the Accessories window.

3 Start Clock.

4 Click on Settings.

5 Click on Digital (to select it).

6 Size the Clock window to about 3" wide by 1" high.

7 Move Clock to the bottom right corner of the desktop.

8 Start and maximize Write.

9 Select Clock (since it is hidden, use the rotation method, page 58).

10 Click on Clock's ⬜.

11 IF Always on Top is deselected (i.e., there is no ✓ by it), then click on Always on Top.

12 Exit Write.

13 Open Paintbrush, and then maximize it.
NOTE: Clock stayed on top.

14 Restore Paintbrush, and then Exit Paintbrush.

15 RETURN CLOCK TO ITS ORIGINAL STATE:
- Click on Settings, and select Analog.
- Click on Settings. IF Seconds is *deselected*, select it.
  OR, IF Seconds is *selected*, click off of the menu.
- Click on Settings. IF Date is *deselected*, select it.
  OR, IF Date is *selected*, click off of the menu.
- Size the clock to about 2" by 2".
- Click on ⬜, and deselect *Always on Top*.
- Move the clock to the top left corner of the screen.

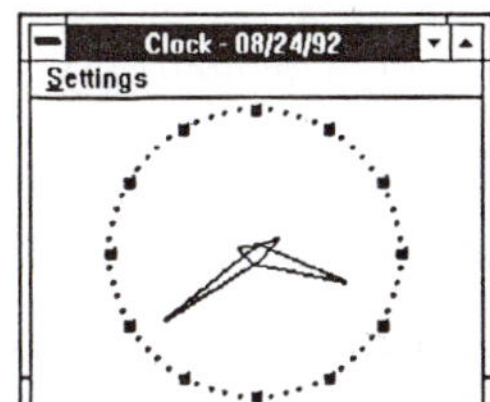

16 Exit Windows.

Tasks Reviewed:
Start Windows
Open group windows
Start programs
Use menu bar
Size a window
Move a window
Maximize a window
Select a window
Exit Windows

Lesson One
Review of Windows Basics Exercises

Lesson One (Windows Basics) covers tasks that:

Start and Exit Microsoft Windows.

Open and Close Group Windows.

Start and Exit Program Windows.

Select Application and Document Windows.

Use the Menu Bar and Choose Commands from Menus.

Cancel Menus, Dialog Boxes, and Windows.

Maximize, Minimize, and Restore Windows.

Move, Size, and Arrange Windows.

Scroll through Windows.

Move and Arrange Icons.

POINTS TO EMPHASIZE

Compare and Contrast

Application Windows <u>and</u> Document Windows <u>and</u> Group Windows:

- Application windows hold running programs.
- Document windows are windows within an application window.
- Group windows are a special kind of document window that are used only within the Program Manager window.

Choose <u>and</u> Select:

- *Choose* means to pick an item from a menu to initiate an action.
- *Select* means to mark an item so that a subsequent action can activate it.

Exit <u>and</u> Close:

- The E<u>x</u>it command is usually found in the <u>F</u>ile menu (only in application windows).
- The <u>C</u>lose command is usually found in the Control menu (in application *and* document windows).
- Both Exit and Close are commands that let you leave Windows.

Start <u>and</u> Open:

- *Start* usually refers to beginning *application windows* (programs).
- *Open* usually refers to beginning *document* and *group windows.*

Minimize *Group Windows* <u>and</u> Minimize *Application Windows*:

- When a *group window* (or document window) is *minimized,* it is closed.
- When an *application window* is *minimized,* it becomes a *running icon* (it is still open).

Control box for *application windows* <u>and</u> control box for *document windows*:

- The control box for *application* and *dialog box* windows holds a "spacebar icon" ⊟ (longer).
- The control box for *group* and *document* windows holds a "hyphen icon" ⊟ (shorter).

Continued ...

Important Skills

- Canceling (backing out of or exiting) unwanted menus, dialog boxes, and windows (see page 63).
- Selecting icons, windows, and menu items.
- Being able to find "hidden" windows.
- Using the mouse to **click** or **double-click** on an item, and to **drag** an item.

Three methods to select application windows

- Click on window with mouse (use only for windows that can be seen).
- Rotation method (rotates through each open window one at a time).
- Task list method (lists all open windows).

Three methods to select group windows

- Click on window with mouse (use only for windows that can be seen).
- Rotation method (rotates through each open window one at a time).
- Click on <u>W</u>indows, then click on the desired document window.

Different ways <u>selected</u> items may be displayed

- a highlighted title bar, icon name, or menu item.
- a check mark on a menu item.
- a dotted rectangle around an option.
- a highlighted border around a dialog box option.

The double-click mouse action

- the action must be quick and precise.
- the mouse must remain stationary when you press the button.

The title bar of a maximized document window

When a document window is maximized, it shares the title bar and menu bar of the application it is in.

Title bar before window is maximized

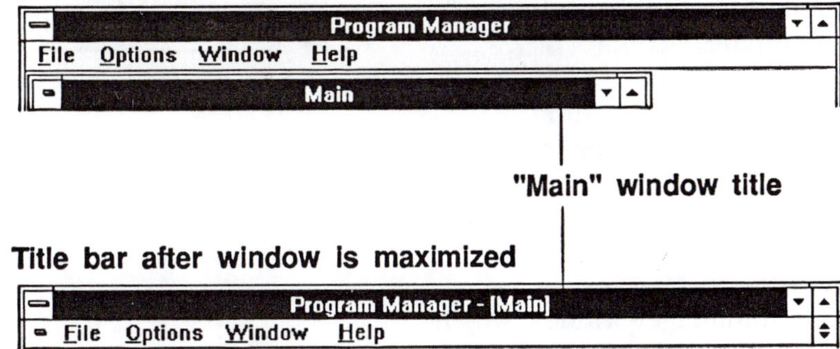

Title bar after window is maximized

The relationship of the maximize and restore buttons

When a window is maximized, the maximize button is replaced with a restore button (⬍); and when a window is restored, the restore button is replaced with a maximize button (▲).

WORKSHEET 16

WINDOWS BASICS <u>TERMS</u>

NAME ______________________________

DIRECTIONS: Match the terms listed below to the definition that best fits the term.

click	title bar	double-click	group window icons
icon	desktop	control menu	group windows
window	dialog box	control box	

1. The background (screen) on which windows and icons appear.

   1) ______________________________

2. A small picture that represents an element such as a document, program, group of programs, command, or the pointer.

   2) ______________________________

3. The rectangular work area for a task, program, document, or Windows group. There are several kinds (application, document, group, and dialog).

   3) ______________________________

4. The box at the left end of the title bar which opens the Control menu.

   4) ______________________________

5. A menu that you can use to manipulate a window. It contains commands such as restore, move, size, maximize, minimize, close, and open.

   5) ______________________________

6. The horizontal bar at the top of a window that holds the window's name.

   6) ______________________________

7. 1) Move the pointer on the desired item, and
   2) quickly press and release the left mouse button twice.

   7) ______________________________

8. A box that appears when a menu item with an ellipsis (...) is chosen. It requests additional information before performing the original command.

   8) ______________________________

9. 1) Move the pointer on the desired item, and
   2) quickly press and release the left mouse button.

   9) ______________________________

10. Icons at the bottom of the Program Manager window which represent *group windows*.

    10) ______________________________

11. Windows within the Program Manager window which hold "groups" of program icons.

    11) ______________________________

(This page may be copied.)

WORKSHEET 17

WINDOWS BASICS <u>TERMS</u>

NAME ________________________

> **DIRECTIONS:** Match the terms listed below to the definition that best fits the term.
>
> | | | | | |
> |---|---|---|---|---|
> | drag | an ellipsis | click off | close a menu | application window |
> | choose | menu bar | group window | program icon | |
> | select | workspace | active window | document window | |

1. A picture in a *group window* that represents a program.
   1) ________________________

2. To click <u>outside</u> of an area in order to "back out" of an action.
   2) ________________________

3. The inner part of a window, where the work on an application is done.
   3) ________________________

4. A window that holds a program.
   4) ________________________

5. The window that you are currently using or that is currently selected.
   5) ________________________

6. A special kind of *document window* that displays program icons that are used to *start* programs.
   6) ________________________

7. The bar located under the title bar on application windows that lists the available *menus*.
   7) ________________________

8. A window within an application window.
   8) ________________________

9. To back out of a menu without choosing a command.
   9) ________________________

10. To pick an item from a menu that initiates an action.
    10) ________________________

11. To *mark* an item so that a subsequent action can activate it. *Highlighting* and *using a check mark* are two ways to mark a command.
    11) ________________________

12. Three dots (...) that follow the name of menu items that open a *dialog box* when selected.
    12) ________________________

13. Move the pointer onto an item, press and hold the left button, slide the mouse to a new location, and release the mouse button.
    13) ________________________

WORKSHEET 18

WINDOWS BASICS <u>TERMS</u>

NAME _______________________________

DIRECTIONS: Match the terms listed below to the definition that best fits the term.

tile	scroll bar	maximize button	minimize button
scroll box	shortcut keys	dimmed command	double-headed arrow
cascade	scroll arrow	restore button	

---

1. The shape the pointer takes when it is used to size a window.

   1) _______________________________

2. Key combinations that can be used to activate certain commands instead of using menus.

   2) _______________________________

3. The box located at the right end of the title bar of a maximized window; it replaces the maximize button when a window is maximized.

   3) _______________________________

4. A bar that appears at the right and/or bottom of a window whose contents are not completely visible.

   4) _______________________________

5. The arrow at each end of a scroll bar, used to *scroll* through the contents of the window.

   5) _______________________________

6. A menu command that is shown in gray instead of black. It cannot be used in the current situation.

   6) _______________________________

7. The box located at the right end of the title bar; it is used to enlarge a window to its greatest size.

   7) _______________________________

8. The small square in a scroll bar that shows the position of the information *displayed* in relation to the *entire contents* of the window.

   8) _______________________________

9. To layer and resize the open group windows so that the title bar of each group window is visible.

   9) _______________________________

10. The box located at the right of the title bar (just before the maximize button) and used to shrink a window to an icon.

    10) _______________________________

11. To resize and arrange the open group windows side by side.

    11) _______________________________

(This page may be copied.)

WORKSHEET 19

WINDOWS BASICS TASKS

NAME ______________________________

DIRECTIONS: Match the tasks listed below to the definition that best fits the task.

cancel   start a program   close a group window
use the menu bar   open a group window   select a group window
exit Windows   exit a program   select an application window
start Windows

---

1. To enlarge a *group window icon* to a window.

1) ______________________________

2. To leave Microsoft Windows and return the computer to a DOS prompt.

2) ______________________________

3. To begin Microsoft Windows from a DOS prompt and/or (for some systems) by turning the computer on.

3) ______________________________

4. To use Windows to leave a program.

4) ______________________________

5. To use Windows to run a program.

5) ______________________________

6. To reduce a group window to an icon.

6) ______________________________

7. To make an *application window* active. A *highlighted title bar* indicates that a window is active.

7) ______________________________

8. To undo or "back out of" an action.

8) ______________________________

9. To *choose* a menu from the menu bar.

9) ______________________________

10. To make a *group window* active. A *highlighted title bar* indicates that a window is active.

10) ______________________________

WORKSHEET 20

WINDOWS BASICS <u>TASKS</u>

NAME ___________________________

DIRECTIONS: Match the tasks listed below to the definition that best fits the task.

move icons	arrange icons	scroll through a window
move a window	arrange group windows	restore a window
size a window	minimize a window	maximize a window

---

1. To shrink a window to an icon.

   1) ___________________________

2. To enlarge a window to its greatest size.

   2) ___________________________

3. To return a maximized window to its previous size.

   3) ___________________________

4. To move through information in a window in order to view parts that are beyond the window's borders.

   4) ___________________________

5. To change the dimensions of a window.

   5) ___________________________

6. To change the location of a window.

   6) ___________________________

7. To use one of Windows' two methods (cascade or tile) to position the open group windows on the screen so that they can all be seen.

   7) ___________________________

8. Use the Windows command to distribute <u>group</u> icons in a row at the bottom of the Program Manager's window, or to distribute <u>program-item</u> icons evenly within the selected group window.

   8) ___________________________

9. To change the location of group window icons in the Program Manager's workspace and application icons on the desktop.

   9) ___________________________

(This page may be copied.)

Lesson Two — Beyond Basics

Table of Contents

EXERCISE 23
Save Desktop Arrangement

Exercises 23 and 24 should be done during the same session.

save desktop arrangement
To save the arrangement of <u>Program Manager group windows and icons</u> so that Windows will remember that arrangement when you start Windows the next time.

select
To <u>mark</u> an item so that a subsequent action can activate it.

Keyboard Users

SELECT "SAVE SETTINGS ON EXIT"

1. Press **Alt** + **O** (Options)

IF ✓ is <u>not</u> next to "Save Settings on Exit":
- Press **S**
  (Save Settings on Exit)
- Press **Alt** + **O** (Options)
  to verify that there is a ✓ by the "Save Setting on Exit" command.

2. Press **Alt**
   to close the options menu.

---

1 **Start Windows** (review, page 52), if necessary.

Starting Windows Screen

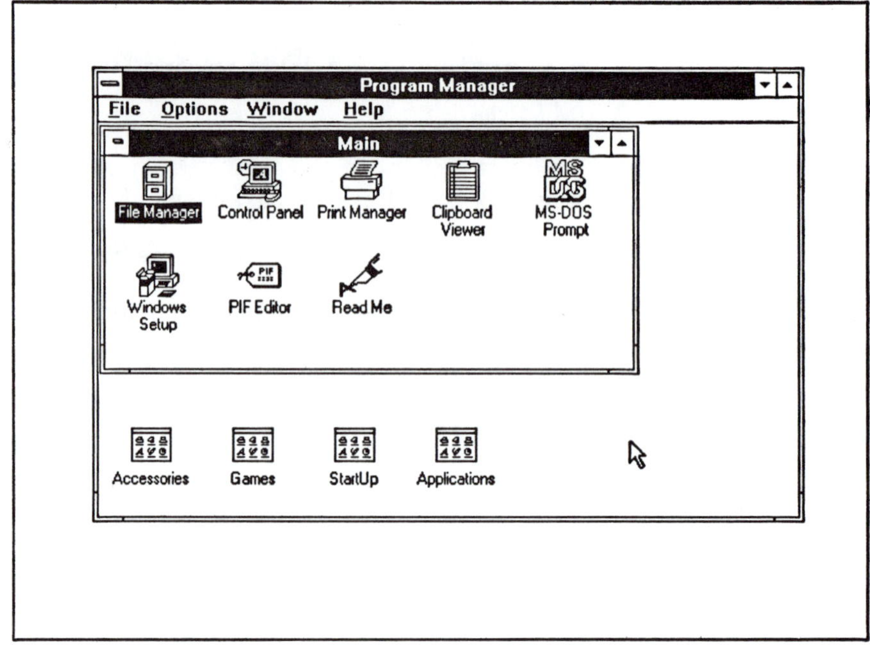

NOTE: After Microsoft Windows is installed, a screen that is arranged like the one above is displayed the first time Windows is started. This exercise explains how to save a new Program Manager <u>desktop arrangement</u>.

2 **SELECT "SAVE SETTINGS ON EXIT" OPTION:**

- **Click** on **Options** (to drop down the menu).

NOTE: When selected, a check mark appears by the "Save Settings on Exit" option.

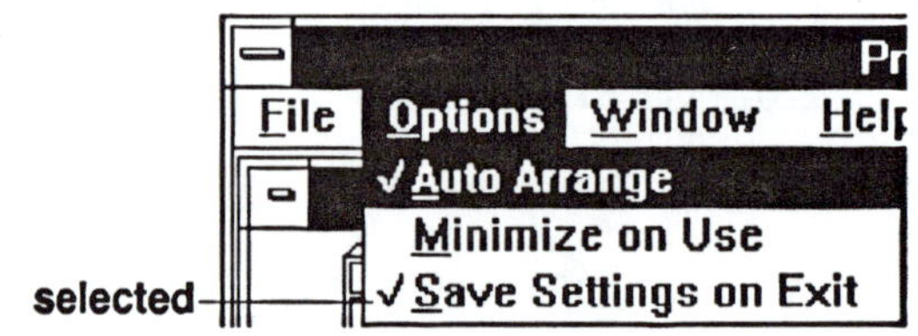

IF ✓ does **not** appear by "Save Settings on Exit":
- **Click** on **Save Settings on Exit**.
- **Click** on **Options again** (to verify that the option is checked).
- **Click** anywhere <u>off</u> of the Options menu (to **close** it).

OR

IF ✓ does appear by "Save Settings on Exit":
- **Click** anywhere <u>off</u> of the Options menu (to **close** it).

---

3 **Open** the **Accessories** group window (review, page 54).

4 **Open** the **Games** group window (review, page 54).

Continue Exercise 23 on the next page

5 **Arrange** the *group windows* in a **tile** format (review, page 73).

Tiled Group Windows

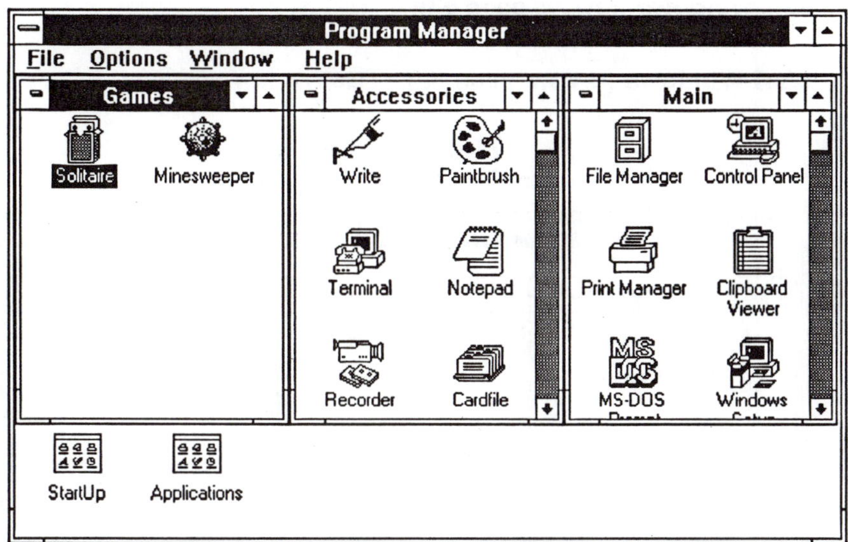

6 **Exit Windows** (review, page 53).

7 **Start Windows** (review, page 52).
NOTE: The screen should appear like that in the illustration above.

8 **DESELECT "SAVE SETTINGS ON EXIT" OPTION:**
NOTE: When deselected, no check mark appears by the "Save Settings on Exit" option.

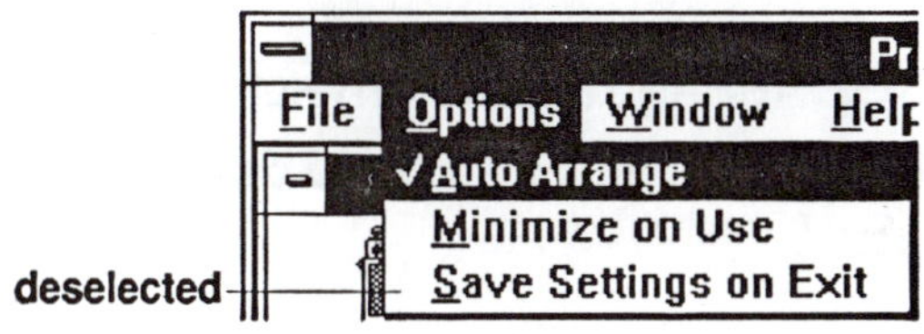

- **Click** on **Options**.

> **IF** ✓ appears by "Save Settings on Exit":
> - **Click** on **Save Settings on Exit**.
> - **Click** on **Options again** (to verify that the option is *not* checked).
> - **Click** anywhere *off* of the Options menu (to **close** it).

OR

> **IF** ✓ does **not** appear by "Save Settings on Exit":
> - **Click** anywhere *off* of the Options menu (to **close** it).

---

deselect
To _unmark_ an item so that a future action will _not_ activate the item.

<u>WARNING</u>:

The "Save Settings on Exit" menu item should remain <u>deselected</u>, that is, there should <u>not</u> be a ✓ by it.

The reason for this is to avoid disturbing the "starting Windows screen," which is the starting point for exercises in this book.

Keyboard Users

DESELECT "SAVE SETTINGS ON EXIT"

1. **Press** Alt + O (Options)

IF ✓ is next to "Save Settings on Exit":

- **Press** S
  (Save Settings on Exit)

- **Press** Alt + O (Options)
  to verify that there is a *no* check mark on the "Save Settings on Exit" command.

2. - **Press** Alt (to close the options menu and leave the menu bar active).

OR

- **Press** Esc (to close the options menu and return to the previous active point).

Continue Exercise 23 on the next page

EXERCISE 23 (continued)
SAVE DESKTOP ARRANGEMENT

save desktop arrangement without exiting Windows

A shortcut method to save the current desktop arrangement.

NOTE: The "Save Settings on Exit" option does NOT have to be checked to save the desktop arrangement this way.

NOTE: The reason this book introduces you to the "Save Settings on Exit" command is to make you aware of how it works, so you will not use it unknowingly in the future.

Keyboard Users

SAVE CURRENT DESKTOP ARRANGEMENT WITHOUT EXITING WINDOWS:

Press and hold **Shift** while you:

• **Press** **Alt** + **F** (**F**ile)
• **Press** **X** (E**x**it)

OR

• **Press** **Alt** + **F4** (shortcut keys)

Exercise 23 (continued)

⑨ **Arrange** the *group windows* in a **cascade** format (review, page 72).

⑩ **Exit Windows** (review, page 53).

⑪ **Start Windows** (review, page 52). This window appears:

**Tiled Group Windows
(previous screen arrangement)**

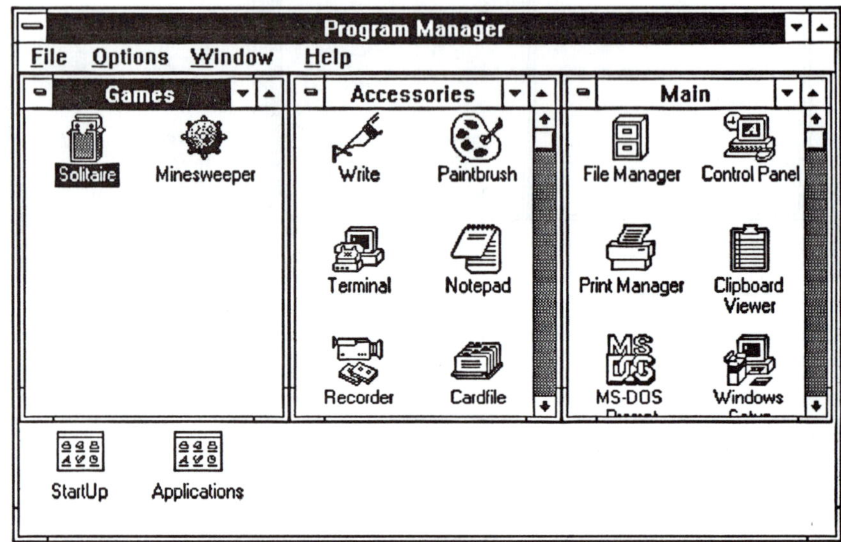

⑫ **Arrange** the *group windows* in a **cascade** format again (review, page 72).

⑬ SAVE DESKTOP ARRANGEMENT WITHOUT EXITING WINDOWS:
• **Press** and **hold down** **Shift** while you **double-click** on the Program Manager's ⊟ (Control box).

⑭ **Exit Windows** (review, page 53).

⑮ **Start Windows** (review, page 52).
Is the **cascade** arrangement displayed?

⑯ Using **size** and **move** as desired, **arrange** the Program Manager's group windows and icons a different way.

⑰ Follow step 13 to "save" the desktop arrangement.

⑱ **Exit Windows** (review, page 53).

⑲ **Start Windows** (review, page 52).
Is your new desktop arrangement displayed?

Go on to Exercise 24

① Close <u>all</u> of the *group windows* that may be open (review, page 55).

② Size the *Program Manager window* to about the size shown in the illustration below (review, page 69).

③ Move the *Program Manager window* to the center of the desktop (review, page 68).

④ Use the <u>A</u>rrange Icons command to arrange the group window icons (review, page 71).

⑤ Open the *Main group window* (review, page 54).

⑥ Size the *Main group window* just large enough to show all the *program items* without *scroll bars* appearing.
IF the *Program Manager window* is too short to show all the *group window icons:*
- Size the *Program Manager window* by pulling the bottom border down a little.
- Click on one of the <u>group window</u> icons (to select it).
- Click off of the icon (to close the menu but it still remains selected).
- <u>A</u>rrange Icons using the command.

⑦ Move the *Main group window* to fit in the Program Manager window as shown below.

⑧ Make any necessary adjustments to match your screen to the illustration below.

Starting Windows Screen

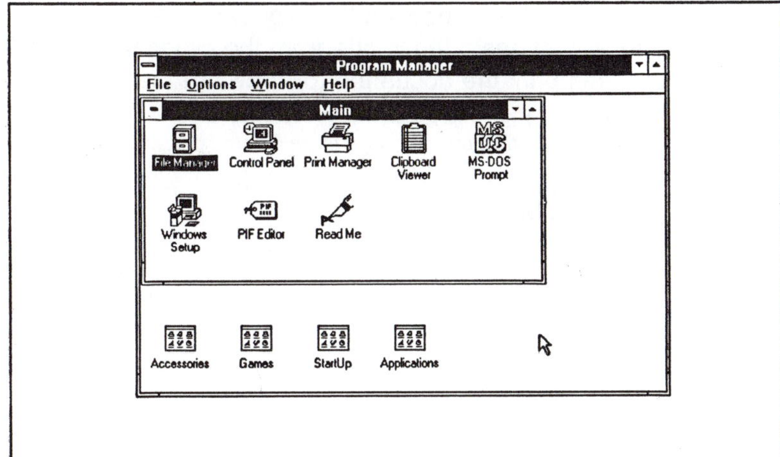

⑨ Save the desktop arrangement without exiting Windows (Review, page 88, step 13).

⑩ Go on to Exercise 25.

OR

Exit Windows (review, page 53).

EXERCISE 24
Create "Starting Windows Screen"

Continue from Exercise 23, doing both during the same session.

create "starting windows screen"
To manipulate the Program Manager window, Main group window, and group window icons to approximate Windows' original opening screen.

EXERCISE 25
Capture an Application Window

Exercises 25, 26, and 27 should be done during the same session.

capture an application window

To copy an image of the <u>active application window</u> onto the <u>clipboard</u>.

<u>IMPORTANT</u>: There are two kinds of captures. An <u>application window capture</u> and a <u>screen capture</u>. The application window capture is done in this exercise. The screen capture is done in Exercise 28 (screen captures can be performed only in the 386 enhanced mode).

clipboard

A temporary storage area used to hold information that is being transferred from one program (or document) to another. The clipboard is also used to hold application window and screen captures.

capture (verb)

To perform the keystrokes to <u>copy the image</u> that is visible on your monitor, either an application window or an entire screen, onto the clipboard.

capture (noun)

The <u>image</u> of an application window or the entire screen that has been copied onto the clipboard.

Keyboard Users

CAPTURE AN APPLICATION WINDOW

See Step 2.

---

1 **Start Windows** (review, page 52), if necessary.

Starting Windows Screen

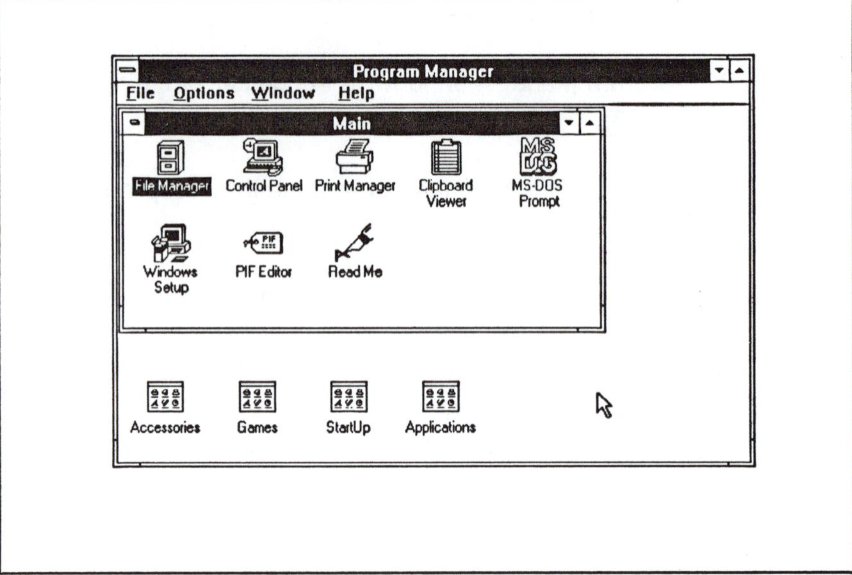

NOTE: This exercise instructs you to <u>capture</u> the Program Manager window. Other application windows can be <u>captured</u> if you first:
- *Select the desired window, and then*
- *Continue with step 2 below.*

2 **Press Alt + Prnt Scrn** (capture an application window).

<u>Nothing seems to happen</u>, but if all went right, an image of the Program Manager window was captured and placed on the *clipboard*. Go on to Exercise 26.

<u>IMPORTANT</u>: Using **Alt** + **Prnt Scrn** does <u>not print</u> the window, but only "captures" an image of the window on the clipboard. To print the "capture," you must first *paste* the image from the clipboard into Write (or Paintbrush) and then print the document (or drawing) (see page 92).

NOTE: Some keyboards may <u>not</u> recognize this procedure. Do the next exercise (Use the Clipboard Viewer) to find out if it <u>does</u> work before trying this alternate procedure:
- *Press **Shift** + **Prnt Scrn**.*

Go on to Exercise 26

1 **Start** the **Clipboard Viewer** (located in the Main group window) (review, page 56).

2 **Maximize** the **Clipboard Viewer** (review, page 64). Does your screen look like the illustration below?

Maximized Clipboard Viewer Showing
Captured Program Manager Window

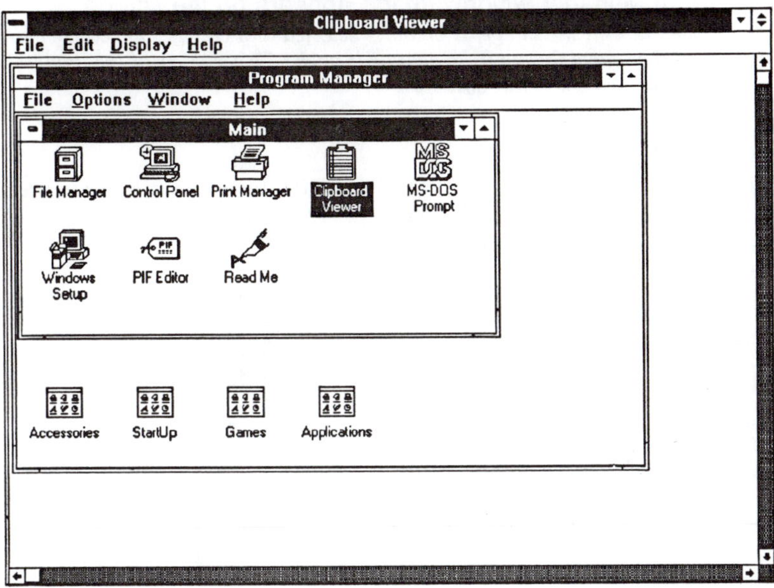

ONLY IF the Clipboard Viewer does <u>not</u> display an image of the Program Manager window:
- **Exit** the **Clipboard Viewer** window (review, page 57).
- Perform the option shown in the NOTE for step 2 of Exercise 25 and continue from there.

3 CLEAR THE CLIPBOARD VIEWER:
- **Click** on <u>E</u>dit.
- **Click** on <u>D</u>elete.
- **Click** on [<u>Yes</u>].

4 **Restore** the **Clipboard Viewer** window (review, page 65).

5 **Exit** the **Clipboard Viewer** window (review, page 57).

6 **Capture** the **Program Manager** window again (press **Alt** + **Prnt Scrn**).

7 **Use** the **Clipboard Viewer** to see if the window was captured, but DO NOT **CLEAR** THE CLIPBOARD VIEWER.

8 **Exit** the **Clipboard Viewer** (review, page 57).

Go on to Exercise 27

EXERCISE 26
Use the Clipboard Viewer

Continue from Exercise 25, doing Exercise 25-27 during the same session.

use the Clipboard Viewer
To <u>open</u> the Clipboard Viewer window and <u>view</u>, <u>save</u>, <u>open</u>, or <u>delete</u> clipboard images; and then <u>close</u> the Clipboard Viewer. The Clipboard Viewer lets you see if you successfully captured a window or screen.

Clipboard Viewer
A program that lets you <u>view</u> the contents of the clipboard. You can also <u>save</u> or <u>delete</u> the contents of the clipboard, or <u>open</u> a previously saved clipboard image.

Keyboard Users
USE THE CLIPBOARD VIEWER
1. **Start** Clipboard Viewer (review, p.56).
2. **Maximize** the window (review, p.64).
3. Clear the Clipboard Viewer:
   - **Press** **Alt** + **E** (Edit)
   - **Press** **D** (Delete)
4. **Restore** Clipboard Viewer (review, p.65).
5. **Exit** Clipboard Viewer (review, p.57).

EXERCISE 27
Print a Capture

Continue from Exercise 26, doing Exercises 25-27 during the same session.

<u>ASSUMPTION:</u>

It is assumed that your printer has been properly installed and that it will print graphics.

print a capture
To "paste" the contents of the clipboard into a program and then print it.

paste
To <u>copy</u> information from the clipboard into a program.

Keyboard Users
PRINT A CAPTURE

1. **Start** Write (review, p.52).
2. **Maximize** the window (review, p.64).
3. Paste clipboard image:
   - Press **Alt** + **E** (Edit)
   - Press **P** (Paste)
4. Print document:
   - Press **Alt** + **F** (File)
   - Press **P** (Print)
   - Press **↵**
     (to accept the default of **OK** to print)
5. **Restore** Write's window (review, p.65).
6. Close Write:
   - Press **Alt** + **F4** (Close)
   - Press **N** (No)
     (No, you do <u>not</u> want to save the document.)

---

① **Open** the **Accessories window** (review, page 54).

② **Start Write** (review, page 56).

③ **Maximize** Write's window (review, page 64).

④ **Click on** <u>E</u>**dit, then on** <u>P</u>**aste.**
The Program Manager window image appears on the screen.
NOTE: If you click on the image, it becomes selected and changes to reverse video. Click off of the image (below it) to change it back. To see parts of the image that may not show, use the scroll bar.

⑤ **Click on** <u>F</u>**ile, then on** <u>P</u>**rint.**
NOTE: Be careful not to confuse the real Write "<u>F</u>ile" command with the image of the captured "<u>F</u>ile" command, which, of course, will not work.
The *Print* dialog box appears:

your printer will be listed here → 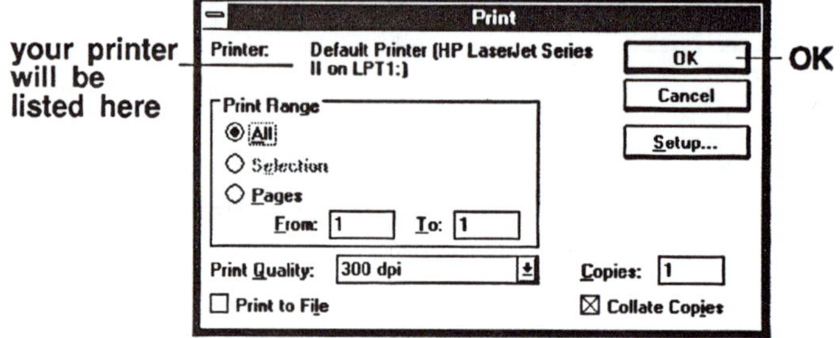 ← **OK**

⑥ Make sure the printer is ready to receive data.

⑦ **Click on** OK (to print).

⑧ **Restore Write's window** (review, page 65).

⑨ **Double-click** on the Control box for **Write.**
The *Write* dialog box appears:

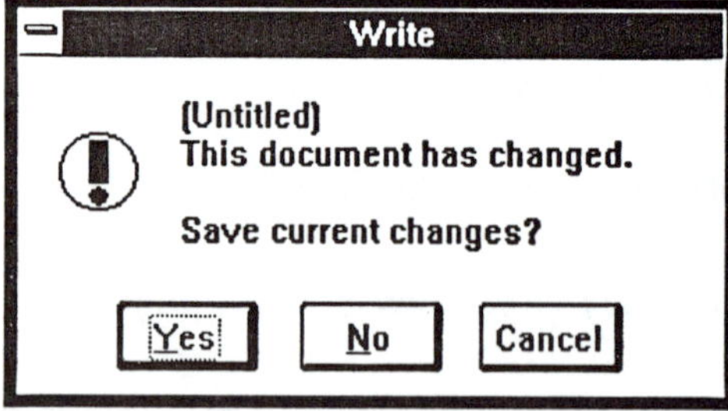

⑩ **Click on** No .
(You do <u>not</u> want to save the document.)

⑪ **Close the Accessories window** (review, page 55).

⑫ **Go on to Exercise 28.**
OR
Exit Windows (review, page 53).

① Start Windows (review, page 52), if necessary.

FROM THE *STARTING WINDOWS* SCREEN:

② Open the **Accessories window** (review, page 54).

③ Arrange the *group windows* in a **tile** format (review, page 73).

④ Start and minimize **Write**.
NOTE: It becomes an application icon that is still running (open).

⑤ Press **Prnt Scrn**. <u>Nothing seems to happen</u>, but an image of the *entire screen* should have been captured and placed on the Clipboard.

⑥ Use the **Clipboard Viewer** to verify that the image was copied (review, page 91). You may have to scroll through the Accessories window to find it. Do not clear the Clipboard Viewer. Be sure to **Exit** the Clipboard Viewer.
NOTE: Some keyboards may <u>not</u> recognize the procedure in step 5.
  ONLY IF the image was <u>not</u> copied, try one of the procedures below and repeat step 6:

  • **Press Alt + Prnt Scrn.**
  OR
  • **Press Shift + Prnt Scrn.**

⑦ Double-click on the **minimized Write icon** at the bottom of the screen.

⑧ Maximize **Write** (review, page 64).

⑨ Print the capture (do steps 4-11 on the previous page).
NOTE: You can use the scroll bar to view the top of the document if desired.

Captured Screen

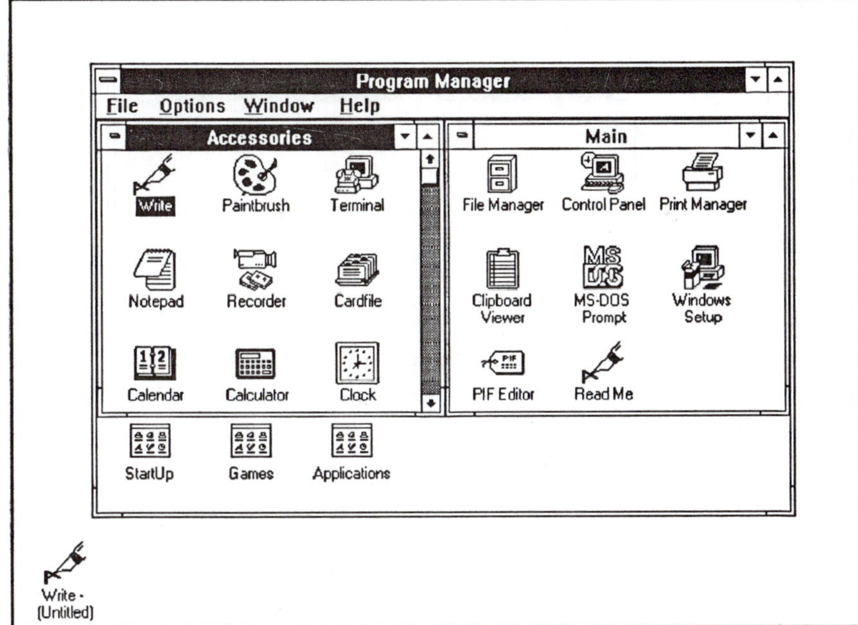

⑩ Exit Windows (review, page 53).

EXERCISE 28
Capture the Screen (386 only)

capture the screen
To copy an image of the <u>entire screen</u> onto the <u>clipboard</u>.

<u>WARNING</u>: You <u>cannot</u> do this exercise unless Windows is using 386 Enhanced mode.

To check the mode you are using,
From the Program Manager Window:

• **click** on **Help**

• **click** on **About Program Manager**

• a dialog box appears. The third line from the bottom tells you the mode Windows is using, either Standard or 386 Enhanced.

NOTE: The default margin settings in Write may not allow the entire width of the captured screen to print. The right side may be cut off a little.

Keyboard Users
CAPTURE THE SCREEN
See Steps 5 and 6.

EXERCISE 29
Create a Group Window

Exercises 29-34 should be done during the same session.

create a group window
To make a new group window.

group windows
Windows within the Program Manager window that hold "groups" of <u>program items</u>.

option buttons
Circles in a dialog box from which you may select only one of a <u>related</u> group.

text box
A box that provides space for typing information needed to carry out a command.

Keyboard Users
CREATE A GROUP WINDOW
1. **Press Alt + F** (File)
2. **Press N** (New)
3. **Press G** (Program Group)
4. **Press ↵**
5. **Type:** New Group
   NOTE: You may type a different description if you desire.
6. **Press ↵**

---

1 **Start Windows** (review, page 52).

FROM THE *STARTING WINDOWS* SCREEN:

2 **Click on File.**

3 **Click on New.**
The *New Program Object* dialog box appears:

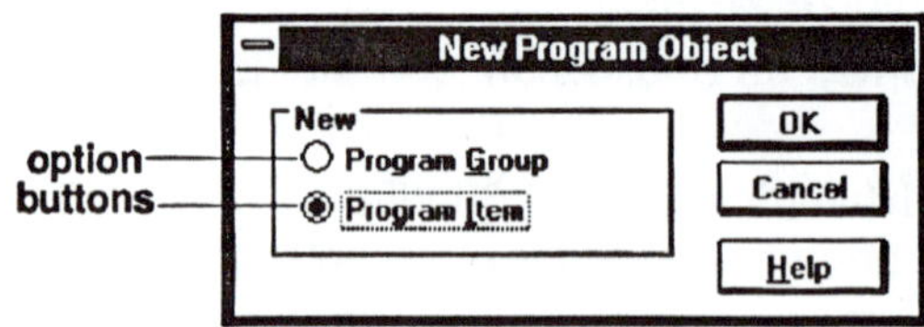

NOTE: When an option button is selected, a dark dot appears inside the circle (⊙).

4 **Click on ○ Program Group.**
A dark dot appears inside the circle.

5 **Click on OK .**
The *Program Group Properties* dialog box appears with the cursor in the *Description* text box:

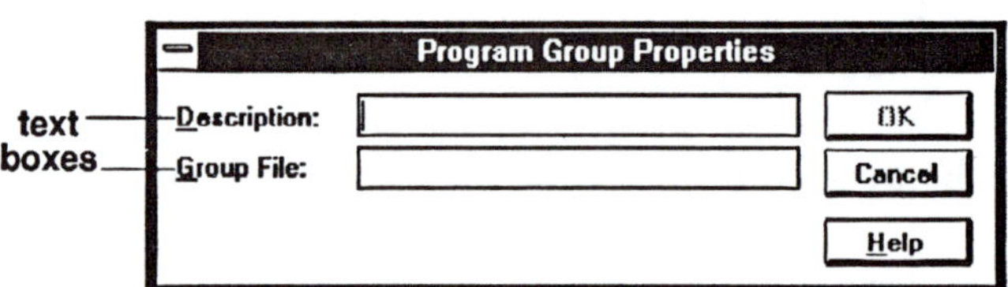

6 **Type:** New Group
NOTE: The description you type here will appear in the title bar of the new group window and below the group icon.

7 **Click on OK .**
The *New Group* window appears:

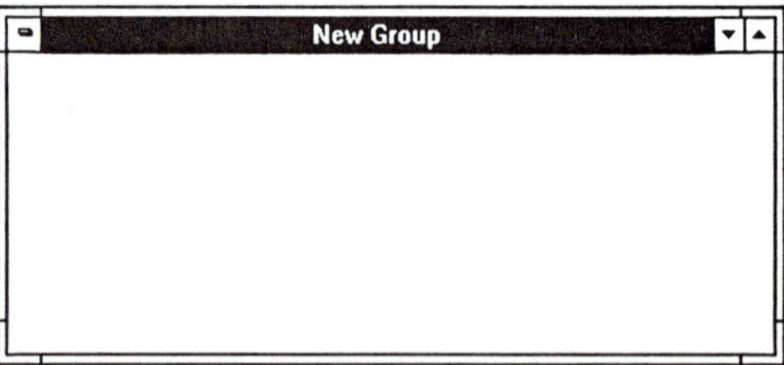

8 **Minimize the New Group window** (review, page 66).
The *New Group* window icon appears at the bottom of the Program Manager window.

New Group

NOTE: If the New Group icon does not appear, it is behind the Main group window. Move the Main group window to find it.

Go on to Exercise 30

1 **Open** the **New Group** window (review, page 54).

2 **Click** on **F̲ile**.

3 **Click** on **N̲ew**.

4 **Click** on ○ **Program Item**.

5 **Click** on [OK].

The *Program Item Properties* dialog box appears with the cursor in the *Description* text box:

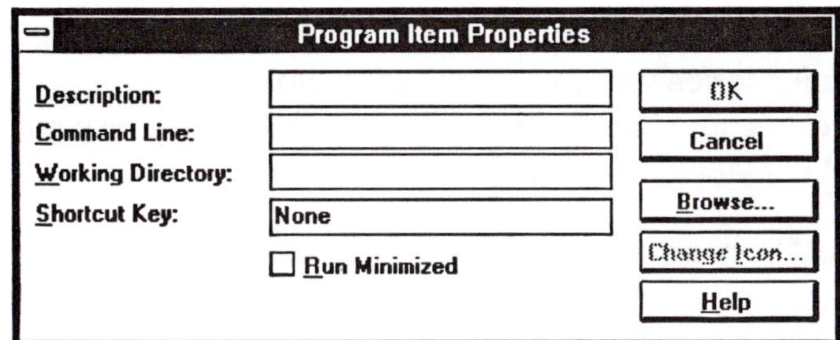

6 **Type:** `Clock`
NOTE: You can substitute your own program item description here.

7 **Click** on the **C̲ommand Line** text box.
The *insert* cursor (|) moves to the *Command Line* text box.

8 **Type:** `Clock.exe`
This is the *file* that "executes" (starts) the *Clock* program.
NOTE: If you are creating a different program item, you should type the name of the file which executes that program in place of Clock.exe.
NOTE: Other Program Item Properties can be changed from this dialog box, including: Working Directory, Shortcut Keys (create your own), Run Minimized, and Change Icon.
NOTE: If you get an "Invalid Path" message, check the way you typed clock.exe. There should not be a space within "clock.exe." Check for typos, and retype the "Command Line."

9 **Click** on [OK].
The Clock program item appears in the New Group window.

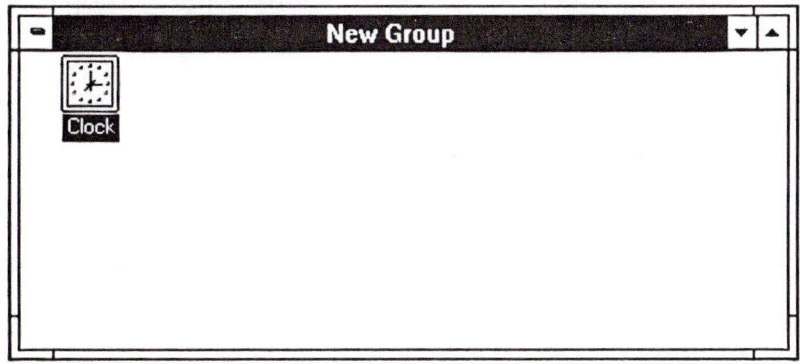

Go on to Exercise 31

EXERCISE 30
Create a Program Item

Continue from Exercise 29, doing Exercises 29-34 during the same session.

create a program item
To name a program item and tell Windows the name of the file that will execute (start) that program.

program items
Program items (represented as icons in a group window) are the programs (and sometimes, documents) that make up a group in the Program Manager.

NOTE: When you create a program item, it will be added to the group window that is selected (i.e., its title bar is highlighted).

Keyboard Users
CREATE A PROGRAM ITEM
1. Press **Alt**+**F** (F̲ile)
2. Press **N** (N̲ew)
3. Press **↵**
4. **Type:** `Clock`
   NOTE: You may type a different description if you desire.
5. • Press **Tab**
   OR
   • Press **Alt**+**C** (C̲ommand Line)
6. **Type:** `Clock.exe`
   NOTE: If you use a different program item, type the filename which executes that program here.
7. Press **↵**

EXERCISE 31
Move a Program Item

Continue from Exercise 30, doing Exercises 29-34 during the same session.

move a program item
To move a <u>program item</u> from one program group to another program group.

<u>IMPORTANT</u>:

Auto Arrange (located in the <u>O</u>ptions menu) should be <u>deselected</u> (no check mark by it) for this exercise (this is the default).

auto arrange
When <u>selected</u>, Auto Arrange automatically rearranges program-item icons every time you move items, add items, or change window size. When <u>deselected</u>, a blank space remains when a program item is moved from a group window.

Keyboard Users
MOVE A PROGRAM ITEM

1. **Open** the group window that has the program item you want to move.

2. **Select** (highlight) the *name* of the program item to be moved by **using arrow keys.**

3. **Press** Alt + F (*F*ile)

4. **Press** M (*M*ove)
   (The *Move Program Item* dialog box appears.)

5. Read the information in the dialog box.

6. OPEN THE LIST BOX:
   Press Alt + ↓

7. SELECT GROUP WINDOW TO MOVE PROGRAM ITEM TO:
   Press ↑ and ↓ until the window to move the program item to is highlighted.

8. **Press** ↵

NOTE: Try not to move the program-item icons around so much that you cannot return them to their original group windows. However, if you do have a problem, Appendix B has directions to instruct Windows to rebuild the original group windows.

1   <u>DESELECT</u> AUTO ARRANGE:
- **Click** on **O**ptions.
  IF **A**uto Arrange does <u>not</u> have a check mark by it,
  - **click** off of the menu to close it.
  IF **A**uto Arrange <u>does</u> have a check mark by it,
    - **click** on **A**uto Arrange to deselect it.

2   **Close** the **Main** window (review, page 55).

3   **Open** the **Accessories** window (review, page 54).
The **New Group** and **Accessories** windows should be the only group windows that are open.

4   **Maximize** the **Program Manager** window (review, page 64).

5   **Arrange** the windows in a **tile** format (review, page 73).
Your screen should look similar to this one:

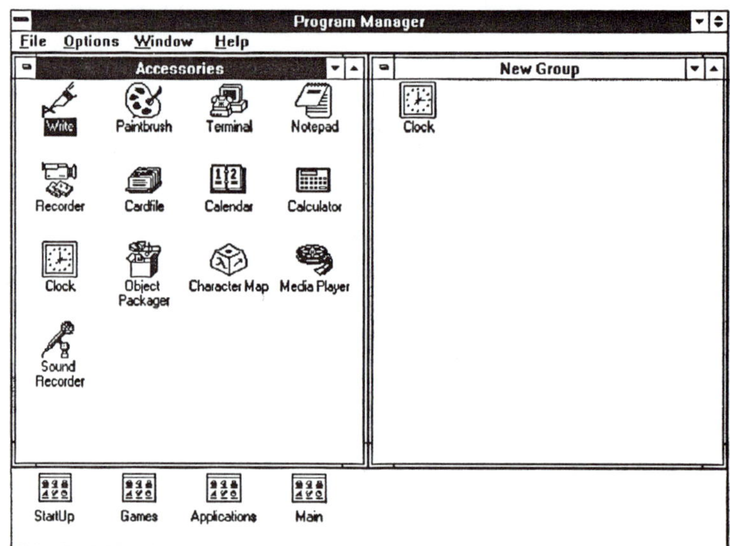

6   Position the pointer on the **Calculator** program-item icon. Notice where it is located in the Accessories window.

7   **Drag** the **Calculator** icon *from* the Accessories window *to* the New Group window. A blank space should appear in the Accessories window where the **calculator** was located.

8   **Drag** the **Calculator** icon back *from* the New Group window *to* the Accessories window, trying to position it where it was originally located.

9   **Drag** the **Notepad** icon from the Accessories window to the New Group window.

10   **Drag** the **Notepad** icon back from the New Group window to the Accessories window.

Go on to Exercise 32

1 Position the pointer on the **Calculator** program-item icon.

2 **Press** and **hold down** `Ctrl` <u>while</u> you **drag** the **Calculator** icon *from* the Accessories window *to* the New Group window.

3 Follow the directions in step 2 above to **copy Paintbrush** to the New Group window.

4 **Copy Calendar** to the New Group window.

5 **Copy Notepad** to the New Group window.

6 **Close** the **Accessories** window (review, page 55).

7 **Restore** the **Program Manager** window (review, page 65).

8 **Arrange** the group windows in a **Cascade** format (review, page 72).

9 **Arrange** icons using the command (review, page 71).
Your screen should look similar to this:

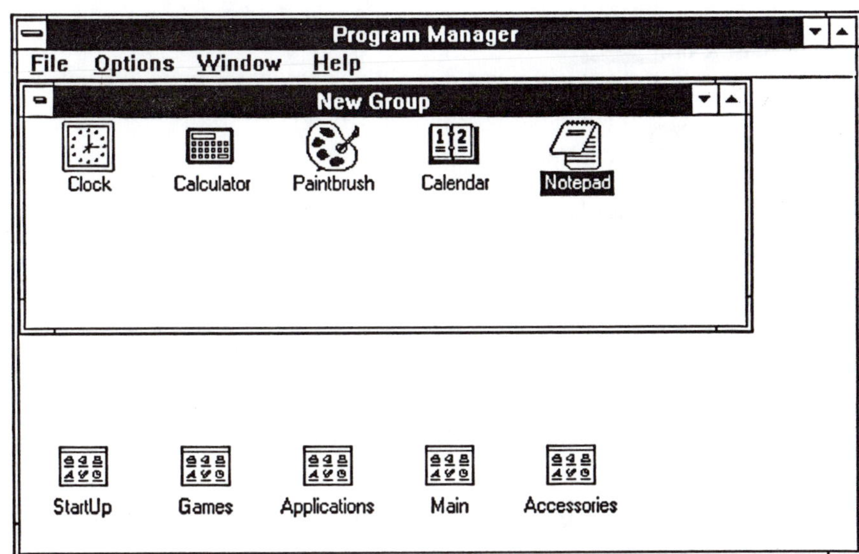

10 **Capture** the **Program Manager** window (review, page 90).

11 **Print** the captured window (review, page 92).
Be sure to **exit** Write and **close** Accessories.

Go on to Exercise 33

EXERCISE 32
Copy a Program Item

Continue from Exercise 31, doing Exercises 29-34 during the same session.

copy a program item
To copy a <u>program item</u> from one program group to another program group.

<u>IMPORTANT</u>: Whenever you are instructed to <u>copy</u> a program item, remember to hold down `Ctrl` as you drag the program item.

Keyboard Users
COPY A PROGRAM ITEM

1. **Open** the group window that has the program item you want to move.
2. **Select** (highlight) the *name* of the program-item icon to be moved by **using arrow keys.**
3. **Press** `Alt` + `F` (<u>F</u>ile)
4. **Press** `C` (<u>C</u>opy)
   (The *Copy Program Item* dialog box appears.)
5. Read the information in the dialog box.
6. OPEN THE LIST BOX:
   Press `Alt` + `↓`
7. SELECT WINDOW TO MOVE PROGRAM ITEM TO:
   Press `↑` and `↓` until the window to move the program item to is highlighted.
8. **Press** `↵`

EXERCISE 33
Delete a Program Item

Continue from Exercise 32, doing Exercises 29-34 during the same session.

delete a program item
To delete a <u>program item</u> from a program group.

---

*NOTE: It is easy to accidentally <u>delete</u> the wrong **program item** or **group window**. To avoid this, always <u>read</u> the dialog boxes that appear to be sure you are performing the intended action. (See Appendix B, page 225, to find instructions to <u>rebuild</u> the original group windows.)*

1
- Make sure you are in the New Group window.
- **Click** on the **Clock** program-item icon (to **select** it).

2
- **Click** on **File**.
- **Click** on **Delete**.

OR

- **Press** Del.

The *Delete* dialog box appears:

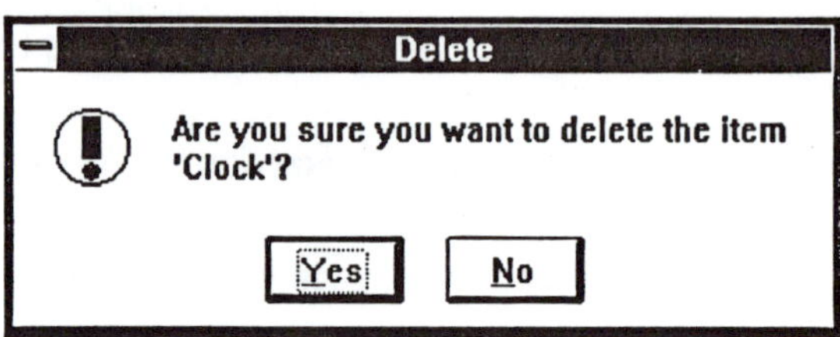

3
- **Click** on Yes.

OR

- **Press** ↵.

4 **Click** on the **Calculator** program-item icon.

5 **Click** on **File**.

6 **Click** on **Delete**.

7 Oops! You do not want to delete **Calculator**.
Click on No.

*NOTE: You cannot use ESC or the <u>Control box</u> to <u>cancel</u> this action...you must use the **N**o command button.*

8 Repeat steps 2 and 3 to **delete** the **Calculator** program item.

9 **Delete** the **Paintbrush** program item.

10 **Delete** the **Calendar** program item.

*NOTE: The **Notepad** program-item icon remains in the New Group window.*

Keyboard Users
DELETE A PROGRAM ITEM

1. **Open** the group window that has the program item you want to delete.

2. **Select** (highlight) the *name* of the program-item icon to be deleted by **using arrow keys**.

3.
   - **Press** Del

   OR

   - **Press** Alt + F (File)
   - **Press** D (Delete)

   The *delete* dialog box appears.

4. **Press** ↵

Go on to Exercise 34

1 **Close** the **New Group** window (review, page 55).

NOTE: If a group window contains program items, it must be an icon in order to be deleted.

2 **Click** on the **New Group** group window icon (to **select** it).

IF the Control menu pops up,

- **Click** off of the icon (to close the menu). Be sure the **New Group's** *icon name* remains highlighted.

3
- **Press** Del.

OR

- **Click** on **File**.
- **Click** on **Delete**.

4
- **Press** ⏎.

OR

- **Click** on Yes.

NOTE: If a group window holds program items, they will also be deleted when the group window is deleted.

5 **Create a group window**; name it **HELLO** (review, page 94).

The *HELLO* group window appears in the Program Manager window.

6 DELETE THE HELLO GROUP WINDOW:

With the title bar for the new window still highlighted,

- **Press** Del.
- **Press** ⏎.

7 **Create a group window**; name it **Super Window** (review, page 94).

8 **Delete** the **Super Window** group window that you just created.

9 **Open** the **Main** group window (review, page 54).

10
Go on to Exercise 35.

OR

Exit Windows (review, page 53).

EXERCISE 34
Delete a Group Window

Continue from Exercise 33, doing Exercises 29-34 during the same session.

delete a group window
To remove a group window from the Program Manager window.

Keyboard Users

DELETE A GROUP WINDOW

1. **Close** the group window to be deleted.

2. **Press** Ctrl + Tab until the *name* of the group window icon to be deleted is **selected** (highlighted).

3. **Press** Del
   (The *Delete* dialog box appears.)

4. **Press** ⏎

EXERCISE 35
Use the Startup Group

use the startup group

To place a program (or programs) in the startup group window so that when you start Windows, that program (or programs) will automatically start.

startup group window

A special group window that has been designed so that programs items which appear in it start when you start Windows.

Keyboard Users

USE THE STARTUP GROUP

Keyboard instructions to perform each step in this exercise are described on the same review pages shown in the exercise.

---

1   **Start Windows** (review, page 52), if necessary.

2   **Close** the **Main** group window (review, page 55).

3   **Open** the **Accessories** group window (review, page 54).

4   **Open** the **Startup** group window (review, page 54).

*NOTE: You may have to **move** the Accessories window in order to see the Startup window icon (review, page 68). Or you may **select** the Startup group window using the menu bar or the rotation method (review, page 59).*

5   **Maximize** the **Program Manager** window (review, page 64).

6   **Arrange** the group windows in a **tile** format (review, page 73).

7   **Copy** the **Clock** from the Application window to the Startup window (review, page 97).

8   **Close** the **Accessories** group window (review, page 55).

9   **Close** the **Startup** group window (review, page 55).

10   **Exit Windows** (review, page 53).

*NOTE: You can exit Windows without closing all the open windows and rearranging disordered icons, and when you start Windows your original desktop arrangement will appear (if "Save Settings on Exit" is deselected—as it should be). If **applications** are open, Windows will warn you before exiting.*

11   **Start Windows** (review, page 52).

A screen similar to this appears:

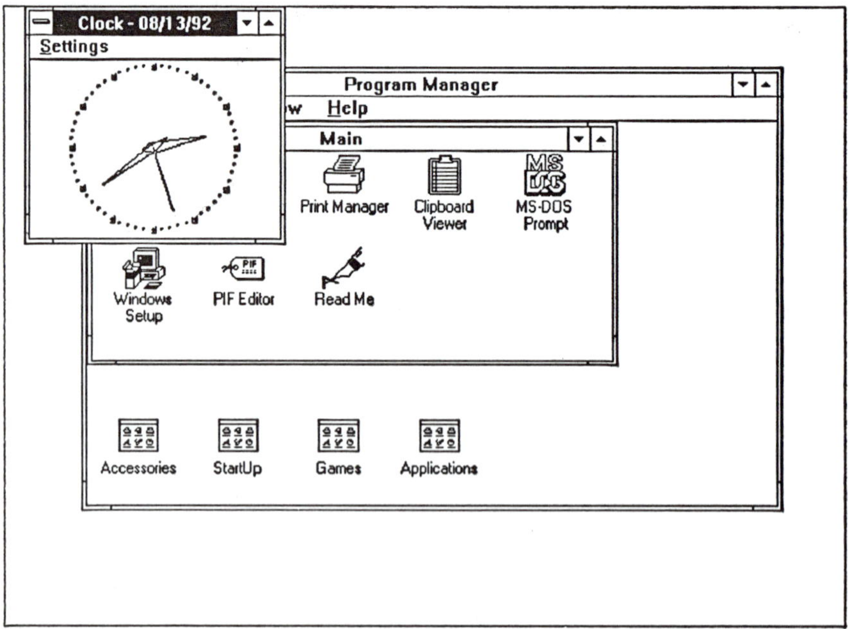

NOTE: Because the Clock program item is in the Startup group window, it appears when Windows is started.

Continue Exercise 35 on the next page

12 **Open** the **Startup** group window (review, page 54).

13 **Delete** the **Clock** program item (review, page 98).

14 **Close** the **Startup** group window (review, page 55).

15 **Exit Windows** (review, page 53).

16 **Start Windows** (review, page 52).
The Clock does <u>not</u> start when you start Windows this time.

17 **Open** the **Startup** window.

18 **Open** the **Accessories** window.
IF the Accessories group icon is hidden, **select** it (review, page 59).

19 **Arrange** the Program Manager window in a **tile** format
(review, page 73).

20 **Copy Write** from the **Accessories** window to the **Startup** window.

21 **Exit Windows** (review, page 53).

22 **Start Windows** (review, page 52).
Did **Write** start?

23 **Exit Write.**

24 **Open Startup.**

25 **Delete** the **Write** Program item from the **Startup** window
(review, page 98).

26 **Exit Windows** (review, page 53).

EXERCISE 36
Practice

Lesson Two
Beyond Basics

Tasks Reviewed:

Start Windows

Open group windows

Size a window

Scroll through a window

Start a program

Close group windows

Move a window

Select a window

Capture a window

Use the Clipboard Viewer

Print a capture

Exit a program

Exit Windows

1 Start Windows.

2 Open the Accessories window.

3 Starting with the *right* border of the Accessories window, size the window to about half of its width.
IF necessary, size the window longer to match the illustration below.

4 Scroll through the window from the top to the bottom. Leave it with the *scroll box* at the top of the *scroll bar*.

5 Close the Main group window.

6 Move the group window icons as shown below:
NOTE: If you have additional group window icons, arrange them below the other group icons.

Match This Illustration

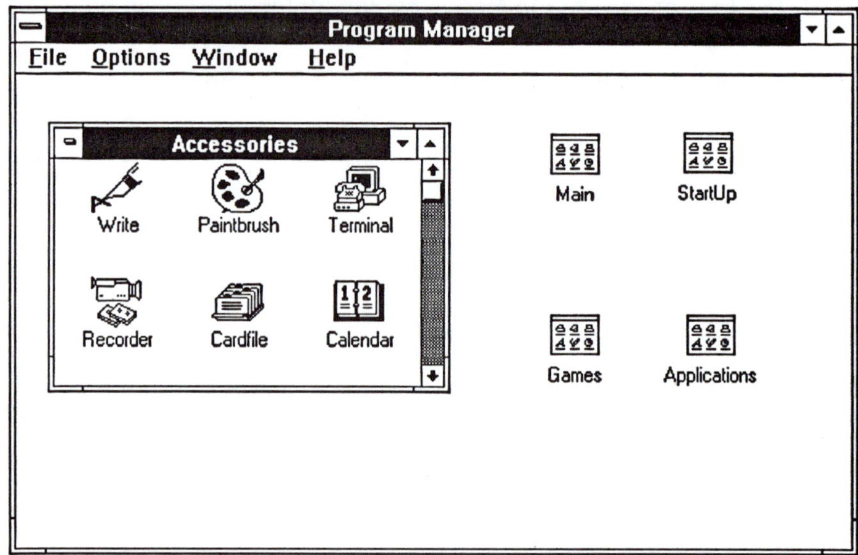

7 Select the Accessories window.

8 Capture the Program Manager window (review, page 90).

9 Open the Main group window.

10 Use the Clipboard Viewer to look at the image. Do <u>not</u> delete the image. Exit the Clipboard Viewer.

11 Select the Accessories window.

12 Print the "captured" window using Write (review, page 92).

13 Exit Windows.

1 Start Windows.

2 CREATE A GROUP WINDOW (review, page 94):
- **Click** on **File**, then **click on New**.
- **Click** on ○ **Program Group**, then **click on** [OK].
- **Type:** FUN WITH WINDOWS
- **Click on** [OK].

The new group window appears and is selected (active).

3 CREATE A PROGRAM ITEM (review, page 95):
- **Click** on **File**, then on **New**.
- **Click** on ○ **Program Item**.
- **Click on** [OK].
- **Type:** Calculator
- **Press** [Tab], then **type:** Calc.exe
- **Press** [↵].

The icon for the new program item appears in the new group window.

NOTE: If necessary, scroll through the Main window to find the program items that are to be moved and copied in steps 4 and 5.

4 MOVE A PROGRAM ITEM (review, page 96):
- **Arrange** the Program Manager in a **tile** format.
- **Move** the **Clipboard Viewer** from the Main window to the FUN WITH WINDOWS window.
- **Move** the **Clipboard Viewer** from the FUN WITH WINDOWS window back to its original position in the Main window.

5 COPY A PROGRAM ITEM (review, page 97):
- **Copy** the **Clipboard Viewer** from the Main window to the FUN WITH WINDOWS window.
- **Copy Readme** from the Main window to the *new* window.

6 DELETE A PROGRAM ITEM (review, page 98):
Delete program items which are in the FUN WITH WINDOWS window:
- **Select** the **Clipboard Viewer** (highlight its name).
- **Press** [Del], and then **press** [↵].
- **Delete** the **Readme** program item the same way.
- **Delete** the **Calculator**.

7 DELETE A GROUP WINDOW (review, page 99):
- Be sure that the title bar for the FUN WITH WINDOWS window is highlighted (if you continue from the step above, it should be).
- **Press** [Del], and then **press** [↵].
  The *new* group window disappears.

8 **Exit Windows.**

EXERCISE 37
Practice
Lesson Two
Beyond Basics

Tasks Reviewed:

Start Windows
Create a group window
Create a program item
Move a program item
Copy a program item
Delete a program item
Delete a group window
Exit Windows

Lesson Two
Review of Beyond Basics Exercises

Lesson Two covers tasks that:

Save the Desktop Arrangement.

Create the "Starting Windows Screen."

Capture Application Windows or the Entire Screen.

Use the Clipboard Viewer.

Print Application and Screen Captures.

Create and Delete Group Windows.

Create, Delete, Move, and Copy Program Items.

Use the Startup Group.

POINTS TO EMPHASIZE
Compare and Contrast

Capture an Application Window <u>and</u> Capture an Entire Screen:

- Capturing an application window copies a picture of the contents of *just* the *active application window* onto the clipboard.

- Capturing the entire screen copies a picture of the contents of the *entire screen* onto the clipboard. Windows must be using the *386 Enhanced mode* to perform a screen capture.

Create a Group Window <u>and</u> Create a Program Item:

- Creating a group window means to make a new group window (that can hold program items—just like other group windows do).

- Creating a program item means to name a program item (which represents a certain program) and tell Windows the name of the file that *executes* that program.

Select <u>and</u> Deselect:

- *Select* means to mark an item so that a subsequent action can activate it.

- *Deselect* means to unmark an item so that a future action will not activate it.

Save by Using "Save Settings on Exit" <u>and</u> Save without Exiting Windows:

- Saving the desktop arrangement by using the "Save Settings on Exit" method requires you to *select* the "Save Settings on Exit" option, and then to exit Windows. Further, if you do not *deselect* the command, Windows will continue to save your *desktop arrangement* every time you exit Windows.

- Saving the *desktop arrangement* without exiting Windows is a method whereby you use a single command to save the *desktop arrangement* (hold down **Shift** <u>while</u> you double-click on the Program Manager's control box) without exiting Windows.

Continued ...

Performing Screen and Window Captures

Different keyboards may use different keystrokes to perform *captures*.

To capture an application window, use:

Alt + **Prnt Scrn**

OR

Shift + **Prnt Scrn**

To capture the entire screen, use:

Prnt Scrn

OR

Alt + **Prnt Scrn**

OR

Shift + **Prnt Scrn**

Save Settings on Exit

The "Save Settings on Exit" menu item should remain **deselected**, that is, there should <u>not</u> be a ✓ by it. The reason for this is to avoid disturbing the "starting Windows screen," which is the starting point for exercises in this book.

Group Windows and Program Items

Windows uses **group windows** to organize **program items**. When Windows is installed, certain groups are automatically created (see page 15).

But, you can also *customize* **group windows** and the **program items** in the **group windows**. You can create and delete **group windows**; and you can create, move, copy, and delete the **program items** that are placed in the **group windows**.

Remember that **program items** represent the *commands that start* the programs that are named, and **program-item icons** represent the **program items** in the **group windows**.

Program items can represent *documents* as well as *commands to start programs*.

Startup Group

The **startup group window** is a special group window that is designed so that **program items** that appear in it automatically start when Windows is started.

WORKSHEET 21

BEYOND BASICS <u>TERMS</u>

NAME ___________________________

DIRECTIONS: Match the terms listed below to the definition that best fits the term.

paste	text box	capture (noun)	Clipboard Viewer
select	clipboard	option buttons	startup group window
deselect	program items	group windows	capture (verb)

---

1. A temporary storage area used to hold information that is being transferred from one program (or document) to another.

   1) ___________________________

2. To *unmark* an item so that a future action will <u>not</u> activate the item.

   2) ___________________________

3. To *mark* an item so that a subsequent action can activate it.

   3) ___________________________

4. The *image* of an application window or the entire screen that has been copied onto the clipboard.

   4) ___________________________

5. To *perform the keystrokes to copy* the image that is visible on your monitor (either an application window or the entire screen) onto the clipboard.

   5) ___________________________

6. A special group window that has been designed so that *program items* that appear in it *start* when you start Windows.

   6) ___________________________

7. A program that lets you *see* the contents of the clipboard.

   7) ___________________________

8. Circles in a dialog box from which you may select only one of a *related* group.

   8) ___________________________

9. To *copy* information from the clipboard into a program.

   9) ___________________________

10. A box that provides space for typing information needed to carry out a command.

    10) ___________________________

11. What are the programs that make up a *group* in the Program Manager called? They are represented as icons in a group window.

    11) ___________________________

12. Windows within the Program Manager window which hold "groups" of *program items*.

    12) ___________________________

    (This page may be copied.)

WORKSHEET 22

NAME ___________________________

BEYOND BASICS <u>TASKS</u>

DIRECTIONS: Match the tasks listed below to the definition that best fits the task.

create a group window   create a program item   capture an application window
delete a group window   delete a program item   save desktop arrangement
copy a program item   use the startup group   use the Clipboard Viewer
print a capture   move a program item   create "Starting Windows Screen"
capture the screen

---

1. To copy an image of the *active application window* onto the clipboard.

   1) ___________________________

2. To remove a group window from the Program Manager window.

   2) ___________________________

3. To manipulate the Program Manager window, Main group window, and group window icons to approximate Windows' original opening screen.

   3) ___________________________

4. To save the arrangement of *Program Manager group windows and icons* so that Windows will remember that arrangement when you start Windows the next time.

   4) ___________________________

5. To "paste" the contents of the clipboard into a program and then print it.

   5) ___________________________

6. To *view, save, open,* or *delete* clipboard images.

   6) ___________________________

7. To copy an image of the *entire screen* onto the clipboard.

   7) ___________________________

8. To *name* a program item and tell Windows the name of the file that will *execute* (start) that program.

   8) ___________________________

9. To relocate a *program item* from one program group to another program group.

   9) ___________________________

10. To make a new group window.

    10) ___________________________

11. To duplicate a *program item* from one program group to another program group.

    11) ___________________________

12. To place a program (or programs) in a certain window so that when you start Windows, that program (or programs) will automatically *start*.

    12) ___________________________

13. To remove a *program item* from a program group.

    13) ___________________________

Lesson Three — Help

Table of Contents

EXERCISE 38
Help

Help

A quick, easy way to look up information about Windows tasks, features, and commands.

<u>IMPORTANT</u>: The purpose of this exercise is to explore the <u>different ways to access</u> **Help**. Although the **move** menu item is used frequently in this exercise, it is used only to demonstrate different ways to access Help.

<u>ASSUMPTION</u>:

It is assumed that you know how to perform the following basic Windows tasks:

① **Start Windows.**

FROM THE *STARTING WINDOWS* SCREEN:

② **Click on Help.**

The *Help* drop-down menu appears:

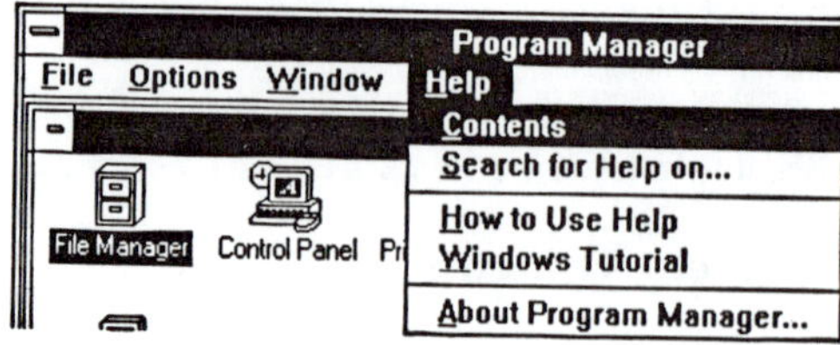

③ **Click off of the Help drop-down menu to close it.**
NOTE: The items shown in the drop-down menu will be examined later.

④ **Press F1 (shortcut key for Help).**

The *Program Manager Help* window appears:

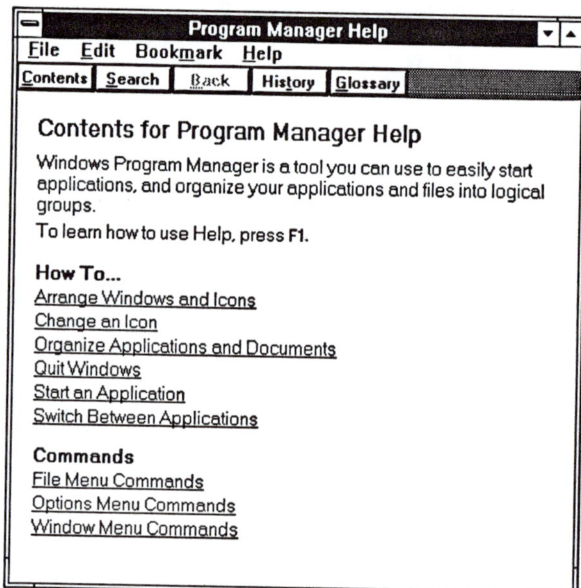

⑤ **Exit the Program Manager Help window.**
NOTE: This Help window will be examined later.

⑥ **Click on File.**

⑦ **Press the left mouse button on Move, but do <u>not</u> release it, and <u>while</u> the Move item remains highlighted...**

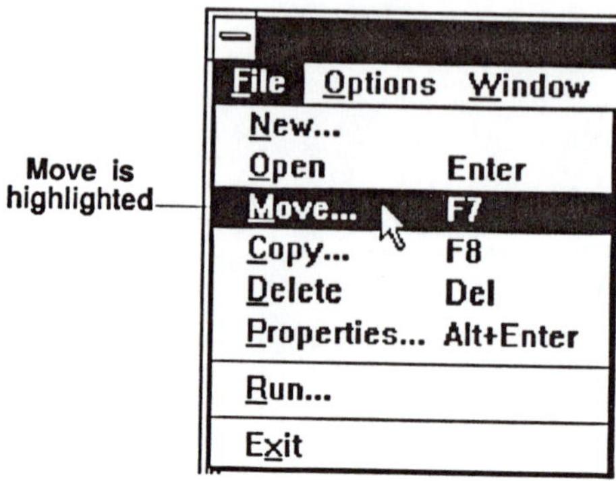

Continue Exercise 38 on the next page

This shadow box, containing information about maximize, appears:

> **maximize**
> To enlarge a window to its maximum size by using the Maximize button (at the right of the title bar) or the Maximize command on the Control menu.

12 **Click** anywhere (to remove the shadow box).

13 **Click** on ⬍ to **restore** the **How to Use Help** window.

14 **Click** on ⎿ Back ⏌.

15 **Scroll** through the entire **How to Use Help** window, and read the *How to Use Help* topics.

16 **Scroll** until <u>Choose a Jump</u> is showing.

17 **Click** on <u>Choose a Jump</u>.
*NOTE: A jump is what you did in step 11, when you "jumped" to the **maximize** shadow box.*

jump
Jumps are Help topics that have a link to other Help topics or to more information about the current topic.

18 **Maximize** the window and read the information about **choosing a jump**.

19 **Restore** the window.
The title bar name is: **How to Use Help.**

20 **Click** on ⎿ Back ⏌. The title bar name is still: **How to Use Help.**

21 **Scroll** to the top of the window. The heading should display: **Contents for How to Use Help.**

22 **Click** on ⎿ Back ⏌ again.
The title bar changes to: **Program Manager Help.**

23 **Click** on ⎿ History ⏌, and look through the list to see where you have been.

24 **Exit** the **Windows Help History** window.

25 **Exit** the **Program Manager Help** window.

26 **Go on to Exercise 40.**
OR
Exit Windows.

EXERCISE 40
Help, Search

Help, search

Search locates information about a Help topic. You can either look through a <u>list of topics</u>, or type a <u>keyword</u> or <u>phrase</u> in a <u>search for</u> text box.

text box

A box that provides space for typing information needed to carry out a command.

list box

A box that displays a list of options from which to choose.

Keyboard Users

HELP, SEARCH

ACCESS HELP, SEARCH MENU:

1. Press **Alt** + **H** (Help)
2. Press **S** (Search)

MOVE FROM OPTION TO OPTION

(left to right and top to bottom):

   Press **Tab**

SCROLL LIST BOXES:

   Press **↑** to move up and press **↓** to move down in the list box.

CHOOSE A TOPIC:

   Press **⏎** to choose the highlighted topic.

CHOOSE A COMMAND BUTTON:

1. Press **Tab** to highlight desired button.
2. Press **⏎**

114

---

① Start Windows (review, page 52), if necessary.

FROM THE *STARTING WINDOWS* SCREEN:

②
- Click on **Help**.
- Click on **Search for help on...** .

OR

- Press **F1**.
- Click on **Search for help on...** .

The **Search** *dialog box* appears:

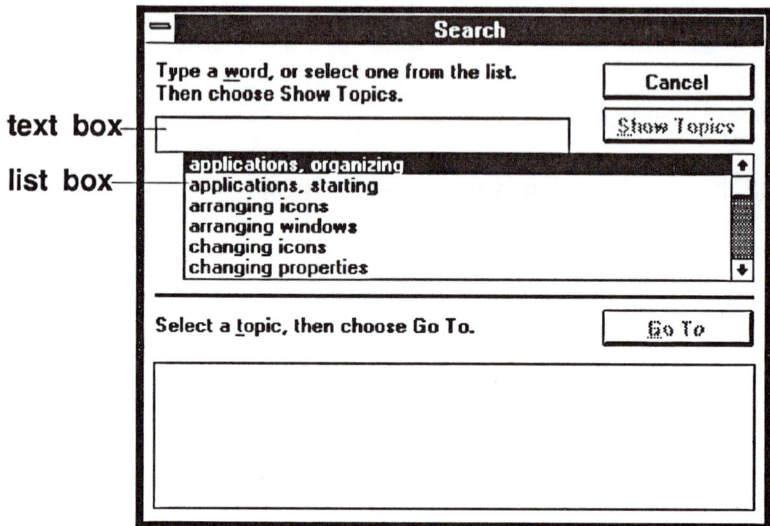

text box

list box

NOTE: When the Search window first appears, the cursor is in the text box, ready for you to type information.

③ SEARCH FOR "WINDOWS ARRANGEMENT":

Press **W** (the highlighting in the *list box* skips to *"windows, arranging"*).

NOTE: Typing a letter, word, or phrase in the text box causes the list box to scroll, as it tries to find an alphabetical match for that letter, word, or phrase in the list of topics.

④ Click on **Show Topics** .

"Arranging Windows and Icons" appears in the Search window's bottom box:

⑤ Click on **Go To** .

*NOTE: Windows changes from the Search window to the Program Manager Help window and displays information about **arranging windows and icons**.*

Continue Exercise 40 on the next page

6 **Click** on **S**earch.

7 **Scroll** through the *list box* until <u>starting applications</u> appears in the list box.

8 **Click** on **starting applications**.
NOTE: "Starting applications" is also displayed in the <u>text box</u>.

9 **Click** on | **S**how Topics |.
Several related topics appear in the Search window's bottom box, with "Starting an Application" highlighted:

Starting an Application
Starting an Application by Using MS-DOS Prompt
Starting an Application by Using the Run Command
Starting an Application from a Group
Starting an Application When You Start Windows

10 **Click** on **Starting an Application When You Start Windows.**

11 **Click** on | **G**o To |.

12 Read the information.

13 **Click** on **S**earch.

14 Use *Search* to find information about a topic of your choice. Either type something in the *text box* or scroll through the *list box*. Complete the actions necessary to display the information about the topic.

15 **Exit** the **Program Manager Help** window.

16 **Go** on to Exercise 41.

OR

Exit Windows.

EXERCISE 41
Help, Glossary

Help, glossary

Glossary provides an alphabetical list of
Windows terms. Choosing a term
displays its definition.

Keyboard Users

HELP, GLOSSARY

ACCESS HELP GLOSSARY
MENU:
1. **Press** **Alt** + **H** (Help)
2. **Press** **G** (Glossary)
SCROLL TERMS:
    Press **↑** (to scroll up)
    Press **↓** (to scroll down)
SELECT TERM:
    Press **Tab** (to move down)
    Press **Shift** + **Tab** (to move up)
DISPLAY DEFINITION:
    Press **↵**
CLOSE DEFINITION:
    Press any key

---

1   **Start Windows** (review, page 52), if necessary.

FROM THE *STARTING WINDOWS* SCREEN:

2
- **Click on Help.**
- **Click on Contents.**

OR

- **Press F1.**

3   **Click on** Glossary.

The *Glossary* window appears:

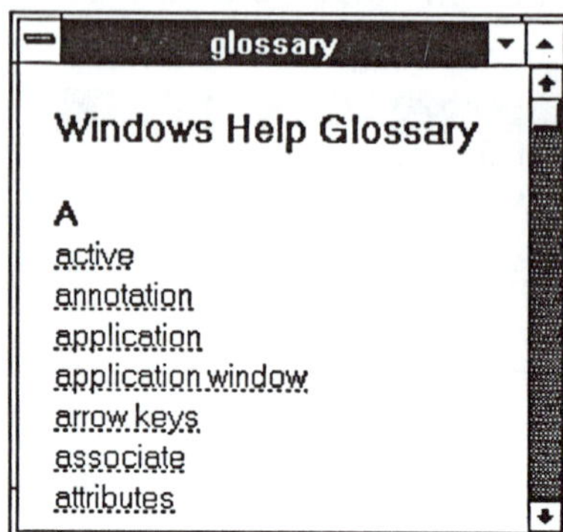

4   **Scroll** down until the terms beginning with "D" are displayed.

5   **Keep scrolling** until the "D" is at the top of the window.

6   **Move** the pointer onto the term "desktop." The pointer turns into a 🖑 shape.

7   **Click** on *desktop*.

The definition for *desktop* appears in a shadow box:

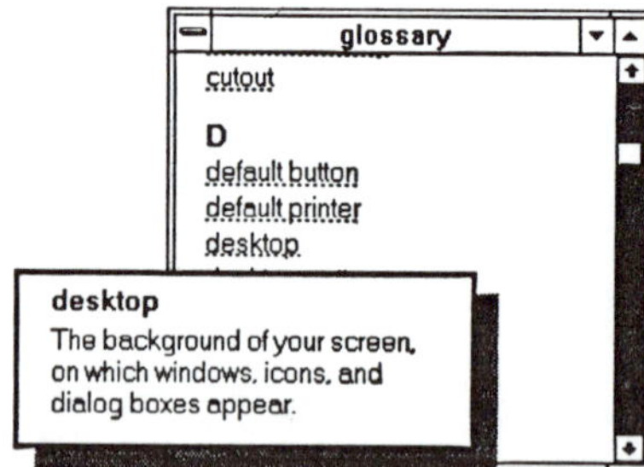

8   **Click** anywhere (to close the shadow box).

9   **Exit** the **Glossary** window.

10   **Exit** the **Program Manager Help** window.

11   Go on to Exercise 42.

OR

Exit Windows.

1 Start Windows (review, page 52), if necessary.

FROM THE *STARTING WINDOWS* SCREEN:

2 Click on **H**elp.

3 Click on **A**bout Program Manager... .
A dialog box similar to this one appears:

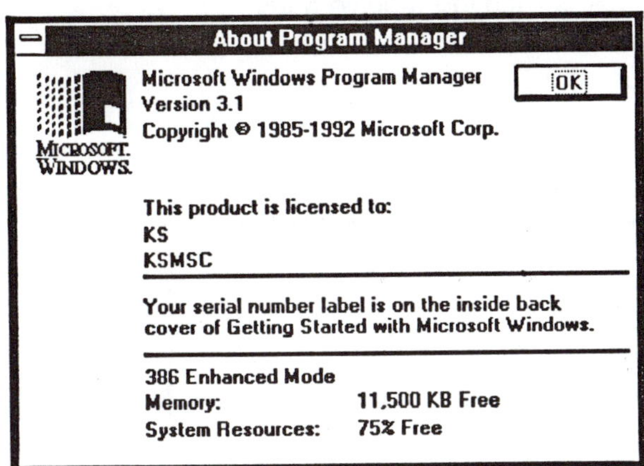

4 **Capture** the **About Program Manager** window (review, page 91).
NOTE: Dialog boxes are also referred to as windows.

5 Click on [OK] (to exit the dialog box).

6 **Print** the captured window (review, page 92).
Be sure to **exit** Write and **close** Accessories.

7 **Open** the **Accessories** window.

8 **Start Calendar.**

9 Click on **H**elp.

10 Click on **A**bout Calendar... .
A dialog box similar to the one above appears.

11 **Exit** the **About Calendar** window.

12 **Exit Calendar.**

13 **Close** the **Accessories** window.

14 Go on to Exercise 43.
OR
Exit Windows.

EXERCISE 42
Help, About (Application)

Help, about (application)
This Help option offers information about
Windows and the application you are
currently using, including:

- copyright,
- Windows version,
- application name,
- licensed owner,
- the mode Windows is using, and
- the amount of memory and
  resources available in your computer.

Keyboard Users

HELP, ABOUT (APPLICATION)
ACCESS ABOUT (APPLICATION)
1. Press **Alt** + **H** (Help)
2. Press **A**
   (About (Application)...)
EXIT ABOUT (APPLICATION)

- Press **↵**

OR

- Press **Space**

OR

- Press **Esc**

EXERCISE 43
Help, Print Topic

Help, print topic

To print a Help topic using the Print Topic command.

NOTE: You cannot print information in a pop-up window using the Print Topic command. The only way to copy a pop-up window is to perform a __screen capture__ (386 Enhanced mode only).

① Start Windows (review, page 52), if necessary.

FROM THE *STARTING WINDOWS* SCREEN:

② Press F1.

The **Program Manager Help** window appears.

③ Click on **File** (on the *Help* menu bar).

Be sure that your printer is ready to receive data.

④ Click on **Print Topic.**

RESULT:

Contents for Program Manager Help

Windows Program Manager is a tool you can use to easily start applications, and organize your applications and files into logical groups.
To learn how to use Help, press F1.

How To...
Arrange Windows and Icons
Change an Icon
Organize Applications and Documents
Quit Windows
Start an Application
Switch Between Applications

Commands
File Menu Commands
Options Menu Commands
Window Menu Commands

⑤ Click on Switch Between Applications.

*NOTE: If you get the wrong item, **click on** ⎡ Back ⎤, and try again.*

⑥ Click on **File** (on the *Help* menu bar).

Be sure that your printer is ready to receive data.

⑦ Click on **Print Topic.**

RESULT:

Switching Between Applications

There are a number of ways to switch between applications. You can use any of the following methods.

To switch to another application

- Click anywhere in an application's inactive window.
- Press ALT+ESC until the window you want is active.
- Press and hold down ALT while pressing TAB repeatedly to cycle through running applications. When you release TAB, the application comes to the foreground.
- Press CTRL+ESC or double-click the desktop to open Task List. Select the application, and then choose the Switch To button. Or select the application, and then press ENTER.
- Choose Switch To from the Control menu of any running application.
- Choose the application's icon.

⑧ Press F1.

The **How to Use Help** window replaces the **Program Manager Help** window.

Keyboard Users

HELP, PRINT TOPIC

With the desired Help window which displays a **File** menu:

1. **Press Alt + F** (File)
2. **Press P** (Print Topic)

Continue Exercise 43 on next page

⑨ Scroll through the box until you see <u>Print a Help Topic</u>.

⑩ Click on <u>Print a Help Topic</u>.

⑪ Click on <u>F</u>ile.
Be sure your printer is ready to receive data.

⑫ Click on <u>P</u>rint Topic.
RESULT:

Printing a Help Topic

You can print any Help <u>topic</u>. A topic prints on the <u>default printer</u>. If you have installed more than one printer, you can make any of them the default printer. You can also change the options for the default printer.

To print the current Help topic
▶ From the File menu in Help, choose Print Topic.

To change printers and printer options
1 From the File menu in Help, choose Print Setup.
2 Select the printer you want to use.
3 To change the default printer options, choose the Setup button.
   The options vary, depending on the printer you select.
4 Select the options you want.
5 Choose the OK button to close the printer's Setup dialog box.
6 Choose the OK button.

For help with the Setup dialog box, choose the Help button or press F1 while using the dialog box.

Note: You cannot print information that is in a pop-up window.

⑬ Exit the **How to Use Help** window.

⑭ Open the **Accessories** window and **start Calculator**.

⑮ Press **F1**, and **click** on <u>F</u>ile, then on <u>P</u>rint Topics.
RESULT:

Contents for Calculator Help

You can use Windows Calculator to perform simple calculations or solve scientific mathematical problems.
To learn how to use Help, press F1.

How To...
<u>Convert Values to Other Number Systems</u>
<u>Enter Calculations</u>
<u>Switch Calculators</u>
<u>Use Advanced Statistical Functions</u>
<u>Use Calculator with the Clipboard</u>
<u>Use Memory Functions</u>
<u>Use Number-Base Functions</u>
<u>Use Operators</u>
<u>Use Other Advanced Functions</u>
<u>Use Scientific Calculator's Statistical Functions</u>
<u>Use Standard Calculator Functions</u>

Commands
<u>Edit Menu Commands</u>
<u>View Menu Commands</u>

⑯ Exit Help and then **Calculator**.

⑰ Close the **Accessories** window.

⑱ **Go** on to Exercise 44.
OR
Exit Windows.

EXERCISE 44
Help, Windows Tutorial

Help, Windows tutorial

Hands-on lessons in two areas:

1) How to use the mouse, and

2) Windows Basics.

NOTE: Your computer system must have a color monitor in order to use Windows Tutorial.

Windows Basics lessons:

    Instructions

    Starting an Application

    Moving and Sizing Windows

    Using Menus and Commands

    Using Dialog Boxes

    Switching Between Applications

    Closing Applications

Keyboard Users

HELP, WINDOWS TUTORIAL

START WINDOWS TUTORIAL:

From the Program Manager:

1. **Press Alt + H** (<u>H</u>elp)
2. **Press W** (<u>W</u>indows Tutorial)
3. • **Press M** (Mouse)

   OR

   • **Press W**

    (Windows Basics)

NOTE: The rest of the tutorial requires the <u>mouse</u> to activate commands.

EXIT WINDOWS TUTORIAL:

1. **Press Esc**
2. **Press Y** (Yes)

---

① **Start Windows** (review, page 52), if necessary.

FROM THE *STARTING WINDOWS* SCREEN:

② START THE WINDOWS TUTORIAL:

- **Click on <u>H</u>elp.**
- **Click on <u>W</u>indows Tutorial.**

The *Windows Tutorial* program starts—it is <u>not</u> in a window:

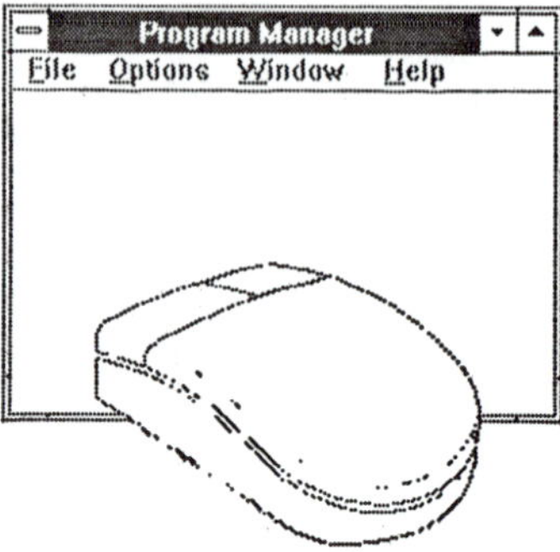

Press the ESC key to exit the Tutorial.

③ EXIT WINDOWS TUTORIAL:

From anywhere in the Windows tutorial:

- **Press Esc.**
- **Press Y** (yes, you do want to exit).

④ DO THE MOUSE LESSON:

NOTE: Do not do this step if you have already done the Mouse Lesson and feel comfortable with the mouse.

- **Start** the **Windows Tutorial** (see step 2).
- **Press M** (for the Mouse lesson).
- Follow the directions to run the mouse tutorial.
- **Exit** the **Windows Tutorial** (see step 3).

⑤ DO THE WINDOWS BASICS LESSON:

NOTE: Do not do this step if you have already done the Windows Basics Lesson and feel comfortable with basic Windows procedures.

- **Start** the **Windows Tutorial** (see step 2).
- **Press W** (for the Windows Basics lesson).
- Follow the directions to run the Windows Basics tutorial.
- **Exit** the **Windows Tutorial** (see step 3).

⑥ ACCESS THE DIALOG BOXES LESSON:

- **Start** the **Windows Tutorial** (see step 2).
- **Press W** (for the Windows Basics lesson).
- **Click** on `Contents` (located in the bottom right corner of the screen).

A contents box with "Windows Basics Lessons" on the right side appears.

Continue Exercise 44 on the next page

- **Click** on the box by "Using Dialog Boxes."
  The following screen appears:

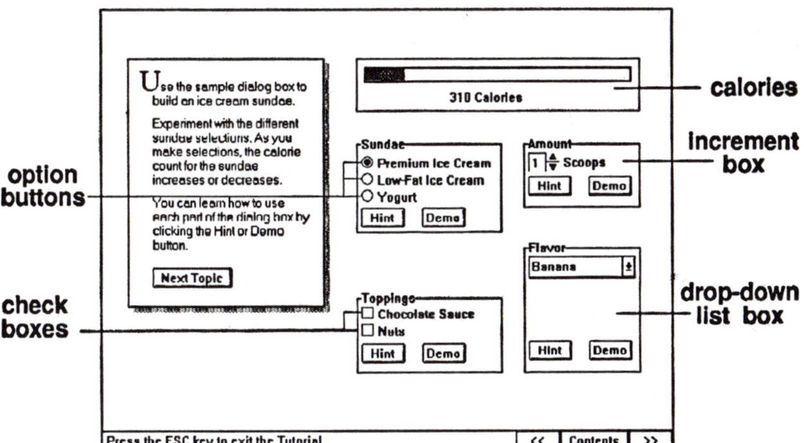

7   **Click** on the ⬚Demo⬚ box for **Toppings** (check box).

8   USE THE OPTION BUTTONS (Sundae):

- **Click** on the **option button** for the desired **Sundae** choice. Notice the calories (in the top box) change when you select different Sundae options.
  NOTE: You may select only one option button at a time.

9   USE THE CHECK BOX (Toppings):

- **Click** on the blank **box** next to each **Topping** you want on your sundae (to **select** it). Notice the calories change as you select different toppings.
  *NOTE: An "X" appears in the box when it is **selected**.*
- **Click** on a selected **box** to deselect it (if you do not want **a** selected Topping).

10   USE THE INCREMENT BOX (Amount):

- **Click** on the ⬆ or ⬇ until the **Amount** of scoops you want appears in the box. Notice the calories change as you change the number of scoops.

11   USE THE DROP-DOWN LIST BOX (Flavor):

- **Click** on the drop-down list arrow in the **Flavor** box.
- **Scroll** through the list until the flavor you want appears.
- **Click** on the **flavor** (to select it).

12   Change the Sundae, Toppings, Amount, and Flavor options. How many total calories?

13   Change the options to create a Sundae with the fewest calories possible.

14   **Exit** the **Windows Tutorial.**

15   **Exit Windows.**

EXERCISE 45
Practice
Lesson Three
Help

Exercises 45 and 46 should be done during the same session.

Tasks Reviewed:

Help
Help, Contents
Help, Glossary
Help, Search

1 Start **Windows**, if necessary.

2 Click on **File**.

3 Click on **New**

4 Click on [Help].

5 **Maximize** the **Help** window. Read the information.

6 **Restore** the **Help** window.

7 **Exit** the **Help** window.

8 **Cancel** the **new program object** dialog box.

9 **Open Accessories.**

10 **Start Character Map.**

11 **Press** **F1** (to access the Help menu). Read the *Contents for Character Map Help.*
NOTE: **Contents** *always contains information about the window you are using.*

12 Click on **Glossary**.

13 **Scroll** through the glossary terms.
NOTE: **Glossary** *always contains the <u>same</u> terms no matter which window you access it from.*

14 **Exit Glossary.**

15 Click on **Search**.
NOTE: **Search** *always contains <u>topics</u> about the window you are using.*

16 Click on **selecting fonts.**

17 Click on [Show Topics].

18 Click on [Go To]. Read about selecting fonts.

19 **Exit** the **Help** window.

20 **Exit Character Map.**

Go on to Exercise 46

① **Start Write.**

② **Click** on **H**elp.

③ **Click** on **C**ontents.

④ **Scroll** through the list until <u>Open Documents</u> appears.

⑤ **Click** on <u>Open Documents</u>.

⑥ **Click** on **F**ile. Be sure the printer is ready to receive data.

⑦ **Click** on **P**rint Topic.
RESULT:

> **Opening Documents**
>
> **To open a Write document**
> 1 From the File menu, choose Open.
> 2 Type or select the filename.
> 3 Choose the OK button.
> To open a document that does not use the Windows character format, you must convert the document to Write format.
>
> **To open a document that is not in Write format**
> 1 From the File menu, choose Open.
> 2 Type or select the filename. You can use the List Files Of Type, Drives, and Directories lists to locate the file.
> 3 Choose the OK button.
> 4 Choose one of the following buttons to open the file.
>
> | Use | To |
> | --- | --- |
> | No Conversion | Open documents created by using a Windows application, including Write documents saved as <u>text-only</u>. |
> | Convert | Open Microsoft Word documents. Or open documents created with a <u>non-Windows application</u>, saved as text-only. |

⑧ **Exit Write Help.**

⑨ **Exit Write.**

⑩ **Exit Accessories.**

⑪ **Start** the Clipboard Viewer, access Help Contents, **print** the Contents for Clipboard Viewer Help (using Print Topics), **exit** Help, and then **exit** the Clipboard Viewer.
RESULT:

> **Contents for Clipboard Viewer Help**
> Windows Clipboard Viewer is a tool you can use to see the contents of the Clipboard. When you cut or copy information from an application, it is placed onto the Clipboard. You then paste that information from the Clipboard into other documents or applications.
> To learn how to use Help, press F1.
>
> **How To...**
> <u>Transfer Information When Running Non-Windows Applications</u>
> <u>Transfer Information When Running Windows Applications</u>
> <u>View Clipboard Contents in Other Formats</u>
>
> **Commands**
> <u>File Menu Commands</u>
> <u>Edit Menu Commands</u>
> <u>Display Menu Commands</u>

⑫ **Exit Windows.**

EXERCISE 46
Practice
Lesson Three
Help

Continue from Exercise 45, doing both during the same session.

Tasks Reviewed:
Help
Help, Contents
Help, Print Topic

Lesson Three
Review of Help Exercises

Lesson Three (Help) covers tasks that:

Use Help

Use Help Contents, Search, and Glossary features

Show Information about Applications

Print Help Topics

Use the Windows Tutorial

POINTS TO EMPHASIZE

Help menu options

- **Contents** — an alphabetical list of Help topics available for the application you are currently using.
- **Search for Help on...** — locates information about a topic when you either look through a list of topics or type a keyword or phrase in a text box.
- **How to Use Help** — displays information about Windows Help features.
- **Windows Tutorial** — offers hands-on help in two areas: 1) how to use the mouse, and 2) introductory Windows procedures.
- **About (Application)** — displays information about Windows and the application you are current using.

Additional Help features found in some Help windows

- **Glossary** — an alphabetical list of Windows terms from which you can *choose* a term to display its defintion.
- **Back** — an option that returns you to the previous Help screen, retracing your steps each time you choose **back** again.
- **History** — a sequential list of every Help topic you have chosen during the current Help session.

Ways to request Help

- **Choose** <u>H</u>elp on the menu bar.
- **Press** **F1**.
- **Choose** | Help | command button (available in many dialog boxes).
- **Highlight** a menu item and then press **F1** for a description of that item.
- **Select** a dialog box option or command, and press **F1** or the | Help | button for an explanation of that option or command.

Choosing a Jump

Jumps are Help topics that have a link to other Help topics or to more information about the current topic. Jumps are usually identified within a Help topic by different color and a dotted underline. **Click** on "jump" topic to display information about that topic.

Printing a Topic

Help topics can be printed if the Help window contains **<u>F</u>ile** menu with a **<u>P</u>rint Topic** commands.

WORKSHEET 23

NAME ___________________________

HELP TERMS AND TASKS

DIRECTIONS: Match the terms listed below to the definition that best fits the term.

F1	search	glossary	Windows tutorial	print topic
back	history	list box	about (application)	
Help	contents	text box	Help window buttons	

1. This Help feature provides an alphabetical list of *Windows terms* from which you may choose a term to display its definition.

   1) ___________________________

2. This Help feature provides an alphabetic list of *Help topics* related to the application you are currently using.

   2) ___________________________

3. A quick, easy way to look up information about Windows tasks, features, or commands.

   3) ___________________________

4. A row of boxes displayed *below* the *menu bar* in a Help window.

   4) ___________________________

5. This Help feature locates information about a Help topic. You can either look through a list of topics, or type a keyword or phrase to be looked for.

   5) ___________________________

6. A box in a dialog box that displays a list of options from which to choose.

   6) ___________________________

7. A box in a dialog box that provides space for typing information needed to carry out a command.

   7) ___________________________

8. This Help option offers information about Windows and the application you are currently using.

   8) ___________________________

9. This Help option displays a sequential list of every Help topic you have chosen during the current Help session.

   9) ___________________________

10. What Help option lets you transfer information about a Help topic to paper?

    10) ___________________________

11. This Help option returns you to the previous Help screen.

    11) ___________________________

12. What is the single Help key that provides help if Help is available in the current situation?

    12) ___________________________

13. Hands-on lessons in two areas: 1) How to use the mouse, and 2) Windows Basics.

    13) ___________________________

Lesson Four — Write

Table of Contents

EXERCISE 47
Start Write

Exercises 47-53 should be done during the same session.

start Write
To use Windows to run the Write Program.

Write
Write is Windows' word processor. Write uses many of the same features as Windows, such as a similar menu bar, dialog boxes, file commands, and window control elements.

insertion point
The insertion point is a blinking vertical line that shows where text will appear when you type.

end mark
The end mark is a small design (☒) that identifies the end of a document.

I-beam pointer
The mouse-pointer shape in Write's work area. Click the I-beam in the desired location to move the <u>insertion point</u> to that spot. (The insertion point cannot be placed beyond the end mark.)

page-status area
The page-status area tells you what page is showing on the screen, but until you <u>repaginate</u> (a File menu command), it displays only "Page 1."

Keyboard Users
START WRITE

1. Press **Ctrl** + **Tab** until the Accessories icon name is highlighted.
2. Press **⏎**
3. Press arrow keys until Write's icon name is highlighted.
4. Press **⏎**

① Start Windows, if necessary.

FROM THE *STARTING WINDOWS* SCREEN:

② Open the **Accessories** window.

③ Start Write.

The Write window appears:

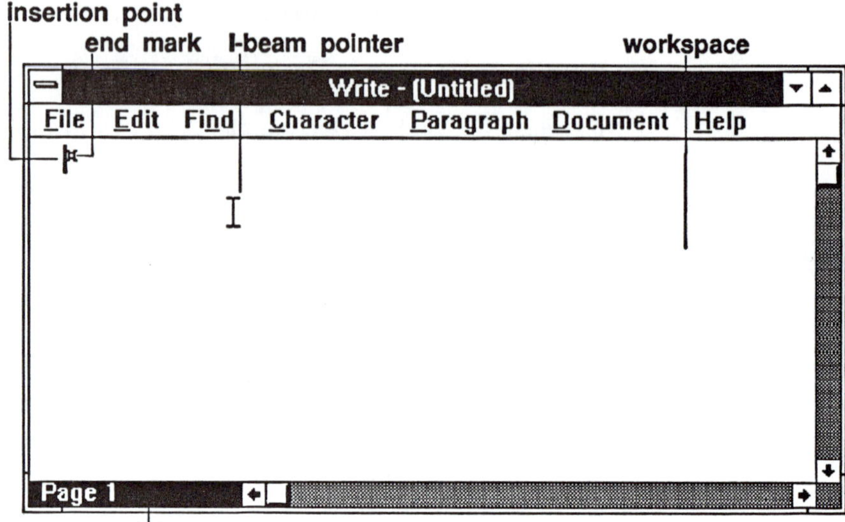

*NOTE: The name in the title bar is **Write - [Untitled]**. When a document has a filename (i.e., it is saved or opened), [Untitled] will change to reflect that document's filename.*

④ Maximize Write.

NOTE: Because Write allows only one document window, the <u>application title bar</u> and the <u>document title bar</u> are shared; and maximize, minimize, and restore buttons exist only for the Write application window.

Go on to Exercise 48

 LOOK AT EACH DROP-DOWN MENU:

- **Click on <u>F</u>ile.**
- **Click on <u>E</u>dit.**
- **Click on Fi<u>n</u>d.**
- **Click on <u>C</u>haracter.**
- **Click on <u>P</u>aragraph.**
- **Click on <u>D</u>ocument.**
- **Click on <u>H</u>elp.**

Each **drop-down** menu is shown below:

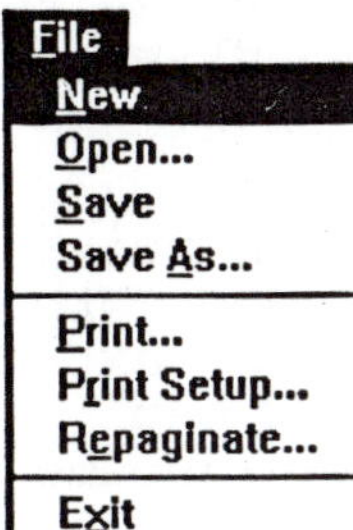

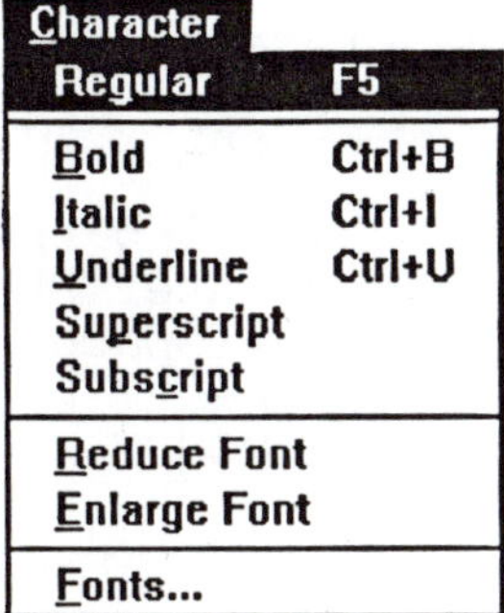

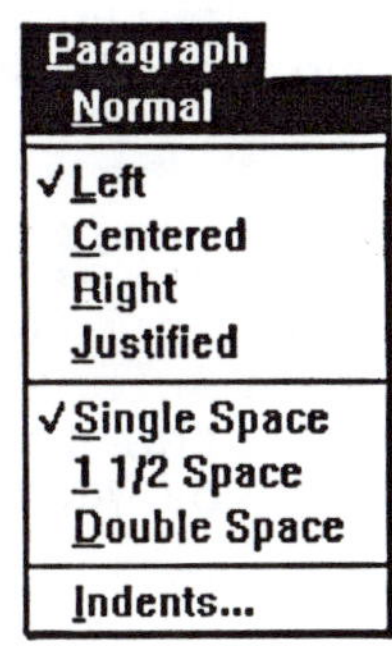

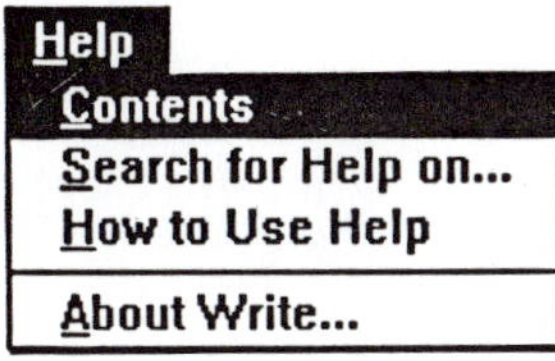

Click off of the menus to cancel any menu that may still be open.

Go on to Exercise 49

EXERCISE 48
Write Menus

Continue from Exercise 47, doing Exercises 47-53 during the same session.

Write menus

The menus showing on the menu bar when you are in Write, some of which are similar to other Windows menus (such as File and Help) and others which are specific to Write.

Keyboard Users
WRITE MENUS

OPEN AND CLOSE MENUS:

1. **Press `Alt` + `F`** (to open <u>F</u>ile)
2. **Press `Alt`** (to close <u>F</u>ile)
3. Repeat steps 1 and 2, replacing `F` with the underlined letter of each of the other menus.

129

EXERCISE 49
Create a Document

Continue from Exercise 48, doing Exercises 47-53 during the same session.

create a document
To type text in the Write window's workspace.

new
The <u>new</u> file option clears the screen (i.e., opens a <u>new</u> document). If you have any unsaved data in Write, <u>new</u> offers you a chance to save it before the new screen appears.

Keyboard Users

CREATE A DOCUMENT
MOVE THE CURSOR:*

To move the insertion
point to the: <u>Press</u>

next space   →
previous space   ←
one line up   ↑
one line down   ↓
next word   Ctrl + →
previous word   Ctrl + ←
end of line   End
beginning of line   Home
end of document   Ctrl + End
beg. of document   Ctrl + Home
next sentence   ** 5 + →
previous sentence   5 + ←
next paragraph   5 + ↓
previous paragraph   5 + ↑
next screen down   PgDn
next screen up   PgUp
bottom of window   Ctrl + PgDn
top of window   Ctrl + PgUp
next page   5 + PgDn
previous page   5 + PgUp

*NOTE: You cannot move the
        insertion point past the end
        of the document.*

**Use the 5 located on the numeric keypad <u>with the Num Lock light turned OFF</u>.

IMPORTANT: When typing text, press ⏎ only at the end of short lines and paragraphs. Automatic **word wrap** will move a word that is within a paragraph to the next line when it no longer fits on the present line. Use BkSp (deletes character to the left of cursor) or Del (deletes character to the right of cursor) to correct errors while typing.

① CREATE A DOCUMENT:
- **Type:**
  When the Write program is started, the cursor (a blinking vertical line) is displayed in the top left corner of the workspace. The cursor is called an "insertion point" because it shows where the next character you type will be inserted.
- **Press** ⏎ twice.
- **Type:**
  The small design following the insertion point is called the "end mark." In a "new document" the "insertion point" and the "end mark" are next to each other at the beginning of the document, indicating that there is nothing in the document.
- **Press** ⏎ twice.
- **Type:**
  You create a document by typing. Press the ENTER key only at the end of short lines, paragraphs, or to insert blank lines. Write will automatically move a word within a paragraph to the next line when it is too long to fit on the present line.
- **Press** ⏎ twice.
- **Type:**
  You can move the "insertion point" by using the arrow keys or the mouse. The mouse pointer shape appears as an "I-beam" in the Write workspace. To move the cursor with the mouse, move the "I-beam" to the desired location AND CLICK THE MOUSE BUTTON.

② MOVE THE CURSOR (INSERTION POINT):
- **Move** the **I-beam** shaped pointer to the top line.
- **Click** on the middle of the top line.
- **Press** End
  to move the cursor to the <u>end of the line</u>.
- **Press** Home
  to move the cursor to the <u>beginning of the line</u>.
- **Press** Ctrl + End
  to move the cursor to the <u>end of the document</u>.
- **Press** Ctrl + Home
  to move the cursor to the <u>beginning of the document</u>.
- **Press** Ctrl + →
  to move the cursor to the <u>next word</u>.
- **Press** Ctrl + ←
  to move the cursor to the <u>previous word</u>.

③ CLEAR THE SCREEN (OPEN A <u>NEW</u> DOCUMENT):
- **Click** on <u>F</u>ile.
- **Click** on <u>N</u>ew.
- **Click** on <u>N</u>o (you do not want to save the document).
  NOTE: The document is erased and cannot be retrieved.

Go on to Exercise 50

IMPORTANT: This book instructs you to save your files on Drive A: (or B:).
Start with a blank, formatted floppy disk. Use a high-density disk if possible.

1 CREATE A DOCUMENT:

- **Type:** `Your Name`
- **Press** ⏎ twice, and then **type:**
  ```
  The "File" menu has file handling options that
  will perform such tasks as Save, Save As, Open,
  and Print files.
  ```
- **Press** ⏎ twice, and then **type:**
  ```
  "Save As" lets you save a new document or save a
  previously named document with a new name.
  ```
- **Press** ⏎ twice, and then **type:**
  ```
  "Save" saves the "changes" to the document you are
  working on.  Your document must be named to use
  this option.  If the document you are working on
  is untitled, "Save" will automatically open the
  "Save As" dialog box.
  ```

2 SAVE A NEW DOCUMENT TO DRIVE A: (OR B:):

- Place a blank disk in Drive A: (or B:) and close the door.
- **Click** on **F**ile, then on **Save A**s... .
  The *Save As* dialog box appears:

File Name list box

File Name text box   **Directories list box**

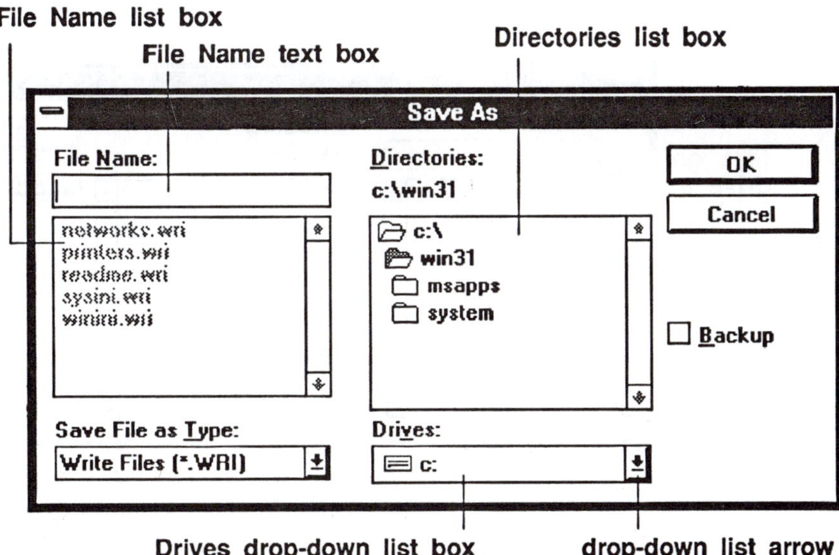

Drives drop-down list box   **drop-down list arrow**

- **Click** on the **drop-down arrow** to open the **Dri**ves drop-down list box.
- **Click** on 🖴 **a:** (or b:).
  NOTE: You have just changed to Drive A: (or B:).
- **Click** on the **File N**ame text box.
- **Type:** `SAVEIT`
- **Press** ⏎.
  NOTE: Look at the name in the title bar. The filename is displayed, and Write
  automatically adds a .wri extension to the filename.

Go on to Exercise 51

Continue from Exercise 49,
doing Exercises 47-53 during
the same session.

save a document
To store a document on a disk.

save
Saves changes to a previously named
document that you are working on.

save as...
Saves new documents or lets you rename
a previously saved document.

file
A file is a set of data that is saved on a
disk as a named unit.

drop-down list box
A box that is similar to a list box except
that it must be opened by clicking on the
drop-down list arrow next to it.

Keyboard Users
SAVE A DOCUMENT

SAVE NEW DOCUMENT OR
RENAME FILE:

1. **Press** `Alt` + `F` (**F**ile)
2. **Press** `A` (S**a**ve As...)
   IF you want to change the
   drive:
   - **Press** `Alt` + `V` (Dri**v**e)
   - **Press** ⬇
   - Use arrows to highlight the
     desired drive.
   - **Press** ⏎
3. **Press** `Alt` + `N` (File **N**ame)
4. Type a filename.
5. **Press** ⏎

SAVE PREVIOUSLY NAMED
DOCUMENT:

1. **Press** `Alt` + `F` (**F**ile)
2. **Press** `Alt` + `S` (**S**ave)

EXERCISE 51
Open a Document

Continue from Exercise 50, doing Exercises 47-53 during the same session.

open a document
To retrieve a saved document file from a disk, bringing it into the Write program.

Keyboard Users

OPEN A DOCUMENT

CLEAR THE SCREEN:

1. Press **Alt** + **F** (File)
2. Press **N** (New)

    IF unsaved text is present, a message asks if you want to "Save current changes."

    - Press **N** (No)

    OR

    - Press **Y** (Yes)
    - Type a filename.
    - Press ⏎

OPEN A DOCUMENT:

1. Press **Alt** + **F** (File)
2. Press **O** (Open)

    IF you want to change the drive:
    - Press **Alt** + **V** (Drive)
    - Press ⬇
    - Use arrows to highlight the desired drive.
    - Press ⏎

3. Press **Alt** + **N** (File Name)

    - Type a filename.
    - Press ⏎

    OR

    - Press **Tab**
    - Use arrows to highlight desired file.
    - Press ⏎

---

① CLEAR THE SCREEN (open a new document):

- **Click on File, then on New.**

    NOTE: Since you just saved your document, Write immediately clears the screen with no questions asked. If there were changes, a dialog box would appear asking if you want to "Save current changes."

② Exit Write.

③ Start Write.

IMPORTANT: Because you exited Write since the last time you accessed your file, the default drive has changed back to Drive C:. Each time you **start** Write, you must change to Drive A: (or B:) if you want to **save** and **open** files on that drive. This is done most conveniently the first time you **save** or **open** a document file.

④ OPEN A DOCUMENT FILE:

- **Click on File, then on Open.**

    The *Open* dialog box appears. Notice that, except for its title, it is like the *Save As* dialog box on the previous page.

- **Click on the Drives drop-down list box.**

- **Click on ▭ a: (or b:).**

    The *Open* dialog box now displays the files on the disk in Drive A: (or B:):

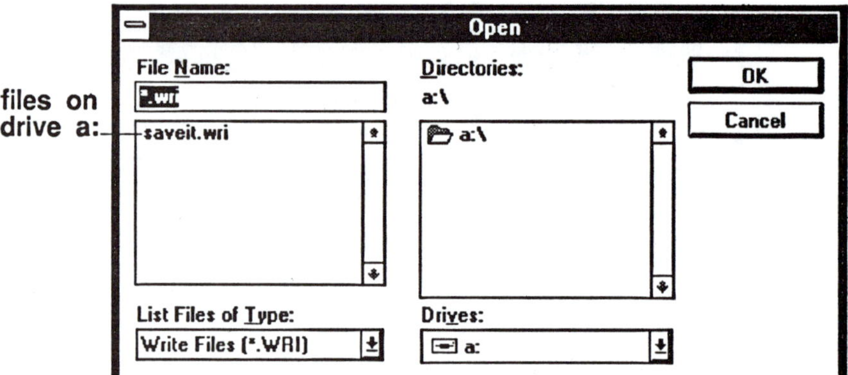

- **Double-click on saveit.wri in the File Name *list box*.**

OR

- **Click on saveit.wri in the File Name *list box*.**
- **Click on OK .**

⑤ CLEAR THE SCREEN:

- **Click on File, then on New.**

    NOTE: The new document is displayed in the title bar as: Write - [Untitled]. The document, saveit.wri, is still saved and can be retrieved again.

⑥ Exit Write.

Go on to Exercise 52

1 Start Write.

2 **Open** the document file named **saveit.wri** (review, previous page).

*NOTE: Always be sure to close the drive door after you put the disk in. If you do not, you will get an error message saying: Cannot read drive a:... . If this happens, close the door and **click** on **Retry** in the error message dialog box.*

*NOTE: If you have made <u>any</u> changes in Write's work area, you will get a message which asks: Save current changes? **Click** on **No**, and Write will continue to process your original command.*

3 PRINT A DOCUMENT:

*NOTE: Write has **default** settings in the **printer setup** that best fit most standard situations, which include what is needed for exercises in this book.*

- **Make** sure your printer is ready to receive data.
- **Click** on **File**, then on **Print...** .
- **Click** on [OK] .

*NOTE: A message briefly appears that allows you to **cancel** the print job if desired.*

RESULT — **SAVEIT**:
Line endings may vary slightly.

Your Name

The "File" menu has file handling options that will perform such tasks as Save, Save As, Open, and Print files.

"Save As" lets you save a new document or save a previously named document with a new name.

"Save" saves the "changes" to the document you are working on. Your document must be named to use this option. If the document you are working on is untitled, "Save" will automatically open the "Save As" dialog box.

---

4 **Clear the screen** (review, previous page, step 5). If you get a message to "Save current changes," **click** on **No**.

5 **Maximize Write.**

Go on to Exercise 53

EXERCISE 52
Print a Document

Continue from Exercise 51, doing Exercises 47-53 during the same session.

<u>ASSUMPTION:</u>

It is assumed that your printer has been properly installed.

print a document

To copy information from a document in the Write program onto paper.

Keyboard Users

PRINT A DOCUMENT

1. Press **Alt** + **F** (*F*ile)
2. Press **P** (*P*rint)
3. Make sure your printer is ready to receive data.
4. Press **↵**

EXERCISE 53
Change Fonts

Continue from exercise 52, doing Exercises 47-53 during the same session.

change fonts
To choose a different typeface, and/or a different type style, and/or a different size.

font
A font is the complete set of characters in a given size, type style, and typeface.

typeface
Typeface is the design of characters (also called font).

type style
Type style is the treatment of characters, for example, bold, italic, and underline.

size
The height of characters is measured in points (one point is 1/72 of an inch). The larger the point size, the larger the font.

sample box
Displays a <u>sample</u> of the selected font in the selected type style and the selected size.

Keyboard Users
See pages 135 and 136 for directions to CHANGE FONTS.

FROM THE WRITE WINDOW:

1 **Click** on **<u>C</u>haracter**, then on **<u>F</u>onts... .**
The *Font* dialog box appears:

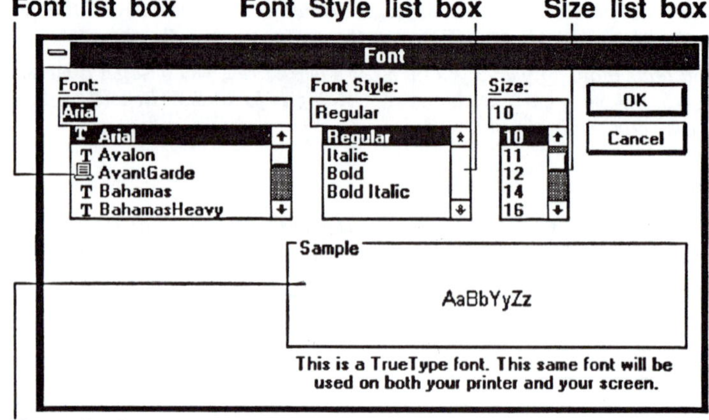

Sample box

2
- **Scroll** through the **<u>F</u>ont** *list box*, and **click** on **Arial.**
- **Scroll** through the **<u>S</u>ize** *list box*, and **click** on **20.**
  NOTE: The font in the Sample box jumps to a larger size.
- **Click** on [OK] .

3 Type the text shown in the box below:

RESULT — FONTS1:
Line endings may vary.

NOTE:
1. Large text will appear on screen when you type.
2. Press ⏎ *twice after short lines and paragraphs. Do not press* ⏎ *within paragraphs.*
3. Space once after numbers.
4. Use the scroll bars to access text that is beyond the Write window.
5. Correct errors by using **BkSp** *to delete the previous character or* **Del** *to delete the next character.*
6. TrueType is one word.

> Your Name
>
> FONTS
>
> Three elements define fonts:
>
> 1. The design of characters is called typeface.
>
> 2. The size of characters is measured in points.
>
> 3. The treatment of characters, such as **bold**, *italic*, or underline, is called type style.
>
> A font is the complete set of characters for a single typeface in one size and one type style.
>
> Windows uses TrueType fonts. These fonts are scalable and are sometimes generated as bitmaps or soft fonts, depending on the capabilities of your printer. TrueType fonts can be sized to any height, and they print exactly as they appear on the screen.

4 **Save** the document on Drive A: (or B:) using **Save <u>A</u>s...** (review, page 131); name it **FONTS1.**

5 **Print** the document.

Continue Exercise 53 on the next page

6 **HIGHLIGHT A WORD:**
- Use the Scroll bar to scroll to the top of the document.
- **Double-click** on FONTS. FONTS is highlighted.

FONTS

HIGHLIGHT A BLOCK OF TEXT:
- Point to the first e in elements.
- **Drag** the *insertion point* <u>from</u> the e <u>to</u> just past the n in design, **and** then release the button. The block is highlighted:

Three **elements define fonts:**

1. The design of characters is called typeface.

HIGHLIGHT A LINE:
- **Move** the **pointer** to the beginning of the line Three elements define fonts:
Notice that the pointer switches between an arrow and an I-beam when it is close to the left edge.
- While the pointer is an arrow, **click** at the beginning of the line. The line is highlighted:

Three elements define fonts:

REMOVE HIGHLIGHTING:
- **Click** anywhere in the work area (not in the menu area).

7 **BOLD TEXT:**
- **Double-click** on FONTS to highlight the word.
- **Click** on **C**haracter, then on **Bold**.

8 **UNDERLINE TEXT:**
- **Highlight** the third line, which begins Three elements... .
- **Click** on **C**haracter, then on **U**nderline.

9 **ITALICIZE TEXT:**
- **Highlight** design in the line numbered 1.
- **Click** on **C**haracter, then on **I**talic.

10 **RETURN TEXT TO REGULAR:**
- **Double-click** on FONTS to highlight the word.
- **Click** on **C**haracter, then on **Regular**.
- **Highlight** the third line, which begins Three elements... .
- **Click** on **C**haracter, then on **Regular**.
- **Highlight** design in the line numbered 1.
- **Click** on **C**haracter, then on **Regular**.

11 **Bold** the word FONTS again.

12 **Underline** the third line, which begins Three elements... again.

13 **Italicize** design in the line numbered 1, again.

Continue Exercise 53 on the next page

---

highlight
To use a procedure that reverses the color on a portion of text, thereby selecting it. Highlighted text will be affected by your next action.

Keyboard Users
CHANGE FONTS
TO HIGHLIGHT:
1. Use arrow keys to move the *insertion point* to the first character to select.
2. **Press** and hold **Shift** <u>while</u> you use arrow keys to move the *insertion point* just past the last character to select.

CHANGE TYPE STYLE:
1. Highlight desired text.
2. To bold:
   - **Press** **Ctrl** + **B**
   To underline:
   - **Press** **Ctrl** + **U**
   To italicize:
   - **Press** **Ctrl** + **I**

Keyboard Users

CHANGE FONTS

CHANGE TYPEFACE, TYPE
STYLE, AND TYPE SIZE:

1. **Press Alt + C** (Character)
2. **Press F** (Fonts...)
3. Change one or all of the
   following options:

> FONT:
> - **Press Alt + F** (Font)
> - **Scroll** through the Font list
>   box using ↓ and ↑ until
>   the desired *font* is
>   highlighted. The name
>   appears in the Font text
>   box.

AND/OR

> FONT STYLE:
> - **Press Alt + Y**
>   (Font Style)
> - **Scroll** through the Font
>   Style list box using ↓ and
>   ↑ until the desired *font
>   style* is highlighted. The
>   name appears in the Font
>   Style text box.

AND/OR

> SIZE:
> - **Press Alt + S** (Size)
> - **Scroll** through the Size list
>   box using ↓ and ↑ until
>   the desired *size* is
>   highlighted. The name
>   appears in the Size text
>   box.

*NOTE: The Sample box displays
the font that is currently
selected.*

4. **Press** ↵

Exercise 53 (continued)

14 Bold, italicize, and underline text to match this sample:

RESULT – **FONTS2:**
*Line endings may vary
slightly.*

> Your Name
>
> **FONTS**
>
> Three elements define fonts:
>
> 1. The *design* of characters is called **typeface.**
>
> 2. The *size* of characters is measured in **points.**
>
> 3. The *treatment* of characters, such as bold,
> italic, or underline, is called **type style.**
>
> A **font** is the complete set of characters for a
> single *typeface* in one *size* and one *type style.*
>
> Windows uses **TrueType** fonts. These fonts are
> scalable and are sometimes generated as
> bitmaps or soft fonts, depending on the
> capabilities of your printer. TrueType fonts can
> be sized to any height, and they print exactly as
> they appear on the screen.

15 **Save** the document on Drive A: (or B:) using **Save As...**
(review, page 131); name it **FONTS2.**

16 **Print** the document (review, page 133).

17 **Clear the screen** (review, page 132, step 5).

18 CHANGE FONT:
- **Click** on **Character**, then on **Fonts... .**
- **Scroll** through the **Font** *list box*, and **click** on **Courier New.**
- **Scroll** through the **Size** *list box*, and **click** on **36.**
- **Click** on | OK | .

19
- **Type:** This is Courier New, point size 36.
- **Press** ↵ twice.

20 CHANGE FONT:
- **Click** on **Character**, then on **Fonts... .**
- **Scroll** through the **Font** *list box* and **click** on **Times New Roman.**
- **Scroll** through the **Size** *list box*, and **click** on **48.**
- **Click** on | OK | .

21
- **Type:** This is Times New Roman, point size 48.
- **Press** ↵ twice.

Continue Exercise 53 on the next page

 **CHANGE FONT:**
- **Click** on **Character**, then on **Fonts...** .
- **Scroll** through the **Font** *list box*, and **click** on **Wingdings**.
- **Scroll** through the **Size** *list box*, and **click** on **28**.
- **Click** on ⬚ OK ⬚ .

- **Type** the alphabet using upper case (wingdings will appear instead of letters): ABCDEFGHIJKLMNOPQRSTUVWXYZ
  NOTE: Use either ▮Caps Lock▮ or ▮Shift▮, but not both.
- **Press** ⬑ twice.
- **Type** (the number row): `'1234567890-=\`
- **Press** ⬑ twice.
- **Type** (uppercase number row): `~!@#$%^&*()_+|`
  NOTE: You must use the ▮Shift▮ key.

- **Save** the document on Drive A: (or B:); name it **FUN**.
- **Print** the document.

RESULT — **FUN:**
*Line endings may
vary slightly.*

This is Courier New,
point size 36.

This is Times New
Roman, point size 48.

 **Exit Write** and **close Accessories.**

Go on to Exercise 54.

OR

Exit Windows.

EXERCISE 54
Edit a Document

Exercises 54 and 55 should be done during the same session.

edit a document
To change the content (words) of a document. Editing consists mainly of inserting, deleting, moving, and copying text.

cut
To move selected (highlighted) data from a document into the Clipboard. <u>Cut</u> removes data from a document.

copy
To copy selected (highlighted) data in a document into the Clipboard. <u>Copy</u> leaves the original data intact.

paste
To copy the data in the Clipboard into a document. <u>Paste</u> leaves the original data in the Clipboard so it can be pasted again.

Keyboard Users

EDIT A DOCUMENT
INSERT:
- Use arrows to move the *insertion point* to the desired location.
- Type text.

DELETE:
- **Press** and hold **Shift** <u>while</u> you use arrow keys to highlight text.
- **Press** **Del**

CUT:
- **Highlight** desired text.
- **Press** **Alt** + **E** (<u>E</u>dit)
- **Press** **T** (Cu<u>t</u>)

COPY:
- **Highlight** desired text.
- **Press** **Alt** + **E** (<u>E</u>dit)
- **Press** **C** (<u>C</u>opy)

PASTE:
- Move *insertion point* where data is to be inserted.
- **Press** **Alt** + **E** (<u>E</u>dit)
- **Press** **P** (<u>P</u>aste)

---

(1) Start Windows, if necessary.

(2) Open Accessories.

(3) Start Write

(4) Maximize Write.

(5) Open the **FONTS2** document file (review, page 132).
NOTE: Remember to change to Drive A: (or B:) if necessary.

(6) INSERT TEXT:
- **Click** the *insertion point* immediately before `or underline` in the third numbered sentence.
- **Type:** `outline,`
- **Press** **Space**.
- **Click** the *insertion point* at the <u>end</u> of the next-to-last paragraph, which begins `A` **`font is....`**
- **Press** **Space** twice, and **type:** `Therefore, one typeface may contain many fonts of different sizes and type styles.`
NOTE: If the text is italic, change to regular (it may pick up the italic command from the words "type style").

(7) DELETE TEXT:
- **Double-click** on the word `complete` in the next-to-last paragraph (to highlight it).
- **Click** on **Edit**, then on **Cut**.
- Use the **drag** mouse action to **highlight** the second sentence in the last paragraph, which begins `These`.
- **Press** **Del** or **BkSp**.
NOTE: Be sure to leave two spaces, and only two spaces, between the remaining sentences.

(8) CUT AND PASTE TEXT:
NOTE: You are going to switch the sentence following 2 with the sentence following 3.
- **Highlight** the sentence which begins `The size`.
- **Click** on **Edit**, then on **Cut**.
- **Click** the *insertion point* immediately before the `T` at the start of the sentence which begins `The treatment....`
- **Click** on **Edit**, then on **Paste**.
- **Highlight** the sentence which begins `The treatment....`
- **Click** on **Edit**, then on **Cut**.
- **Click** the *insertion point* just after the `2.` (and the space which follows it).
- **Click** on **Edit**, then on **Paste**.
NOTE: Make adjustments, if necessary, to keep one blank line, and only one blank line, between paragraphs.

Continue Exercise 54 on the next page

9 COPY TEXT:

- **Highlight** `Windows uses TrueType fonts.`
- **Click** on **Edit**, then on **Copy**.
- **Click** the *insertion point* at the start of the line `Three elements define fonts:`.
  NOTE: *Click the insertion point when the pointer is an I-beam, not when it is an arrow.*
- **Click** on **Edit**, then on **Paste**.
- **Press** ⏎ twice.

10 **Save** the document on Drive A: (or B:) using **Save As...** (review page 131); name it **FONTS3**.

11 **Print** the document.

RESULT — **FONTS3:**
Line endings may vary slightly.

Your Name

FONTS

Windows uses **TrueType** fonts.

Three elements define fonts:

1. The *design* of characters is called **typeface**.

2. The *treatment* of characters, such as bold, italic, outline, or underline, is called **type style**.

3. The *size* of characters is measured in **points**.

A **font** is the set of characters for a single *typeface* in one *size* and one *type style*. Therefore, one typeface may contain many fonts of different sizes and type styles.

Windows uses **TrueType** fonts. TrueType fonts can be sized to any height, and they print exactly as they appear on the screen.

Go on to Exercise 55

EXERCISE 55
Change Text Alignment

Continue from Exercise 54, doing both during the same session.

change text alignment

To change a line (or paragraph) of text to be <u>centered</u> between the margins, aligned at the <u>left</u> margin, aligned at the <u>right</u> margin, or <u>justified</u> (having an even left margin and an even right margin).

Keyboard Users

CHANGE TEXT ALIGNMENT

1. Position the *insertion pointer* anywhere on the line or paragraph to be justified.
2. Press **Alt** + **P** (Paragraph)
3. Select <u>one</u> of the following options:

   <u>L</u>eft:
   - Press **L**

   <u>R</u>ight:
   - Press **R**

   <u>C</u>entered:
   - Press **C**

   <u>J</u>ustified:
   - Press **J**

1 ALIGN TEXT RIGHT:
- **Click** the *insertion point* anywhere on the line with `Your Name`.
- **Click** on **Paragraph**, then on **Right**.

2 ALIGN TEXT CENTER:
- **Click** the *insertion point* anywhere on the line with `FONTS`.
- **Click** on **Paragraph**, then on **Centered**.

3 **Center** the sentence (the first one), `Windows uses` **`TrueType`** `fonts`.

4 ALIGN TEXT LEFT:
- **Click** the *insertion point* anywhere on the line of the sentence you just *centered*, `Windows uses` **`TrueType`** `fonts`.
- **Click** on **Paragraph**, then on **Left**.

5 JUSTIFY TEXT:
- **Click** the *insertion point* anywhere in the next-to-last paragraph.
- **Click** on **Paragraph**, then on **Justified**.

6 **Justify** the last paragraph.

7 **Click** the *insertion point* at the <u>end</u> of the last paragraph.

8 **Press** ⏎ twice.

9 **Click** on **Paragraph**, then on **Centered**.

10 **Type:** `This is a` **`TrueType`** `story.`

11 **Press** ⏎ twice.

12 **Click** on **Paragraph**, then on **Right**.

13 **Type:** `The end`

14 **Save** the document on Drive A: (or B:) using **Save As...** (review, page 131); name it **FONTS4**.

Continue Exercise 55 on the next page

15 **Print** the document.

RESULT – FONTS4:
Line endings may vary slightly.

Your Name

FONTS

Windows uses **TrueType** fonts.

<u>Three elements define fonts:</u>

1. The *design* of characters is called **typeface**.

2. The *treatment* of characters, such as bold, italic, outline, or underline, is called **type style**.

3. The *size* of characters is measured in **points**.

A **font** is the set of characters for a single *typeface* in one *size* and one *type style*. Therefore, one typeface may contain many fonts of different sizes and type styles.

Windows uses **TrueType** fonts. <u>TrueType fonts can be sized to any height, and they print exactly as they appear on the screen.</u>

This is a **TrueType** story.

The end

---

16 **Clear the screen.**

17 **Exit Write.**

18 **Close Accessories.**

19 **Go** on to Exercise 56.

OR

Exit Windows.

EXERCISE 56
Change Margins

change margins
To adjust the width of the left, right, top, and bottom borders around text on a page.

margins
The white space which creates a border around the body of data on a page.

Keyboard Users

CHANGE MARGINS

1. Press **Alt** + **D** (Document)
2. Press **P** (Page Layout....)
3. SELECT MARGIN TO CHANGE:

   • Press **Tab** until the desired margin *text box* is *selected*.

   OR

   • Press **Alt** +
     ← (Left margin), or
     → (Right margin), or
     T (Top margin), or
     B (Bottom margin).

4. **Type** the desired margin setting.
5. Repeat steps 3 and 4 until all desired margins are set.
6. Press **↵**

---

① **Start Windows**, if necessary.

② **Open Accessories.**

③ **Start Write.**

④ **Maximize Write.**

⑤ **Open** the **FONTS4** document.
NOTE: Remember to change to Drive A: (or B:), if necessary.

⑥ DELETE BOTTOM SECTION OF DOCUMENT:
   • **Drag** to **highlight** *from* <u>immediately after the period</u> at the end of the sentence that begins: `A font is...`, *to* the <u>end</u> of the document.
   • **Click** on **Edit.**
   • **Click** on **Cut.**

⑦ INSERT A WORD:
   • **Click** the insertion point <u>immediately</u> after the **e** in: `A font is the....`
   • **Press** **Space**.
   • **Type:** `complete`

⑧ CHANGE MARGINS:
   • **Click** on **Document**, then on **Page Layout... .**
     The *Page Layout* dialog box appears:

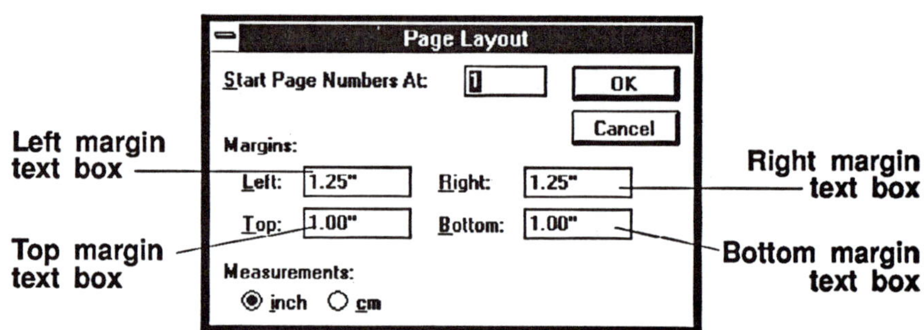

   • **Press** **Tab** (to move to the *Left* text box), and **type:** 3
   • **Press** **Tab** (to move to the *Right* text box), and **type:** 3
   • **Click** on **OK**.
NOTE: Three-inch margins on each side of the document leave a narrow column of text.

⑨ **Save** the document on Drive A: (or B:) using **Save As...** ; name it **FONTS5.**

⑩ CHANGE MARGINS:
   • **Click** on **Document**, then on **Page Layout... .**
   • **Press** **Tab** (to move to the *Left* text box), and **type:** 2
   • **Press** **Tab** (to move to the *Right* text box), and **type:** 2
   • **Press** **Tab** (to move to the *Top* text box), and **type:** 2
   • **Press** **Tab** (to move to the *Bottom* text box), **type:** 2
   • **Click** on **OK**.

Continue Exercise 56 on the next page

11   **Justify** the <u>last</u> paragraph (review, page 140, step 5).

12   **Resave** the document using **<u>F</u>ile, <u>S</u>ave**.

13   **Print** the document.

RESULT — **FONTS5:**
Line endings may vary slightly.

Your Name

FONTS

Windows uses **TrueType** fonts.

<u>Three elements define fonts:</u>

1. The *design* of characters is called **typeface**.

2. The *treatment* of characters, such as bold, italic, outline, or underline, is called **type style**.

3. The *size* of characters is measured in **points**.

A **font** is the complete set of characters for a single *typeface* in one *size* and one *type style*.

14   **Clear the screen.**

15   **Exit Write.**

16   **Close Accessories.**

17   **Exit Windows.**

EXERCISE 57
Practice

Lesson Four
Write

Tasks Reviewed:

Start Write

Use Menus

Save a Document

Open a Document

Print a Document

Change Fonts
  (Use Bold, Underline, and Italic)

Edit a Document

Change Text Alignment

Change Margins

NOTE: You can often change text characteristics either <u>before</u> you type (by issuing the command and then typing), or <u>after</u> you type (by highlighting text and then issuing the command to change).

*NOTE: When typing text, you may find it easier to use the keyboard rather than the mouse to issue commands. **Alt** + [the underlined key in a menu item] drops the menu down from the menu bar. Press [the underlined letter of an item in a drop-down menu] to select it.*

SHORTCUT KEYS TO:

  bold: **Ctrl** + **B**

  underline: **Ctrl** + **U**

  italicize: **Ctrl** + **I**

RETURN TO REGULAR TEXT:

  Issue the original command again to <u>end</u> bold, underline, or italic

---

1
- **Start Windows.**
- **Open Accessories.**
- **Start Write.**
- **Maximize Write.**

2 Change **font** to **Times New Roman, size 16.**

3 Change the left and right **margins** to 1 inch each.

4 **Align text** right.

5
- **Type:** Your Name
- **Press** ⏎ twice.

6 **Align text** left.

7
- **Type:** Using Write
- **Press** ⏎ twice.

8 **Type the following text, pressing** **Tab** **at the beginning of each paragraph, pressing** ⏎ **twice after each paragraph, and using bold, underline, and italic on words as shown:**

> Write is an *easy-to-use* word processor that comes with your Windows program. This book covers only **basic** Write procedures.
>
> You may explore other Write features by working through the menus and using <u>Help</u> when you are unsure about something. For example, let's see how easy it is to use the *Indent* feature. The Write <u>Help</u> feature tells you that "you can indent an entire paragraph from the left or right margin." The following paragraph is a description from <u>Help</u>:

NOTE: Remember to press ⏎ twice after typing each paragraph.

9 USE INDENT FEATURE:
- **Click on** <u>**P**</u>**aragraph.**
- **Click on** <u>**I**</u>**ndents... .**
- **Change** <u>**L**</u>**eft Indent to 1.**
- **Change** <u>**F**</u>**irst Line to .25.**
- **Change** <u>**R**</u>**ight Indent to 1.**
- **Click on** OK .

10 Change the **font** <u>**size**</u> to 12 (keep the Times New Roman font).

11 **Type:**

> The values in the Left Indent and Right Indent boxes specify how much to indent a paragraph from the left and right margins. The value in the First Line box indicates how much to indent the first line of the paragraph from the rest of the paragraph.

- **Press** ⏎ twice.

Continue Exercise 57 on the next page

12 **RETURN INDENTS TO ORIGINAL SETTINGS:**
- Access the *Indents* dialog box (see step 9 above).
- Change *Left Indent*, *First Line*, and *Right Indent*, all to 0 (zero).
- **Click** on [OK].

13 Change the **font size** back to 16 (keep the Roman font).

14 **Type:**
```
    See how easy it is to learn more about Write?
Some of the Write tasks that are covered in this
book are

Start Write and Examine the Menus
Create, Save, Open, and Print a Document
Edit a Document
Change Fonts
Change Text Alignment
Change Margins
```

15 **Save** the document on Drive A: (or B:) using **Save As...;** name it **USEWRITE.**

16 **Clear the screen.**

17 Type a couple of lines of anything you want.

18 **CLEAR THE SCREEN WITHOUT SAVING:**
- **Click** on **File,** then on **New.**
- **Click** on **No** (you do not want to save *current changes*).

19 **Open** the document named **usewrite.wri.**

20 **CHANGE THE TITLE:**
- **Center** the title, Using Write.
- **Bold** the title.
- Change the **size** of the title to 36 (highlight it first, then issue the command to change the font size).

21 **Bold** the indented paragraph.

22 Insert the words, want to, in the second paragraph after You may.

23 Insert the following text in the second paragraph after You may want to explore other Write features:
Type: (such as setting tabs, using headers and footers, changing line spacing, and using Find)
NOTE: Be sure spaces are correct before and after the inserted text.

24 Highlight the tasks at the bottom of the document, starting with:
Start Write and Examine the Menus

Continue Exercise 57 on the next page

Exercise 57 (continued)

(25) **Center** the highlighted text.

(26) **Copy** your name, inserting it a double space below the list of tasks at the bottom. **Right-align** it, if necessary.

(27) **Align text** to **Justify** all the paragraphs.

(28) **Delete** For example, in the second paragraph, and capitalize the L in let's.

(29) • **Delete** the title.
• **Oops!** you want the title back.
• **Click** on **Edit**, then on **Undo**.

(30) • **Save** the document using **Save**.
• **Print** the document.
RESULT — **USEWRITE:**
Line endings may vary slightly.

Your Name

Using Write

Write is an *easy-to-use* word processor that comes with your Windows program. This book covers only **basic** Write procedures.

You may want to explore other Write features (such as setting tabs, using headers and footers, changing line spacing, and using Find) by working through the menus and using Help when you are unsure about something. Let's see how easy it is to use the *Indent* feature. The Write Help feature tells you that "you can indent an entire paragraph from the left or right margin." The following paragraph is a description from Help:

The values in the Left Indent and Right Indent boxes specify how much to indent a paragraph from the left and right margins. The value in the First Line box indicates how much to indent the first line of the paragraph from the rest of the paragraph.

See how easy it is to learn more about Write? Some of the Write tasks that are covered in this book are

Start Write and Examine the Menus
Create, Save, Open, and Print a Document
Edit a Document
Change Fonts
Change Text Alignment
Change Margins

Your Name

---

(31) **Clear the screen.**

(32) **Exit Write.**

(33) **Close Accessories.**

(34) **Exit Windows.**

Lesson Four
Review of Write Exercises

Lesson Four (Write) covers tasks that:

Start Write and Examine the Menus

Create, Save, Open and Print a Document

Edit a Document

Change Fonts, Text Alignment and Margins

POINTS TO EMPHASIZE

Compare and Contrast

Save <u>and</u> Save As:

- *Save* is used to save **changes** in a previously saved (and named) file.
- *Save As* is used to **name** and save a **new** file or to save a previously named file under a **new name.**

Write's Title Bar for a New Document <u>and</u> Write's Title Bar for a Saved Document:

- When starting with a **clear screen** (also called a *new document*) or if there is data in the work area that has <u>not</u> been saved, Write's *title bar* displays: Write - [Untitled].
- When a document has a **name** (i.e., it has been saved or opened), Write's *title bar* displays: Write - FILENAME.WRI, (where the real filename replaces FILENAME).

Saving Files

To minimize the potential for causing errors on the hard disk, this book directs you to save your files on a floppy disk drive. Files saved in this lesson and the next lesson are used in the File Manager lesson.

Naming Files

Write automatically puts the filename extension .WRI at the end of your filename to identify the file as a Write file. For more information about files and file naming, review "File Manager" (page 27).

Fonts

An assortment of Windows' *TrueType* fonts is part of your Windows program. TrueType fonts should be available for use with *dot matrix, ink jet,* and *laser* printers (but not with *daisy wheel* printers). Your built-in printer fonts are available also. Fonts have three aspects that affect their appearance.

1. *Design of characters* is called <u>typeface</u> (or <u>font</u>).
2. *Treatment of characters* (i.e., bold, italic, etc.) is called <u>type style</u>.
3. *Size of characters* in TrueType fonts is measured in <u>points</u> (the larger the point size, the larger the font).

Editing Documents

Except for simple deletions and insertions, text to be edited must first be highlighted. Once data is highlighted, it can be *cut, copied,* or *pasted* by using the Edit menu.

Aligning Text

Text alignment is changed from the <u>P</u>aragraph menu by choosing one of four options: *centered, left, right,* or *justified.*

WORKSHEET 24

WRITE TERMS

NAME _______________________________

DIRECTIONS: Match the terms listed below to the definition that best fits the term.

New	I-beam	Write	drop-down list box
file	end mark	insertion point	
Save	Save As...	page-status area	

1. Which <u>F</u>ile option clears the screen (i.e., opens a new document?

   1) _______________________________

2. What is the small icon (¤) that identifies the end of a document?

   2) _______________________________

3. What command saves new documents or lets you rename a previously saved document?

   3) _______________________________

4. What is the pointer shape used in Write's work area?

   4) _______________________________

5. What is a <u>set of data</u> that is saved on a disk as a <u>named</u> unit?

   5) _______________________________

6. What is the blinking vertical line that shows where text will appear when you type?

   6) _______________________________

7. What area in Write tells you what page is showing on the screen (only after you repaginate the document)?

   7) _______________________________

8. What command saves changes to a previously named document file that you are working on?

   8) _______________________________

9. What kind of box is opened by clicking on the arrow next to it?

   9) _______________________________

10. What is Windows' word processor?

    10) _______________________________

(This page may be copied.)

WORKSHEET 25

WRITE <u>TERMS</u>

NAME _______________________________

DIRECTIONS: Match the terms listed below to the definition that best fits the term.

cut	copy	typeface
font	paste	highlight
size	margins	type style

1. To move highlighted data from a document into the Clipboard.

1) _______________________________

2. What is the treatment of characters, for example, bold, italic, and underline?

2) _______________________________

3. What is the white space that creates a border around the body of data on a page?

3) _______________________________

4. What is the design of characters?

4) _______________________________

5. What is the complete set of characters in a given size, type style, and design?

5) _______________________________

6. To duplicate highlighted data in a document into the Clipboard.

6) _______________________________

7. What aspect of characters is changed by changing points?

7) _______________________________

8. What procedure reverses the color on a portion of text, thereby selecting it (also called reverse video)?

8) _______________________________

9 To copy data from the Clipboard into a document.

9) _______________________________

WORKSHEET 26

WRITE <u>TASKS</u>

NAME _______________________

DIRECTIONS: Match the tasks listed below to the definition that best fits the task.

start Write	change margins	save a document
Write menus	open a document	print a document
change fonts	edit a document	change text alignment
create a document		

---

1. To adjust the width of the left, right, top, and bottom borders around text on a page.

   1) _______________________

2. To retrieve a saved document file from a disk, bringing it into the Write program.

   2) _______________________

3. The menus showing on the menu bar, some of which are similar to other Windows menus and others that are specific to Write.

   3) _______________________

4. To change a line (or paragraph) of text so that (a) the text is <u>centered</u> between the margins; or (b) all lines start at the <u>left</u> margin; or (c) all lines end at the <u>right</u> margin; or (d) the text is <u>justified</u> (having flush left and right margins).

   4) _______________________

5. To transfer the information in the Write program to a disk (a permanent storage area).

   5) _______________________

6. To choose characters in a different typeface and/or a different type style and/or a different size.

   6) _______________________

7. To copy information from a document in the Write program onto paper.

   7) _______________________

8. To use Windows to run the Write program.

   8) _______________________

9. To change the content (words) of a document by inserting, deleting, moving, and copying text.

   9) _______________________

10. To type text in the Write window's workspace.

    10) _______________________

(This page may be copied.)

Lesson Five — Paintbrush

Table of Contents

EXERCISE 58
Start Paintbrush

Exercises 58-61 should be done during the same session.

start Paintbrush
To use Windows to run the Paintbrush program.

Paintbrush
Paintbrush is Windows' drawing program. Paintbrush uses many of the same features as Windows, such as a similar menu bar, dialog boxes, file commands, and window control elements.

toolbox
The toolbox holds tools that are used to create drawings.

linesize box
The linesize box holds lines of varying widths from which drawing widths can be selected.

palette
The palette holds colors and patterns that may be used in the background of the drawing area and with the drawing tools.

drawing area
The area where you create drawings.

Keyboard Users
START PAINTBRUSH

1. Press **Ctrl** + **Tab** until the Accessories icon name is highlighted.
2. Press **↵**
3. Press arrow keys until Paintbrush's icon name is highlighted.
4. Press **↵**

IMPORTANT: When **clicking** the mouse, always use the <u>left</u> mouse button <u>unless otherwise instructed</u>.

1 **Start Windows**, if necessary.

FROM THE *STARTING WINDOWS* SCREEN:

2 **Open** the **Accessories** window.

3 **Double-click** on .

The *Paintbrush* window appears:

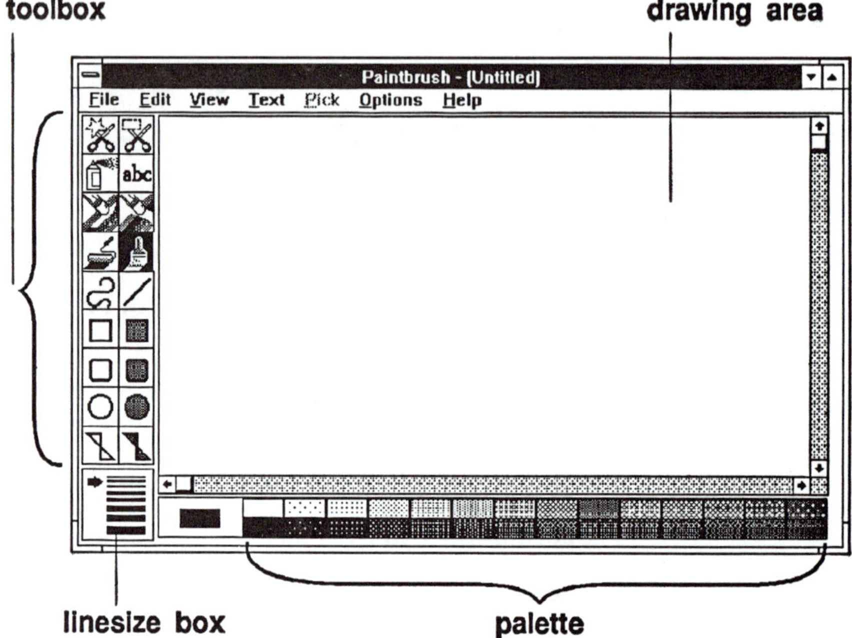

*NOTE: The name in the title bar is **Paintbrush - [Untitled]**. When a document has a filename (i.e., it is saved or opened), [Untitled] will change to reflect that document's filename.*

4 **Maximize Paintbrush.**

Go on to Exercise 59

① LOOK AT EACH DROP-DOWN MENU:

- **Click** on **F**ile.
- **Click** on **E**dit.
- **Click** on **V**iew.
- **Click** on **T**ext.
- **Click** on **P**ick.

  *NOTE: No drop-down menu will appear for **Pick**. Something (i.e., a drawing) must be <u>selected</u> before the **Pick** menu can be accessed.*

- **Click** on **O**ptions.
- **Click** on **H**elp.

Each **drop-down** menu is shown below:

File
New	
Open...	
Save	Ctrl+S
Save As...	
Page Setup...	
Print...	
Print Setup...	
Exit	

Edit
Undo	Ctrl+Z
Cut	Ctrl+X
Copy	Ctrl+C
Paste	Ctrl+V
Copy To...	
Paste From...	

View
Zoom In	Ctrl+N
Zoom Out	Ctrl+O
View Picture	Ctrl+P
√ Tools and Linesize	
√ Palette	
Cursor Position	

Text
√ Regular	
Bold	Ctrl+B
Italic	Ctrl+I
Underline	Ctrl+U
Outline	
Shadow	
Fonts...	

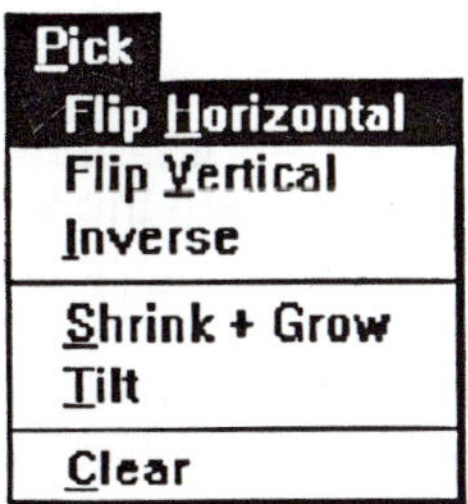

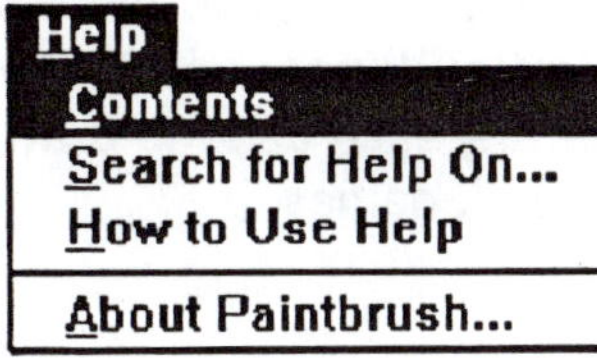

② **Click off** of the menus to cancel any menu that may still be open.

Go on to Exercise 60

EXERCISE 59
Paintbrush Menus

Continue from Exercise 58, doing Exercises 58-61 during the same session.

Paintbrush menus

The menus displayed on the menu bar, some of which are similar to other Windows menus (such as File and Help) and others that are specific to Paintbrush.

Keyboard Users

PAINTBRUSH MENUS

OPEN AND CLOSE MENUS:

1. Press **Alt** + **F** (to open **F**ile)
2. Press **Alt** (to close **F**ile)
3. Repeat steps 1 and 2, replacing **F** with the underlined letter of each of the other menus.
4. Press **Alt** to return to the drawing area.

EXERCISE 60
Paintbrush Tools

Continue from Exercise 59, doing Exercises 58-61 during the same session.

Paintbrush tools
The various tools found in the toolbox that are used to create a drawing.

types of tools

two <u>cutout</u> tools
(Scissors & Pick)

two <u>free-form</u> drawing tools
(Airbrush & Brush)

one <u>fill</u> tool
(Paint Roller)

two <u>erasing</u> tools
(Color Eraser & Eraser)

one <u>text</u> tool
(Text tool)

two <u>line</u> drawing tools
(Curve & Line)

eight <u>shape</u> drawing tools
(Box, Rounded Box, Circle/Ellipse, Polygon, Filled Box, Filled Rounded Box, Filled Circle/Ellipse, and Filled Polygon)

Keyboard Users

PAINTBRUSH TOOLS

SELECT A TOOL:

1. **Press Tab** until the pointer moves to the *toolbox*.
2. **Press** arrow keys to move the pointer to the desired tool.
3. **Press Ins** to *select* the tool.

---

*NOTE: When you first start **Paintbrush**, the <u>selected</u> drawing tool is **Brush**.*

1 **Click** on the desired tool to **select** it.

Toolbox tools

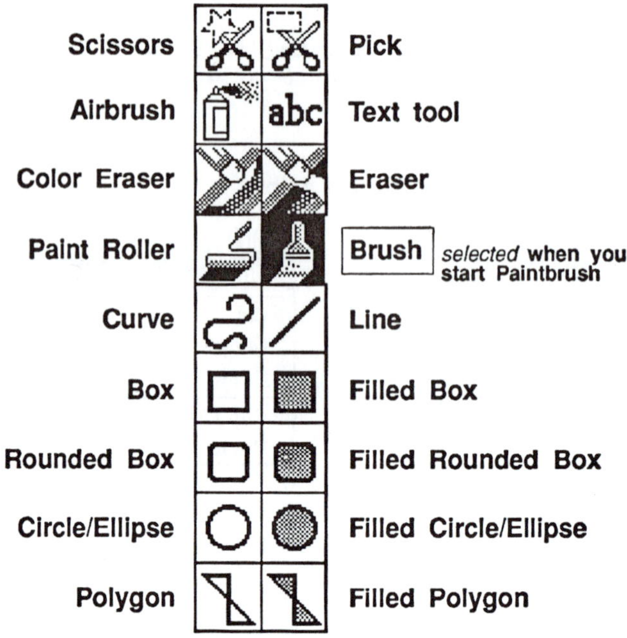

Scissors is a <u>free-form cutout</u> tool.

Pick is a <u>rectangular cutout</u> tool.

Airbrush is a <u>free-form drawing</u> tool which produces a circular spray of dots.

Text tool lets you <u>type</u> text in the drawing area.

Color Eraser lets you change color in all or part of your drawing.

Eraser erases the portions of the drawing that it touches.

Paint Roller lets you <u>fill</u> any closed shape or area with the foreground color.

Brush is used to draw <u>free-form</u> shapes and lines that are the width of the selected line.

Curve is used to draw curved <u>lines</u> in the width of the selected line.

Line is used to draw straight <u>lines</u> that are the width of the selected line.

Box, **Rounded Box**, **Circle/Ellipse**, and **Polygon** are each used to draw the hollow <u>shape</u> it names.

Filled Box, **Filled Rounded Box**, **Filled Circle/Ellipse**, and **Filled Polygon** are each used to draw the solid <u>shape</u> it names.

Go on to Exercise 61

PAINTBRUSH LINESIZE BOX

*NOTE: When you first start **Paintbrush**, the selected line is the top line (the narrowest line).*

NOTE: The width of the selected line determines the width of the line used by the various drawing tools.

1 **Click** on the desired line to **select** it.

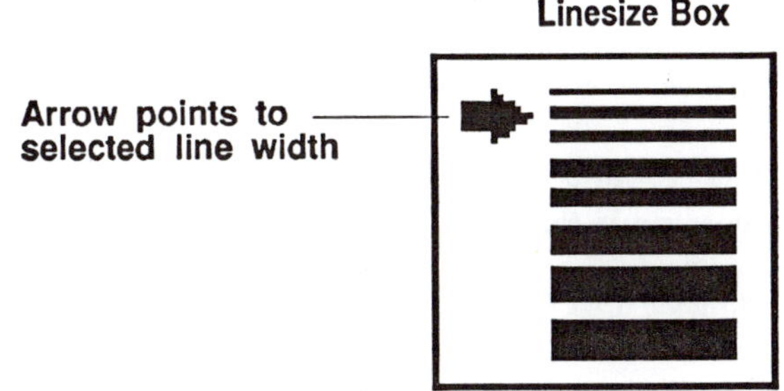

PAINTBRUSH PALETTE

*NOTES: When you first start **Paintbrush**, the selected foreground color is black, and the selected background color is white.*
*The **selected** foreground color determines the color or pattern used by the drawing tools.*
If your monitor is monochrome, the palette will display black-and-white patterns. If your monitor is color, the palette will display colors. Color monitors can be changed to display black-and-white by selecting Options, Image Attributes..., Colors, Black and White.

Palette

selected foreground color/pattern
selected background color/pattern

2 **Click** on the desired *foreground* color or pattern using the *left* mouse button.

3 **Click** on the desired *background* color or pattern using the *right* mouse button.

4 **Exit Paintbrush.**
IF there is any change to the Paintbrush drawing area, a dialog box appears that asks: Do you want to save current changes?
- **Click** on [No].

5 Go on to Exercise 62.
OR
Exit Windows.

Continue from Exercise 60, doing Exercises 58-61 during the same session.

Paintbrush linesize box
The box in the bottom left corner of the Paintbrush window that displays line widths available to draw with.

Paintbrush palette
The box across the bottom of the Paintbrush window that displays colors and patterns that may be selected for background or drawing.

background color or pattern
The color or pattern used to cover the drawing area before creating a drawing.

foreground color or pattern
The color or pattern used by the tools to draw with and fill areas.

Keyboard Users
PAINTBRUSH LINESIZE BOX AND PALETTE

SELECT A LINE WIDTH:
1. **Press** [Tab] until the pointer moves to the *linesize box*.
2. **Press** [↓] and [↑] to select the desired line width.
3. **Press** [Ins] to *select* the line.

SELECT COLOR:
1. **Press** [Tab] until the pointer moves to the *palette*.
2. **Press** arrow keys to select the desired color or pattern.
3.
   - **Press** [Ins] to *select* foreground color.

   OR

   - **Press** [Del] to *select* background color.

EXERCISE 62
Create a Drawing

Exercises 62-64 should be done during the same session.

create a drawing
To use the drawing tools to make images in the drawing area.

new
The <u>new</u> file option clears the screen (i.e., opens a <u>new</u>, blank drawing area).

Keyboard directions to CLEAR THE SCREEN are on page 158.

Keyboard Users

CREATE A DRAWING
SELECT A TOOL:
  See page 154.
SELECT A LINE WIDTH:
  See page 155.
SELECT A FOREGROUND COLOR:
  See page 155.
SELECT A BACKGROUND COLOR:
  See page 155.

USE KEYBOARD TO DRAW:
1. **Press** **Tab** until the pointer appears in the drawing area.
2. **Use** **←**, **→**, **↑**, and **↓** to move the pointer to the desired location.
3. **Use** the keys listed below on the left to replace the mouse actions on the right.

<u>Keyboard</u>	<u>Mouse Action</u>
Ins	Click <u>left</u> mouse button.
Del	Click <u>right</u> mouse button.
F9 + **Ins**	Double-click <u>left</u> mouse button.
F9 + **Del**	Double-click <u>right</u> mouse button.
Ins + an arrow key	Drag the pointer in direction of arrow key.

1
- **Start Windows**, if necessary.
- **Open** the **Accessories** window.
- **Start Paintbrush.**
- **Maximize Paintbrush.**

NOTE: The pointer is a small dot when it is in the drawing area.

2 **Move** the pointer around on the drawing area without pressing the mouse buttons.

NOTE: When you use the mouse to position the pointer, it does <u>not</u> leave a mark in the drawing area.

3 **Drag** the pointer around on the screen, holding down the left mouse button <u>while</u> you move the mouse.

NOTE: When you hold down the <u>left</u> mouse button while you slide the mouse, it draws in the drawing area.

4 **Move** and **drag** the pointer around in the drawing area to create a drawing.

5 CLEAR THE SCREEN (OPEN A <u>NEW</u> DRAWING):
- **Click** on **File.**
- **Click** on **New.**
- **Click** on [No] (you do not want to save the drawing).

NOTE: The drawing will be erased and cannot be retrieved.

6 **Draw** your own picture with the brush tool.

7 USE THE TEXT TOOL:
- **Click** on [abc] (text tool).
- **Click** on **Text.**
- **Click** on **Fonts... .**
- **Select Arial** Font.
- **Select Bold** Font Style.
- **Select Size 24.**
- **Click** on [OK].
- **Click** the *insertion point* in the top left corner of the *drawing area*.
- **Type** your name.

8 **Clear** the screen (step 5 above).

9
- **Click** on [brush] (brush tool).
- **Draw** another picture with the brush tool.

10
- **Click** on [abc] (text tool).
- **Click** on **Text**, and then **Fonts... .**
- **Select** a **Font, Font Style**, and **Size** of your choice.
- **Click** on [OK].
- **Type** something in the drawing area.

11
- **Clear** the screen (step 5 above).
- **Click** on [brush] (brush tool).

Go on to Exercise 63

IMPORTANT: This book instructs you to save your files on Drive A: (or B:). Continue using the disk on which you saved files during the Write exercises.

1 **Draw** a picture using the brush tool.

2 PUT YOUR NAME ON THE DRAWING:
- **Click** on abc (text tool).
- **Click** on **Text**, and then **Fonts....**
- **Select** Arial **Font**, bold **Font Style**, and **Size** 36.
- **Click** on [OK].
- **Click** an **insertion point** in the top left corner of the drawing area.
- **Type** your name.

3 SAVE A NEW DRAWING ON DRIVE A: (OR B:):
- **Place** your disk in Drive A: (or B:) and close the door, if necessary.
- **Click** on **File**.
- **Click** on **Save As...** .
  The *Save As* dialog box appears:

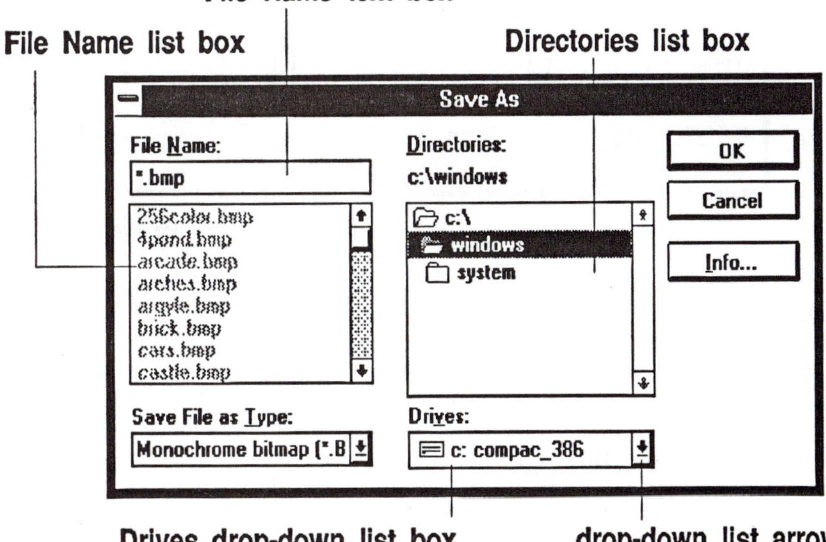

- **Click** on the **down arrow** for the **Drives** drop-down list box.
- **Click** on a: (or b:).
- **Click** on the **File Name** text box.
- **Type:** DRAW1
- **Click** on [OK].

NOTE: Paintbrush adds the three-letter filename extension .BMP (stands for bitmap). See "File Manager," page 27, for an explanation of file terms.

4
- **Click** on (brush tool).
- **Draw** something else on the drawing.

5 RESAVE A DRAWING:
- **Click** on **File**.
- **Click** on **Save**.

Go on to Exercise 64

EXERCISE 63
Save a Drawing

Continue from Exercise 62, doing Exercises 62-64 during the same session.

save a drawing
To store a drawing in the Paintbrush program on a disk.

save
Saves changes to a previously named drawing that you are working on.

save as...
Saves new drawings or lets you rename a previously saved drawing.

file
A file is a <u>set of data</u> that is saved on a disk as a <u>named</u> unit.

drop-down list box
A box that is similar to a <u>list box</u> except that it must be opened by clicking on the drop-down list arrow next to it.

Keyboard Users
SAVE A DRAWING

SAVE NEW DRAWING OR RENAME FILE:
1. **Press** Alt + F (**File**)
2. **Press** A (Save As...)
   IF you want to change the drive:
   - **Press** Alt + V (Dri**v**e)
   - **Press** ↓
   - Use arrows to highlight the desired drive.
   - **Press** ↵
3. **Press** Alt + N (File **N**ame)
4. Type a filename.
5. **Press** ↵

SAVE PREVIOUSLY NAMED DRAWING:
1. **Press** Alt + F (**File**)
2. **Press** (**S**ave)

EXERCISE 64
Open a Drawing

Continue from Exercise 63, doing Exercises 62-64 during the same session.

open a drawing
To retrieve a saved drawing from a disk into the Paintbrush program.

Keyboard Users

OPEN A DRAWING

CLEAR THE SCREEN:

1. Press **Alt** + **F** (Eile)
2. Press **N** (New)

   IF unsaved data is present, a message asks if you want to "Save current changes?"

   - **Press N** (No)

   OR

   - **Press Y** (Yes)
   - Type a filename.
   - **Press** ↵

OPEN A DRAWING:

1. Press **Alt** + **F** (Eile)
2. Press **O** (Open)

   IF you want to change the drive:

   - Press **Alt** + **V** (Drive)
   - Press ↓
   - Use arrows to highlight the desired drive.
   - Press ↵

3. Press **Alt** + **N** (File Name)

   - Type a filename.
   - **Press** ↵

   OR

   - **Press Tab**
   - Use arrows to highlight desired file.
   - **Press** ↵

---

1 Clear the screen (review, page 156, step 5).

2 Exit Paintbrush.

3 Open Paintbrush.

4 OPEN A DRAWING FILE:

IMPORTANT: Because you have exited Paintbrush since the last time you accessed the disk drive, the default drive has changed back to Drive C:. Each time you start Paintbrush, you must change to Drive A: (or B:) if you are going to **save** and **open** files on that drive. This is most conveniently done the first time you **save** or **open** a drawing file.

- **Click** on **File.**
- **Click** on **Open.**

  The *Open* dialog box appears:

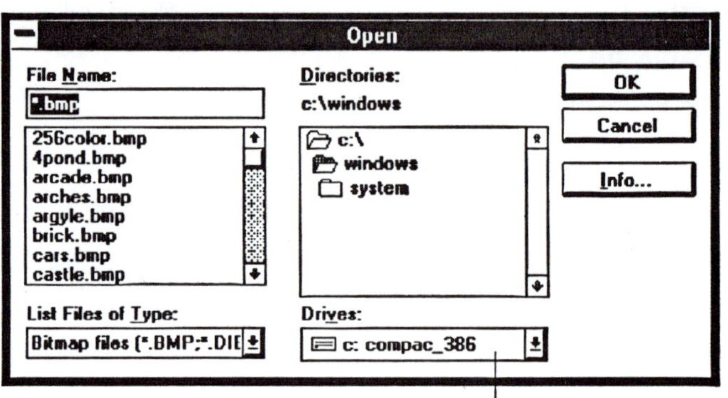

Drives drop-down list box

- **Click** on the **Drives** drop-down list box.
- **Click** on a: (or b:).
- - **Double-click** on **draw1.bmp.**

  OR

  - **Click** on **draw1.bmp.**
  - **Click** on | OK |.

5 Clear the screen.

6 CREATE A NEW DRAWING:

- **Click** on (airbrush tool).
  The pointer becomes ⊥ (a crosshair) when it is in the drawing area.
- **Draw** a picture with airbrush.

7 Save the drawing using **Save As...**; name it DRAW2.

8 Exit Paintbrush.

9 Go on to Exercise 65.

   OR

   Exit Windows.

1
- **Start Windows** and **Open Accessories,** if necessary.
- **Start** and **maximize Paintbrush.**

2 **Open** the file **DRAW1.BMP** (review, page 158).

*NOTES: Always be sure to close the disk drive door after you put the disk in it. If you do not, you will get an error message saying: Cannot read drive a:... . **IF** this happens, close the door and • click on **Retry**.*

*   **IF** you have made any changes in Paintbrush's drawing area, you will get a message that asks: Do you want to save current changes? • **Click on No,** and Paintbrush will continue to process your original command.*

3 PRINT A DRAWING:
- **Make** sure your printer is ready to receive data.
- **Click** on **File.**
- **Click** on **Print.**
- **Click** on [OK].

RESULT — **DRAW1**

Your drawing will be different.

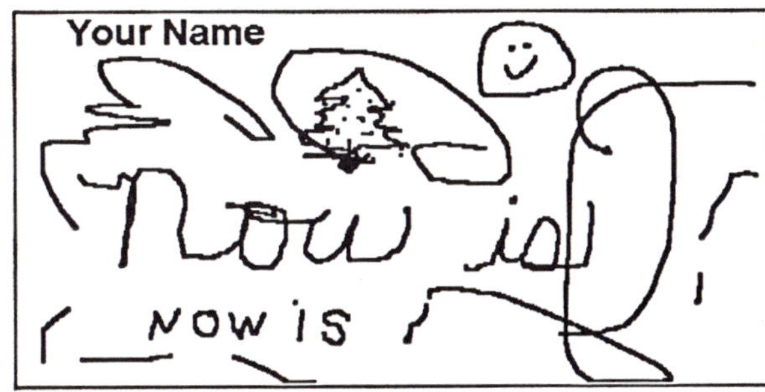

4 **Open** the file **DRAW2.BMP** (review, page 158).

5 PRINT AND SCALE A DRAWING:
- **Make** sure your printer is ready to receive data.
- **Click** on **File.**
- **Click** on **Print.**
- **Click** on the **Scaling** *text box.*
- **Delete** 100 and **type** 50.
- **Click** on [OK].

RESULT — **DRAW2**

Your drawing will be different. Notice that it prints at 50% of its original size.

6 **Exit Paintbrush.**

7 Go on to Exercise 66.

OR

 Exit Windows.

EXERCISE 65
Print a Drawing

<u>ASSUMPTION:</u>

It is assumed that your printer has been properly installed and will print graphics.

print a drawing
To transfer a drawing in the Paintbrush program onto paper.

Keyboard Users
PRINT A DRAWING
1. Press **Alt** + **F** (*F*ile)
2. Press **P** (*P*rint)
3. Make sure your printer is ready to receive data.
4. Press ↵

PRINT AND SCALE A DRAWING:
1. Press **Alt** + **F** (*F*ile)
2. Press **P** (*P*rint)
3. Press **Tab** until the *S*caling *text box* is highlighted.
4. **Delete** the 100.
5. **Type** the desired value.
6. Make sure your printer is ready to receive data.
7. Press ↵

EXERCISE 66
Use Line Tools

Exercises 66-68 should be done during the same session.

use line tools
To draw with the <u>curve</u> and <u>line</u> tools.

1
- **Start Windows** and **Open Accessories**, if necessary.
- **Start** and **maximize Paintbrush.**

2 USE CURVED LINE:
- **Click** on ▢ (curve tool).
- **Draw** a line across the drawing area one third of the way from the top.

Example:

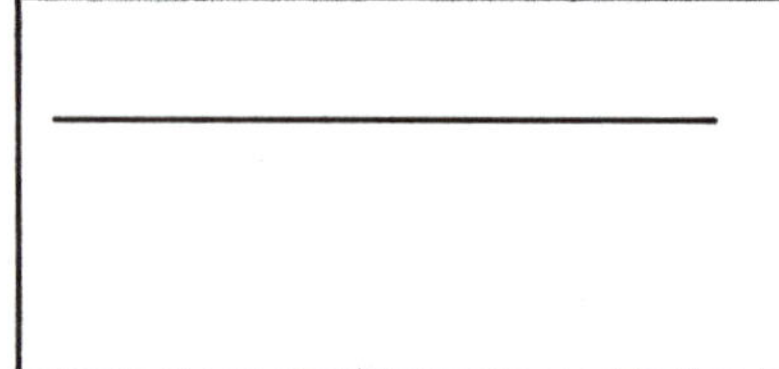

- **Click** once at the center top of the drawing area.
- **Click** once at the center bottom of the drawing area.

Example:

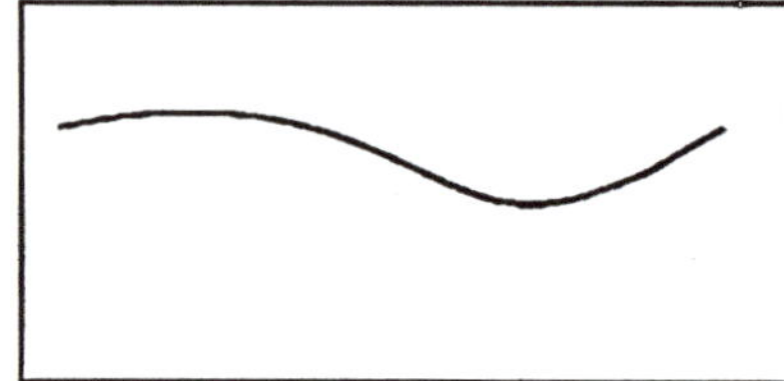

3 CHANGE LINE WIDTH:
- **Click** on the **bottom line** in the **linesize box** (located in the bottom left corner of the screen).

4
- **Draw** a line about an inch below the first line.
- **Click** once at the center top of the drawing area.
- **Click** once at the center bottom of the drawing area.

5 USE LINES:
- **Click** on ▢ (line tool).
  To **draw** a line, **move** the pointer to the starting point, **drag** the pointer to the ending point, and then release the button.
- **Draw** lines to match the illustration below.

RESULT — **LINES**

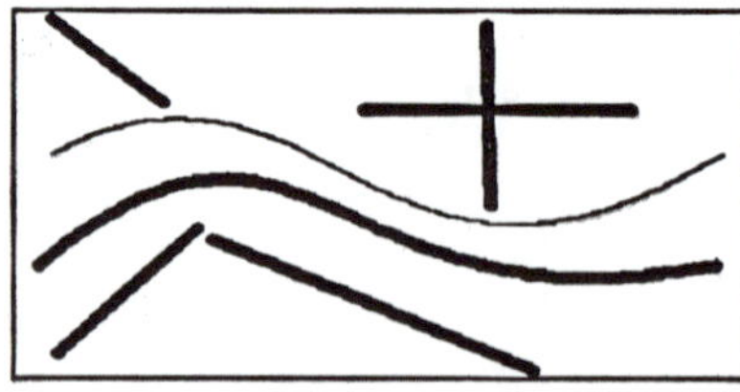

6
- **Print** the drawing.
- **Clear** the screen (review, page 56, step 5).

*NOTE: Because Paintbrush files use very large amounts of disk space, you are not instructed to **save** any more drawings in this lesson.*

Keyboard Users

USE LINE TOOLS
SELECT A TOOL:
  See page 154.
USE KEYBOARD TO DRAW:
  See page 156.

Go on to Exercise 67

① **Click** on the next-to-top line width in the line size box.

② USE BOX AND FILLED BOX:
- **Click** on ▢ (box tool).
- **Draw** a rectangle at the location shown in the illustration below (start in the top left corner and **drag** the pointer diagonally down and right).
- **Draw** a <u>square</u> box under the rectangle as shown below:
  - Move the pointer just under the rectangle.
  - **Press** and **hold** **Shift** <u>while</u> you **drag** the pointer in any direction.
- **Click** on ▣ (filled box tool).
- Repeat steps above to create filled boxes as shown below.

③ USE ROUNDED BOX AND FILLED ROUNDED BOX:
- **Click** on ▢ (rounded box tool).
- **Draw** a rectangular *rounded box* as shown below.
- **Draw** a <u>square</u> *rounded box* as shown below.
- **Click** on ▣ (*filled rounded box tool*).
- **Draw** a rectangular *filled rounded box* as shown below.
- **Draw** a <u>square</u> *filled rounded box* as shown below.

④ USE CIRCLE/ELLIPSE AND FILLED CIRCLE/ELLIPSE:
- **Click** on ◯ (circle/ellipse tool).
- **Draw** an *ellipse* as shown below.
- **Draw** a <u>circle</u> as shown below.
- **Click** on ▣ (filled rounded box tool).
- **Draw** a *filled ellipse* as shown below.
- **Draw** a *filled <u>circle</u>* as shown below.

⑤ USE POLYGON AND FILLED POLYGON:
- **Click** on ◹ (polygon tool).
- **Draw** a triangle:
  - **Draw** the first line.
  - **Click** on a point about an inch away from the line.
  - **Click** at the beginning of the line.
  - *NOTE: The final **click** must be at the very <u>start</u> of the <u>first</u> line.*
- **Click** on ◤ (filled polygon tool).
- **Draw** the polygon in the bottom right corner:
  - **Draw** the first line as shown here.
  - **Click** at 1, **click** at 2, and **click** at 3.

RESULT — **SHAPES**

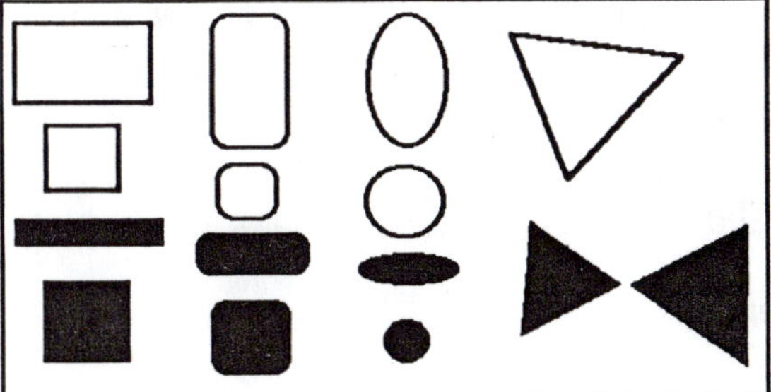

⑥ **Print** the drawing (review, page 159).

Go on to Exercise 68

EXERCISE 67
Use Shape Tools

Continue from Exercise 66, doing Exercises 66-68 during the same session.

NOTE: In this exercise you will make a drawing similar to the one at the bottom of the page. You do not need to match it exactly.

use shape tools
To draw with tools which create geometric shapes: the box, rounded box, circle/ellipse, polygon, and the <u>filled</u> box, <u>filled</u> rounded box, <u>filled</u> circle/ellipse, and <u>filled</u> polygon.

draw precise circles, squares, and rounded squares
- **Select** desired **shape** tool.
- **Press** and **hold** **Shift** <u>while</u> you **drag** the pointer in the desired direction.

Keyboard Users
USE SHAPE TOOLS
SELECT A TOOL:
  See page 154.
USE KEYBOARD TO DRAW:
  See page 156.

EXERCISE 68
Use Erase and Undo

Continue from Exercise 67, doing Exercises 66-68 during the same session.

use erase

The erase tool changes the foreground color that it touches to the selected background color, thus erasing the image.

use undo

The undo command will erase the changes that have been made in the drawing area since the last time you selected a new tool (or used a scroll bar, switched to another application, or resized the window).

Keyboard Users

USE ERASE AND UNDO

SELECT ERASE:

   See page 154.

USE KEYBOARD TO DRAW (OR ERASE):

   See page 156.

UNDO:

1. Press **Alt** + **E** (**E**dit)
2. Press **U** (**U**ndo)

---

①
- **Clear** the screen.
- **Click** on ☐ (box tool).
- **Draw** a **rectangle** in the center of the screen.
- **Click** on ◯ (circle/ellipse tool).
- **Draw** a **circle** inside the rectangle.
  The drawing area should look something like this:

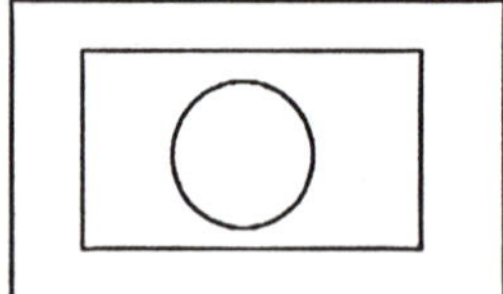

② USE UNDO:
- **Click** on **Edit**, and then **click** on **Undo**.
  The circle disappears.
  NOTE: Undo erases all the changes that have been made since the last time you selected a tool (in this case, the circle/ellipse tool).
- **Click** on **Edit**, and then **click** on **Undo**, again.
  The circle reappears.
- **Click** on 🖌 (brush tool).
- **Click** on **Edit**, and then **click** on **Undo**, again.
  Nothing happens.
  NOTE: When you select a new tool, the drawing becomes "set" and undo has no effect.

③ USE ERASE:
- **Click** on 🧹 (erase tool).
  The pointer shape changes to a small box when it is in the drawing area.
- **Drag** the box pointer across the top line of the rectangle to erase it.
- **Click** on **Edit**, and then **click** on **Undo**.
  The top line reappears.
- **Press** and **hold** **Shift** while you **drag** the eraser across the top line of the rectangle again.
  *NOTE: Holding **Shift** while you **drag** the eraser keeps the eraser moving in a straight line.*

④
- **Click** on 🖌 (brush tool).
- **Create** a drawing of your choice using the brush tool.
  - At some point, **press** **Shift** while you **draw** with the **brush** tool (to create a straight line).
- **Click** on the **bottom line** in the **linesize box**.
- **Click** on 🧹 (erase tool).
  The pointer shape changes to a **large** box when it is in the drawing area.
- **Erase** the drawing as desired.

⑤ **Clear** the screen.

⑥ **Exit Paintbrush.**

⑦
   Go on to Exercise 69.

OR

   Exit Windows.

1
- **Start Windows**, if necessary.
- **Start** and **maximize Paintbrush**.

2 CREATE A DRAWING:
- **Select** the next-to-top line width (review page 155).
- **Click** on ☐ (box tool).
- **Draw a square** with about 1" sides in the top left corner of the screen.
  NOTE: Remember to press **Shift** *while you drag the cursor to make precise squares and circles.*
- **Click** on ⃝ (circle/ellipse tool).
- **Draw an exact circle** about ½" in diameter below the square.

3 DEFINE A CUTOUT USING THE PICK TOOL:
- **Click** on ▧ (pick tool).
  NOTE: Do not confuse the pick tool ▧ *with the* **Pick** *menu option.*
- **Position** the pointer <u>above</u> and to the <u>left</u> of the circle.
- **Drag** the pointer right and down until the circle is surrounded by a dashed line.
  NOTE: If the entire circle is not defined repeat the procedure.

4 ANCHOR A CUTOUT (REMOVE DASHED BORDER):

- **Click** anywhere in the drawing area outside the *defined* cutout.

OR

- **Drag** the pointer as desired to *define* a new cutout.

OR

- **Select** a new tool.

5 **Define** the circle as a **cutout** again (step 3).

6 MOVE A CUTOUT:
- **Position** the pointer *inside* the defined cutout area.
- **Drag** the cutout until the **circle** is in about the middle of the **square**.

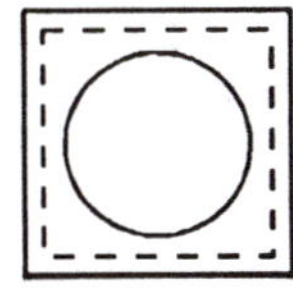

- **Anchor** the circle (step 4).

7 CUT A CUTOUT:
- **Use** the **pick** tool to *define* the square.
- **Click** on **Edit**, then on **Cut**.
  NOTE: The cutout is moved from the drawing area to the clipboard when it is cut.

Continue Exercise 69 on the next page

EXERCISE 69
Use Cutout Tools

use cutout tools
To use <u>scissors</u> or <u>pick</u> to <u>define</u> an area. You can perform the following actions on a cutout:

Move	Copy to (save)
Cut	Paste from (retrieve)
Copy	Sweep (transparent)
Paste	Sweep (opaque)
Flip	Shrink and enlarge
Tilt	Invert

cutout
A portion of the drawing area <u>defined</u> by a dashed-line border surrounding it. Using **scissors** creates a line with short dashes, while using **pick** creates a line with longer dashes.

scissors
Scissors is a free-form cutout tool used to define an <u>irregular</u> cutout area.

pick
Pick is a rectangular cutout tool that is used to define a <u>rectangular</u> cutout area.

NOTE: When the <u>cut</u> menu option is used, the cutout is erased from the drawing area and placed in the clipboard.

Keyboard Users
USE CUTOUT TOOLS

Use cutout tools to define an area, then use shortcut keys to perform these actions:

<u>Action</u>	<u>Shortcut keys</u>
Cut	**Ctrl** + **X**
Copy	**Ctrl** + **C**
Paste	**Ctrl** + **V**

EXERCISE 69 (continued)

USE CUTOUT TOOLS

*NOTE: When the <u>Paste</u> menu option
is used, the last cutout that
was either cut or copied is
<u>copied from the clipboard to
the top left corner of the
drawing area</u>.*

*NOTE: When the <u>Copy to...</u> option is
used, the cutout is <u>saved</u> to
the disk and can be <u>retrieved</u>
from the disk when desired.*

*NOTE: When the <u>Copy</u> option is used,
the cutout is placed in the
Clipboard.*

*NOTE: The <u>Clipboard</u> is a temporary
storage area that can hold
only one cutout. When a new
cutout is cut or copied to the
Clipboard, the previous cutout
is erased.*

Exercise 69 (continued)

8 PASTE A CUTOUT:

- **Click** on **Edit**, then on **Paste**.
  The cutout appears in the top left corner of the drawing area with a
  dashed box around it:

  *NOTE: The **pick tool** is automatically selected when you paste a cutout.*
- **Move** the cutout to the top right corner of the drawing area (step 6).

9 SAVE A CUTOUT:

With the cutout still defined (a dashed box around it):

- **Click** on **Edit**, then on **Copy To... .**
- **Change** the Drive to **A:** (or B:) (review, page 157).
- **Click** on the **File Name** *text box*.
- **Delete** the text in the text box.
- **Type:** cut
- **Click** on [OK].

10 COPY A CUTOUT:

With the cutout still defined (a dashed box around it):

- **Click** on **Edit**, then on **Copy**.
  NOTE: The cutout does <u>not</u> disappear from the drawing area when it is <u>copied</u>.

11
- **Paste** the **cutout** (step 8).
- **Move** the **cutout** to the bottom right corner of the drawing **area**.
- **Paste** the **cutout** again.
- **Move** the **cutout** to the bottom left corner of the drawing **area**.
- **Paste** the **cutout** again.
- **Move** the **cutout** to the center of the drawing area.
- **Paste** the **cutout** again.
- **Move** the **cutout** to the top left corner of the drawing area.
  The drawing should look similar to this:
  RESULT – **CUTOUT**

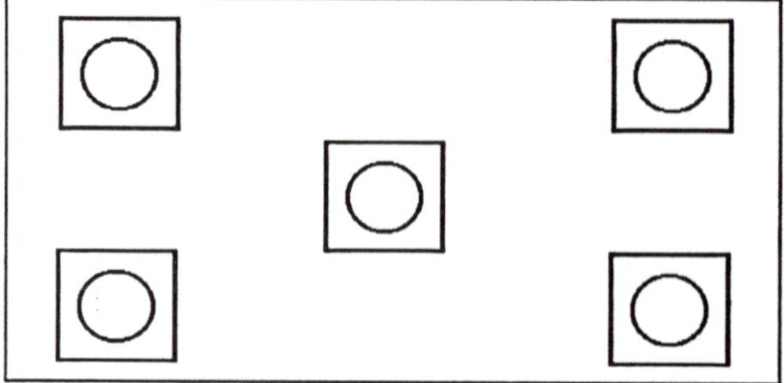

12
- **Print** the drawing (review, page 159).
- **Clear** the screen.

Continue Exercise 69 on the next page

 **SWEEP A CUTOUT (TRANSPARENT):**

- **Select** the top (narrowest) line width (review, page 155).
- **Click** on ◯ (circle/ellipse tool).
- **Draw** a precise **circle** about ½" in diameter in the top left corner of the drawing area.
- **Define** the **circle** as a cutout using the **pick** tool.
- **Press** and **hold** **Shift** while you **drag** the cutout around on the screen, using the left mouse button.

  Your drawing may look something like this:

  RESULT — **TRANSPAR**

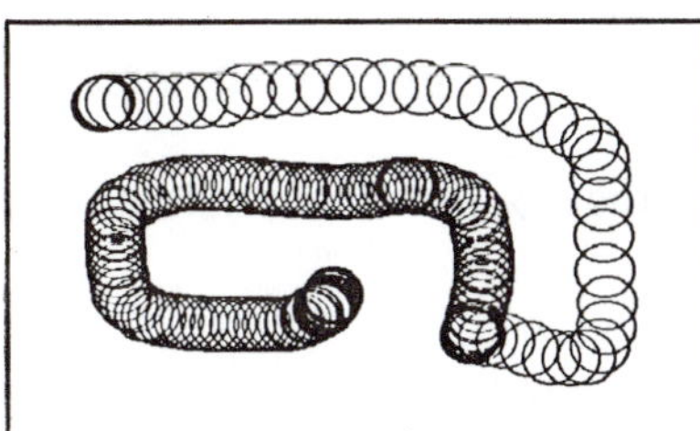

- **Print** the drawing, then **clear** the screen.

 **SWEEP A CUTOUT (OPAQUE):**

- **Click** on ▫ (box tool).
- **Draw a square** with about 1"-long sides in the top left corner of the screen.
- **Define** the **square** as a cutout using the **pick** tool. <u>Keep the dashed lines as close as possible to the square.</u>
- **Press** and **hold** **Shift** while you **drag** the cutout around on the screen, using the right mouse button.

  Your drawing may look something like this:

  RESULT — **OPAQUE**

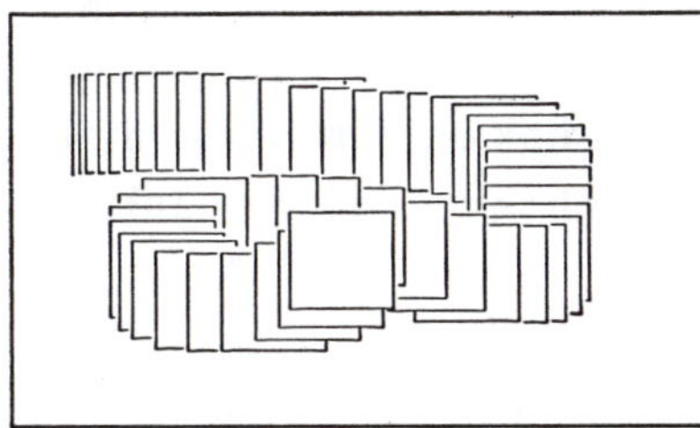

- **Print** the drawing, then **clear** the screen.

- **Click** on <u>T</u>ext, then on <u>F</u>onts... .
- **Select Arial** Font, **Bold** Font Style, and **Size 72**.
- **Click** on [OK].
- **Click** on abc (text tool).
- **Click** the *insertion point* toward the bottom and slightly left of the center in the drawing area.
- **Type:** `Tilt`
- **Use** ✄ (pick tool) to **define** a box around the word.

Continue Exercise 69 on the next page

Exercise 69 (continued)

The drawing area should look something like this:

16 TILT A CUTOUT:

- **Click** on **Pick** (on the menu bar).
- **Click** on **Clear** (to select it).
- **Click** on **Pick** again.
- **Click** on **Tilt** (to select it).
- **Position** the pointer just <u>above</u> the top and just <u>left</u> of the left side of the word.
- **Drag** the pointer about ¼ inch to the left, and **release** the mouse button.
- **Click** on **Pick** again.
- **Click** on **Tilt** (to deselect it).
- **Click** outside the cutout (to anchor it).

  The drawing area should look something like this:

*NOTE: When you <u>select</u> the **Clear** and **Tilt** options from the **Pick** menu, they stay selected until you either <u>deselect</u> them or <u>exit</u> Paintbrush.*

17
- **Use** (pick tool) to **define** a box around the word.
- **Copy** the cutout (step 10).

*NOTE: When you <u>choose</u> the **Flip Horizontal** or **Flip Vertical** option from the **Pick** menu, it <u>does not</u> stay selected.*

18 FLIP A CUTOUT:

With the word still defined:

- **Click** on **Pick**, and **click** on **Flip Horizontal**.
  Oops! You do not want to flip horizontally.
- **Click** on **Pick**, and **click** on **Flip Horizontal** again.
- **Click** on **Pick**, and **click** on **Flip Vertical**.

19
- **Paste** the **cutout** (step 8).
- **Move** the **cutout** until it is directly above the *flipped* word.
- **Click** outside the **cutout** (to anchor it).

  The drawing area should look something like this:

*NOTE: When you <u>select</u> the **Shrink & Grow** option from the **Pick** menu, it stays selected until you either <u>deselect</u> it or <u>exit</u> Paintbrush.*

20 SHRINK AND ENLARGE A CUTOUT:

- **Use** (pick tool) to **define** a box around the two words.
- **Click** on **Pick** (on the menu bar).
  NOTE: Clear should still be selected (✓ by it).

Continue Exercise 69, step 20 on the next page

166

- **Click** on <u>S</u>hrink + Grow.
- Starting close to the top left corner of the drawing area, **drag** the **pointer** <u>down</u> and <u>right</u> to create a rectangle about 1 inch square, and release the mouse button. The image is *reduced* in size and *moved* to the new location.
- Starting close to the top left corner of the drawing area, **drag** the **pointer** down and right to create a rectangle about 4 inches wide and 2 inches high, and release the mouse button.
  NOTE: You can <u>stretch</u> cutouts as well as <u>shrink and grow</u> them using the shrink + grow feature.
- **Click** on **<u>P</u>ick,** and **click** on **<u>S</u>hrink + Grow** (to deselect it).
- **Click** outside the cutout (to deselect it).

㉑ RETRIEVE A CUTOUT:
- **Click** on **<u>E</u>dit.**
- **Click** on **Paste <u>F</u>rom.**
- **Double-click** on **cut.bmp.**
  It appears in the top left corner of the drawing area.
- While it is still selected, **move** it to the bottom center of the drawing area.

RESULT — **TILT**

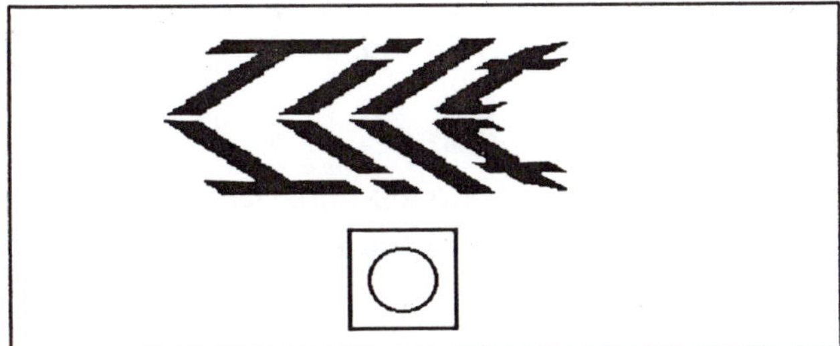

㉒ **Print** the drawing (review, page 159).

㉓ DEFINE A CUTOUT USING SCISSORS:
With the TILT.BMP still in the drawing area:
- **Click** on 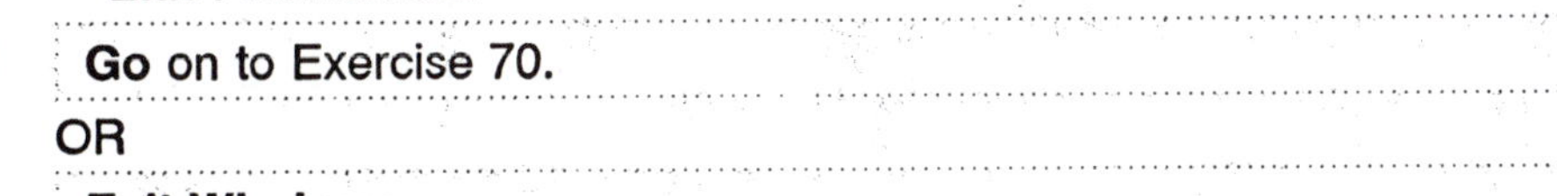 (scissors tool).
- Use the **pointer** to draw a circle around the first "T" in the top "Tilt." Do not worry if you do not define it perfectly. You can try again, if you wish.
- **Move** the **cutout** to the bottom of the drawing area.
- **Move** the **cutout** back to its original position.

㉔
- **Clear** the screen <u>without</u> saving the drawing.
- **Exit Paintbrush.**

㉕ Go on to Exercise 70.

OR

Exit Windows.

NOTE: When the <u>Paste From...</u> menu option is used, Paste From dialog box appears from which you may select the desired file. These files remain on the disk and can be <u>retrieved</u> as many times as desired.

EXERCISE 70
Use the Palette

use the palette

To change the foreground and/or background colors or patterns.

Directions are given for systems with color monitors. If your monitor is <u>not</u> color, substitute patterns of your choice for the colors.

1   CHANGE A BACKGROUND COLOR:

- **Click** on **yellow** in the palette <u>using the **right mouse button**</u>.
- **Clear** the screen.

  NOTE: Selecting New from the File menu fills the background with the newly selected background color or pattern.

2
- **Click** on ☐ (box tool).
- **Draw** a **rectangle** in the top left portion of the drawing area.
- **Click** on ▱ (paint roller tool).
- **Click** somewhere inside the **rectangle**.

  NOTE: The rectangle fills with the <u>foreground</u> color (which should be black).

3   CHANGE THE FOREGROUND COLOR:

- **Click** on **red** in the palette <u>using the **left mouse button**</u>.

4
- **Click** on ☐ (rounded box tool).
- **Draw** a **rounded rectangle** in the bottom left portion of the drawing area.
- **Click** on ▱ (paint roller tool).
- **Click** somewhere inside the **rounded rectangle**.
  The rounded rectangle fills with red.

5
- **Click** on ◯ (circle/ellipse tool).
- **Draw** a **circle** or **ellipse** in the top right portion of the drawing area.
- Change the foreground color to **blue**.
- **Click** on ▱ (paint roller tool).
- **Click** somewhere inside the **circle**.
  The rounded rectangle fills with blue.

6
- **Click** on ▨ (brush tool).
- **Draw** a <u>closed</u> **shape** of your choice in the lower right portion of the drawing area.
- **Click** on ▱ (paint roller tool).
- **Click** somewhere inside the **closed shape**.
  Oops! You do not want blue here.
- **Click** on **Edit**, and then **click** on **Undo**.
- Change the foreground color to **green**.
- **Click** somewhere inside the **closed shape**.

  *NOTE: If there are any "holes" in your shape, the color will leak out and color the background. If this happens, use **undo** to delete the color, **click** on **brush** and close the "hole," **click** on the **paint roller**, and **click** inside the shape again.*

7   **Print** the drawing and **clear** the screen.

Continue Exercise 70 on the next page

RESULT – **PALETTE1**

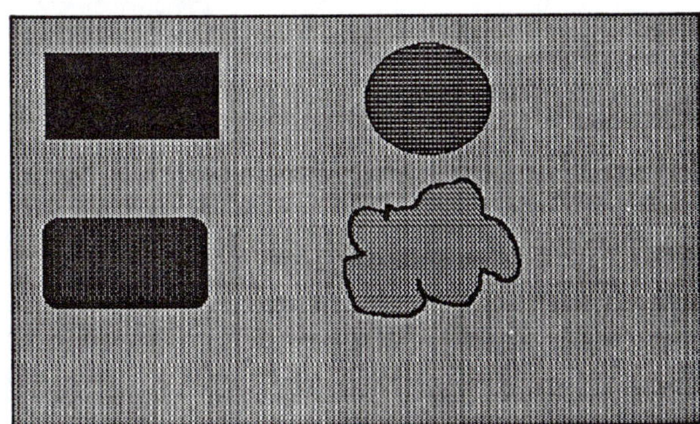

8
- Change the **foreground** color to **black**.
- Change the **background** color to **white**.

9 USE THE COLOR ERASER:
- Use the **box** tool to create a rectangle in each corner of the drawing area.
- Change the **foreground** color to **red**.
- **Click** on 🖌 (paint roller tool).
- **Click** in the top left rectangle to fill it with red.
- Change the **foreground** color to **blue**.
- **Click** in each of the remaining three rectangles to fill them with blue.

  To change colors:
  - Change the **foreground** color to **red**.
  - Change the **background** color to **yellow**.
  - **Click** on 🖌 (color eraser tool).
  - **Drag** the **color eraser** over the red box (to change the red to yellow).

  To change every occurrence of one color to another color:
  - Change the **foreground** color to **blue**.
  - Change the **background** color to **green**.
  - **Double-click** on 🖌 (color eraser tool) (to change every occurrence of blue to green).
- **Clear** the screen.

10 ACCESS PALETTE PATTERNS:
- **Click** on **Options.**
- **Click** on **Image Attributes... .**
- **Click** on the **option button** for "Black and White."
- **Click** on [**OK**].

NOTE: *The following numbers represent pattern locations on the palette so you can more easily identify the correct patterns when doing this exercise.*

1	2	3	4	5	6	7	8	9	10	11	12	13	14
15	16	17	18	19	20	21	22	23	24	25	26	27	28

NOTE: *Background colors other than white will print over a larger area than displayed on the screen. The default page size is 7.5" (wide) x 4.36" (high). This is what the screen displays for PALETTE1:*

NOTE: *The Color Eraser can be used in two ways:*
1. *Drag the Color Eraser pointer over an area to change the selected foreground color to the selected background color.*
2. *Double-click on the Color Eraser tool to change every occurrence of the selected foreground color to the selected background color.*

Continue Exercise 70 on the next page

Exercise 70 (continued)

11
- Change the **background** pattern to #2 (page 168, step 1).
  NOTE: Remember to use the right mouse button to click for the background, and then "clear the screen" to fill in the background.
- **Click** on the next-to-top **line width**.
- **Click** on  (circle/ellipse tool).
- Create six **circles**.
- **Click** on (paint roller tool).
- **Click** on the number 3 pattern in the palette.
- **Click** in the first circle (to fill it with pattern number 3).
- Fill each of the remaining circles with patterns numbers 4, 5, 7, 10, and 15, respectively.

12 **Print** the drawing and **clear** the screen.

RESULT — **PALETTE2**

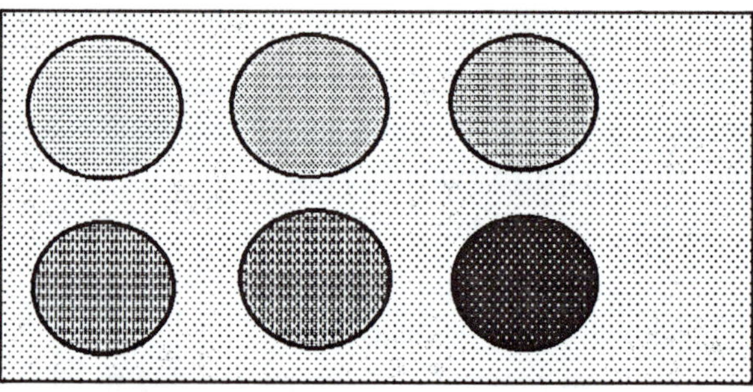

13 ACCESS THE COLOR PALETTE:
- **Click** on **O**ptions.
- **Click** on **I**mage Attributes... .
- **Click** on the **option button** for "Color."
- **Click** on OK .

14
- Change the **foreground** color to **black**.
- Change the **background** color to **white**.
- Clear the screen.

15 **Exit Paintbrush.**

16
Go on to Exercise 71.

OR

Exit Windows.

① • **Start Windows,** if necessary.
  • **Start Paintbrush** and **maximize** it.

② • **Click** on **T**ext, then on **F**onts... .
  • **Select** the **Arial** Font in **bold** Type Style and size 36.
  • **Click** on [OK   ].
  • **Click** on [abc] (text tool).
  • **Click** an *insertion point* in about the center of the drawing area.
  • **Type:** 1

③ ZOOM IN TO EDIT:
  • **Click** on **V**iew, then on **Zoom In**.
    When you move the pointer into the drawing area, the shape changes
    to a movable rectangle.
  • **Move** the rectangle over the 1 (like this) | **1** | and **click.**

  The screen looks like this:

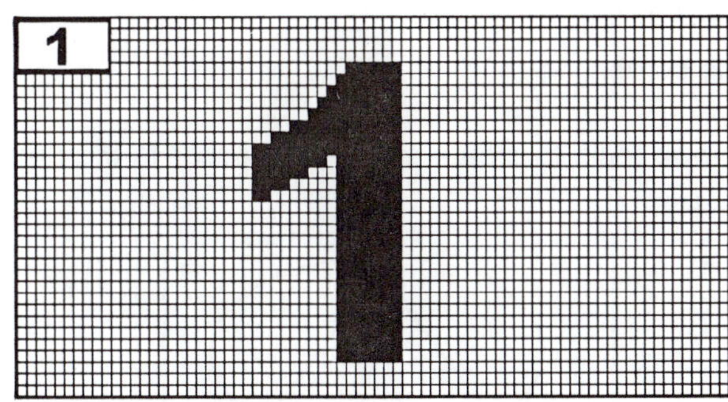

> *NOTE: The portion of the screen that was in the rectangle is now enlarged to fill the*
> *entire screen. A small rectangle in the top left corner displays the screen*
> *area that is magnified in its original size. As you make changes, they are*
> *shown in the small rectangle as well as in the magnified area.*

④ DELETE THE "FLAG" ON THE 1:
  • **Click** the <u>RIGHT</u> mouse button on the pixels that make up the "flag"
    on the "1" until just a straight number one remains. One or two pixels
    are missing in the top left corner of the 1.

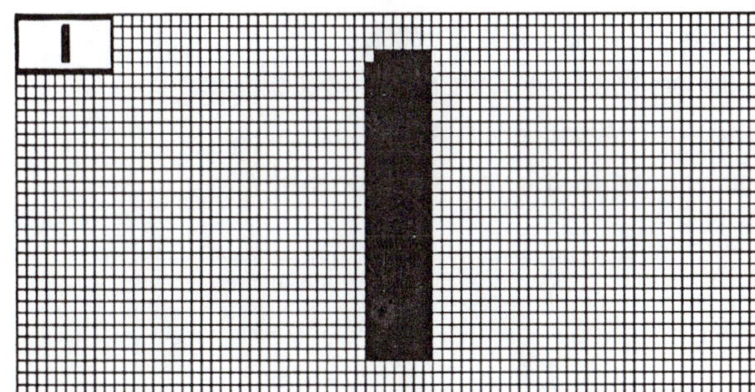

  • **Click** the <u>LEFT</u> mouse button on the missing pixel(s) in the top left
    corner of the number to fill it in.

⑤ ZOOM OUT TO RETURN TO NORMAL SCREEN:
  • **Click** on **V**iew, then on **Zoom O**ut.

⑥ **Exit Paintbrush** and **Windows** without printing the drawing.

EXERCISE 71
Zoom In to Edit

zoom in to edit
To magnify a portion of a drawing so that
you can make changes one pixel at a
time.

pixel
A single dot that represents the smallest
graphic unit that can be displayed on the
screen.

Keyboard Users
ZOOM IN
1. **Press** [Ctrl] + [N] (Zoom In) to
    magnify an area.
    A rectangle appears.
2. Use arrows to **move** the
    rectangle until it covers the
    desired area.
3. **Press** [Ins]
4. Use arrow keys to **move** the
    pointer to the desired pixel.
5. **Press** [Ins] to change the pixel
    to the **foreground** color.

    OR

    Press [Del] to change the pixel
    to the **background** color.
6. **Press** [Ctrl] + [O] (Zoom **O**ut) to
    return to the normal screen.

EXERCISE 72
Practice

Lesson Five
Paintbrush

NOTE: Try to approximate the drawing illustrations, but do not worry if your screen is different from the illustration.

Tasks Reviewed:

Create a Drawing
Use Line Tools
Paintbrush Linesize Box
Save a Drawing
Print a Drawing
Use Shape Tools
Use the Palette

1
- **Start Windows**, and **start** and **maximize Paintbrush**.
- **Click** on (curve tool).
- **Select** the **fifth linesize** from the top in the linesize box.
- **Draw** a line from the top left corner to the bottom right corner.
- **Click** in the top right corner and then in the bottom left corner.
- **Click** on (text tool).
- **Select** Arial, bold, size 20 font.
- **Type** your name in the top right corner of the drawing.

RESULT — **P1**

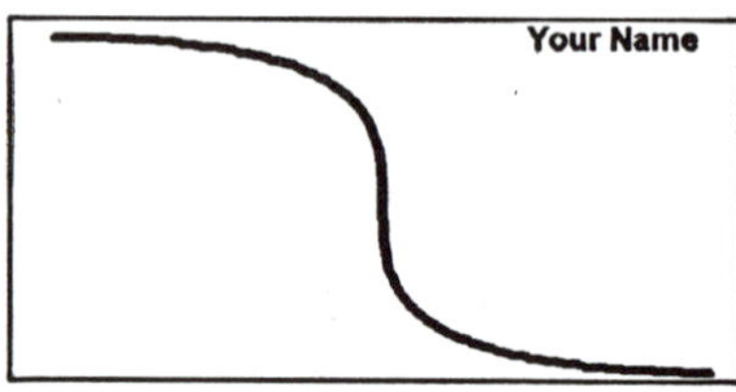

2
- **Print** the drawing.
- **Clear** the screen.

3
Use the **shape** tools to create a drawing similar to the one below:

RESULT — **P2**

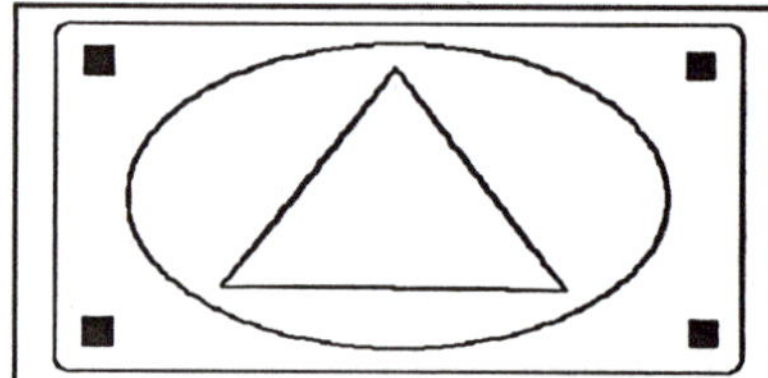

4
- **Print** the drawing.
- **Clear** the screen.

5
- **Select** yellow **background** and green **foreground**.
- **Clear** the screen (to change the background to yellow).
- **Draw** a tree with the **air brush** tool.
- **Change** foreground color to **red**.
- **Draw** balls on the tree with the **filled circle**.
- **Select** the font: Arial, bold, size 24.
- **Type** your name in the top right corner.

RESULT — **P3**

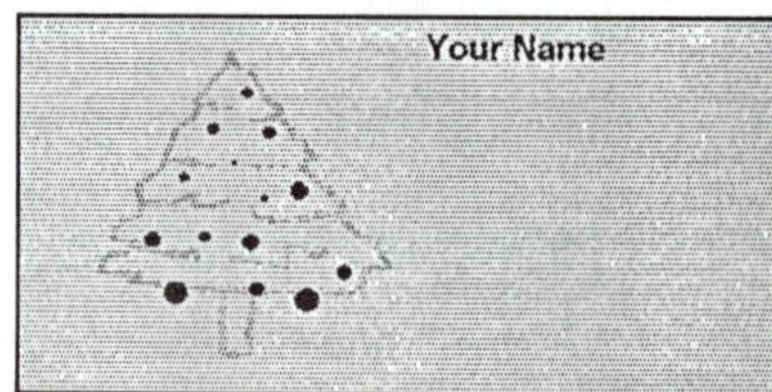

6
- **Print** the drawing.
- **Exit Paintbrush** and **Windows**.

Go on to Exercise 73

1
- **Start Windows, and start and maximize Paintbrush.**
- **Create a drawing** similar to the one below:

RESULT — **P4**

2
- **Print** the drawing.

3 Make the following changes to match the illustration **below**:
- **Move** the **box.**
- **Copy, paste,** and **move** the **filled box.**
- **Erase** part of the **filled rounded box** as shown.
- **Copy, paste,** and **move** the **filled rounded box.**
- **Cut** the **rounded box.**
- **Cut** and **paste** the **filled circle.**

RESULT — **P5**

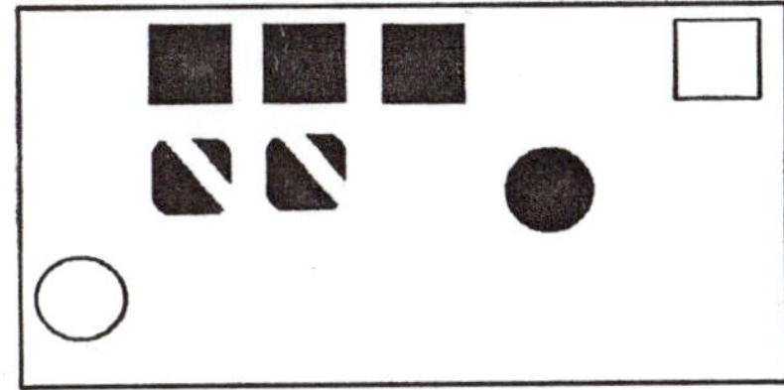

4
- **Print** the drawing.

5 Make the following changes to match the illustration below:
- **Tilt** the **box** (check Clear also, and deselect Tilt when done).
- **Enlarge** the **filled circle** (deselect Shrink and Grow when done).
- **Horizontally flip** the **filled rounded box** on the right.
- Use ✂ (scissors tool) to define the small corner of the **rounded box** on the left, and **move** it out a little as shown.
- Use the **Zoom In** feature to magnify the larger part of the **rounded box**, and draw a face using the <u>right</u> mouse button to erase (change to background color).
- **Sweep** the **circle.**
- **Move** the left two **filled squares** to the left.

RESULT — **P6**

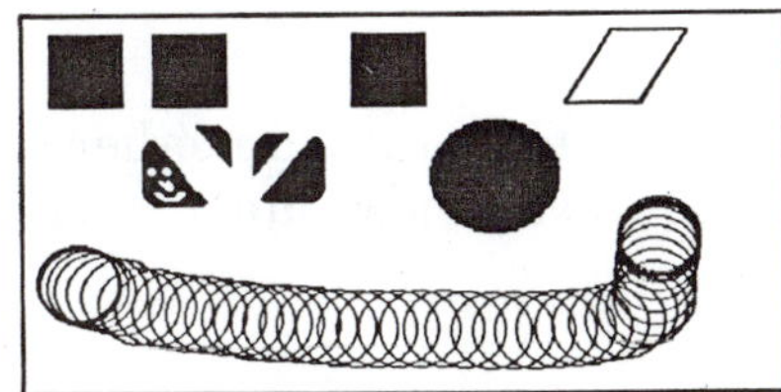

6
- **Print** the drawing.
- **Exit Paintbrush** and **Windows.**

EXERCISE 73
Practice

**Lesson Five
Paintbrush**

Tasks Reviewed:

Create a Drawing
Use Shape Tools
Save a Drawing
Print a Drawing
Use Erase
Use Cutout Tools
Use Zoom In

Lesson Five
Review of Paintbrush Exercises

Lesson Five (Paintbrush) covers tasks that:

Start Paintbrush and Examine the Menus

Examine Paintbrush Tools, Linesize Box, and Palette

Create, Save, Open, and Print a Drawing

Use Line Tools, Shape Tools, Erase and Undo, Cutting Tools, and the Palette

Zoom In to Edit

POINTS TO EMPHASIZE

Compare and Contrast

Foreground Color <u>and</u> Background Color
- The *foreground color* is used to draw with and fill areas.
- The *background color* is used to fill the background of the drawing area.

Scissors cutout tool <u>and</u> Pick cutout tool
While both tools are displayed in the toolbox with scissors,
- *Scissors* shows a jagged cutout and is used to define an irregular cutout.
- *Pick* shows a rectangle and is used to define a rectangular cutout.

Paintbrush Defaults

The selected drawing tool is *brush*, the selected linesize is the *top* line, the selected foreground color is *black*, and the selected background color is *white*.

Using **Shift** with Tools

Keeps tools moving in a straight line with *eraser*, *brush*, and in *Zoom In* mode.
Makes precise circles and squares with the *shape* tools.
Draws exact horizontal, vertical, or diagonal lines with the *line* tool.

Using the Undo Command

The *Undo* command is especially handy in the Paintbrush program, where it is easy to make a change that is not exactly what you wanted. **Undo** erases all the changes that have been made since the last time you selected a tool, used a scroll bar, resized the window, or switched to another program.

Using the New Command

Selecting <u>N</u>ew from the <u>F</u>ile menu *clears the screen (you cannot retrieve what was on the screen unless it was saved)* and *fills the background* with the selected background color or pattern. If you select a new background color, you must use the *New* command to fill the background with that color.

Using the Clipboard

The *Clipboard* is a temporary storage area that holds *cutouts* that are either cut or copied. The *Clipboard* can hold only one cutout at a time, so when a new cutout is cut or copied to the *Clipboard*, the previous cutout is erased.

Using Zoom In to Edit

The *Zoom In* command changes the pointer shape to a *rectangle*. You position the rectangle over the part of the drawing you want to magnify, and *then click* the mouse button to select the area. The portion of the screen in the rectangle enlarges to fill the entire screen. A small rectangle in the top left corner displays the magnified screen area in its original size. As you make changes, they are reflected in the small rectangle as well as in the magnified area. You can scroll the magnified area to other parts of the screen.

WORKSHEET 27

NAME ________________________

PAINTBRUSH <u>TERMS</u>

DIRECTIONS: Use the following terms to fill in the blanks below:

New	pixel	scissors	linesize box
pick	cutout	Save As...	drop-down list box
Save	toolbox	Paintbrush	background color or pattern
file	palette	drawing area	foreground color or pattern

1. What holds the tools that are used to create drawings?

1) ________________________

2. What is a single dot that represents the smallest graphic unit that can be displayed on the screen?

2) ________________________

3. What holds the colors and patterns that may be used with the drawing tools?

3) ________________________

4. What is the color or pattern that is used by the <u>tools</u> to draw with and fill areas?

4) ________________________

5. What command stores new drawings or lets you rename a previously saved drawing?

5) ________________________

6. What is a portion of the drawing area that is <u>defined</u> by a dashed-line border that surrounds it?

6) ________________________

7. What is the color or pattern that is used to cover the <u>drawing area</u> before creating a drawing?

7) ________________________

8. What holds lines of varying widths from which drawing widths can be selected?

8) ________________________

9. What file option clears the screen?

9) ________________________

10. What is a <u>set of data</u> that is saved on a disk as a <u>named</u> unit?

10) ________________________

11. What is Windows' drawing program?

11) ________________________

12. What box is similar to a <u>list box</u> except that it must be opened by clicking on the drop-down list arrow next to it?

12) ________________________

13. What cutout tool is used to define an <u>irregular</u> cutout area?

13) ________________________

14. What command stores changes to a previously named drawing that you are working on?

14) ________________________

15. What is the space where you create drawings?

15) ________________________

16. What cutout tool is used to define a <u>rectangular</u> cutout area?

16) ________________________

"

WORKSHEET 28

NAME ________________________

PAINTBRUSH <u>TASKS</u>

DIRECTIONS: Use the following tasks to fill in the blanks below:

zoom in	linesize box	use the palette	Paintbrush tools
palette	open a drawing	use shape tools	Paintbrush menus
use undo	save a drawing	print a drawing	start Paintbrush
use erase	use line tools	create a drawing	use cutout tools

1. To draw with tools that create geometric shapes.

    1) ________________________

2. To magnify a portion of a drawing so that you can make changes one pixel at a time.

    2) ________________________

3. To retrieve a saved drawing from a disk into the Paintbrush program.

    3) ________________________

4. To use Windows to run the Paintbrush program.

    4) ________________________

5. The various tools found in the toolbox that are used to create a drawing.

    5) ________________________

6. To use the drawing tools to make images in the drawing area.

    6) ________________________

7. To transfer a drawing in the Paintbrush program onto paper.

    7) ________________________

8. The menus displayed on the menu bar, some of which are similar to other Windows menus (such as File and Help) and others that are specific to Paintbrush.

    8) ________________________

9. To store a drawing in the Paintbrush program on a disk.

    9) ________________________

10. To draw using the <u>curve</u> and <u>line</u> tools.

    10) ________________________

11. To delete parts of the drawing by changing the foreground color (or pattern) to the selected background color (or pattern).

    11) ________________________

12. The box across the bottom of the Paintbrush window that displays colors and patterns that may be selected for the background or drawing.

    12) ________________________

13. To remove the changes that have been made in the drawing area since the last time you selected a new tool.

    13) ________________________

14. The box in the bottom left corner of the Paintbrush window that displays line widths available to draw with.

    14) ________________________

15. To use <u>scissors</u> or <u>pick</u> to <u>define</u> an area.

    15) ________________________

16. To change the foreground and/or background colors or patterns.

    16) ________________________

(This page may be copied.)

Lesson Six — File Manager

Table of Contents

EXERCISE 74
Start File Manager

Exercises 74-76 should be done during the same session.

start File Manager
To use Windows to run the File Manager program.

File Manager window
The application window which holds the File Manager program and one or more directory windows (document windows).

Directory window
The window within the File Manager window that displays the files, directories, and subdirectories on your disk.

directory tree
The directory structure (root directory, directories, and subdirectories) displayed on the left side of the directory window.

contents of current directory
A list of the files and subdirectories located within the directory which is highlighted in the directory tree. These files and directories are displayed on the right side of the Directory window.

status bar
The bar at the bottom of the File Manager window that displays information about the current drive and directory.

Keyboard Users

START FILE MANAGER

With the Program Manger and Main windows both open, and the Main window *selected*:

1. **Press** arrow keys until File Manager's icon name is highlighted.

2. **Press** ⏎

The File Manager is a program that oversees your files.

The Directory window (within the File Manager) displays the **disk structure** and the files within the disk structure.

Disk structure (or directory tree) refers to the way a disk is organized (which is similar to a filing cabinet):
   root directory (filing cabinet)
   directories (file drawers)
   subdirectories (subcategories within a file drawer)

There may be many, many files on a disk, and it is important—especially on a hard disk—to keep track of files by arranging them into <u>related groups</u>.

The root directory, directories, and subdirectories create the disk structure into which <u>related groups of files</u> are organized.

❶ Start Windows.

FROM THE *STARTING WINDOWS* SCREEN:
(With the Program Manager <u>and</u> the Main Group windows open.)

❷ Double-click on File Manager .

The File Manager window, and the *current* Directory window within it, appears:

File Manager window

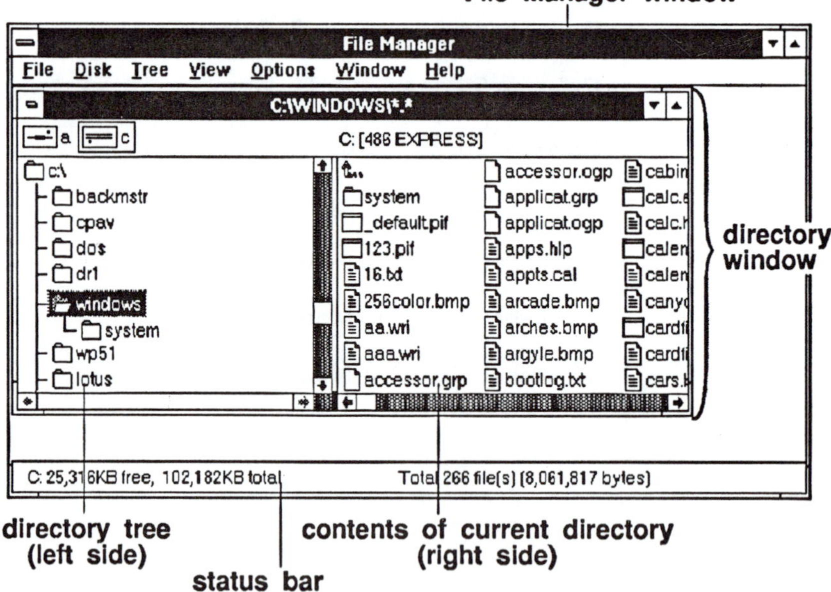

directory tree (left side)   **contents of current directory (right side)**   **status bar**

NOTE: Your directory window will display different directories and files.

Continue Exercise 74 on the next page

❸ Examine the *Directory window, directory tree,* and *contents of current directory*.

Directory Window:

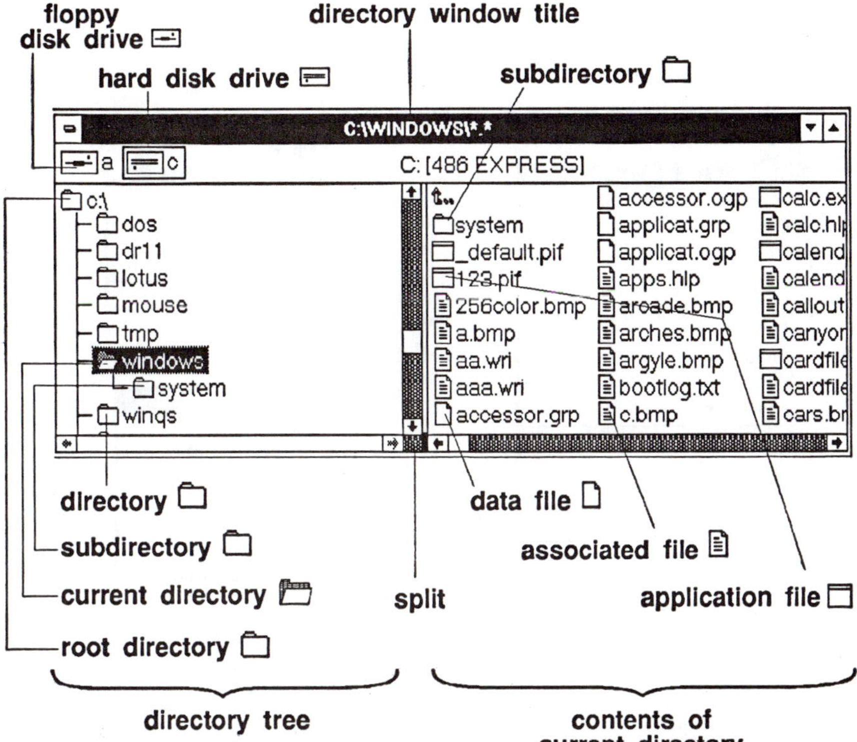

NOTE: *The Directory window defaults to being <u>split</u>, displaying the directory tree on the left side and the contents of the <u>current</u> directory on the right side. This default can be changed to display only the directory tree (left side) or only the contents of the current directory (right side) in the window by accessing the **<u>V</u>iew** menu and choosing **Tr<u>e</u>e Only, Directory <u>O</u>nly**. Select **<u>T</u>ree and Directory** to return to a split screen.*

Go on to Exercise 75

Directory window title
The <u>name of the current (highlighted) directory</u> that is displayed in the title bar of the Directory window.

hard disk drive 
The part of the computer system that transfers files back and forth between the computer and the hard disk (usually Drive C:).

floppy disk drive
The part of the computer system that transfers files back and forth between the computer and the floppy disks (usually Drive A: and possibly Drive B: also).

directory
The part of the disk structure that holds files and/or other directories (called subdirectories).

current directory
The active directory which is <u>highlighted</u>.

root directory
The original (or highest level) directory on a disk.

subdirectory
Directories that are within other directories.

file
A set of data that is saved on a disk as a <u>named</u> unit.

data file
A file that consists of data created in a program, such as a letter typed into a word processor.

application (program) file
A file that holds a set of instructions that perform a task, such as word processing.

associated file
A file that is identified as belonging to a certain application, such as a Write (.WRI) or a Paintbrush (.BMP) file.

EXERCISE 75
File Manager Menus

Continue from Exercise 74, doing Exercises 74-76 during the same session.

File Manager menus

The drop-down menus that are displayed on the menu bar, some of which are similar to other Windows menus (such as File and Help) and others that are specific to File Manager (such as Disk, Tree, and View).

Keyboard Users

VIEW FILE MANAGER MENUS
OPEN AND CLOSE MENUS:

1. Press **Alt** + **F** (to open File)
2. Press **Alt** (to close File)
3. Repeat steps 1 and 2, replacing **F** with the underlined letter of each of the other menus in turn.
4. Press **Alt** to leave menus.

180

---

1 LOOK AT EACH DROP-DOWN MENU:

- **Click** on **F**ile.
- **Click** on **D**isk.
- **Click** on **T**ree.
- **Click** on **V**iew.
- **Click** on **O**ptions.
- **Click** on **W**indow.
- **Click** on **H**elp.

Each **drop-down** menu is shown below:

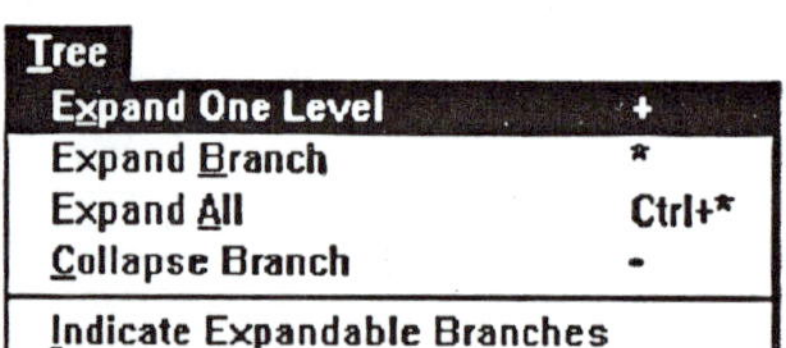

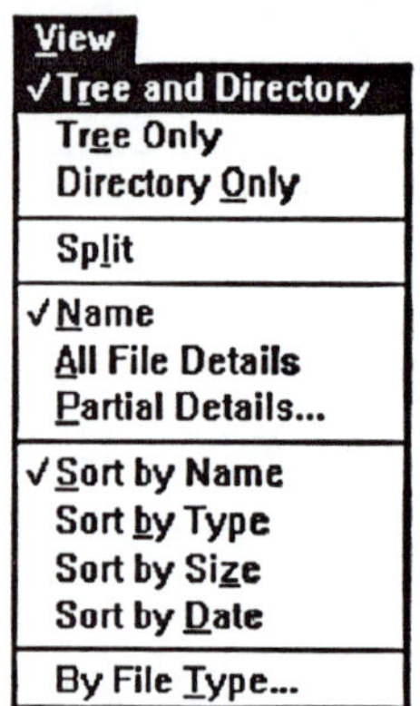

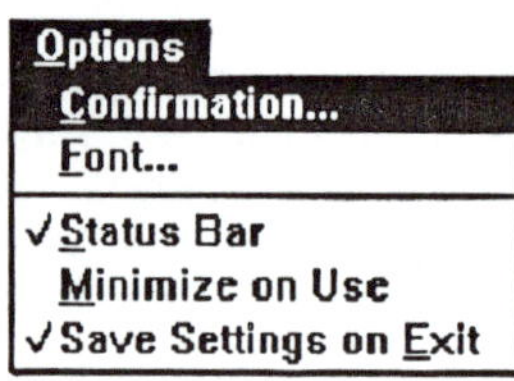

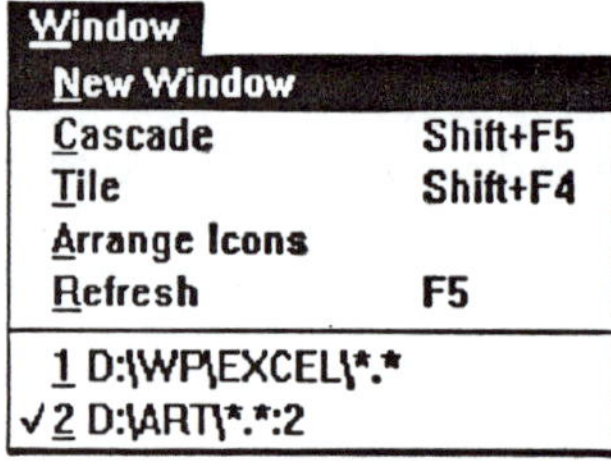

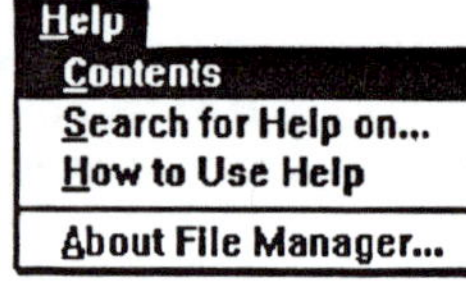

IMPORTANT!

2 DESELECT "SAVE SETTINGS ON EXIT":

- **Click** on **O**ptions.

- IF ✔ *does* appear by "Save Settings on Exit," then:
  - **Click** on **Save Settings on Exit** (to deselect it).

  OR

  IF ✔ *does not* appear by "Save Settings on Exit," then:
  - **Click** anywhere *off* of the menu bar (to close the menu).

- **Click** on **O**ptions, again, to confirm that there is <u>not</u> a check mark by "Save Settings on Exit."
- **Click** anywhere *off* of the menu bar (to close the menu).

3 **Exit File Manager.**

Go on to Exercise 76

IMPORTANT: You must prepare "mock" files for the File Manager Lesson in order to complete the exercises in the lesson. Use a <u>blank</u>, formatted disk of any size or density to save the "mock" files on. Notepad is a good program to use for this job since it saves files using less disk space than any other Windows Program. When through, you should have all the filenames that are listed on the next page saved on your floppy disk.

NOTE: If you continue using the data disk used in Lessons 4 and 5, the files should be deleted from it before you proceed.

❶ • **Start Windows.**

 • **Open Accessories.**

❷ • **Double-click on**  (the program-item icon for Notepad).

The *Notepad* window appears:

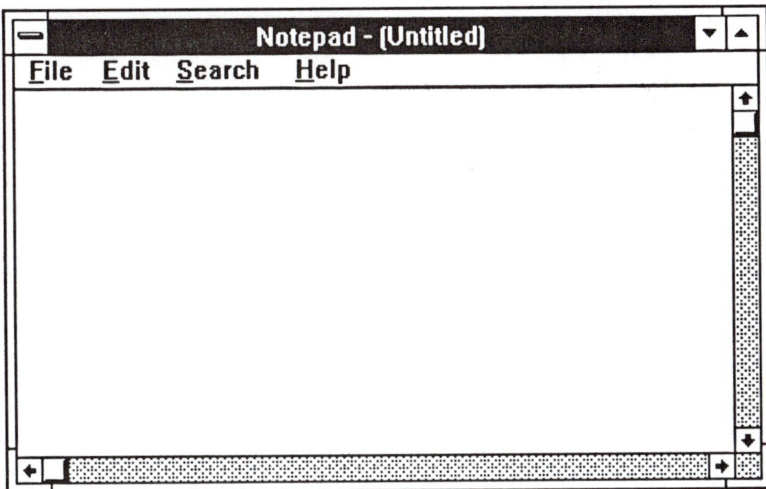

NOTE: The Notepad program is a "text editor" similar to, but not as complex as, Write. You can use Notepad to edit small "text files." "Text files" contain only letters, numbers and symbols, and are saved as ASCII files. They contain little or no formatting information, and they take up very little disk space.

❸ Place a blank, formatted disk in Drive A: (or B:).

❹ **Type** the first filename on the list of filenames on the next page:
`cut.bmp`

❺ SAVE THE "MOCK" FILE:

 • **Click** on **F̲ile**, then on **Save A̲s... .**

 • **Click** on the **down arrow** for the **Dri̲ves** *drop-down list box*, then on *a:* (or *b:*).

 • **Click** on the **File N̲ame** text box and **delete** the text in it.

 • **Type:** `cut.bmp`
 (Do <u>not</u> put any spaces in the filename.)
 *NOTE: Unless you direct Notepad to do otherwise, it saves and displays files with a .TXT extension. In this procedure you are directed to save files with .BMP and .WRI extensions. If you want to view your saved files during this process: click on the **List Files of Type box**, then on **All Files *.***.*

 • **Click on** ☐ OK ☐ .

IMPORTANT: If, at any point in the following exercises, the files on your disk become "messed up," you can start with a blank disk again, create "mock" files again, and redo the exercises. There is nothing important that can be lost.

Continue preparing "mock" files on the next page

Prepare Mock Files for Lesson Six (continued)

6
- **Click** on **File**, then on **New** (to clear the screen).
- **Type** the next filename on the list below.
- **Save** the file on Drive A: (or B:) using **Save As...**; use its filename and extension as the name.

7 Repeat step 6 above for each of the remaining filenames below.

```
cut.bmp
cutout.bmp
draw1.bmp
draw2.bmp
fonts1.wri
fonts2.wri
fonts3.wri
fonts4.wri
fonts5.wri
fun.wri
lines.bmp
p1.bmp
p2.bmp
p3.bmp
p4.bmp
p5.bmp
p6.bmp
palette1.bmp
palette2.bmp
saveit.wri
shapes.bmp
tilt.bmp
usewrite.wri
```

8 **Exit Notepad.**

9
Go on to Exercise 76.

OR

Exit Windows.

1. **Start File Manager**, if necessary.

2. Place your floppy disk, which contains the "mock" files, in Drive A: (or B:).

3. **Click on** [⊟] a (or b) (the floppy disk drive icon).

   NOTE: **IF** *this message window appears:*

   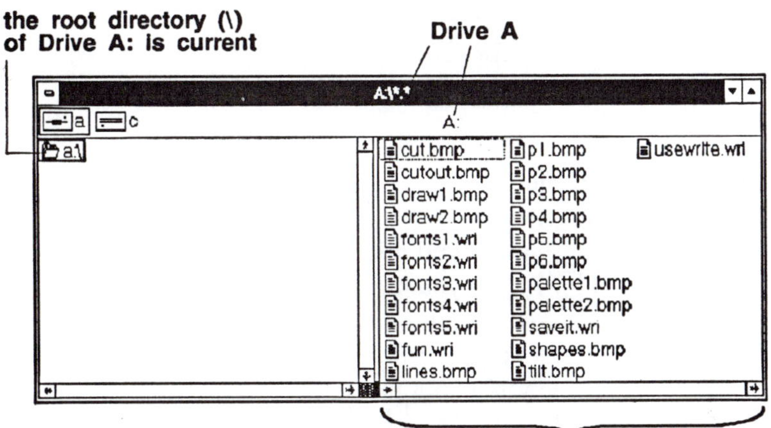

   *be sure your disk is in the proper disk drive, that the door is closed, and that you have selected the appropriate drive, then **click** on* Retry*.*

   The Directory window should appear similar to this:

   **the root directory (\)
   of Drive A: is current**   **Drive A**

   **these files are stored in the root
   directory on the disk in Drive A:**

4. **Click on** [═] (the hard disk drive icon).

5. **Change** back to the **floppy** disk drive.

6. **Change** back to the **hard** disk drive.

7. **Exit the File Manager.**

8. **Go** on to Exercise 77.

   OR

   Exit Windows.

EXERCISE 76
Change the Disk Drive

Continue from Exercise 75, doing Exercises 74-76 during the same session.

change the disk drive
To switch between the drives shown in the Directory window.

WARNING: Because of the possibility of destroying important files on the hard disk, this book instructs you to work with the files that have been stored on a floppy disk in Drive A: (or B:) to complete the exercises in the File Manager Lesson.

The following files should be on your floppy disk:

cut.bmp	p1.bmp
cutout.bmp	p2.bmp
draw1.bmp	p3.bmp
draw2.bmp	p4.bmp
fonts1.wri	p5.bmp
fonts2.wri	p6.bmp
fonts3.wri	palette1.bmp
fonts4.wri	palette2.bmp
fonts5.wri	saveit.wri
fun.wri	shapes.bmp
lines.bmp	tilt.bmp
	usewrite.wri

WARNING: **Click only once** on the drive icon to **change the disk drive** displayed in the current directory window (double-clicking will "open another directory window").

Keyboard Users
CHANGE THE DISK DRIVE
From the File Manager Window:
1. **Press** Tab until a disk drive icon is highlighted.
2. **Use** → or ← to select the desired disk drive.
3. **Press** Space

EXERCISE 77
Select and Deselect Files

Exercises 77-80 should be done during the same session.

select files
To <u>highlight</u> files. Once files are selected, commands can be carried out that affect them, such as <u>moving</u>, <u>copying</u>, or <u>deleting</u> the files.

deselect files
To remove the highlighting from files.

Keyboard Users

SELECT AND DESELECT FILES

1. Press **Tab** until the cursor moves to the list of files (right side) on the Directory window.
2. Perform an action:

   SELECT A FILE:
   - Use arrow keys to select the desired file.

   SELECT MULTIPLE FILES:
   a. Use arrow keys to highlight the first file to select.
   b. Press **Shift** + **F8** (The cursor starts blinking.)
   c. Use arrow keys to move to the next file to select.
   d. Press **Space**
   e. Repeat c and d until all files are selected.
   f. Press **Shift** + **F8**

   SELECT ADJOINING FILES:
   - Use arrow keys to move the cursor to the first file to select.
   - **Press** and **hold** **Shift** while you use arrow keys to select files.

   DESELECT MULTIPLE FILES:
   - Press **Space**
     (One file will remain selected until you move to another area.)

1
- **Start Windows**, if necessary.
- **Start File Manager.**
- **Put** your floppy disk (used with this book) in Drive A: (or B:) and close the door, if necessary.
- **Change to Drive A:** (or B:).

2 SELECT A FILE:
- **Click** on ▤ **cutout.bmp** (located on the right side of the Directory window).
  cutout.bmp becomes highlighted (it is selected):

```
▤ cut.bmp       ▤ fun.wri
▤ cutout.bmp    ▤ lines.bmp
▤ draw1.bmp     ▤ p1.bmp
▤ draw2.bmp     ▤ p2.bmp
```

3 DESELECT A FILE:
- **Press** and **hold** **Ctrl** while you **click** on ▤ **cutout.bmp**.
  The **deselected** file looks something like this:

```
▤ cut.bmp       ▤ fun.wri
▤ cutout.bmp    ▤ lines.bmp
▤ draw1.bmp     ▤ p1.bmp
▤ draw2.bmp     ▤ p2.bmp
```

4 SELECT MULTIPLE FILES:
- **Click** on ▤ **cutout.bmp**.
- **Press** and **hold** **Ctrl** while you **click** on ▤ **draw2.bmp**.
- **Press** and **hold** **Ctrl** while you **click** on ▤ **P1.bmp**.
  The selected files look something like this:

5 DESELECT MULTIPLE FILES:
- **Click** on ▤ **cutout.bmp**. All the files except ▤ **cutout.bmp** are **deselected**.
  NOTE: Clicking anywhere will deselect all the selected files, but the file you click on will stay (or become) selected.
- **Deselect** ▤ **cutout.bmp** (step 3).
  The **deselected** file looks something like this:

```
▤ cut.bmp       ▤ fun.wri
▤ cutout.bmp    ▤ lines.bmp
▤ draw1.bmp     ▤ p1.bmp
▤ draw2.bmp     ▤ p2.bmp
```

6 SELECT MULTIPLE ADJOINING FILES:
- **Click** on ▤ **cutout.bmp**.
- **Press** and **hold** **Shift** while you **click** on ▤ **fonts1.wri**.
  The selected files look something like this:

7 **Deselect** the files that are highlighted (step 5).

Go on to Exercise 78

① • **Click** on ▭ **a:** (or **b:**) (the *root directory* located on the left side of the Directory window).

② CREATE A DIRECTORY:
• **Click** on **File**.
• **Click** on **Create Directory... .**
  The *Create Directory* dialog box appears:

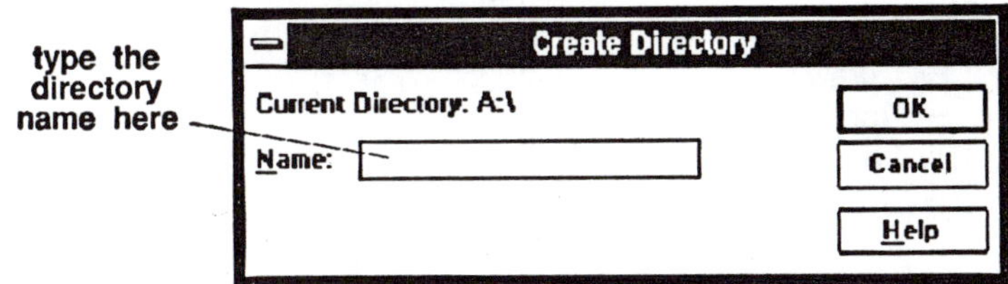

• **Type:** `write`
• **Click** on [OK] .
  The new directory appears on both sides of Directory window:

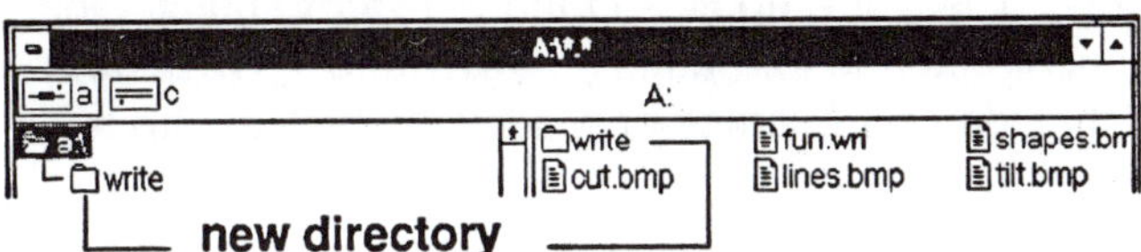

③ Follow step 2 above to **create** another Directory; name it **paint**.
The new directory appears:

④ CREATE A SUBDIRECTORY (A DIRECTORY UNDER ANOTHER DIRECTORY):
• **Click** on ▭ **write** (on the <u>left</u> side of the window).
• **Create** a Directory; name it **fonts**.
  The *fonts* subdirectory appears under the *write* directory:

⑤ • **Click** on ▭ **paint** (on the <u>left</u> side of the window).
• **Create** a Directory; name it **draw**.
• **Create** a Directory; name it **practice**.
  The two subdirectories appear under *paint*:

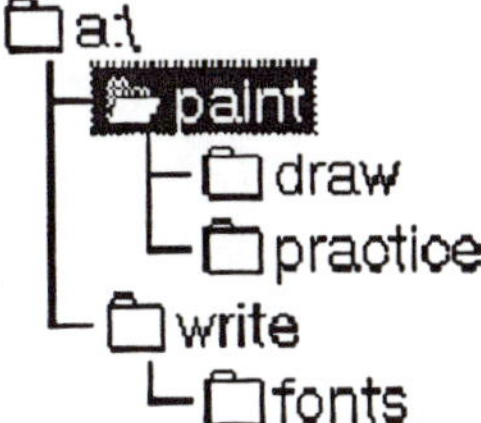

Go on to Exercise 79

EXERCISE 78
Create a Directory

Continue from Exercise 77, doing Exercises 77-80 during the same session.

create a directory
To use commands in the File Manager to make a new directory.

NOTE: <u>Subdirectories</u> of the <u>current directory</u> are displayed at the top on the <u>right side</u> of the Directory window.

Keyboard Users
CREATE A DIRECTORY

From the File Manager Window:
1. **Press** [Tab] until the cursor is on the left side of the Directory window.
2. **Use** [↑] or [↓] to select the directory under which to create the new directory.
3. **Press** [Alt]+[F] (File)
4. **Press** [E] (Create Directory...)
5. **Type** a directory name.
6. **Press** [↵]

EXERCISE 79
Select a Directory

Continue from Exercise 78, doing Exercises 77-80 during the same session.

select a directory

To <u>highlight</u> a directory, making it <u>current</u> (and changing its icon from 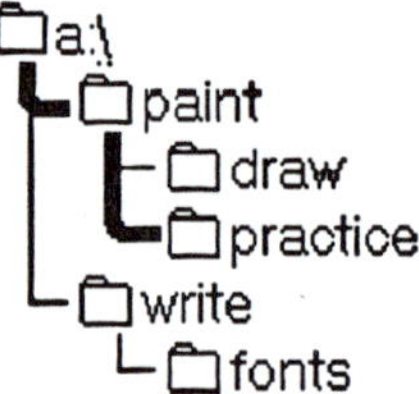).

directory path

The <u>path</u> shows the location of a file within the <u>directory tree</u>. For example, the path to the PRACTICE directory shown in the illustration below is

A:\PAINT\PRACTICE

Each directory in the <u>path</u> is separated from other directories by a backslash (\). The root directory (A in this case) is always followed by a colon (:).

Continue from Exercise 78 with the 🗁 **paint** subdirectory still highlighted. The Directory window looks similar to this:

selected directory   the Directory window's name is the path of the selected directory

The "contents of the selected directory" are displayed on the right side of the window. There are <u>no</u> files in the 🗁 **paint** subdirectory, but notice that the subdirectories for paint (🗀 **draw** and 🗀 **practice**) are displayed on the right side of the directory window as well as the left side.

❶ SELECT A DIRECTORY:
- **Click** on 🗀 **a:** (or **b:**) (the root directory).
- Notice that the name in the *Directory window's* <u>title bar</u> changes to the name of the **selected** directory: A:*.* (or B:*.*).

  *NOTE: An asterisk (*) is called a "wildcard" because it represents one or more characters (any characters). When *.* is used, it means to list <u>all files</u>. The first asterisk represents any filename, and the second asterisk represents any file extension.*

- Notice that the right side of the window displays the two <u>subdirectories</u> and <u>all the files</u> that are within the 🗀 **a:** (or **b:**) directory.

❷
- **Click** on 🗀 **practice**.
- Notice the **path** to the practice directory in the Directory window's name:

  A:\PAINT\PRACTICE*.* (or B:\PAINT\PRACTICE*.*)

❸
- **Select** 🗀 **write**.
- Notice the name in the *Directory window's* <u>title bar</u>.

❹
- **Select** 🗀 **fonts**.
- Notice the name in the *Directory window's* <u>title bar</u>.

Keyboard Users

SELECT A DIRECTORY

1. **Press Tab** until the cursor moves to the "directory tree" (left side) of the Directory window.

2. **Press** ⬆ and ⬇ to highlight the desired directory.

Go on to Exercise 80

1 COLLAPSE A BRANCH (ALL LEVELS OF DIRECTORIES WITHIN A DIRECTORY):

NOTE: Double-click on the directory above the directories to be collapsed.

With the directory tree fully expanded:

before collapse

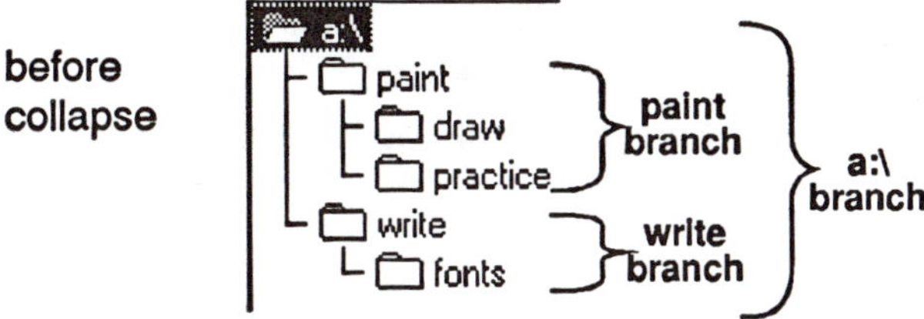

- **Double-click on ⬜ a:\ (or b:\) (the root directory).**

NOTE: The directories are not really gone; they just do not show.

after collapse

2 EXPAND DIRECTORIES ONE LEVEL AT A TIME:

NOTE: Double-click on the directory to be expanded.

- **Double-click on ⬜ a:\ (or b:\).**
- **Double-click on ⬜ paint.**
- **Double-click on ⬜ write.**

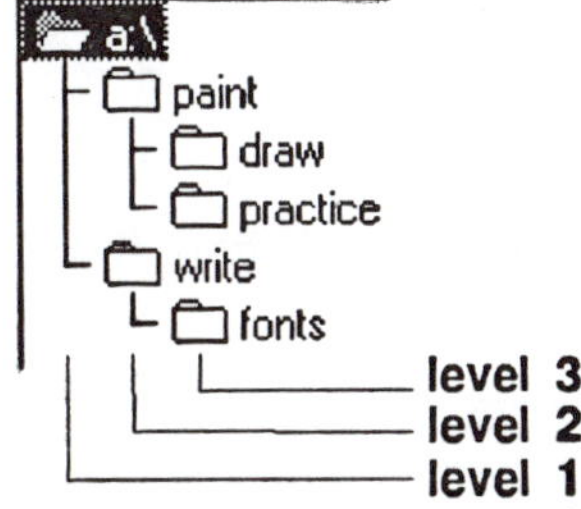

3 COLLAPSE ONE LEVEL AT A TIME:

NOTE: Double-click on the directory above the level to be collapsed.

- **Double-click on ⬜ write.**
- **Double-click on ⬜ paint.**
- **Double-click on ⬜ a:\ (or b:\).**

4 EXPAND ALL DIRECTORY LEVELS:

- **Click on Tree.**
- **Click on Expand All.**

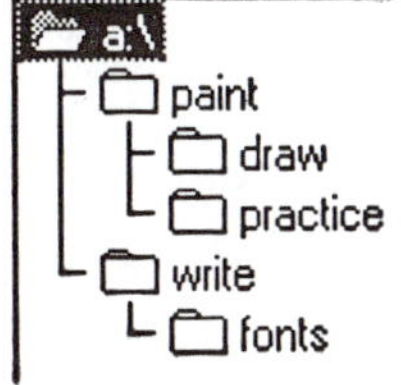

5 **Exit File Manager.**

6 **Go on to Exercise 81.**

OR

Exit Windows.

EXERCISE 80
Expand and Collapse Directories

Continue from Exercise 79, doing Exercises 77-80 during the same session.

expand and collapse directories
To control the levels of directories shown in the directory tree.

expand directories
To display unseen directory levels in the <u>directory tree</u>.

collapse directories
To <u>hide</u> directory levels in the <u>directory tree</u>.

directory branch
All the levels of subdirectories within a specific directory.

directory levels
The tiers of subdirectory layers, starting with the root directory.

Keyboard Users

COLLAPSE AND EXPAND DIRECTORIES

1. **Select** the desired directory.
2. Perform an action below:

   EXPAND ONE LEVEL
   - Press ⏎ or ➕

   EXPAND ONE BRANCH
   - Press ✱

   EXPAND ALL BRANCHES
   - Press **Ctrl** + ✱

   COLLAPSE DIRECTORIES
   - Press ➖

EXERCISE 81
Move, Copy, and Delete Files

<u>WARNING</u>: It is a good idea to back up the files on your data disk before doing this exercise.

move and copy files
To transfer files from one directory to another directory. <u>Copy</u> leaves the original file intact, while <u>move</u> removes the original file.

delete files
To remove files from a disk.

shortcut keys to:
  move: **F7**
  copy: **F8**

Keyboard Users

MOVE, COPY, AND DELETE FILES

MOVE OR COPY FILES:

1. Select the file or files to be moved or copied.
2. Press **Alt** + **F** (<u>F</u>ile)
3.
   Move files:
   - Press **M** (<u>M</u>ove)

   The *Move* dialog box appears:

   OR

   Copy files:
   - Press **C** (<u>C</u>opy)

   The *Copy* dialog box appears:
4. Type the pathname. (See **path** term on page 186.)
5. Press **↵**
   The *Confirm File Replace* dialog box appears.
6. Press **↵**
   Repeat step 6 for each file that is being moved or copied.

DELETE FILES:

- Select the files to be deleted.
- Press **Del**
- Press **↵**
- Press **↵**

---

❶
- **Start Windows,** if necessary.
- **Start File Manager.**
- **Put** your floppy data disk in Drive A: (or B:) and close the door, if necessary.
- **Change to Drive A:** (or B:) (review, page 183).
- **Expand all directories** (review, page 187).
- **Click on**  **a:** (or **b:\)** (to select it), if necessary.

❷ COPY ONE FILE:

- **Press** and **hold** **Ctrl** while you **drag** cut.bmp to paint.

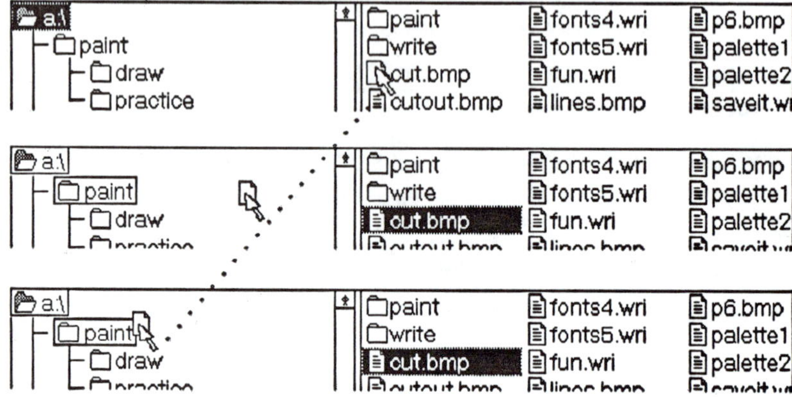

When you release the mouse button, the *Confirm Mouse Operation* dialog box appears:

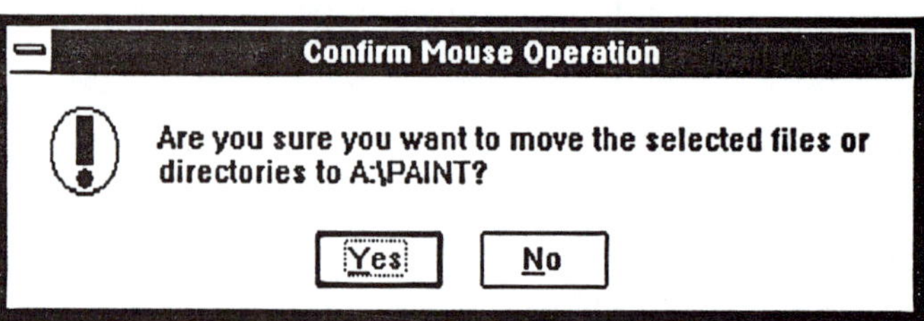

NOTE: Always read the information in the dialog box to be sure that the desired action is going to take place.

- **Click on** [Yes].

   A dialog box briefly appears to explain what is happening.

❸ MOVE ONE FILE:

NOTE: Compare <u>move</u> files with <u>copy</u> files. When <u>moving</u> files, DO NOT hold **Ctrl** *while you drag the files.*

- **Drag** cutout.bmp to paint.

   The *Confirm Mouse Operation* dialog box appears.
- **Click on** [Yes].
- **Click on** paint (to display the files stored in it).

   Look on the right side of the Directory window. The two files (cut.bmp and cutout.bmp) should be showing.
- **Click on** a:\ (or b:\) (to return to the files listed in the root directory).

Continue Exercise 81 on the next page

188

4 COPY MULTIPLE FILES:
- **Select** 📄**draw1.bmp** and 📄**draw2.bmp** (review, page 184).
- **Press** and **hold** **Ctrl** while you **drag** one of the selected files to 📁 **draw**.
  NOTE: All the selected files will be copied.
  The *Confirm Mouse Operation* dialog box appears.
- **Click on** Yes .
NOTE: A dialog box briefly appears to explain what is happening.

5 Follow step 4 to copy **fonts1.wri, fonts2.wri, fonts3.wri, fonts4.wri,** and **fonts5.wri** to the *fonts* subdirectory.

6 Copy **p1.bmp, p2.bmp, p3.bmp, p4.bmp, p5.bmp,** and **p6.bmp** to the *practice* subdirectory.

7 MOVE MULTIPLE FILES:
- **Select** the following files:

  lines.bmp   shapes.bmp
  palette1.bmp   tilt.bmp
  palette2.bmp
- **Drag** one file of the *block of selected files* to 📁 **paint** (the rest will follow, with an icon like this 🗐).
  The *Confirm Mouse Operation* dialog box appears.
- **Click on** Yes .
NOTE: A dialog box briefly appears to explain what is happening.

8 Move the following files to 📁 **write**:
  fun.wri, saveit.wri, and usewrite.wri.

9 DELETE FILES:
- **Click on** 📄**cut.bmp** (to select it).
- **Press** Del .
  The *Delete* dialog box appears.
- **Click on** OK .
  The *Confirm File Delete* dialog box appears.
- **Click on** Yes .

10
- **Select** the following files.

  draw1.bmp   p1.bmp   p3.bmp   p5.bmp
  draw2.bmp   p2.bmp   p4.bmp   p6.bmp
- **Click on** **File**, then **Delete...**, then OK .
- **Click on** Yes for each of the files to delete.

11 Delete the remaining *files* in 📁 **A:** (or **B:**). WARNING: DO NOT DELETE the subdirectories (📁 **paint** and 📁 **write**).

12 Select each of the directories (paint, draw, practice, write, fonts, and then a:\ (or b:\)) and look at the files in each directory.

13 **Exit File Manager.**

14 **Go on to Exercise 82.**
OR
Exit Windows.

WARNING:

If you try to move or copy files to a directory that already contains those files (which may happen, for example, if you try to repeat the steps in this exercise), a Confirm File Replace dialog box will appear. It tells you what action is about to happen and asks for confirmation for each file. This is designed to prevent you from replacing an important file accidentally.

OVERVIEW OF FILE MOVEMENT:

In this exercise, the following files are being moved or copied from 📁 **a:** (or **b:**) to:

📁 paint	📁 draw	📁 practice
cut	draw1	p1
cutout	draw2	p2
lines		p3
palette1		p4
palette2		p5
shapes		p6
tilt		

📁 write	📁 fonts
fun	fonts1
saveit	fonts2
usewrite	fonts3
	fonts4
	fonts5

The files remaining in 📁 **a:** (or **b:**) are then deleted.

EXERCISE 82
View File Details

Exercises 82-84 should be done during the same session.

view file detail
To display additional information about files, beyond the file's name and extension. The following kinds of file information can be displayed:

  file size

  last modification date

  last modification time

  file attributes

NOTE:

A <u>check box</u> with an "X" (⊠) in it is <u>selected</u>.

An empty <u>check box</u> (☐) is <u>deselected</u>.

Keyboard Users
VIEW FILE DETAILS
VIEW ALL FILE DETAILS:
1. Press **Alt** + **V** (<u>V</u>iew)
2. Press **A** (<u>A</u>ll File Details)
VIEW PARTIAL FILE DETAILS:
1. Press **Alt** + **V** (<u>V</u>iew)
2. Press **P**
   (<u>P</u>artial File Details...)
3. Select options as desired:
   ☐ Size
   ☐ Last Modification Date
   ☐ Last Modification Time
   ☐ File Attributes
4. Press **⏎**
VIEW ONLY FILENAME:
1. Press **Alt** + **V** (<u>V</u>iew)
2. Press **N** (<u>N</u>ame)

190

1
- **Start Windows**, if necessary.
- **Start File Manager.**
- **Put** your floppy data disk in Drive A: (or B:) and close the door, if necessary.
- **Change** to Drive A: (or B:) (review, page 183).
- **Expand all directories** (review, page 187).

2 COPY FILES BACK TO THE ROOT DIRECTORY:
a. **Select** ☐ **paint.**
b. **Select** and then **copy** <u>all</u> the files to ☐ **a:** (or **b:**) (review, page 189).
c. Using steps a and b above, **copy** <u>all</u> of the files *from* ☐ **draw,** ☐ **practice,** ☐ **write,** and ☐ **fonts** *to* ☐ **a:** (or **b:**).
d. **Select** ☐ **a:** (or **b:**).
   There should now be 23 files and 2 subdirectories on the right side.

3 VIEW ALL FILE DETAILS:
- **Click** on **V**iew, then on **All File Details.**
   The Directory window now displays "all file details."

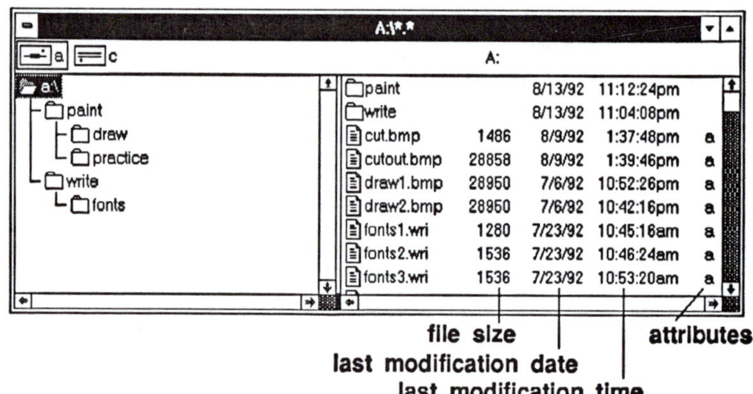

4 VIEW PARTIAL FILE DETAILS:
- **Click** on **V**iew, then on **Partial Details...**
   The *Partial Details* dialog box appears with all the check boxes *selected* (because the last option used was to view *All File Details*):

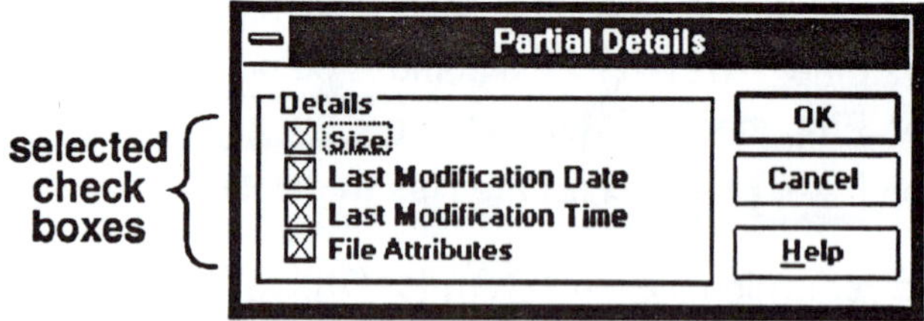

- **Click** on ⊠ Last Modification Time (to deselect it).
- **Click** on ⊠ File Attributes (to deselect it).
- **Click** on [OK].
   The *Last Modification Time* and *File Attributes* disappear.

5 VIEW ONLY FILENAME:
- **Click** on **V**iew, then on **Name.**
   The files appear with just their name showing.

Go on to Exercise 83

① SORT BY FILE TYPE:

- **Click** on **View**, then on **Sort by Type**.
  The files are displayed so that all the files with .BMP extensions are listed before the files with .WRI extensions: (They are also alphabetized *within* each file type.)

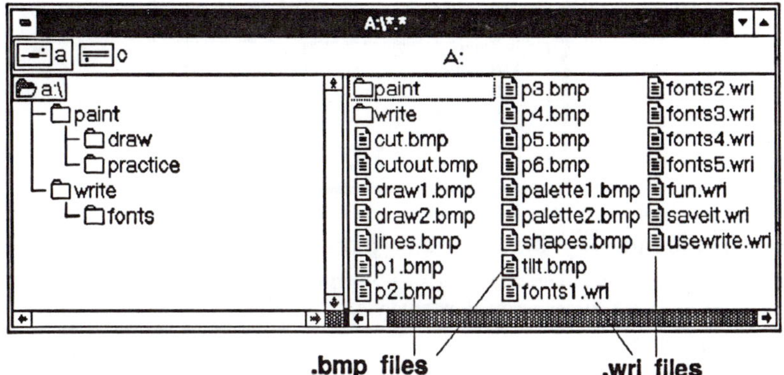

② SORT BY SIZE:

- **Click** on **View**, then on **Partial Details... .**
- **Click** on ☐ **Size**, then on 〔   OK   〕 .
- **Click** on **View**, then on **Sort by Size**.
  The files are listed with the largest file at the top, and the smallest file at the bottom.
- **Scroll** down through the files until you get to the smallest file.

③ SORT BY "LAST MODIFICATION DATE":

- **Click** on **View**, then on **Partial Details... .**
- **Click** on ☒ **Size** (to deselect it).
- **Click** on ☐ **Last Modification Date** (to select it).
- **Click** on ☐ **Last Modification Time** (to select it).
- **Click** on 〔   OK   〕 .
- **Click** on **View**, then on **Sort by Date**.
  The files are listed with the most current file at the top, and the oldest file at the bottom. Since the files were probably created on the same date, they are all the same and cannot be sorted according to date. However, notice the times that are displayed for each file. The files <u>are</u> sorted by the *Last Modification Time*.
  *NOTE: If the right side of the Directory window is too narrow to display the entire date, **drag** the <u>split bar</u> to the left or enlarge the window.*
- **Scroll** down through the files until you get to the oldest file.

④ SORT BY NAME:

- **Click** on **View**, then on **Name**.
- **Click** on **View**, then on **Sort by Name**.
  The files are sorted in their original order, alphabetically.

Go on to Exercise 84

EXERCISE 83
Sort Files

Continue from Exercise 82, doing Exercises 82-84 during the same session.

sort files
To arrange files in different orders, such as by alphabetic order, by size, by file type, or by last modification date.

file type
The extension on a filename (often called the file type) is often used to organize files into groups. For example, files ending with .wri belong with the Write program, files ending with .bmp belong with Paintbrush, and files ending with .exe are application files.

NOTE: When you <u>sort by type</u>, Windows sorts by the filename extension. When you <u>view by File Type</u> Windows shows only the files you specify.

Keyboard Users
SORT FILES
SORT BY TYPE:
1. **Press** [Alt] + [V] (View)
2. **Press** [T] (Type)
SORT BY SIZE:
1. **Press** [Alt] + [V] (View)
2. **Press** [Z] (Size)
SORT BY DATE:
1. **Press** [Alt] + [V] (View)
2. **Press** [D] (Date)
SORT BY NAME:
1. **Press** [Alt] + [V] (View)
2. **Press** [N] (Name)

NOTE: See "View File Details" (previous page) for instructions on how to show the information you are sorting on.

EXERCISE 84
View Specific Files

Continue from Exercise 83, doing Exercises 82-84 during the same session.

view specific files

To display only certain specified files in the directory window—files whose conditions you control. For example, to show only files ending with the extension .BMP, or to show only files beginning with the letter "P." In addition to files with specific parameters, four different <u>kinds</u> of files can be <u>selected</u> using check boxes.

types of files

There are four different kinds of files that can be shown on the right side of the Directory window. The default is to display all four:

   directories

   programs (applications)

   or   documents (data files)

   other files

Keyboard Users

VIEW SPECIFIC FILES

1. Press **Alt** + **V** (View)
2. Press **T** (By File Type...)
3. ENTER SPECIFIC CONDITIONS:

   Type conditions as desired, for example:

   ***.bmp** lists all files ending with .bmp.

   or

   p*.* lists all files beginning with "P."

   SELECT KIND OF FILE:

   ☐ Directories
   ☐ Program
   ☐ Documents
   ☐ Other Files

4. **Press** ⏎

---

1 VIEW SELECTED FILES:

- **Click on View.**
- **Click on By File Type.**
  The *By File Type* dialog box appears:

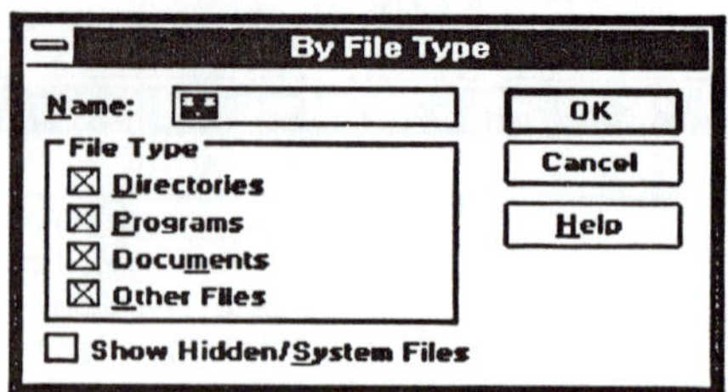

- Notice the ▛▜ that is in the Name *text box*.
  *NOTE: Remember, the asterisk (*) is a wildcard, and *.* means to show <u>all</u> filenames and <u>all</u> extensions.*
- **Type:** *.bmp
  NOTE: If text in a <u>text box</u> is highlighted, the previous text will disappear when you type, and what you type will be entered.
- **Click on** [OK].
  The right side of the Directory displays only files with .bmp extensions:

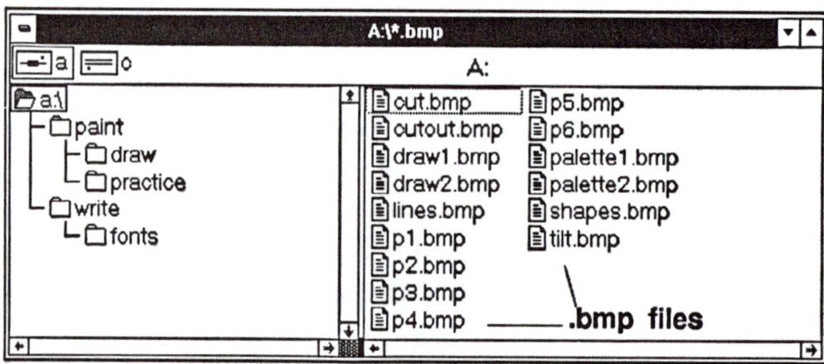

2
- **Capture** an application window (review, page 90).
- **Select** the Program Manager window (press **Ctrl** + **Esc** (Task List) and double-click on **Program Manager**).
- **Print** the **capture** (review, page 92).
- Use the Task List to **select** the **File Manager** window.

3 View only files that begin with "P" (step 1).
Hint: Type p*.* in the Name *text box*.

4 DISPLAY ALL FILES:
- **Click on View**, then on **By File Type**.
  The *By File Type* dialog box appears.
- **Type:** *.*
- **Click on** [OK].

5 Exit File Manager.

6 Go on to Exercise 85.
OR
Exit Windows.

1
- **Start Windows**, if necessary.
- **Start File Manager.**

2 CHOOSE A DISK TO FORMAT:

IMPORTANT! Formatting a disk is risky because it erases all the information on a disk. <u>Your data disk is needed in the next exercise</u>, so EITHER do Exercise 86 and then come back to this exercise, OR do not use your data disk in this exercise.
- Be sure the disk you format <u>does not</u> have any important files on it.
- **Put** the disk in Drive A: (or B:) and close the door.

3 FORMAT A DISK:

- **Click** on <u>D</u>isk, then on <u>F</u>ormat Disk... .
  The *Format Disk* dialog box appears:

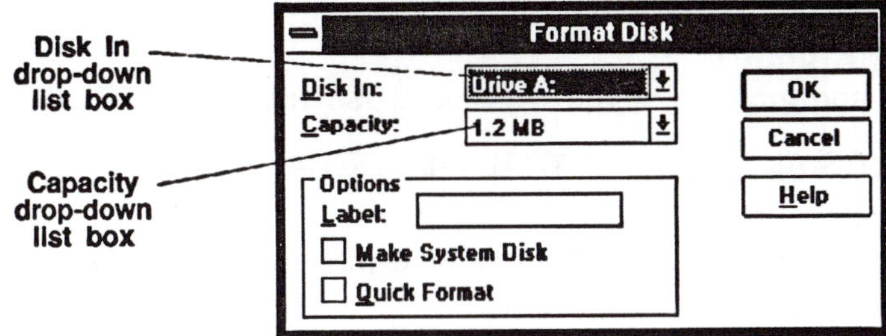

- Look at the <u>D</u>isk In drop-down list box.
  IF the disk drive you want to use is <u>not</u> displayed, **click** on the arrow and **select** the correct disk drive.
- Look at the <u>C</u>apacity drop-down list box.
  IF the disk formatting capacity you want to use is <u>not</u> displayed, **click** on the arrow and **select** the correct disk formatting capacity.
- **Click** on OK .

  The *Confirm Format Disk* dialog box appears:

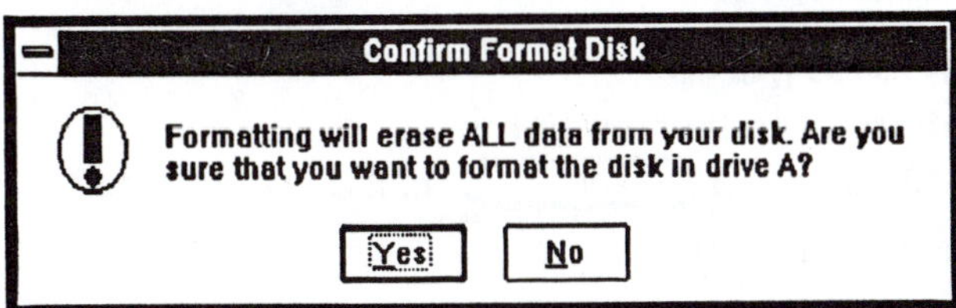

- **Click** on Yes .
  The *Formatting Disk* message window keeps you informed.
  After a while, the *Format Complete* dialog box appears.
- **Click** on No .
  The format is complete.

4
- **Click** on  a: (or b:). The Directory window shows that there are "no files found."

5 **Exit File Manager.**

6
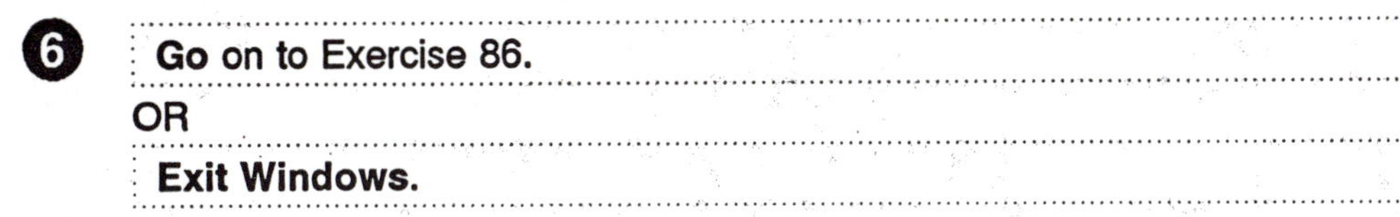
Go on to Exercise 86.

OR

Exit Windows.

---

format a disk
To prepare a disk for holding information. Formatting erases any information that may be on a disk.

disk capacity
5 1/4" <u>high density</u> disks
   hold 1.2 MB (megabytes)

5 1/4" <u>double density</u> disks
   hold 360 K (kilobytes)

3 1/2" <u>high density</u> disks
   hold 1.4 MB

3 1/2" <u>double density</u> disks
   hold 720 K

NOTE: The <u>Quick Format</u> "Option," found in the "Format Disk" dialog box lets you format previously formatted disks quickly. Disks are <u>not</u> scanned for bad sectors if you use this option.

Keyboard Users

FORMAT A DISK
From the File Manager:

1. **Press** Alt + D (<u>D</u>isk)
2. **Press** F (<u>F</u>ormat Disk...)
   The *Format Disk* dialog box appears.
3. If the disk drive displayed in the *Disk In* box is <u>not</u> correct:
   - **Press** Tab until the *Disk In* box is selected.
   - **Press** ↓ (to open it)
   - **Select** correct drive.
4. If the disk formatting capacity displayed in the *Capacity* box is <u>not</u> correct:
   - **Press** Tab until the *Capacity* box is selected.
   - **Press** ↓ (to open it)
   - **Select** correct capacity.
5. **Press** ↵ (the Confirm Format Disk window appears)
6. **Press** ↵ (the Format Complete window appears)
7. **Press** ↵

EXERCISE 86
Practice

Lesson Six
File Manager

Tasks Reviewed:

Start File Manager

Change the Disk Drive

View File Manager Menus

Expand and Collapse Directories

Create a Directory

Select a Directory

Select and Deselect Files

Move, Copy, and Delete Files

View File Details

Sort Files

View Specific Files

1
- **Start Windows**, if necessary.
- **Start File Manager.**
- **Put** your floppy data disk in Drive A: (or B:) and close the door, if necessary.
- **Change** to Drive A: (or B:) (review, page 183).
- **Expand all directories** (review, page 187).

2 CREATE A DIRECTORY; MOVE, COPY, AND DELETE FILES:
- **Create a directory** under 🗀 write; name it **letters** (review, page 185).
- **Select** 🗀 **a:\ (or b:\).**
- **Select** the files 📄 **saveit.wri** and 📄 **usewrite.wri** (review, page 186).
- <u>Move</u> the selected files to 🗀 **letters.**
- **Select** 📄 **fun.wri** and <u>copy</u> it to 🗀 **letters.**
- **Select** 🗀 **letters.** Are the three files in it?
- **Select** the file 📄 **fun.wri.**
- **Delete** 📄 **fun.wri.**
- **Select** and <u>move</u> 📄 **saveit.wri** and 📄 **usewrite.wri** to 🗀 **a:\ (or b:\).**

3 SORT FILES AND VIEW PARTIAL FILE DETAILS:
- **Select** 🗀 **a:\ (or b:\).**
- **Change <u>P</u>artial detail...** to show **Size** (review, page 190).
- **Sort** by Si<u>z</u>e (review, page 191).
- **View <u>N</u>ame** only.
- **<u>S</u>ort** by Name.

4 VIEW SPECIFIC FILES:
- **View** the specific files that start with "F" and have the .WRI extension. Hint: enter f*.wri in the <u>N</u>ame *text box* (review, page 192).
- **View <u>a</u>ll** files. Hint: use *.* in the <u>N</u>ame *text box*.

5 COLLAPSE AND EXPAND DIRECTORIES (review, page 187):
- **Collapse** the directories so that only 🗀 **a:\ (or b:\)** is showing.
- **Expand all directories.**

6 CHANGE FONT SIZE (NEW):
- **Click** on **<u>O</u>ptions**, and then on **<u>F</u>onts... .**
- **Select** size 12, and then [OK]. Is it easier to read?
- **Change** back to size 8 font.

7 DELETE A SUBDIRECTORY (NEW):
- **Select** 🗀 **letters** and then **Press** [Del]. The *Delete* dialog box appears.
- **Click** on [OK]. The *Confirm Directory Delete* dialog box appears.
- **Click** on [Yes].

8 DELETE FILES AND SUBDIRECTORIES:
- **Select** 🗀 **fonts** (on the left side).
- **Delete** all the files in 🗀 **fonts** (on the right side).
- **Delete** 🗀 **fonts.**
- **Select** each of the remaining <u>subdirectories</u> (NOT 🗀 **a:\ (or b:\)**), delete all the files in each subdirectory, and then delete the subdirectory itself. The 🗀 **a:\ (or b:\)** directory and 23 files in it should be all that is remaining on the floppy disk.

9 **Exit File Manager** and **Windows.**

Lesson Six
Review of File Manager Exercises

Lesson Six (File Manager) covers tasks that:

Start File Manager and View the Menus

Change the Disk Drive

Select and Deselect Files

Create a Directory and Select a Directory

Expand and Collapse Directories

Move, Copy, and Delete Files

View File Details

Sort Files and View Specific Files

POINTS TO EMPHASIZE

Compare and Contrast

File Manager Window _and_ Directory Window:

- The *File Manager* window is an *application window*. It holds the File Manager program and contains one or more Directory windows.
- The *Directory window* is a *document window* that is within the File Manager window and that displays files and directories on the active disk drive.

Directory Tree _and_ Contents of Current Directory:

- The *directory tree* is a representation of the directory structure on your disk. It is displayed on the <u>left side</u> of the Directory window.
- The *contents of current directory* is a list of the subdirectories and files that are in the current (selected) directory. The contents are displayed on the <u>right side</u> of the Directory window.

Directory _and_ Subdirectory _and_ Root Directory _and_ Current Directory:

- A *directory* is the part of the disk structure that holds files and other directories (also called subdirectories).
- A *subdirectory* is a directory that is within another directory. It is *both* a *directory* and a *subdirectory* and may be referred to as either.
- The *root directory* is the original (or highest level) directory.
- The *current directory* is the active (or selected) directory.

File _and_ Data File _and_ Program (Application) File _and_ Associated File:

- A *file* is a "set of data" that is saved on a disk as a named unit.
- A *data file* contains data that was created in a program, such as a letter.
- A *program file* holds instructions that do a task, such as word processing. A program file usually has a filename extension of .EXE, .COM, .PIF, .BAT or .PIF.
- An *associated file* is a data file that belongs to a certain program, such as Write.

Continued ...

File Manager

Managing files is a serious job. The disk you store files on is your *filing cabinet*. It is important to create a system in which you can quickly locate files when necessary.

The File Manager program makes it easy to work with your files by letting you:

- view your files
- organize your files into directories and subdirectories
- create new directories
- move, copy, and delete files
- sort your files in different ways
- select out specific groups of files
- search for files
- format disks
- start applications or look at a document file (as easy as **double-clicking** on the file)

Directory Branch

A branch is all the levels of subdirectories within a particular directory.

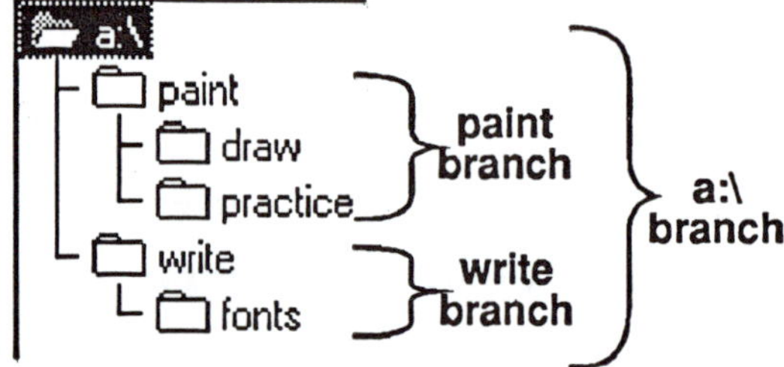

Directory Levels

Levels are the tiers of directory layers, starting with the root directory.

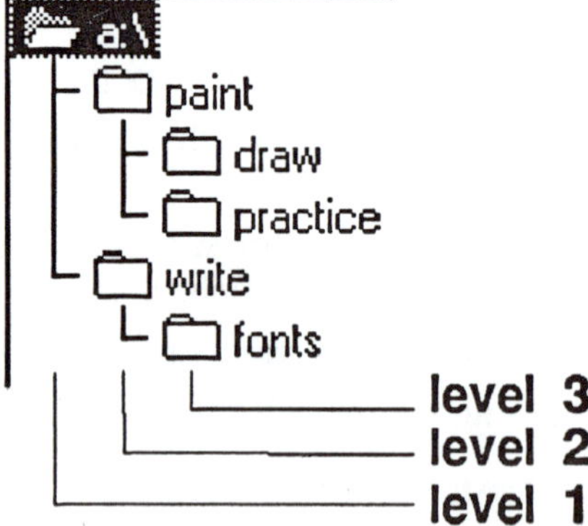

Directory Path

The **path** shows the location of files within the **directory tree**. Each directory in the **path** is separated from other directories by a backslash (\). The root directory (A in this case) is always followed by a colon (:).

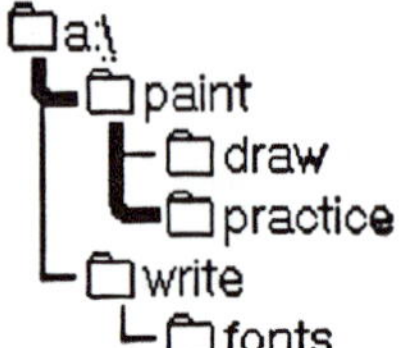

The path to the PRACTICE directory is

A:\PAINT\PRACTICE

Continued ...

View File Details

To show certain information about a file, such as its size, the date and time of the last modification, and its attributes (read only, active, hidden, and system).

Sort Files

Files can be sorted four ways:

alphabetically by	NAME
alphabetically by	FILE TYPE (file type refers to the filename extension here)
numerically by	FILE SIZE
chronologically by	LAST MODIFICATION DATE

Wildcard

A *wildcard* is a symbol that represents other characters.

? can represent any <u>single</u> character.

* can represent any <u>single</u> character or <u>group</u> of characters.

Wildcards are used to help you select specific *groups of files*.

For example:

*.EXE is used to select the *group of files* that have .EXE file extensions.

M*.* is used to select the *group of files* that start with the letter "M."

. is used to select <u>all</u> the files in a directory. The first * represents <u>any</u> filename, and the second * represents <u>any</u> filename extension.

View Specific Files and File Types

1. To indicate certain guidelines that affect which *group of files* is selected to be viewed by using wildcards in specifying file restrictions.

2. To indicate whether the *contents* (right) side of the Directory window will display

   directories,

   program files (files ending with .EXE, .COM, .PIF, and .BAT),

   document files, or

   other files (any file that does not fall under one of the categories above).

WORKSHEET 29

FILE MANAGER <u>TERMS</u>

NAME _______________________________

1. What is the part of the disk structure that holds files and/or other directories (called subdirectories)?

   1) _______________________________

2. What is the bar at the bottom of the File Manager window that displays information about the <u>current</u> drive and directory?

   2) _______________________________

3. What is the active directory, the one that is <u>highlighted</u>?

   3) _______________________________

4. What window within the File Manager window displays the files, directories, and subdirectories on your disk?

   4) _______________________________

5. What is the part of the computer system that transfers files back and forth between the computer and the hard disk?

   5) _______________________________

6. What do you call the list of the files and subdirectories that are located within the <u>directory highlighted in the directory tree</u> and that is displayed on the right side of the Directory window?

   6) _______________________________

7. What is the <u>name of the current directory</u> that is displayed in the title bar?

   7) _______________________________

8. What application window holds the File Manager program and one or more directory windows (document windows)?

   8) _______________________________

9. What is the part of the computer system that transfers files back and forth between the computer and the floppy disk?

   9) _______________________________

10. What do you call the directory structure (root directory, directories, and subdirectories) displayed on the left side of the <u>directory window</u>?

    10) _______________________________

(This page may be copied.)

WORKSHEET 30

FILE MANAGER <u>TERMS</u>

NAME _______________________________

DIRECTIONS: Use the following terms to fill in the blanks below:

directory path	file type	root directory
file	data file	collapse directories
directory branch	expand directories	associated file
directory levels	subdirectories	application (program) file

1. To display unseen directory levels in the <u>directory tree</u>.

   1) _______________________________

2. What are directories that are within other directories?

   2) _______________________________

3. What do you call the tiers of subdirectory layers, starting with the root directory?

   3) _______________________________

4. What is a set of data that is saved on a disk as a <u>named</u> unit?

   4) _______________________________

5. To <u>hide</u> directory levels in the <u>directory tree</u>.

   5) _______________________________

6. What is a file that is identified as belonging to a certain application, such as a Write or Paintbrush file?

   6) _______________________________

7. What is a file that consists of data that is created in a program, such as a letter typed into a word processor?

   7) _______________________________

8. What is the original (or highest level) directory on a disk?

   8) _______________________________

9. What is a file that holds a set of instructions that perform a task, such as word processing?

   9) _______________________________

10. What shows the location of a file within the <u>directory tree</u>?

   10) _______________________________

11. What do you call a filename extension, which is often used to organize files into groups?

   11) _______________________________

12. What is the term for all the levels of subdirectories within a specific directory?

   12) _______________________________

WORKSHEET 31

NAME ___________________________

FILE MANAGER <u>TASKS</u>

1. To *highlight* a directory, making it *current* (changing its icon from ☐ to 📁).

1) ___________________________

2. To *highlight* files so that commands can be carried out that affect them, such as *moving, copying,* or *deleting* the files.

2) ___________________________

3. To transfer files from one directory to another directory, but *leaving the original file intact.*

3) ___________________________

4. To remove the highlighting from files.

4) ___________________________

5. To use commands in the File Manager to make a new directory.

5) ___________________________

6. To use Windows to run the File Manager program.

6) ___________________________

7. To arrange files in different orders, such as by alphabetical order, by size, by file type, or by last modification date.

7) ___________________________

8. To control the levels of directories shown in the directory tree.

8) ___________________________

9. To transfer files from one directory to another directory and *removing the original file.*

9) ___________________________

10. To remove files from a disk.

10) ___________________________

11. To look at the drop-down menus that are displayed on the menu bar.

11) ___________________________

12. To display only the certain files in the directory window—files whose conditions you control.

12) ___________________________

13. To display additional information about the files, beyond the file's name and extension.

13) ___________________________

14. To switch between the drives shown in the Directory window.

14) ___________________________

15. To prepare a disk for holding information.

15) ___________________________

(This page may be copied.)

Lesson Seven — Integration

Table of Contents

EXERCISE 87
Integrate Text

integrate text

To transfer text from one document to another document. You use <u>cut</u> or <u>copy</u> (to the clipboard) and <u>paste</u> (from the clipboard) to integrate data between documents.

clipboard

A temporary storage area in the computer's memory used to hold information that is being cut (or copied) and pasted

- from place to place within a document,
- from document to document, or
- from program to program.

shortcut keys to:

copy   **Ctrl** + **C**
cut   **Ctrl** + **X**
paste   **Ctrl** + **V**

Keyboard Users

INTEGRATE TEXT

1. Start Write.
2. Create a document.
3. Highlight the text to be integrated.
4.
   - Press **Alt** + **E** (<u>E</u>dit)
   - Press **T** (Cu<u>t</u>)

   OR

   - Press **C** (<u>C</u>opy)
5. Start another Write program.
6. Position the insertion point where the text is to be inserted.
7. Press **Alt** + **E** (<u>E</u>dit)
8. Press **P** (<u>P</u>aste)

NOTE: Data can be integrated between all programs that recognize the data format.

(1) **Start Windows, if necessary.**

FROM THE *STARTING WINDOWS* SCREEN:

(2)
- **Open Accessories.**
- **Start** and **maximize Write.**

(3) CREATE A DOCUMENT:
- **Change to center justification** (review, page 140).
- **Change font to Arial, size 14** (review, page 134).
- Turn **bold** on (review, page 135).
- **Type:** `Simple Integration`
- **Press ⏎ twice.**
- **Change to regular text.**
- **Change to left justification.**
- Pressing ⏎ twice at the end of the paragraph and twice after each numbered line, **type:**

```
Integration, transferring information from one
document to another document, can be accomplished
simply by using cut and paste.

1. Type the text to be integrated.

2. Highlight the text to be integrated.

3. Copy (or cut) the text to be integrated.

4. Switch to the document to receive the text.

5. Paste the text into the new document.
```

(4) COPY TEXT:
- **Highlight** the numbered lines.
- **Copy** the selected text to the clipboard (review, page 139).

(5)
- **Save** the document on <u>Drive A:</u> (or B:); name it **DOC1.**

  NOTE: You can save on Drive A: without first changing to Drive A:, by typing the drive designation in front of the document name, for example, <u>A:DOC1</u>.
- **Print** the document.
- **Clear** the screen (**click on <u>F</u>ile, and then on <u>N</u>ew**).

(6) INTEGRATE TEXT:
- **Change font to Arial, size 14.**
- **Type:** `Here is the integrated text:`
- **Press ⏎ twice.**
- **Paste** the data from the clipboard (review, page 138).

(7)
- **Save** the document on <u>Drive A:</u> (or B:); name it **DOC2.**
- **Print** the document.

(8) **Exit Write.**

(9)
> **Go on to Exercise 88.**

OR

> **Exit Windows.**

NOTE: Not all programs can use the <u>embed</u> feature. Paintbrush and Write are two that can.

EMBED A DRAWING *STARTING* FROM PAINTBRUSH

❶ CREATE A DRAWING:

- **Open Paintbrush.**
- **Use** ◯ (circle/ellipse tool) to draw a circle about 1" in diameter in the top left corner.
- **Use** ✂ (pick tool) to **define** the circle as a cutout (review, page 163).
- **Copy** the cutout (it is placed onto the *Clipboard*).
- **Save** the drawing on <u>Drive A:</u> (or B:); name it **OBJECT**.
- **DO <u>NOT</u> exit Paintbrush** or clear the screen.
- **Select** (switch to) the **Program Manager** window (review, page 58).

❷ EMBED THE OBJECT:

- **Start** and **maximize Write.**
- **Change** the **font** to **Arial, size 14.**
- **Type:** Here is my circle!
- **Press** ⏎ twice.
- **Click** on **Edit**, and then on **Paste.**
  The drawing appears at the *insertion point*.

❸
- **Save** the Document on <u>Drive A:</u> (or B:); name it **EMBED1.**
- **Print** the **document** and **clear** the screen.

EMBED A DRAWING *STARTING* FROM WRITE

❹ CREATE A DOCUMENT:

- **Change** the **font** to **Arial, size 14.**
- **Type:** Example of Embedding an Object:
- **Press** ⏎ twice.

❺ INSERT OBJECT:

- **Click** on **Edit**, and then on **Insert Object... .**
  The *Insert Object* dialog box appears:

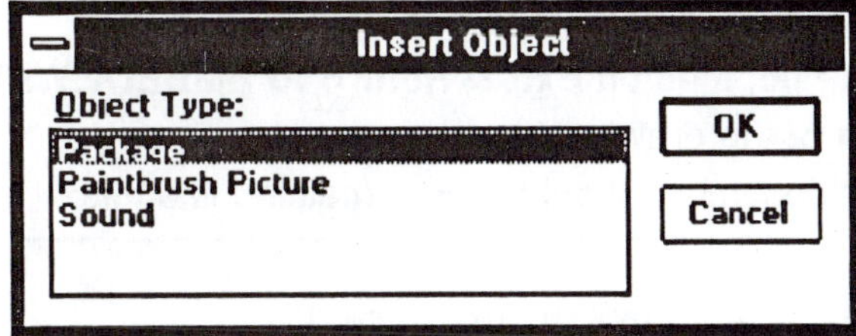

- **Double-click** on **Paintbrush Picture.** Paintbrush opens.
- **Draw** a smiley face in the top left corner.

- **Click** on **File**, then on **Update.**
- **Click** on **File**, then on **Exit & Return to [Untitled].**
  The drawing appears in the Write document, and the *insertion point* jumps to the bottom of the drawing.

❻
- **Scroll** to the top of the document (to view the image).
- **Save** the document on <u>Drive A:</u> (or B:); name it **EMBED2.**
- **Print** the **document** and **clear** the screen.

Go on to Exercise 89

EXERCISE 88
Embed an Object

Exercises 88 and 89 should be done during the same session.

embed an object
To insert information from one program into a <u>different</u> program.

object
An object is a selected <u>set of information</u> created in a Windows application (program). An object can be <u>embedded in</u> and <u>linked to</u> other applications.

embed
To paste an <u>object</u> that was created in one program into another program.

Keyboard Users

EMBED AN OBJECT
STARTING FROM PAINTBRUSH:

1. Start Paintbrush.
2. Create a drawing.
3. Define the drawing as a cutout.
4. Copy the cutout.
5. Start Write.
6. Position the insertion point where the object is to be embedded.
7. **Press** **Ctrl** + **V** (Paste)

STARTING FROM WRITE:

1. Start Write.
2. Position the insertion point where the object is to be embedded.
3. **Press** **Alt** + **E** (Edit)
4. **Press** **I** (Insert Object...)
   A dialog box appears.
5. **Press** **↓** or **↑** to highlight **Paintbrush Picture.**
6. **Press** ⏎
7. Create or open a drawing.
8. **Press** **Alt** + **F** (File)
9. **Press** **U** (Update)
10. **Press** **Alt** + **F** (File)
11. **Press** **X** (Exit & Return to [Untitled])

EXERCISE 89
Edit an Embedded Object

Continue from Exercise 88, doing both during the same session.

edit an embedded object
To access the <u>source program</u> for an embedded object from within the <u>destination document</u> to make changes to that embedded object.

NOTE: If you suddenly lose the object, try using <u>E</u>dit <u>U</u>ndo to bring the image back. (Pressing either the spacebar or delete will delete a highlighted object.)

Keyboard Users
EDIT AN EMBEDDED OBJECT

1. Start Write and open a document with an embedded object.
2. Use 🖳 to highlight the embedded object. (When the cursor moves inside the object, it will become highlighted.)
3. **Press** Alt + E (<u>E</u>dit)
4. **Press** O (Edit Paintbrush Picture <u>O</u>bject) Paintbrush opens.
5. Edit the drawing as desired.
6. **Press** Alt + F (<u>F</u>ile)
7. **Press** U (<u>U</u>pdate)
8. **Press** Alt + F (<u>F</u>ile)
9. **Press** X (E<u>x</u>it & Return to [your document])

---

1 Open EMBED1.

2 EDIT THE DRAWING:
- **Double-click** on the **circle**.
  Paintbrush opens with the drawing displayed.
- **Use** ☐ (box tool) to draw a **square** inside the circle.
- **Click** on <u>F</u>ile, then on <u>U</u>pdate.
- **Click** on <u>F</u>ile, then on E<u>x</u>it & Return to EMBED1.WRI.
  The new document should look something like this:

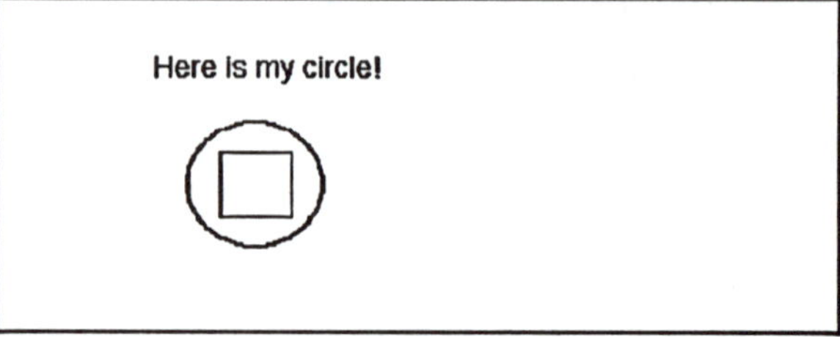

3 DID THE ORIGINAL DRAWING CHANGE?
- **Select** (switch to) **Paintbrush**.
- Notice that the drawing did <u>not</u> change (no square in the circle).

4
- **Select Write – EMBED1.WRI.**
- **Click** in the Write workspace, but out of the picture area (to *deselect* the drawing).

5
- **Save** the updated document.
- **Print** the document and **clear** the screen.

PRACTICE:

6
- **Open EMBED2.**
- **Double-click** on the **face**.
  Paintbrush opens with the face displayed.
- **Draw** a hat.
- **Click** on <u>F</u>ile, then on <u>U</u>pdate.
- **Click** on <u>F</u>ile, then on E<u>x</u>it & Return to EMBED2.WRI.
- **Click off** of the drawing (to *deselect* it).
  The new document should look something like this:

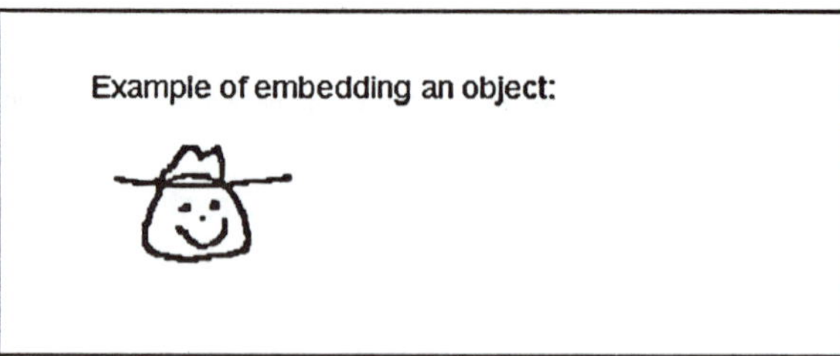

7
- **Save** the updated document.
- **Print** the document and **clear** the screen.
- **Exit Write.**

8 Go on to Exercise 90.

OR

Exit Windows.

NOTE: Not all programs can use the <u>link</u> feature. Paintbrush and Write are two that can.

1 **Start Windows**, if necessary.

2 CREATE A DRAWING (SOURCE DOCUMENT):
- **Start** and **maximize Paintbrush.**
- **Use** ▢ (rounded box tool) to **draw** a square box about 1.5" long x 1.5" wide in the top left corner.
- **Save** the drawing on <u>Drive A:</u> (or B:); name it **BOX.**
- **Use** ✂ (pick tool) to **define** the box as a cutout.
- **Copy** the cutout.
- DO <u>NOT</u> **exit Paintbrush** or clear the screen.
- **Select** the **Program Manager** window.

3 CREATE A DESTINATION DOCUMENT:
- **Start** and **maximize Write.**
- **Change** the **font** to **Arial, size 14.**
- **Type:** LINKED DOCUMENT #1
- **Press** ⏎ twice.
- **Type:** Linking connects an object that has been embedded in one or more destination documents in such a way that when the object is edited in one document, the other documents are also edited.
- **Press** ⏎ twice.
- **Type:** LINKED OBJECT:
- **Press** ⏎ twice.

4 EMBED AND LINK THE OBJECT INTO WRITE:
- **Click** on **E̲dit.**
- **Click** on **Paste L̲ink.**
  The rounded box appears in the document.

5 - **Save** the document on <u>Drive A:</u> (or B:); name it **LINK1.**
- **Print** the **document.** Do <u>not</u> **clear** the screen.
- **Select** the **Program Manager.**
- **Start** and **maximize Write** again (two copies of Write are now open).

6 CREATE A SECOND DESTINATION DOCUMENT:
- **Change** the **font** to **Arial, size 14.**
- **Type:** LINKED DOCUMENT #2
- **Press** ⏎ twice.
- **Type:** This is the second Write document into which you are going to embed and link the rounded box.
- **Press** ⏎ twice.
- **Type:** LINKED OBJECT:
- **Press** ⏎ twice.

7 EMBED AND LINK THE OBJECT INTO WRITE:
- **Click** on **E̲dit.**
- **Click** on **Paste L̲ink.**
  The rounded box appears in the document.

8 - **Save** the document on <u>Drive A:</u> (or B:); name it **LINK2.**
- **Print** the **Document.** Do <u>not</u> clear the screen.

Go on to Exercise 91

Exercises 90-92 should be done during the same session.

link an object
To embed an object with an <u>active connection</u> between the <u>source document</u> and one or more <u>destination documents</u>.

link
An active connection between an object and the different programs into which that object is embedded.

source document
The document in which an object is created.

destination document
The document into which an object is placed.

Keyboard Users
LINK AN OBJECT
1. Start Paintbrush.
2. Create a drawing.
3. Save the drawing.
4. Define the drawing as a cutout.
5. Copy the cutout.
6. Start Write.
7. Type text as desired.
8. Position the insertion point where the object will be inserted.
9. **Press** Alt + E (E̲dit)
10. **Press** L (Paste L̲ink)
    The object appears.
11. Save the document.

EXERCISE 91
Edit a Linked Object

Continue from Exercise 90, doing Exercises 90-92 during the same session.

edit a linked object
To change and save a linked <u>object</u> in the source document, thus changing the <u>object</u> in all of the <u>open</u> destination documents to which it is linked.

NOTE: When you <u>open</u> a document that has a linked object in it, a dialog box appears that asks, "Do you want to update links now?" Select "<u>Y</u>es" so you can be certain that the link is current.

Keyboard Users
EDIT A LINKED OBJECT
1. Start Write.
2. Open a document with a *linked* object in it.
3. Use 🖰 to highlight the embedded object. (When the cursor moves inside the object, the object becomes highlighted.)
4. Press **Alt** + **E** (<u>E</u>dit)
5. Press **O** (Edit Paintbrush Picture <u>O</u>bject) Paintbrush opens.
6. Edit the drawing as desired.
7. Press **Alt** + **F** (<u>F</u>ile)
8. Press **S** (<u>S</u>ave)
9. Press **Alt** + **F** (<u>F</u>ile)
10. Press **X** (E<u>x</u>it)

There are now two Write programs and one Paintbrush program <u>open</u> that contain the linked object, "BOX."

1 PRACTICE:
- **Select Paintbrush - BOX.BMP.**
- **Select Write - LINK1.WRI.**
- **Select Write - LINK2.WRI.**
- **Select the Program Manager.**

2 EDIT A LINKED OBJECT:
- **Select Write - LINK1.WRI.**
- **Double-click** on the rounded box.
  Paintbrush opens with the document that contains the rounded box.
  NOTE: Because Paintbrush - BOX.BMP was already open, it was selected instead of opening a new version of the Paintbrush program.
- **Size the Paintbrush window** to about 4" x 4" and **move** it to the right side of the screen.
  The screen should look something like this:

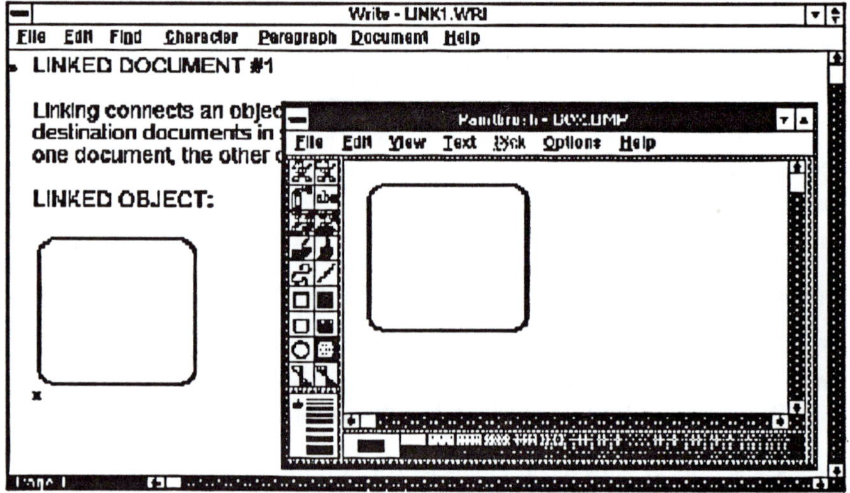

- **Use** 🔲 (box tool) to draw a box inside the rounded box.
  Notice that <u>both</u> images change as you edit the image in Paintbrush.
- **Use** ⬤ (filled circle/ellipse tool) to draw a circle inside the boxes.
  The images should look something like this:

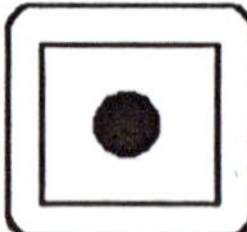

3
- **Save** the drawing (from the Paintbrush <u>F</u>ile menu).
- **Exit Paintbrush.**

4 **Print** and **save** the revised **LINK1**, and then **exit Write.**

5
- **Select WRITE - LINK2.WRI.**
  The image was changed in this document also.
- **Print** and **save** the revised **LINK2**, and then **exit Write.**

Go on to Exercise 92

1 INTEGRATE DATA:

- **Start Write.**
- **Select** the **Program Manager,** and **start Write** again.
- **Type:** This is a quick and simple review of how to integrate information from one document to another. THIS TEXT WILL BE INTEGRATED.
- **Highlight** and **copy:** THIS TEXT WILL BE INTEGRATED.
- **Select** the other **Write window.**
- **Paste** the text into the document.
  The integration is complete.
- **Exit Write** without saving.
  The other Write becomes selected.
- **Exit Write** without saving.

2 EMBED AN OBJECT:

- **Start Write.**
- **Type:** I am going to embed a drawing into this document. It will be inserted at the "insertion point."
- **Press** ⏎ three or four times.
- **Insert Object** (review, page 203, step 5).
- **Create** a **drawing** of your choice in **Paintbrush.**
- **Update** the **object** and **exit Paintbrush.**
- **Scroll** to the top to view the drawing.

3 EDIT AN EMBEDDED OBJECT:

- **Edit** the embedded **object** (review, page 204).
- **Change** the **drawing.**
- **Update** the **object,** and **exit Paintbrush.**
- **Click off** of the object (to deselect it).
- **Print** the **document** and **save** it on Drive A: (or B:); name it **EMBEDDED.**
- **Clear** the screen.

4 LINK AN OBJECT:

- **Select** the **Program Manager,** and **start Paintbrush.**
- **Create** a **drawing** and **save** it on Drive A: (or B:); name it **PICTURE.**
- **Define** the drawing as a **cutout,** and then **copy it.**
- **Exit Paintbrush.**
- **Select Write.**
- **Type:** HERE IS MY LINKED DRAWING:
- **Press** ⏎ a few times.
- **Link** the **object** (review, page 205, step 4).

5 EDIT A LINKED OBJECT:

- **Double-click** on the **object.**
- **Change** the drawing.
- **Save** the drawing and **exit Paintbrush.**
- **Click off** of the object.
- **Print** the **document** and **save** it on Drive A: (or B:); name it **LINKED.**
- **Clear** the screen.

6 - **Exit Write and Windows.**

Tasks Reviewed:

Integrate Text
Embed an Object
Edit an Embedded Object
Link an Object
Edit a Linked Object

Lesson Seven
Review of Integration Exercises

Lesson Seven (Integration) covers tasks that:

Integrate Text

Embed an Object

Edit an Embedded Object

Link an Object

Edit a Linked Object

POINTS TO EMPHASIZE

Object Linking and Embedding (OLE)

Object linking and embedding (or OLE) is the term Windows uses for its powerful integration features. Four of Windows' programs support object linking and embedding. Two are designed to <u>create</u> objects for linking and embedding—Paintbrush and Sound Recorder. They are called *servers*. Two are designed to <u>accept</u> embedded or linked objects—Write and Cardfile. They are called *clients*. Other software that is designed to run under Windows may also support OLE.

Object

An object is a selected *set of information* created in a Windows application (program). An object can be *embedded in* and *linked to* other applications.

Embed

To paste an *object* that was created in one program into another program.

Link

To establish an active connection between an object and the different programs into which that object is embedded.

Source Document

The document in which an object is created.

Destination Document

The document into which an object is placed.

Clipboard

An area in the computer used to hold information that is being *cut (or copied) and pasted*
- from place to place within a document,
- from document to document within a program, or
- from program to program.

Continued ...

Compare and Contrast

Integrate <u>and</u> Embed <u>and</u> Link:

- *Integrate* is a computer term that means to transfer data from one document to another within the same program or between different programs. Windows performs integration by using *cut (or copy) and paste*, with the *clipboard* temporarily holding the data being transferred. Windows has certain programs (Paintbrush and Write are two) that are designed with special integration capabilities (see *embed* below).

- *Embed* means to transfer an *object* between programs using *certain Windows* programs that are specially designed so you can *edit* the embedded object from within the destination document. You actually open the *source program* from within the *destination program*, edit and update the object, exit the *source program*, and return to the original document. The *object* <u>need not be saved</u> to use the *embed* feature.

- *Link* means to transfer an *object* from one program to another program with an *active connection* between the source document and one or more destination documents. When you edit a linked object in the source document, the object is also changed in <u>all</u> of the *open* destination documents (when a document with a linked object is *opened*, you are offered an opportunity to "update" the *linked* object). An *object* <u>must be saved</u> to use the *link* feature.

WORKSHEET 32
INTEGRATION TERMS AND TASKS

NAME _______________________________

DIRECTIONS: Use the following terms to fill in the blanks below:

link	clipboard	edit a linked object	source document
embed	integrate text	destination document	
object	link an object	edit an embedded object	

1. To change and save a linked object in the source document, thus changing it in <u>all</u> of the destination documents that are open.

   1) _______________________________

2. What is the document from which an object is created?

   2) _______________________________

3. To embed an object with an <u>active connection</u> between the <u>source document</u> and one or more <u>destination documents</u>.

   3) _______________________________

4. What is a selected *set of information* created in a Windows application (program)?

   4) _______________________________

5. To access the <u>source program</u> of an embedded object from within the <u>destination document</u> to make changes to that embedded object.

   5) _______________________________

6. To paste an *object* that was created in one program into another program.

   6) _______________________________

7. What is the <u>active connection</u> between an object and the different programs into which that object is embedded?

   7) _______________________________

8. What is the document into which an object is placed?

   8) _______________________________

9. To transfer text from one document to another document.

   9) _______________________________

10. What is the area in the computer that is used to hold information that is being *cut (or copied) and pasted*?

   10) _______________________________

(This page may be copied.)

Lesson Eight — Other Features

Table of Contents

EXERCISE 93
Select a Desktop Wallpaper

Exercises 93-95 should be done during the same session.

select a desktop wallpaper
To select a <u>picture</u> that is repeated to cover the desktop.

desktop wallpaper
A picture that is repeated to create a wallpaper effect across the desktop. Wallpaper is usually a larger design and more elaborate than a <u>desktop pattern</u>. Wallpaper is stored in a file with a .BMP extension. The files are accessible through Paintbrush, and new wallpaper designs can be created in Paintbrush.

Keyboard Users

SELECT A DESKTOP WALLPAPER

From the Starting Windows screen, with the Main window open:

1. **Start** the Control Panel.
2. **Open** Desktop.
3. Press **Alt** + **F** (*F*ile)
4. Press **Alt** + **↓** (open the list box)
5. Press **↓** and **↑** until the desired wallpaper is highlighted.
6. Press **↵**
7. **Close** the Control Panel.

---

1 **Start Windows**, if necessary.

FROM THE *STARTING WINDOWS* SCREEN:
(With the *Main* window open)

2 • **Double-click** on .

The *Control Panel* window opens.

• **Double-click** on .

The *Desktop* window opens:

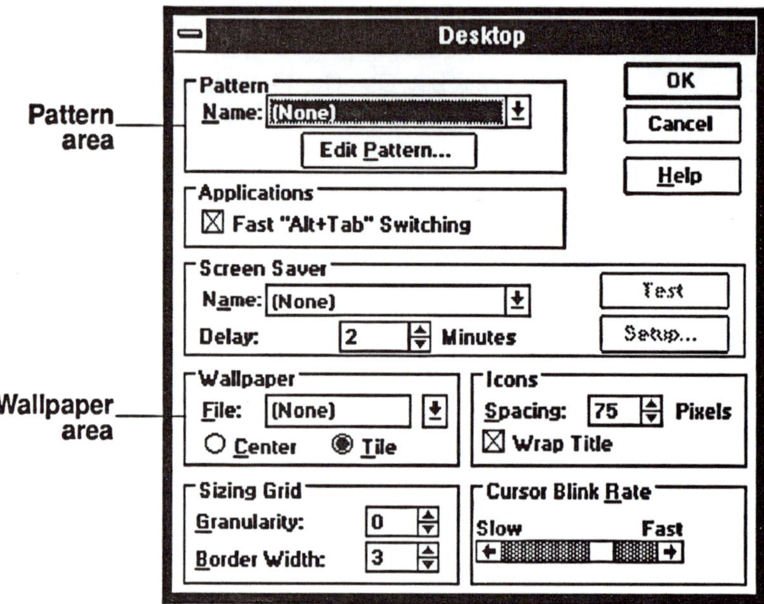

Pattern area

Wallpaper area

3 • **Click** on the *F*ile *drop-down list box.*
A list of wallpaper choices drops down.
• **Scroll** through the list.
• **Click** on **Honey**.
• **Click** on **OK**.

Honey wallpaper covers the desktop.

4 • **Double-click** on the **Desktop** icon.
• **Click** on the *F*ile *drop-down list box.*
• **Scroll** through the list and **click** on the wallpaper of your choice.
• **Click** on **OK**.
• **Repeat** step 4 to view different wallpapers as desired.

5 CHANGE WALLPAPER BACK TO "NONE":
• **Double-click** on **Desktop**.
• **Click** on the *F*ile *drop-down list box.*
• **Scroll** to the top of the list and **click** on **(None)**.
• **Click** on **OK**.

Go on to Exercise 94

❶ SELECT A DESKTOP PATTERN:
With the *Control Panel* open:
- **Double-click** on **Desktop**.
  The *Desktop* window opens (see illustration on previous page).
- **Click** on the **N**ame *drop-down list box*.
  A list of patterns drops down.
- **Scroll** through the list.
- **Click** on **Spinner**.
- **Click** on [OK].
  The Spinner pattern covers the desktop area.

❷ VIEW OR EDIT DESKTOP PATTERNS:
- **Double-click** on **Desktop**.
- **Click** on the **N**ame *drop-down list box*.
- **Click** on **Spinner** (it should already be selected).
- **Click** on **Edit P**attern... .
  The *Desktop - Edit Pattern* dialog box appears:

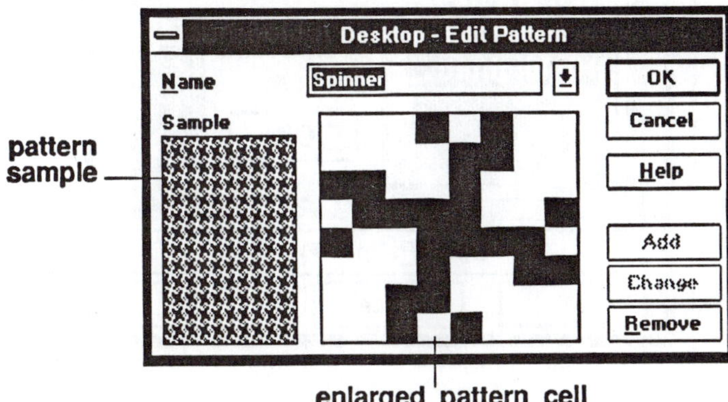

enlarged pattern cell

❸ VIEW PATTERNS AND SELECT A PATTERN:
- **Click** on the **N**ame *drop-down list box*.
- **Scroll** through the box and **click** on any pattern.
  The pattern is displayed in the Sample box.
- Repeat the two directions above until you see a pattern you like.
- **Click** on [OK] (in the *Desktop - Edit Pattern* window).
- **Click** on [OK] (in the *Desktop* window).

❹ CREATE A NEW PATTERN:
- **Double-click** on **Desktop**.
- **Click** on the **N**ame *drop-down list box*.
- **Scroll** to the top of the box and **click** on (None).
- **Click** on **Edit P**attern... .
- Type a name for the new pattern in the **N**ame box.
- **Click** in the enlarged pattern cell to create a new pattern.
- **Click** on **Add**, then on [OK].
- **Click** on [OK] (in the *Desktop* window).

❺ CHANGE PATTERN BACK TO "NONE":
- **Double-click** on **Desktop**.
- **Click** on the **N**ame *drop-down list box*.
- **Scroll** to the <u>top</u> of the list and **click** on (None).
- **Click** on [OK].

❻ - **Close** the **Control Panel**.

Go on to Exercise 95

EXERCISE 94
Select a Desktop Pattern

Continue from Exercise 93, doing Exercises 93-95 during the same session.

select a desktop pattern
To select a <u>design</u> that is repeated to cover the desktop.

desktop pattern
A small design that is repeated to create a pattern across the desktop.

Keyboard Users
SELECT A DESKTOP PATTERN
From the Starting Windows screen, with the Main window open:
1. **Start** the Control Panel.
2. **Open** Desktop.
3. **Press** [Alt] + [N] (Name)
4. **Press** [Alt] + [↓] (to open the list box)
5. **Press** [↓] and [↑] until the desired pattern is highlighted.
6. **Press** [↵]
7. **Close** the Control Panel.

213

EXERCISE 95
Change Desktop Color Scheme

Continue from Exercise 94, doing Exercises 93-95 during the same session.

change desktop color scheme
To select a new color scheme from a predefined list of color schemes, or to change or create your own color scheme.

color scheme
A combination of colors that Windows uses for its screen elements.

sample color scheme area
An area in the Color window with Windows elements that change to match the highlighted color scheme. Use the sample color scheme area to decide if you like a color scheme before selecting it for your desktop.

Keyboard Users

CHANGE DESKTOP COLOR SCHEME
From the Starting Windows Screen, with the Main window open:

1. **Start** Control Panel.
2. **Open** Color.
3. **Press** Alt + S
   (Color Schemes)
4. **Press** Alt + ↓
   (to open the list box)
5. **Press** ↓ and ↑ to scroll through the color schemes, and notice the sample color scheme area change to match the highlighted color scheme.
6. Highlight the desired color scheme.
7. **Press** ↵
8. **Close** the Control Panel.

---

① **Start the Control Panel.**

② **Double-click on** [Color].

The *Color* window opens:

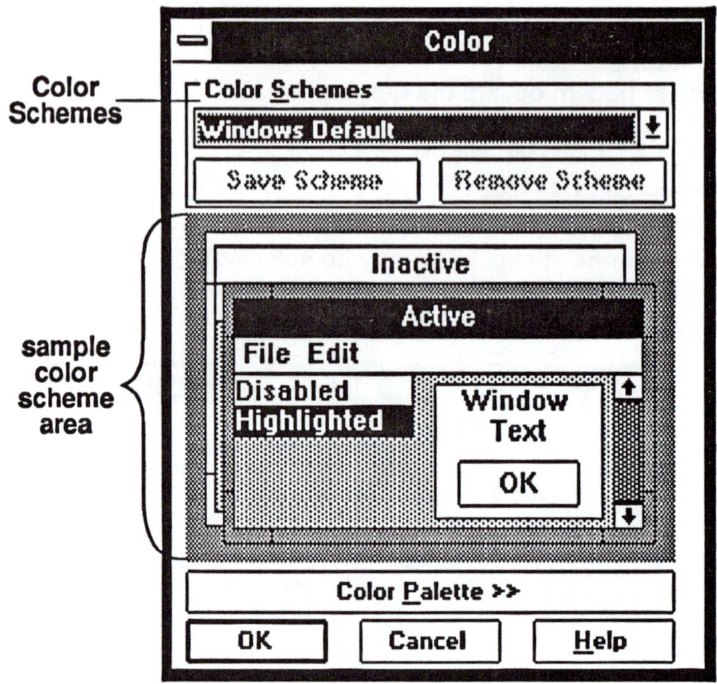

Color Schemes

sample color scheme area

③ VIEW AND SELECT A COLOR SCHEME:
- **Click** on the **Color Schemes** *drop-down list box* **arrow**.
  A list of *Color Scheme* choices drops down.
- **Scroll** through the list.
- **Click** on **Arizona**.
  Notice that the *sample color scheme* changes.
- **Click** on the **Color Schemes** *drop-down list box* **arrow** again.
- **Press** ↓ and ↑ to **scroll** through the list; notice the *sample color scheme* box change to display each highlighted color scheme.
- **Click** on the **color scheme** that you want.
- **Click** on [OK].
  Your desktop color scheme changes to the one you chose.

④ CHANGE THE COLOR SCHEME BACK TO "WINDOWS DEFAULT":
With the *Control Panel* still open:
- **Double-click** on **Color**.
- **Click** on the **Color Schemes** *drop-down list box* **arrow**.
- **Scroll** to the top of the list.
- **Click** on **Windows Default**.
- **Click** on [OK].

Continue Exercise 95 on the next page

 **5** **CREATE A COLOR SCHEME:**

With the *Control Panel* open:

a. **Double-click on Color.**

b. **Click on Color Palette>>.**
   The color palette is added to the *Color* window. It includes a drop-down list of *screen elements*, a palette of *Basic Colors*, and a palette for *Custom Colors*.

c.
   - **Click** on a screen element in the *sample color scheme area* you want to change.

   OR

   - **Click** on the **Screen Elements** *drop-down list box.*
   - **Click** on the desired screen element.

d. **Click** on a **color** in the *Basic Color* palette.
   The color is displayed in the *sample screen*.

e. Repeat steps c and d to change other screen elements as desired.

f. **Click** on [OK] when your screen is done.
   Your desktop color scheme changes to the one you created.
   NOTE: In order to avoid adding color schemes to classroom hard disks, it is recommended that you do not save color schemes unless you own your own computer.

Screen elements in the Sample Color Scheme Area

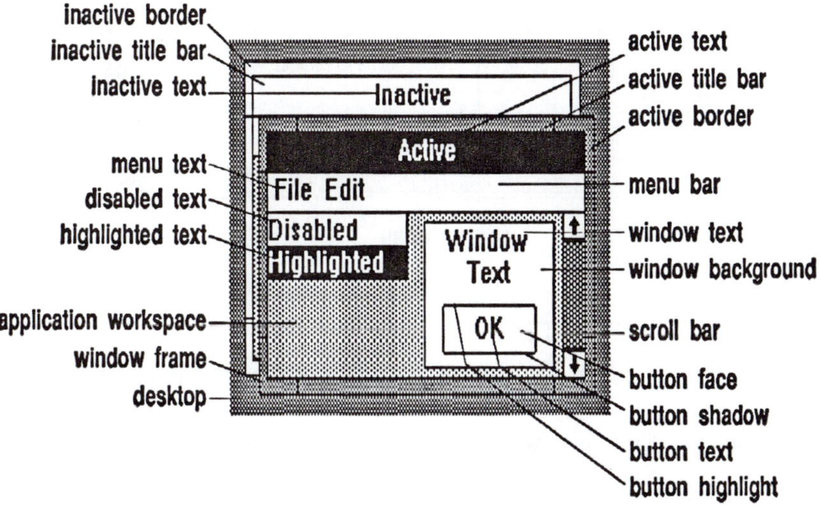

6 **CHANGE THE COLOR SCHEME BACK TO "WINDOWS DEFAULT":**

With the *Control Panel* still open:

- **Double-click** on **Color.**
- **Click** on the **Color Schemes** *drop-down list box* arrow.
- **Scroll** to the top of the list.
- **Click** on **Windows Default.**
- **Click** on [OK].

7
   Go on to Exercise 96.

   OR

   Exit Windows.

---

create desktop color scheme
To change the color for any of the screen elements as desired.

screen elements
   desktop
   application workspace
   window background
   window text
   menu bar
   menu text
   active title bar
   inactive title bar
   active title bar text
   inactive title bar text
   active border
   inactive border
   window frame
   scroll bars
   button face
   button shadow
   button text
   button highlight
   disabled text
   highlight
   highlighted text

Keyboard Users

CREATE DESKTOP COLOR SCHEME

From the Starting Windows Screen, with the Main window open:

1. **Start** the Control Panel.

2. **Open** Color.

3. **Press** [Alt] + [P] (Color Palette)
   The color palette opens.

4. **Press** [Alt] + [E]
   (Screen Elements)

5. **Press** [Alt] + [↓] (to open the list box)

6. **Press** [↓] and [↑] until the desired *screen element* is highlighted.

7. **Press** [Space] (to select a screen element)

8. **Press** [Tab] (to move to the color palette)

9. **Press** [↕↔] (to select the desired color)

10. **Press** [Space] (to choose the color)

11. Repeat steps 4-10 to change other screen elements.

12. **Press** [↵]
   New desktop colors appear.

13. **Close** the Control Panel.

EXERCISE 96
Use the Calendar

use Calendar

To use Windows' Calendar's program to:
> view other dates
> add an appointment
> save a calendar file
> open a calendar file
> toggle <u>day</u> and <u>month</u> view
> insert a <u>special</u> time
> set the alarm
> turn the alarm off
> delete <u>special</u> time

Calendar

A month-at-a-glance calendar, a daily appointment book, and an alarm clock.

Keyboard Users

START FILE MANAGER

From the Starting screen:

1. **Open Accessories.**
2. **Start Calendar.**

VIEW TOMORROW'S SCHEDULE:

1. **Press** `Ctrl` + `PgDn`

ADD AN APPOINTMENT:

1. **Press** `Tab` until *insertion point* is in the appt. area.
2. **Press** `↑` or `↓` to move *insertion point* to desired time.
3. **Type** the desired message.

SAVE A CALENDAR:

1. **Press** `Alt` + `F` (<u>F</u>ile)
2. **Press** `A` (Save <u>A</u>s...)
3. **IF** you want to change the drive:
   - **Press** `Alt` + `V` (Dri<u>v</u>e)
   - **Press** `↓`
   - Use arrows to highlight the desired drive.
   - **Press** `↵`
4. **Press** `Alt` + `N` (File <u>N</u>ame)
5. Type a filename.
6. **Press** `↵`

EXIT CALENDAR:

1. **Exit Calendar.**

continued on next page...

216

---

① **Start Windows,** if necessary.

FROM THE *STARTING WINDOWS* SCREEN:

② START CALENDAR:

- **Open Accessories.**
- **Double-click on** ⬚ .
  Calendar

  The Calendar window appears:

view other dates:
previous next

current time

status bar

date of current page

appointment area

scratch pad

insertion point

③ VIEW OTHER DATES:

- **Click** once on `→` (next to the date) to view tomorrow's schedule.

④ ADD AN APPOINTMENT:

- **Click** an **insertion point** at 12:00 p.m.
- **Type:** Lunch with Hazel

⑤ SAVE A CALENDAR FILE:

- **Place** your disk in Drive A: (or B:) and close the door.
- **Click on <u>F</u>ile.**
- **Click on Save <u>A</u>s... .**
  The *Save As* dialog box appears.
- **Select** Drive A: (or B:) from the **Dri<u>v</u>es** *drop-down list box*.
- **Click on the File <u>N</u>ame** *text box*, and **type:** APPTS
- **Click on** [OK] .

⑥ EXIT CALENDAR:

- **Double-click** on the Calendar's ⬚ (control box).

Continue Exercise 96 on the next page

7
- **Start Calendar**, again.
- Notice that the date defaults back to today's date.

8 OPEN A CALENDAR FILE:
- **Click** on **F**ile.
- **Click** on **O**pen... .
  The *Open* dialog box appears.
- **Select** Drive A: (or B:).
- **Double-click** on **appts.cal** (in the File **N**ame *list box*).

9 DISPLAY THE APPOINTMENT YOU ADDED:
- **Click** once on ▣ (next to the date).
  The lunch appointment should be displayed.
- **Click** once on ▣ to return to current date.

10 TOGGLE BETWEEN *DAY VIEW* AND *MONTH VIEW*:
- **Double-click** on the **current date status bar**.
  The *month view* calendar is displayed.
- **Double-click** on the **current date status bar**.
  The *day view* calendar is displayed.

11 INSERT A SPECIAL TIME, AND SET THE ALARM:
- Note the time displayed on the left end of the status bar and add 3 minutes to the time.
- **Click** on **O**ptions, and then on **S**pecial Time... .
- **Type** the special time (the current time + 3 minutes)
- **Click** on ○ **A**M or ○ **P**M (whichever is appropriate).
- **Click** on | Insert |.
  You are returned to the Calendar with the new time inserted at the appropriate location and the *insertion point* at the right of the time.
- **Click** on **A**larm and then on **S**et.
  A bell appears on the left side of the special time.

  🔔 3:22 |

- Wait for the bell to sound (a dim sound).
  When the alarm goes off, a window appears with the time displayed in a box.
  NOTE: The alarm will ring only if Calendar is active. It can be minimized, but not closed.
- **Click** on | OK |.

12 TURN THE ALARM OFF, AND DELETE THE SPECIAL TIME:
- With the *Insertion Point* still at the *new* time,
- **Click** on **A**larm and then on **S**et (to deselect it).
- **Click** on **O**ptions and then on **S**pecial Time... .
- **Click** on | **D**elete |.

13 **Exit Calendar.**

14
> **Go** on to Exercise 97.

OR

> **Exit Windows.**

Keyboard Users (continued)
OPEN A CALENDAR FILE:
1. **Press** `Alt` + `F` (F̲ile)
2. **Press** `O` (O̲pen)
   IF you want to change the drive: see instructions on previous page.
3. **Press** `Alt` + `N` (File N̲ame)

   > - Type a filename.
   > - **Press** `↵`

   OR

   > - **Press** `Tab`
   > - Use arrows to highlight desired file.
   > - **Press** `↵`

TOGGLE DAY AND MONTH VIEW:
1. **Press** `Alt` + `V` (V̲iew)
2. > **Press** `M` (for M̲onth view)

   OR

   > **Press** `D` (for D̲ay view)

INSERT A SPECIAL TIME:
1. **Press** `Alt` + `O` (O̲ptions)
2. **Press** `S` (S̲pecial Time...)
3. **Type** the desired time.
4. **Press** `Alt` + `A` (for A̲M)

   OR

   Press `Alt` + `P` (for P̲M)
5. **Press** `Alt` + `I` (I̲nsert)

SET THE ALARM:
1. **Move** *insertion point* to desired time.
2. **Press** `Alt` + `A` (A̲larm)
3. **Press** `S` (S̲et)

TURN OFF ALARM:
1. **Move** *insertion point* to desired time where a bell is displayed.
2. **Press** `Alt` + `A` (A̲larm)
3. **Press** `S` (S̲et)

DELETE SPECIAL TIME:
1. **Move** *insertion point* to time to be removed.
2. **Press** `Alt` + `O` (O̲ptions)
3. **Press** `S` (S̲pecial Time...)
4. **Press** `Alt` + `D` (D̲elete)

EXERCISE 97
Use the Calculator

use Calculator

To use Windows' Calculator program to:
- add
- subtract
- multiply
- divide
- edit the display
- store values
- recall values
- clear the memory and
- add to the memory.

Calculator

Windows' Calculator has two modes: Standard and Scientific. The Standard calculator lets you do basic calculations, while the Scientific calculator lets you do advanced scientific and statistical calculations.

display

The <u>display</u> area is where the calculator shows numbers.

display edit buttons

The <u>display edit buttons</u> let you change numbers in the display area and clear a calculation.

memory buttons

The <u>memory buttons</u> let you use the calculator's memory area.

Keyboard Users

USE CALCULATOR

Use the Calculator Functions shown on the right (step 3) to find the keystrokes to perform the action described.

TOGGLE CALCULATOR MODES:

1. Press **Alt** + **V** (<u>V</u>iew)
2. Press **S** (<u>S</u>cientific)

    OR

    Press **T** (S<u>t</u>andard)

---

1 Start Windows, if necessary.

FROM THE *STARTING WINDOWS* SCREEN:

2 START CALCULATOR:

- Open Accessories.

- Double-click on [image] .
  Calculator

  The *Standard Calculator* window appears:

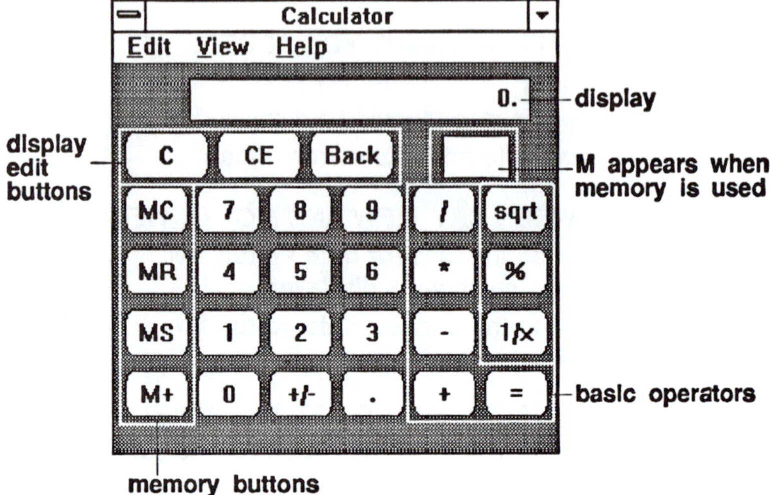

3 Examine Calculator functions:

click on button	or	*press* key	action
+		+	add
-		-	subtract
*		*	multiply
/		/	divide
=		= or ↵	calculate answer
C		Esc	clear calculator
CE		Del	clear last number
Back		BkSp	clear last digit
MC		Ctrl + L	memory, clear
MR		Ctrl + R	memory, recall value
MS		Ctrl + M	memory, store value
M+		Ctrl + P	memory, add value

Continue Exercise 97 on the next page

NOTE: The following instructions ask you to use the mouse with the calculator. If you prefer to use the keyboard, be sure the Num Lock light is <u>on</u>, then use the numeric keypad to <u>type</u> the numbers. To perform the functions, press the appropriate key instead of clicking on the indicated function buttons (see <u>Examine Calculator functions</u> on the previous page).

PERFORM STANDARD CALCULATIONS:

4 ADD 28 AND 56:

- **Click** on [2], then on [8].
  The number is displayed: | 28.
- **Click** on [+].
- **Click** on [5], then on [6].
  The number is displayed: | 56.
- **Click** on [=].
  The answer is displayed: | 84.

5 SUBTRACT 24 FROM 60:

NOTE: You do not need to clear the calculator when you begin a new calculation if the previous calculation ended with [=].

- **Click** on [6], [0], [–], [2], [4], then on [=].
  The answer is displayed: 36

6 MULTIPLY 9 TIMES 6:

- **Click** on [9], [*], [6], then on [=].
  The answer is displayed: 54

7 DIVIDE 50 BY 4:

- **Click** on [5], [0], [/], [4], then on [=].
  The answer is displayed: 12.5

USE FUNCTION BUTTONS TO EDIT THE DISPLAY:

8
- **Click** on [2], [8], [9], [4], [3].
  Oops! You meant to enter 2894<u>6</u>.
- **Click** on [Back], then on [6].
- **Click** on [c] to clear the calculator.
- Add 234 and 678:
  - **Click** on [2], [3], [4], [+], [6], [7], [8].
    Oops! The second number has been changed to 548.
  - **Click** on [CE], then on [5], [4], [8], then on [=].
    The answer is displayed: 782
- **Click** on [c] to clear the calculator (just to see it return the display to 0).

USE MEMORY:

9 Multiply 15 * 4, then add 10, 15, and 20 to the result.

- **Click** on [1], [5], [*], [4], then on [=].
  The answer is displayed: 60

  <u>STORE</u> A VALUE IN MEMORY:
- **Click** on [MS] (60 is stored in the memory).
  "M" appears in the box below the display to indicate that the memory has a value stored in it.
- **Click** [+], then on [1], [0], then on [=].
  The answer is displayed: 70

Continue Exercise 97 on the next page

Exercise 97, step 9 (continued)

<u>RECALL</u> A VALUE FROM MEMORY:
- **Click** on [MR].
  60 appears in the display (and remains in memory).
- **Click** [+], then on [1], [5], then on [=].
  The answer is displayed: 75
- **Click** on [MR]; 60 appears in the display.
- **Click** [+], then on [2], [0], then on [=].
  The answer is displayed: 80
  <u>CLEAR</u> THE MEMORY:
- **Click** on [MC].
  The "M" disappears from the box below the display to indicate that the memory is clear.

10 Use "memory +" to total the results of 3 * 5, 4 * 5, and 5 * 5.
- **Click** on [3], [*], [5], then on [=]; 15 is displayed.
- **Click** on [MS] (to store the value in memory).
- **Click** on [4], [*], [5], then on [=]; 20 is displayed.
  <u>ADD</u> THE VALUE TO MEMORY:
- **Click** on [M+].
  You just added 20 to the original value (15) in memory. The value in memory is now 35.
  <u>CHECK</u> TO SEE IF MEMORY IS HOLDING 35:
- **Click** on [MR] (memory recall); 35 should be displayed.
- **Click** on [5], [*], [5], then on [=]; 25 is displayed.
- **Click** on [M+] (to add the value to memory).
- **Click** on [MR] (memory recall); 60 should be displayed.

VIEW THE SCIENTIFIC CALCULATOR:
11 • **Click** on <u>V</u>iew, then on <u>S</u>cientific.

The *Scientific Calculator* appears:

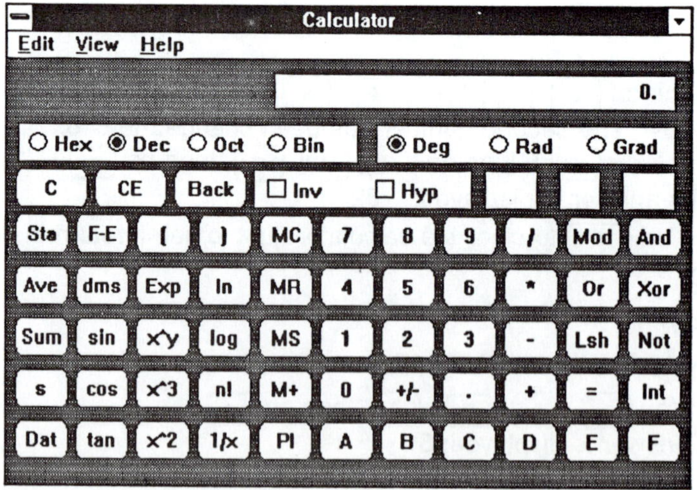

NOTE: You can perform more complex calculations using the Scientific Calculator than you can using the Standard Calculator.

- **Click** on <u>V</u>iew, then on <u>St</u>andard.
- **Exit Calculator.**

12 **Exit Windows.**

Appendix

Table of Contents

NOTE: *If this book is being used in a classroom or for training, the instructor may want to remove Appendices B, C, and D to*
1. *avoid student access to, and possible experimenting with, the instruction to "Reproduce the Original Windows Desktop," and*
2. *avoid student access to worksheet answers.*

APPENDIX A
Check-Off List for Worksheets & Printouts

This check-off list instructs you to jump around a little in the book so that the Getting Started topics toward the end are more closely linked to the related Lessons. The reason for doing this is to get you started on the hands-on exercises sooner and allow you to become acquainted with Windows before encountering the more complex Windows concepts. This affects the Help Topic and Lesson; the File Manager Topic and Lesson; and the Windows Modes, Windows Multitasking, and Integration Topics **and** Integration Lesson.

DIRECTIONS: Check off each item as you complete it

```
______    Do Windows tutorial  (page iv)

          Read pages 2, 3  . . . . . . . . . .  Hardware
______    Do worksheet 1, page 36  . . . . .  Hardware Illustration
______    Do worksheet 2, page 37  . . . . .  Hardware Terms


          Read pages 4, 5  . . . . . . . . .  Software
______    Do worksheet 3, page 38  . . . . .  Software Illustration
______    Do worksheet 4, page 39  . . . . .  Software Terms


          Read pages 6-11  . . . . . . . . .  Windows, Windows Aspects, and Three Basic Parts of Windows
______    Do worksheet 5, page 40  . . . . .  Windows, Windows Aspects, and Three Basic Parts of Windows

          Read pages 12, 13  . . . . . . . .  Windows Elements
______    Do worksheet 6, page 41  . . . . .  Windows Elements Illustration
______    Do worksheet 7, page 42  . . . . .  Windows Elements Terms


          Read pages 14-17 . . . . . . . . .  Windows Organization and Controlling Windows
______    Do worksheet 8, page 43  . . . . .  Windows Organization and Controlling Windows


          Read pages 18-21 . . . . . . . . .  The Mouse, Pointer, and Keyboard
______    Do worksheet 9, page 44  . . . . .  The Mouse, Pointer, and Keyboard


          Read pages 22, 23  . . . . . . . .  Dialog Boxes
______    Do worksheet 10, page 45   . . . .  Dialog Boxes Illustration
______    Do worksheet 11, page 46   . . . .  Dialog Boxes Terms


          DO LESSON ONE — WINDOWS BASICS  (page 51)
______    Do worksheet 16, page 80   . . . .  Windows Basics Terms
______    Do worksheet 17, page 81   . . . .  Windows Basics Terms
______    Do worksheet 18, page 82   . . . .  Windows Basics Terms
______    Do worksheet 19, page 83   . . . .  Windows Basics Tasks
______    Do worksheet 20, page 84   . . . .  Windows Basics Tasks


          DO LESSON TWO — BEYOND BASICS  (page 85)
______    Print, Ex. 27, page 92, #7 . . . .  Capture Program Manager Application Window
______    Print, Ex. 28, page 93, #9 . . . .  Capture screen (tiled)
______    Print, Ex. 32, page 97, #11  . . .  Capture Program Manager Application Window
______    Print, Ex. 36, page 102, #12 . . .  Capture Program Manager Application Window
______    Do worksheet 21, page 106  . . . .  Basics Terms
______    Do worksheet 22, page 107  . . . .  Basics Tasks
```

Continued ..

     (This page may be copied.)

```
_____   Read pages 24, 25 . . . . . . . . Help
        Do worksheet 12, page 48 . . . . . Help


        DO LESSON THREE — HELP (page 109)
_____   Print, Ex. 42, page 117, #6  . . . Capture About Program Manager Window
_____   Print, Ex. 43, page 118, #4  . . . Help Topic, Contents for Program Manager
_____   Print, Ex. 43, page 118, #7  . . . Help Topic, Switching between Applications
_____   Print, Ex. 43, page 119, #12 . . . Help Topic, Printing a Help Topic
_____   Print, Ex. 43, page 119, #15 . . . Help Topic, Contents for Calculator Help
_____   Print, Ex. 46, page 123, #7  . . . Help Topic, Opening Documents
_____   Print, Ex. 46, page 123, #11 . . . Help Topic, Contents for Program Manager Help
_____   Do worksheet 23, page 125  . . . . Help Terms and Tasks


        DO LESSON FOUR — WRITE (page 127)
_____   Print, Ex. 52, page 133, #3  . . . SAVEIT
_____   Print, Ex. 53, page 134, #5  . . . FONTS1
_____   Print, Ex. 53, page 136, #16 . . . FONTS2
_____   Print, Ex. 53, page 137, #24 . . . FUN
_____   Print, Ex. 54, page 139, #11 . . . FONTS3
_____   Print, Ex. 55, page 141, #15 . . . FONTS4
_____   Print, Ex. 56, page 143, #13 . . . FONTS5
_____   Print, Ex. 57, page 146, #30 . . . USEWRITE
_____   Do worksheet 24, page 148  . . . . Write Terms
_____   Do worksheet 25, page 149  . . . . Write Terms
_____   Do worksheet 26, page 150  . . . . Write Tasks


        DO LESSON FIVE — PAINTBRUSH (page 151)
_____   Print, Ex. 65, page 159, #3  . . . DRAW1
_____   Print, Ex. 65, page 159, #5  . . . DRAW2
_____   Print, Ex. 66, page 160, #6  . . . LINES
_____   Print, Ex. 67, page 161, #6  . . . SHAPES
_____   Print, Ex. 69, page 164, #12 . . . CUTOUT
_____   Print, Ex. 69, page 165, #13 . . . TRANSPAR
_____   Print, Ex. 69, page 165, #14 . . . OPAQUE
_____   Print, Ex. 69, page 167, #22 . . . TILT
_____   Print, Ex. 70, page 168, #7  . . . PALETTE1
_____   Print, Ex. 70, page 170, #12 . . . PALETTE2
_____   Print, Ex. 72, page 172, #2  . . . P1
_____   Print, Ex. 72, page 172, #4  . . . P2
_____   Print, Ex. 72, page 172, #6  . . . P3
_____   Print, Ex. 73, page 173, #2  . . . P4
_____   Print, Ex. 73, page 173, #4  . . . P5
_____   Print, Ex. 73, page 173, #6  . . . P6
_____   Do worksheet 27, page 175  . . . . Paintbrush Terms
_____   Do worksheet 28, page 176  . . . . Paintbrush Tasks


        Read pages 26, 27,  . . . . . . . . File Manager
_____   Do worksheet 13, page 48 . . . . . File Manager


        DO LESSON SIX — File Manager (page 177)
_____   Print, Ex. 84, page 192, #2  . . . Capture File Manager application window
_____   Do worksheet 29, page 198  . . . . File Manager Terms
_____   Do worksheet 30, page 199  . . . . File Manager Terms
_____   Do worksheet 31, page 200  . . . . File Manager Tasks


        Read pages 28-31 . . . . . . . . . Windows Modes and Windows Multitasking
_____   Do worksheet 14, page 49 . . . . . Windows Modes and Multitasking
        Read pages 32, 33 . . . . . . . . Windows Integration
_____   Do worksheet 15, page 50 . . . . . Windows Integration
```

Continued ...

```
        DO LESSON SEVEN — Windows Integration (page 201)
______  Print, Ex. 87, page 202, #5  . . . DOC1
______  Print, Ex. 87, page 202, #7  . . . DOC2
______  Print, Ex. 88, page 203, #3  . . . EMBED1
______  Print, Ex. 88, page 203, #6  . . . EMBED2
______  Print, Ex. 89, page 204, #5  . . . EMBED1 (revised)
______  Print, Ex. 89, page 204, #7  . . . EMBED2 (revised)
______  Print, Ex. 90, page 205, #5  . . . LINK1
______  Print, Ex. 90, page 205, #8  . . . LINK2
______  Print, Ex. 91, page 206, #4  . . . LINK1 (revised)
______  Print, Ex. 91, page 206, #5  . . . LINK2 (revised)
______  Print, Ex. 92, page 207, #3  . . . EMBEDDED
______  Print, Ex. 92, page 207, #5  . . . LINKED
______  Do worksheet 32, page 210  . . . . Windows Integration Terms and Tasks


        DO LESSON EIGHT — OTHER FEATURES (page 211)
```

                                          (This page may be copied.)

DO THIS PROCEDURE ONLY IF PROGRAM ICONS ARE MISPLACED OR DELETED FROM THE GROUP WINDOWS. However, it should not cause any problems if you do this procedure (unless you have customized program icons in your group windows and do not want them to change).

If you have done the procedures in Appendix C and/or have correct copies of the .INI and .GRP files, <u>you need not do this procedure</u>. However, if your group windows are missing program icons, this procedure will "rebuild" the group windows and group window files.

1. START WINDOWS
   - Turn the monitor and computer on.
   - If Windows does not appear, **start Windows** (from the **C:\>** prompt, type WIN, then press ⏎).

2. FROM THE STARTING WINDOWS SCREEN,
   with the Program Manager window's top bar (title bar) highlighted:
   - **Press Alt + F** (File) OR **click on** F̲ile.
     The File menu drops down.
   - **Press R** (R̲un...) OR **click on** R̲un... .
     The *Run* dialog box appears.
   - **Type:** setup /p
   - **Press ⏎ OR click on** [OK   ].

3. EXIT WINDOWS
   - **Press Alt + F4** (shortcut keys to exit a window).
   - **Press ⏎**.

APPENDIX C
Reproduce the Original Windows Desktop

The original .INI and .GRP files should be copied on a floppy disk for a back up. In addition, you may want to be able to reproduce the original Windows desktop (starting Windows screen) simply by typing CHANGE at the DOS prompt. Instructions to do both jobs are shown below. The best time to perform these procedures is before any changes are made to your Windows program.

If program icons within the group windows have been deleted, do Appendix B, Rebuild Group Windows, before doing the procedures below.

If you have little or no experience working with DOS (disk operating system), you may prefer to get assistance from someone with expertise in this area.

If the Windows subdirectory on your system is not named WINDOWS, substitute the name of your Windows subdirectory for WINDOWS in the procedures below.

Copy the .INI and .GRP Files on a Floppy Disk for a back up

1. • Turn the monitor and computer on.
     If Windows appears, **press** **Alt** + **F4**, then **⏎** (to exit Windows).
     The DOS prompt, **C:\\>**, appears in the top left corner of the screen.
   • Place a blank, formatted disk in Drive A: or B:. (If you use Drive B:, substitute b: for a: in step 2 below.)

2. • At the **C:\\>** prompt, **type** `cd windows`   **press** **⏎**.
   • At the **C:\\WINDOWS>** prompt, **type** `copy *.ini a:`   **press** **⏎**.
                                      type `copy *.grp a:`   **press** **⏎**.
                                      type `cd\`   **press** **⏎**.

Prepare a System to Reproduce the Original "Starting Windows Screen"

1. • Turn the monitor and computer on.
     If Windows appears, **press** **Alt** + **F4**, then **⏎** (to exit Windows).
     The DOS prompt, **C:\\>**, appears in the top left corner of the screen.

2. • At the **C:\\>** prompt, **type** `cd windows`   **press** **⏎**.
   • At the **C:\\WINDOWS>** prompt, **type** `copy *.ini *.oin`   **press** **⏎**.
                                      type `copy *.grp *.ogp`   **press** **⏎**.
                                      type `cd\`   **press** **⏎**.

3. • At the **C:\\>** prompt, **type** `copy con change.bat`   **press** **⏎**.
                          type `echo off`   **press** **⏎**.
                          type `cd windows`   **press** **⏎**.
                          type `copy *.oin *.ini`   **press** **⏎**.
                          type `copy *.ogp *.grp`   **press** **⏎**.
         (optional)   **type** `cls`   **press** **⏎**.
                          type `cd\`   **press** **⏎**.
                          press **Ctrl** + **Z**   **press** **⏎**.

   NOTE: If you make an error, press **Ctrl** + **Z**, **⏎** *and start step 3 again.*

Reproduce the Original "Starting Windows Screen" Using the CHANGE Batch File

1. • At the **C:\\>** prompt, **type** `change`   **press** **⏎**.

NOTE: For more information about .INI and .GRP files, read the SYSINI.WRI and WININI.WRI files. First open Write, then open the files, one at a time. You may need assistance doing this.

WORKSHEET 1 HARDWARE (ILLUSTRATION)

Missed	Score	Answers
0 -	100	1. monitor
1 -	91	2. floppy disks
2 -	82	3. printer
3 -	73	4. computer
4 -	64	5. floppy disk drive
5 -	55	6. hard disk
6 -	46	7. chips
7 -	37	8. memory
8 -	28	9. processor
9 -	19	10. mouse
10 -	10	11. keyboard
11 -	0	

WORKSHEET 2 HARDWARE (TERMS)

Missed	Score	Answers
0 -	100	1. computer
1 -	92	2. chips
2 -	84	3. hardware
3 -	76	4. mouse
4 -	68	5. hard disk
5 -	60	6. memory
6 -	52	7. printer
7 -	44	8. disk drive
8 -	36	9. floppy disks
9 -	28	10. processor
10 -	20	11. monitor
11 -	12	12. keyboard
12 -	0	

WORKSHEET 3 SOFTWARE (ILLUSTRATION)

Missed	Score	Answers
0 -	100	1. application software
1 -	86	2. system software
2 -	72	3. floppy disks
3 -	58	4. hard disk
4 -	44	5. firmware
5 -	30	6. memory
6 -	16	7. processor
7 -	0	

WORKSHEET 4 SOFTWARE (TERMS)

Missed	Score	Answers
0 -	100	1. software
1 -	91	2. in any order:
2 -	82	a. system software
3 -	73	b. application software
4 -	64	3. in any order:
5 -	55	a. firmware
6 -	46	b. DOS - disk operating
7 -	37	system
8 -	28	4. system software
9 -	19	5. firmware
10 -	10	6. DOS - disk operating
11 -	0	system
		7. application software
		8. Microsoft Windows
		9. program

WORKSHEET 5 ABOUT WINDOWS, WINDOWS ASPECTS, and THREE BASIC PARTS OF WINDOWS

Missed	Score	Answers
0 -	100	1. GUI - graphical user interface
1 -	89	
2 -	78	2. Program Manager
3 -	67	3. multitasking
4 -	56	4. OLE - object linking and embedding
5 -	45	
6 -	34	5. icons
7 -	23	6. windows
8 -	12	7. application
9 -	0	8. document
		9. desktop

WORKSHEET 6 WINDOWS ELEMENTS (ILLUSTRATION)

Missed	Score	Answers
0 -	100	1. title bar
1 -	90	2. control box
2 -	80	3. menu bar
3 -	70	4. minimize button
4 -	60	5. maximize button
5 -	50	6. restore button
6 -	40	7. workspace
7 -	30	8. window borders and corners
8 -	20	
9 -	10	9. pointer
10 -	0	10. scroll bar

WORKSHEET 7 WINDOWS ELEMENTS (TERMS)

Missed	Score	Answers
0 -	100	1. control box
1 -	90	2. pointer
2 -	80	3. title bar
3 -	70	4. scroll bars
4 -	60	5. menu bar
5 -	50	6. maximize button
6 -	40	7. minimize button
7 -	30	8. window borders and corners
8 -	20	9. restore button
9 -	10	10. workspace
10 -	0	

WORKSHEET 8 WINDOWS ORGANIZATION & CONTROLLING WINDOWS

Missed	Score	Answers
0 -	100	1. Program Manager
1 -	94	2. in any order:
2 -	88	a. accessories
3 -	82	b. applications
4 -	75	c. main
5 -	69	d. startup
6 -	63	e. games
7 -	57	3. commands
8 -	50	4. mouse
9 -	44	5. menu bar
10 -	38	6. drop-down menu
11 -	32	7. dialog box
12 -	25	8. control box
13 -	19	9. command button
14 -	13	10. program icon
15 -	7	11. dimmed command
16 -	0	12. default

WORKSHEET 9   THE MOUSE, THE POINTER, and
                  THE KEYBOARD

Missed	Score	Answers
0 -	100	1. mouse
1 -	93	2. click
2 -	86	3. double-click
3 -	79	4. drag
4 -	72	5. pointer
5 -	65	6. keyboard
6 -	58	7. in any order:
7 -	51	a. function keys
8 -	44	b. control keys
9 -	37	8. Alt, Shift, Ctrl
10 -	30	9. shortcut keys
11 -	23	10. plus (+)
12 -	16	11. comma (,)
13 -	9	12. ESC
14 -	0	13. F1

WORKSHEET 10   DIALOG BOXES (ILLUSTRATION)

Missed	Score	Answers
0 -	100	1. drop-down list box
1 -	86	2. drop-down list arrow
2 -	72	3. command with an ellipsis
3 -	58	4. check box
4 -	44	5. option buttons
5 -	30	6. command buttons
6 -	16	7. increment box
7 -	0	

WORKSHEET 11   DIALOG BOXES (TERMS)

Missed	Score	Answers
0 -	100	1. option buttons
1 -	89	2. dialog box
2 -	78	3. check boxes
3 -	67	4. command button
4 -	56	5. text box
5 -	45	6. drop-down list box
6 -	34	7. list box
7 -	23	8. drop-down list arrow
8 -	12	9. increment box
9 -	0	

WORKSHEET 12   HELP

Missed	Score	Answers
0 -	100	1. F1
1 -	86	2. Help
2 -	72	3. Glossary
3 -	58	4. Contents
4 -	44	5. About (application)
5 -	30	6. Search for Help On
6 -	16	7. How to Use Help
7 -	0	

WORKSHEET 13   FILE MANAGER

Missed	Score	Answers
0 -	100	1. directory window
1 -	93	2. File Manager
2 -	86	3. root directory
3 -	79	4. directory
4 -	72	5. subdirectory
5 -	65	6. current directory
6 -	58	7. directory tree
7 -	51	8. directory window
8 -	44	9. filename extension
9 -	37	10. file
10 -	30	11. associated file
11 -	23	12. program file
12 -	16	13. data file
13 -	9	14. filename
14 -	0	

WORKSHEET 14   WINDOWS MODES & MULTITASKING

Missed	Score	Answers
0 -	100	1. 1,000
1 -	94	2. extended memory
2 -	87	3. memory
3 -	80	4. 386 enhanced mode
4 -	74	5. 1
5 -	67	6. microprocessor chip
6 -	61	7. conventional memory
7 -	54	8. in any order:
8 -	47	a. multitasking
9 -	40	b. complex programs
10 -	34	c. graphics environment
11 -	27	9. 1,000,000
12 -	20	10. standard mode
13 -	14	11. multitasking
14 -	8	12. memory managing
15 -	0	13. 386 enhanced mode

WORKSHEET 15   WINDOWS INTEGRATION

Missed	Score	Answers
0 -	100	1. CUA - common user access
1 -	92	2. integration
2 -	84	3. OLE - object linking
3 -	76	and embedding
4 -	68	4. link
5 -	60	5. embed
6 -	52	6. integration
7 -	44	7. object
8 -	36	8. source document
9 -	28	9. clipboard
10 -	20	10. destination document
11 -	12	11. client application
12 -	0	12. server application

WORKSHEET 16   LESSON ONE
                   WINDOWS BASICS (TERMS)

Missed	Score	Answers
0 -	100	1. desktop
1 -	91	2. icon
2 -	82	3. window
3 -	73	4. control box
4 -	64	5. control menu
5 -	55	6. title bar
6 -	46	7. double-click
7 -	37	8. dialog box
8 -	28	9. click
9 -	19	10. group window icons
10 -	10	11. group windows
11 -	0	

WORKSHEET 17 LESSON ONE
WINDOWS BASICS (TERMS)

Missed	Score	Answers
0	100	1. program icon
1	93	2. click off
2	85	3. workspace
3	77	4. application window
4	70	5. active window
5	62	6. group window
6	55	7. menu bar
7	47	8. document window
8	40	9. close a menu
9	32	10. choose
10	24	11. select
11	17	12. an ellipsis
12	9	13. drag
13	0	

WORKSHEET 18 LESSON ONE
WINDOWS BASICS (TERMS)

Missed	Score	Answers
0	100	1. double-headed arrow
1	91	2. shortcut keys
2	82	3. restore button
3	73	4. scroll bar
4	64	5. scroll arrow
5	55	6. dimmed command
6	46	7. maximize button
7	37	8. scroll box
8	28	9. cascade
9	19	10. minimize button
10	10	11. tile
11	0	

WORKSHEET 19 LESSON ONE
WINDOWS BASICS (TASKS)

Missed	Score	Answers
0	100	1. open a group window
1	90	2. exit Windows
2	80	3. start Windows
3	70	4. exit a program
4	60	5. start a program
5	50	6. close a group window
6	40	7. select an application window
7	30	
8	20	8. cancel
9	10	9. use the menu bar
10	0	10. select a group window

WORKSHEET 20 LESSON ONE
WINDOWS BASICS (TASKS)

Missed	Score	Answers
0	100	1. minimize a window
1	89	2. maximize a window
2	78	3. restore a window
3	67	4. scroll through a window
4	56	5. size a window
5	45	6. move a window
6	34	7. arrange group windows
7	23	8. arrange icons
8	12	9. move icons
9	0	

WORKSHEET 21 LESSON TWO
BEYOND BASICS (TERMS)

Missed	Score	Answers
0	100	1. clipboard
1	92	2. deselect
2	84	3. select
3	76	4. capture (noun)
4	68	5. capture (verb)
5	60	6. startup group window
6	52	7. Clipboard Viewer
7	44	8. option buttons
8	36	9. paste
9	28	10. text box
10	20	11. program items
11	12	12. group windows
12	0	

WORKSHEET 22 LESSON TWO
BEYOND BASICS (TASKS)

Missed	Score	Answers
0	100	1. capture an application window
1	93	2. delete a group window
2	85	3. create "Starting Windows Screen"
3	77	
4	70	4. save desktop arrangement
5	62	5. print a capture
6	55	6. use the Clipboard Viewer
7	47	7. capture the screen
8	40	8. create a program item
9	32	9. move a program item
10	24	10. create a group window
11	17	11. copy a program item
12	9	12. use the startup group
13	0	13. delete a program item

WORKSHEET 23 LESSON THREE
HELP (TERMS and TASKS)

Missed	Score	Answers
0	100	1. glossary
1	93	2. contents
2	85	3. Help
3	77	4. Help Window buttons
4	70	5. search
5	62	6. list box
6	55	7. text box
7	47	8. about (application)
8	40	9. history
9	32	10. print topic
10	24	11. back
11	17	12. F1
12	9	13. Windows tutorial
13	0	

WORKSHEET 24 LESSON FOUR
WRITE (TERMS)

Missed	Score	Answers
0	100	1. New
1	90	2. end mark
2	80	3. Save As...
3	70	4. I-beam
4	60	5. file
5	50	6. insertion point
6	40	7. page-status area
7	30	8. Save
8	20	9. drop-down list box
9	10	10. Write
10	0	

WORKSHEET 25 LESSON FOUR
WRITE (TERMS)

Missed	Score	Answers
0 -	100	1. cut
1 -	89	2. type style
2 -	78	3. margins
3 -	67	4. typeface
4 -	56	5. font
5 -	45	6. copy
6 -	34	7. size
7 -	23	8. highlight
8 -	12	9. paste
9 -	0	

WORKSHEET 26 LESSON FOUR
WRITE (TASKS)

Missed	Score	Answers
0 -	100	1. change margins
1 -	90	2. open a document
2 -	80	3. Write menus
3 -	70	4. change text alignment
4 -	60	5. save a document
5 -	50	6. change fonts
6 -	40	7. print a document
7 -	30	8. start Write
8 -	20	9. edit a document
9 -	10	10. create a document
10 -	0	

WORKSHEET 27 LESSON FIVE
PAINTBRUSH (TERMS)

Missed	Score	Answers
0 -	100	1. toolbox
1 -	94	2. pixel
2 -	88	3. palette
3 -	82	4. foreground color or pattern
4 -	75	
5 -	69	5. Save As...
6 -	63	6. cutout
7 -	57	7. background color or pattern
8 -	50	
9 -	44	8. linesize box
10 -	38	9. New
11 -	32	10. file
12 -	25	11. Paintbrush
13 -	19	12. drop-down list box
14 -	13	13. scissors
15 -	7	14. Save
16 -	0	15. drawing area
		16. pick

WORKSHEET 28 LESSON FIVE
PAINTBRUSH (TASKS)

Missed	Score	Answers
0 -	100	1. use shape tools
1 -	94	2. zoom in
2 -	88	3. open a drawing
3 -	82	4. start Paintbrush
4 -	75	5. Paintbrush tools
5 -	69	6. create a drawing
6 -	63	7. print a drawing
7 -	57	8. Paintbrush menus
8 -	50	9. save a drawing
9 -	44	10. use line tools
10 -	38	11. use erase
11 -	32	12. palette
12 -	25	13. use undo
13 -	19	14. linesize box
14 -	13	15. use cutout tools
15 -	7	16. use the palette
16 -	0	

WORKSHEET 29 LESSON SIX
FILE MANAGER (TERMS)

Missed	Score	Answers
0 -	100	1. directory
1 -	90	2. status bar
2 -	80	3. current directory
3 -	70	4. Directory window
4 -	60	5. hard disk drive
5 -	50	6. contents of current directory
6 -	40	
7 -	30	7. Directory window title
8 -	20	8. File Manager window
9 -	10	9. floppy disk drive
10 -	0	10. directory tree

WORKSHEET 30 LESSON SIX
FILE MANAGER (TERMS)

Missed	Score	Answers
0 -	100	1. expand directories
1 -	92	2. subdirectories
2 -	84	3. directory levels
3 -	76	4. file
4 -	68	5. collapse directories
5 -	60	6. associated file
6 -	52	7. data file
7 -	44	8. root directory
8 -	36	9. application (program) **file**
9 -	28	10. directory path
10 -	20	11. file type
11 -	12	12. directory branch
12 -	0	

WORKSHEET 31 LESSON SIX
FILE MANAGER (TASKS)

Missed	Score	Answers
0 -	100	1. select a directory
1 -	94	2. select files
2 -	87	3. copy files
3 -	80	4. deselect files
4 -	74	5. create a directory
5 -	67	6. start File Manager
6 -	61	7. sort files
7 -	54	8. expand and collapse directories
8 -	47	
9 -	40	9. move files
10 -	34	10. delete files
11 -	27	11. view File Manager menus
12 -	20	12. view specific files
13 -	14	13. view file details
14 -	8	14. change the disk drive
15 -	0	15. format a disk

WORKSHEET 32 LESSON SEVEN
INTEGRATION (TERMS and TASKS)

Missed	Score	Answers
0 -	100	1. edit a linked object
1 -	90	2. source document
2 -	80	3. link an object
3 -	70	4. object
4 -	60	5. edit an embedded object
5 -	50	6. embed
6 -	40	7. link
7 -	30	8. destination document
8 -	20	9. integrate text
9 -	10	10. clipboard
10 -	0	

386 enhanced mode The mode Windows automatically runs in if you have a 386 (or higher) processor with 640K of conventional memory plus at least 1 Mb of extended memory. *See also* standard mode.

A

About (application) A Help feature that displays a window with information about the program you are using.

active window The window whose *title bar is highlighted,* indicating that it is currently *selected.*

analog clock The Windows clock mode that displays a circular clock with moving hour and minute hands and, if you choose, a second hand. *See also* digital clock.

application file A file that holds a *set of instructions* that perform a task, such as word processing or database management. Program files usually contain one of the following extensions: .EXE, .PIF, .COM, or .BAT.

application software (programs) Software that does a specific task, such as word processing.

application window A window that holds a program. An application window may hold multiple *document* windows, but it may not hold other *application* windows.

arrow pointer The mouse-pointer shape that appears when you start Windows. It is used to choose items, move windows, and activate applications.

associated file A file that has a *filename extension* that identifies it as "belonging" to a certain application, such as a Write (.WRI) or a Paintbrush (.BMP) file.

B

back A Help feature that returns you to the previous Help screen, retracing your steps each time you choose *back* again.

background color or pattern The color or pattern used to cover the *drawing area* in Paintbrush before you create a drawing.

branch *See* directory branch.

byte A unit of memory that holds one character.

C

Calculator Windows' Calculator, which has two modes: Standard and Scientific. The Standard Calculator lets you do simple calculations, while the Scientific Calculator lets you do advanced scientific and statistical calculations.

Calendar Window's Calendar, which provides a month-at-a-glance calendar, a daily appointment book, and an alarm clock.

cancel To escape, or back out of, a menu or dialog box without completing a command.

capture *(noun)* The *image* of an *application window* or the *entire screen* that has been copied onto the clipboard.

capture *(verb)* To *perform the keystrokes to copy* the image that is visible on your monitor (either an application window or the entire screen) onto the clipboard.

cascade To layer and resize the open group windows within the Program Manager workspace so that the title bar of each group window is visible.

check boxes Squares in a dialog box that you may select as desired. *Selected check boxes* contain an ⊠.

chips Small pieces of silicon wafers that often hold instructions to perform behind-the-scenes tasks, making it possible for you to use the computer. The *processor* and *memory* are especially important chips in the computer system.

choose To pick an item from a menu that initiates an action. (Contrast with *select.*)

click A mouse action in which you move the pointer on an item, and then quickly press and release a mouse button, usually the *left* button.

click off A mouse action in which you click *outside* of an area in order to "back out" of an action.

client application An application whose documents can *accept* embedded or linked objects. *See also* server application.

clipboard A temporary storage area in the computer's memory used to hold information that is being cut (or copied) and pasted. Using the clipboard, data can be transferred from place to place within a document, from document to document, or from one program to another program (in some cases).

Clipboard Viewer A program that lets you *view* the contents of the clipboard. You can also *save* or *delete* the contents of the clipboard, or *open* a previously saved clipboard image.

collapse directories To hide directory levels in the directory tree. *See also* expand directories.

color scheme A combination of colors used for Windows screen elements.

command button A small box holding an icon or a word that will carry out a command, for example, `OK` or `Cancel`. Command buttons are usually found in dialog boxes.

commands Instructions that cause an action to be carried out.

Common User Access *See* CUA.

computer An electronic device that performs complex tasks at high speed and with great accuracy. There are two main parts of a computer—the *processor* and the *memory*. *See also* processor and memory.

contents An alphabetic list of the Help *topics* available for the application you are using.

contents of current directory (File Manager) A list of the files and subdirectories located within the *directory which is highlighted in the directory tree*. These files and directories are displayed on the right side of the Directory window.

control box (or control-menu box) ▭ The box at the left end of the title bar which opens the control menu. *See also* control menu.

control keys Shift, Ctrl, and Alt Keys used in combination with other keys to issue commands.

control menu The menu found in the small box located at the left end of application windows. The *control menu* holds commands that manipulate the *window*, such as Restore, Move, Size, Maximize, Minimize, and Close. *See also* control box.

conventional memory The first 640K of computer memory.

copy To copy *selected* (highlighted) data in a document into the clipboard. *Copy* leaves the original data intact.

copy files To transfer selected files from one directory to another directory, leaving the original files intact.

CUA - Common User Access A common set of commands used in Windows applications.

current directory 📁 The directory you are working in. In the File Manager, the *current directory* is the *highlighted directory*.

cut To move *selected* (highlighted) data from a document into the clipboard. *Cut* removes data from a document.

cutout A portion of the drawing area in Paintbrush which is *defined* by a dashed-line border surrounding it. The *cutout* tools, *pick* and *scissors*, are used to *define* a cutout area. *See also* both scissors and pick.

D

data file 📄 A file that consists of data created in a program, such as a *letter* typed into a *word processor*.

default An automatic setting in a program.

delete files To remove selected files from a disk.

deselect To *unmark* an item so that a future action will *not* activate the item.

desktop The background (screen) upon which *windows* and *icons* appear.

desktop pattern A small design that is repeated to create a pattern across the desktop.

desktop wallpaper A picture that is repeated to create a wallpaper effect across the desktop. Wallpaper is usually a larger design and is more elaborate than a *desktop pattern*.

232

destination document The document into which an *object* is placed. *See also* source document.

dialog box A window that appears when a *menu item with an ellipsis (...)* is chosen. A dialog box requests additional information before performing the original command.

digital clock The Windows clock mode that displays a clock with a precise numeric readout, for example, 1:15:30 P.M. *See also* analog clock.

dimmed command A command that cannot be used in the current situation. A *dimmed command* is shown in gray instead of black.

directories, collapse *See* collapse directories.
directories, expand *See* expand directories.

directory ☐ The part of the disk structure that holds the *files* that are saved on a disk. A directory can also hold other directories (also called subdirectories).

directory, current *See* current directory.
directory, root *See* root directory.

directory branch All the levels of subdirectories within a specific directory.

directory levels Tiers of subdirectory layers, starting with the root directory.

directory path A list of the directory and subdirectories, starting with the root directory, that lead to a file. For example, C:\LETTERS\JUNE is the path that shows where files in the JUNE subdirectory are located.

directory tree A disk's *directory structure* (root directory, directories, and subdirectories) *displayed* on the left side of the *Directory window*.

Directory window A document window within File Manager that displays the *directories, subdirectories,* and *files* on your disk. *See also* Directory window title.

Directory window title The *name of the current (highlighted) directory* that is displayed in the title bar of the Directory window.

disk drive A device that transfers information back and forth between the computer's memory and a disk.

display area Where the Calculator shows numbers.

display edit buttons Calculator buttons that let you change numbers in the display area and/or clear a calculation.

document window A window within an application window. There may be more than one *document* window in an *application* window.

DOS (Disk Operating System) A kind of *system software* that comes on disks and acts as a link between *application software* and the system's hardware. *DOS* must be in the computer's memory before application software can be used.

double-click A mouse action in which you move the pointer on an item, and then quickly press and release the *left* mouse button *twice*.

double-headed arrow ⟷ The shape the pointer takes when it is used to size a window. *See also* sizing pointer.

drag A mouse action in which you move the pointer on an item, hold down the *left* button, slide the mouse to a new location, and then release the button.

drawing area The workspace in which you create drawings in Paintbrush.

drop-down list arrow ⬇ An arrow in a dialog box that has a line under it, which indicates that it can open a *drop-down list box*.

drop-down list box A box similar to a *list box* except that it usually appears in a small or crowded dialog box and is opened by clicking on the *drop-down list arrow* next to it.

drop-down menu A submenu that *drops down* when a *menu* is chosen from the *menu bar*.

E

ellipsis *Three dots (...)* that follow menu commands that open a dialog box when *selected*.

embed To *paste* an *object* that was created in a source document into a destination document. *See also* object, server application, client application, source document, destination document, and object embedding.

end mark ╫ A small icon that identifies the end of a document in Write.

expand directories To display unseen directory levels in the directory tree. *See also* collapse directories.

extended memory General purpose memory above *conventional* and *upper* memory.

F

file ▯ A *set of data* that is saved on a disk as a *named unit*.

file, application *See* application file.

file, associated *See* associated file.

file, data *See* data file.

file, program *See* application file.

file type The filename extension. It is often used to organize files into groups. Also, *kinds* of files that can be shown on the right side of the *Directory window*—directory, program, document, and other.

File Manager A program to help you control your files.

File Manager window The application window that holds the File Manager program and one or more directory windows (document windows).

filename The name you assign to a *set of data* (file) that you save on a disk. The name may have up to eight characters and may include an extension (a period followed by up to the three characters), for example, LETTER.WRI.

filename extension The optional *period and up to three characters* at the end of a *filename*. A *filename extension* is often used to identify *groups* of related files and is automatically added by some Windows applications.

firmware A kind of *system software* that is built into the computer system on chips.

floppy disk drive The part of the computer system that transfers files back and forth between the computer's memory and floppy disks (usually Drive A: or Drive B:).

floppy disks Magnetically coated disks on which information (both programs and data typed from the keyboard) can be stored and retrieved. *Floppy disks* are inserted into and removed from the *floppy disk drive*.

font The complete set of characters in a given *size*, *type style*, and *typeface*.

font sample box A box in the *Font* dialog window that shows a *sample* of the selected *font* in the selected *type style* and the selected *size*.

foreground color or pattern The color or pattern used by the *tools* to draw with and fill areas in Paintbrush.

function keys Twelve (or ten) special keys labeled F1, F2, etc., and located across the top (or at the left side) of the keyboard. *Function keys* are used to issue commands.

G

glossary A Help feature that provides a list of Windows terms from which you *choose* a term to display its definition.

graphical user interface or **GUI** (pronounced "gooey") A phrase that is commonly used to describe Microsoft Windows and similar programs. It simply means that Windows has *pictures* (graphical) that *you use* (user) to *communicate* (interface) with the computer.

group window A *document window* within the Program Manager that holds *groups* of program-item icons that represent commands to *start* programs.

group window icons Icons at the bottom of the Program Manager window which represent *group windows*.

GUI *See* graphical user interface.

H

hand pointer The pointer shape that appears when you can jump between related Help topics. *See also* jump.

hard disk A large capacity, permanent storage area that offers fast access to the information stored on it. Unlike floppy disks, the hard disk (along with its drive) is enclosed in a unit that you do not handle.

hard disk drive The part of the computer system that transfers files back and forth between the computer and the hard disk (usually Drive C:).

hardware The group of parts that make up the computer system and that can be seen and touched.

Help A quick, easy way to look up information about Windows tasks, features, and commands.

Help, about application *See* about (application).
Help, contents *See* contents.
Help, glossary *See* glossary.
Help, print topic *See* print topic.
Help, search *See* search for Help on.

Help, Windows tutorial *See* Windows tutorial.

Help window buttons Buttons that are displayed below the *menu bar* in a Help window.

highlight To indicate that an object or text is *selected* and that it will be affected by your next action. *Highlighting* reverses the color on text (also called reverse video).

History A Help feature that displays a sequential list of every Help topic you have chosen during the current Help session.

hourglass An icon that signals you to wait while Windows processes data.

How to Use Help Information about how to *use* the Help feature.

I-beam pointer The pointer shape in Write's work area. Click the I-beam in the desired location to move the *insertion point* to that spot.

icon A small picture that represents an element such as a document, program, group of programs, command, or the pointer.

increment box A box in a dialog box used to set a value by providing an up and a down arrow, which, when clicked on, changes the original value. A new value can also be *typed* in.

insertion point A blinking vertical line that shows where text will appear when you type.

integration 1) A software system in which *information* can be easily *transferred* back and forth between different programs, and/or 2) a software system in which different programs look and behave alike, thus reducing the time it takes to learn a new program.

J

jump A jump is made from a Help topic that has a link to another related Help topic, or to more information about the current topic. Topics that provide a *jump* opportunity are marked with a *dotted underline* or a *different color*.

K

keyboard A hardware device used to enter data into and issue commands to the computer.

kilobyte A unit of memory that holds about 1,000 characters.

L

levels *See* directory levels.

linesize box (Paintbrush) The box in the bottom left corner of the Paintbrush window that displays lines of varying width from which a drawing width can be selected.

link An active connection between an *object* and the different programs into which that *object* is embedded. *See also* server application, client application, object, embed, and object linking.

list box A box that displays a list of options from which to choose.

M

margins The white space that creates a border around the body of data on a page.

maximize button The small box located at the right end of the title bar and used to enlarge a window to its maximum size.

megabyte A unit of memory that holds about 1,000,000 characters.

memory The area of the computer that holds instructions (programs) and information you give it. When the computer is turned off, everything in the memory disappears. *Memory size* is measured in bytes. *Memory* is also called random access memory (RAM) or main memory.

memory buttons Buttons that let you use the Calculator's memory area.

memory managing programs Programs that organize the computer's memory to prevent different programs from using the same memory at the same time.

menu bar The second horizontal bar (located under the title bar) in an *application* window. The *menu bar* displays the first-level *menu items* for the application it is in.

menu command The options that appear in drop-down menus.

microprocessor chip The computer's processor that identifies a computer. Standard microprocessing chips are 80286, 80386, and 80486. The higher the chip number, the faster the computer's processor.

Microsoft Windows A special kind of *software* that provides a *graphics environment*, that is, *an icon-based* **link** between you, application software, and DOS.

minimize button ▾ The small box located toward the right of the title bar (just to the left of the maximize button) and used to reduce a window to an icon.

monitor A screen that displays information in the computer.

mouse A small, hand-held device used to control a pointer on the screen.

move files To transfer selected files from one directory to another directory, deleting the original files.

move pointer ✥ The pointer shape used to relocate windows when you use the keyboard instead of the mouse.

multitasking The ability to run more than one program at once.

N

New The *File* option that clears the screen (i.e., opens a *new* workspace).

O

object A selected *set of information* created in a Windows application, such as a *drawing* in Paintbrush. An object can be *embedded in* or *linked to* certain other applications.

object embedding A way to copy an *object* from a *source program* (for example, Paintbrush) into a *destination program* (for example, Write) so that it can be edited directly from the *destination program* (for example, you can edit a drawing from the word processor).

object linking Connecting an *object* that has been copied from a *source document* and **embedded** in one or more *destination documents* so that when the *object* is *edited* in one document, all the other documents are also *edited*.

Object Linking and Embedding *See* OLE.

OLE - Object Linking and Embedding A powerful way of integrating developed for Microsoft Windows.

option buttons ◯ Circles in a dialog box from which you may select *only one of a related group*. A dot in the circle ◉ means an option button is selected.

P

Paintbrush Windows' drawing program. Paintbrush uses many Windows features, such as a similar menu bar, dialog boxes, file commands, and window control elements.

palette The box across the bottom of the Paintbrush window that displays colors and patterns that may be selected for background or drawing.

paste To copy the data in the Clipboard into a document. *Paste* leaves the original data in the Clipboard so it can be pasted again (until you cut or copy other data).

path *See* directory path.

pattern *See* desktop pattern.

pick A Paintbrush tool used to define a *rectangular* cutout area. *See also* both scissors and cutout.

pixel A single dot that represents the smallest graphic unit that can be displayed on the screen.

pointer (or mouse pointer) The arrow-shaped cursor on the screen that moves with the mouse as you slide the mouse over a flat surface. The pointer's shape may change depending on the job it is doing.

prevent pointer ⊘ The pointer shape that indicates that you *cannot* perform an action.

print topic A Help feature that lets you print a Help topic.

printer A hardware device that transfers information from the computer to paper.

processor The "brains" of the computer—it processes *instructions* in the computer's *memory*. The 286, 386, and 486 chips are all *processors*. Also called the central processing unit (CPU) or microprocessor chip.

program file *See* application file.

program icon *See* program-item icon.

program-item icon An icon that represents a program that can be started from a *group window*.

program items The programs (and documents) that make up a *group* in the Program Manager. *Program items* are represented as *icons* in Group windows.

Program Manager A menu-like program that lets you *start* applications and organize applications and tasks into *groups*.

R

restore button ⬍ The small box located at the right end of the title bar of a maximized window and used to return a window to its previous size.

root directory ▢ The original (or highest-level) directory on a disk. For example, **C:** is the root directory on most hard disks.

S

sample box *See* font sample box.

sample color scheme area An area in the *Color* window that contains sample Windows elements which change to match the highlighted *color scheme*.

Save The file option that saves changes to a previously named file that you are working on.

Save As... The file option that saves new files or lets you *rename* a previously saved file.

scissors A Paintbrush tool used to define an *irregular* cutout area. *See also* both pick and cutout.

screen *See* monitor.

scroll arrow The arrow at each end of a scroll bar, used to *scroll* through the contents of the window.

scroll bar A *bar* that appears at the right and/or bottom of a window whose contents are not fully visible. Each *scroll bar* contains two *scroll arrows* and a *scroll box*.

scroll box The small box in a scroll bar that shows the position of the information *displayed* in relation to the *entire contents* of the window.

Search for Help On A Help feature that displays a dialog box used to locate information about a specific topic.

select To *mark* an item so that a subsequent action can activate it. *Highlighting* and *a check mark* are two ways to *select* an item. (Contrast with *choose*.)

server application An application that *creates* objects that can be embedded or linked into other documents. *See also* client application.

shortcut keys Easy-to-use key combinations that activate certain commands instead of using menus. If a menu option has a *shortcut*, the key combination is shown to the right of the command on the drop-down menu.

size of fonts The *size* of fonts is usually measured either in points or characters per inch. When using the point system, the *height* of characters is measured in points. One point is 1/72 of an inch. The larger the point size, the larger the font. Some fonts are measured in *characters per inch (CPI)*, that is, the number of characters that fit in a horizontal inch. The larger the number of characters per inch, the smaller the font.

sizing pointer <> The shape the pointer takes when it contacts window borders and corners. The *sizing* pointer is used to change a *window's* size.

software The set of *instructions* (programs) that tell the computer what to do. While *software* is often stored on a disk, *software* is not the disk itself, but rather the *instructions* that are stored *on* the disk. *Software* cannot be seen or touched.

source document The document in which an *object* is created. *See also* destination document and object.

standard mode The only mode Windows runs in if you have a 286 processor with 640K of conventional memory plus no more than 256K of extended memory. Standard mode lets you switch between non-Windows programs, but it does not access virtual memory or let non-Windows programs run in the background or within a window. *See also* 386 enhanced mode.

startup group window A special group window that has been designed so that *the program items* that appear in it *start* when you start Windows.

status bar (File Manager) The bar at the bottom of the File Manager window that displays information about the *current* drive and directory.

subdirectory □ A directory that is within another directory.

system software Programs that run the computer system. System software communicates between the parts that make up the computer system, making it possible for you to operate the computer. Two types of *system software* are *firmware* and *DOS.*

T

text box A box in a dialog box that provides space to type the information needed to carry out a command.

tile To resize and arrange the open group windows *side by side* within the Program Manager workspace.

title bar The horizontal bar at the top of a window that holds the window's name.

toolbox An area along the left side of the Paintbrush drawing area that holds tools used to create drawings.

tools (Paintbrush) Various tools found in the toolbox (along the left side of the Paintbrush window) that are used to create a drawing.

tutorial *See* Windows tutorial.

type style The treatment of characters, for example, *bold, italic,* and *underline.*

typeface The design of characters.

U

upper memory Additional memory (up to 384K) above the 640K of conventional memory that is normally reserved for running the computer's hardware.

W

wallpaper *See* desktop wallpaper.

window The rectangular work area for a task, program, document, or group. There are several kinds of windows: application, document, group, and dialog.

window, active *See* active window.
window, application *See* application window.
window, Directory *See* Directory window.
window, document *See* document window.
window, group *See* group window.

window borders and **corners** Boundaries that mark the edges of a window and are used to *size* a window.

Windows tutorial Hands-on lessons in two areas: 1) How to use the mouse, and 2) Windows Basics.

Windows, Microsoft *See* Microsoft Windows.

workspace The inner part of a window, where the work on an application is done.

Write Windows' word processor. Write uses many Windows features, such as a similar menu bar, dialog boxes, file commands, and window control elements.

Windows

Z

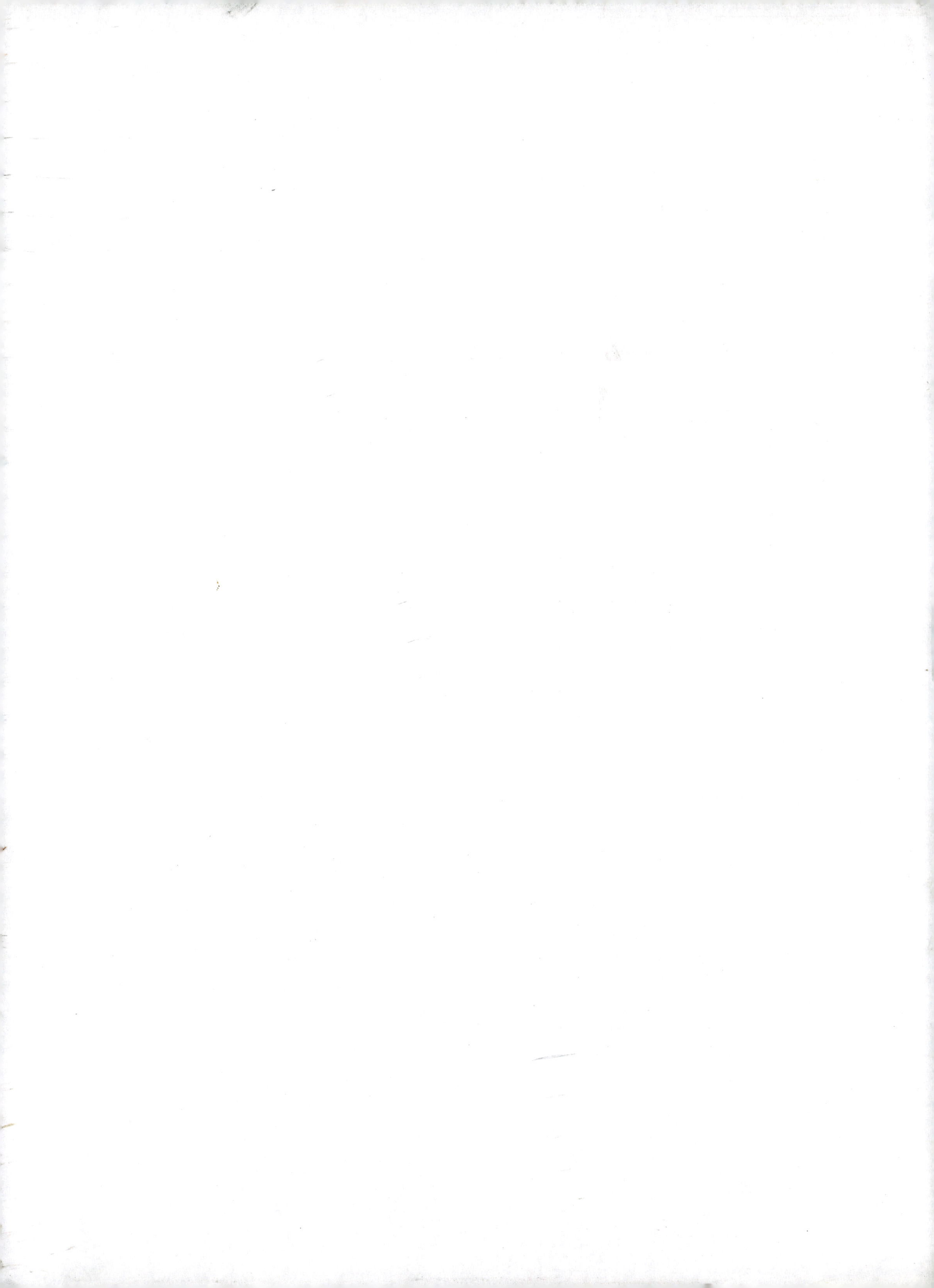